D0096113

Austin,
San Antonio
& the Hill Country

Sara Benson

Contents

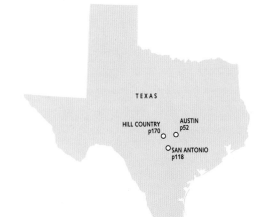

TEXAS

HILL COUNTRY
p170

AUSTIN
p52

SAN ANTONIO
p118

Destination Austin, San Antonio & the Hill Country

Almost everyone's image of the American West comes from this gargantuan state. It was here that the Alamo was defended and lost, here that the rebellious Republic of Texas was born. But the Lone Star experience is far more complex than cowboys, steers and the open range.

With two great cities and abundant natural beauty, south-central Texas deservedly ropes in the most visitors. There's Austin, home to phenomenal live music, the state capitol and over a million Mexican free-tailed bats. There's San Antonio, with its storied Spanish missions, festival-loving Latino culture and lively Riverwalk. Then there's Texas Hill Country, which beckons with its charming towns, country dance halls and natural swimming holes.

The whole region is a wellspring of musical invention, from the 19th-century *conjunto* rhythms of Tejano culture to Austin's modern indie rock and alt-country sounds. It's also a film capital and a mass-market music powerhouse. When it comes to high tech, Austin rivals the West Coast, with literate, highly educated people building a new economy based on brains, not brawn. Meanwhile, well-heeled San Antonio is a haven for the arts, especially culinary ones. Outside of the major cities, the flavor of central Texas is defined by the state's early European settlers. A drive through the Hill Country reveals pockets of Czech bakeries, German breweries and French restaurants. Perhaps you've heard of the Heart of Texas? Well, here it is.

Browse quirky stores along South Congress Ave, also known as SoCo (p54), Austin

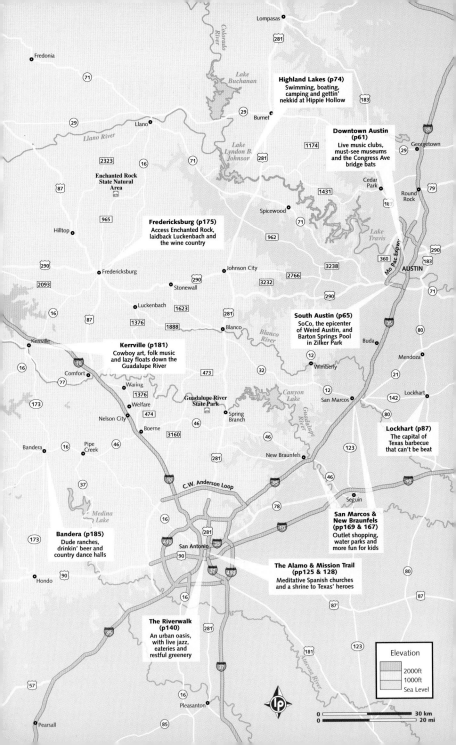

Lompasas

281

Fredonia

71

Colorado River

Lake Buchanan

Highland Lakes (p74)
Swimming, boating, camping and gettin' nekkid at Hippie Hollow

183

29

Llano River

Llano

29

Burnet

281

Downtown Austin (p61)
Live music clubs, must-see museums and the Congress Ave bridge bats

Georgetown

29

79

2323

16

Lake Lyndon B. Johnson

1174

Enchanted Rock State Natural Area

87

1431

Cedar Park

Round Rock

965

Fredericksburg (p175)
Access Enchanted Rock, laidback Luckenbach and the wine country

Spicewood

71

962

Lake Travis

183

360

AUSTIN

290

Hilltop

290

Fredericksburg

290

Johnson City

3238

3232

2766

290

290

183

71

2093

Stonewall

Luckenbach

1623

87

1376

1888

Blanco

Blanco River

South Austin (p65)
SoCo, the epicenter of Weird Austin, and Barton Springs Pool in Zilker Park

Buda

80

16

281

Mo. Pac. Expwy.

Kerrville

70

77

Kerrville (p181)
Cowboy art, folk music and lazy floats down the Guadalupe River

473

32

12

Wimberly

Mendoza

21

Lockhart

142

Comfort

1376

Waring

Welfare

Guadalupe River State Park

12

San Marcos

80

Lockhart (p87)
The capital of Texas barbecue that can't be beat

173

474

Spring Branch

Canyon Lake

Guadalupe River

Nelson City

Boerne

46

123

16

3160

46

16

Bandera

16

Pipe Creek

46

281

New Braunfels

46

Seguin

C.W. Anderson Loop

10

35

80

37

16

78

San Marcos & New Braunfels (pp169 & 167)
Outlet shopping, water parks and more fun for kids

173

Medina River

281

10

410

Bandera (p185)
Dude ranches, drinkin' beer and country dance halls

San Antonio

35

90

90

Hondo

37

410

The Alamo & Mission Trail (pp125 & 128)
Meditative Spanish churches and a shrine to Texas' heroes

80

16

87

87

35

The Riverwalk (p140)
An urban oasis, with live jazz, eateries and restful greenery

281

123

37

181

Pleasanton

Elevation

2000ft
1000ft
Sea Level

57

16

85

Pearsall

0   30 km
0   20 mi

Say howdy to an unforgettable destination, the heart of the Lone Star State. Or state of mind, as the old tune sung by Nanci Griffith goes. Roam the well-trodden halls of the venerable Alamo (p125), hear some live music at one of Austin's 200 clubs, feast at Lockhart's (p87) roadside barbecue shacks or sip a fine Riesling at a Hill Country winery (p173) in an old stone barn. Take a dip in the Highland Lakes (p74) or float lazily along the Guadalupe River outside Kerrville (p181). South-central Texas is a feast for not just the eyes, but all of your senses.

Pay your respects to Stevie Ray Vaughn (p33), Austin's legendary blues-rock hero

Try a brew with a view at the Alamo Drafthouse Cinema (p107), Austin

Wait for dusk, when a million bats swoop from under the Congress Ave bridge (p64), Austin

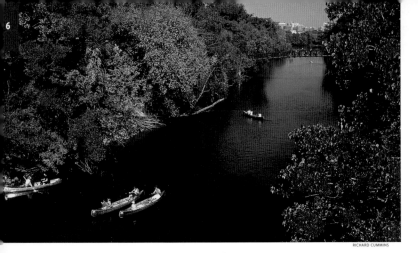

RICHARD CUMMINS

Paddle the jewel-like oasis of Barton Creek Greenbelt in Zilker Park (p72), Austin

Collect curiosities and clothes at San
Antonio's Market Square (p163)

MARK AND AUDREY GIBSON

Climb (p43) challenging outcrops
in the Hill Country

COREY RICH

WITOLD SKRYPCZAK

Tip your hat to Fredericksburg (p175), where Old Europe meets the Old West

Light a votive candle at the historic Mission San Jose (p129), San Antonio

RICHARD CUMMINS

Stroll the festive *Paseo Del Rio*, downtown San Antonio's Riverwalk (p140)

LEE FOSTER

WITOLD SKRYPCZAK

Catch some tunes in Bandera (p185), the cowboy capital of Texas

View the stately buildings of historic New Braunfels (p167).

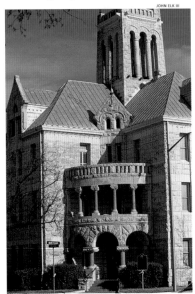

JOHN ELK III

Summit Enchanted Rock (p179), the USA's second-largest granite batholith, Hill Country

WITOLD SKRYPCZAK

Getting Started

Texas truly is a huge state, but you can see a good-size chunk of Austin, San Antonio and the Hill Country in just a week or so. If you have only a few days, limit yourself to Austin and either San Antonio or the Hill Country. You don't need much advance planning unless you're traveling during the peak summer season or attending one of the region's major festivals, such as Austin's SXSW music and media extravaganza or Fiesta San Antonio, in which case you'll need to make arrangements months ahead. At other times it's easy to travel solo, with a couple of friends or as a family – south-central Texas is big enough to accommodate everyone. This region also has a fairly good public transportation network, especially within the major cities, though it is always easier to get around with a car or motorcycle.

WHEN TO GO

South-central Texas' climate makes it possible to visit year-round, but it's not exactly a tropical destination; in winter, temperatures may still dip below freezing at night, even though they stay rather moderate during the day. Winter is definitely the off-season for tourism, and some of the larger theme parks close, such as SeaWorld and Six Flags Fiesta Texas. The best times to visit are during spring (from April to early June) and fall (from September to November), when crowds are thinner, temperatures are more moderate and most attractions are open. Peak summer season – late June through August – can be stiflingly hot, even though there's air-conditioning blasting everywhere. It's also when the region is most crowded. You may want to brave the crowds at other times of year to attend special events.

See Climate Charts (p193) for more information.

COSTS

San Antonio is less expensive than most other large cities in the US, while Austin is definitely a travel bargain. Costs for accommodations vary seasonally, between the cities and the countryside, and between resorts and everywhere else. Generally rates are higher in summer, which is between Memorial Day (the last weekend in May) and Labor Day (the first Monday in September), and for special events, when prices shoot through the roof. Food is reasonable; good restaurant meals can be had for $10. Intracity public transportation is inexpensive. In some areas, such as the Hill Country, a car is the only practical way of getting around, but rentals are reasonably priced, and gasoline still costs less here than in many other US states.

Campers who make most of their own meals and drive their own car might squeeze by on as little as $20 a day. Staying at motels, eating at budget-priced cafés and using public transport, you can expect to spend about $50 a day. Those opting for better hotels with all the amenities, renting a car and splashing out on restaurants and entertainment will pay upwards of $150 per day.

Bargaining is not common, but you can work angles to cut costs. For example, at hotels in the off-season, casually and respectfully mentioning a competitor's rate may prompt a manager to lower the quoted rate. The Internet is an excellent source of lodging and car-rental deals. Discount lodging and dining coupons are widely available – check visitor centers, alternative weeklies and the Sunday papers. Advance tickets to festivals and special events are often much cheaper. Many attractions admit children up to a certain age for free, or sell kids tickets at greatly reduced rates. Look for free days at museums, too.

PRE-DEPARTURE READING

A very short list of Texana titles that are entertaining, witty, quirky and adventurous – as well as educational – might begin with *Shrub: The Short but Happy Political Life of George W Bush* by Molly Ivins and Lou Dubose, which is an excellent, though admittedly left-wing, look at the younger Bush's tenure as Texas governor.

Three Roads to the Alamo: The Lives and Fortunes of David Crockett, James Bowie, and William Barret Travis by William C Davis is a riveting account covering the strange twists of fate that led each man to that epic battle. Many of the short stories in *Woman Hollering Creek* by contemporary Chicana novelist and poet Sandra Cisneros are set in San Antonio (aka the River City). The update of *Lone Star: A History of Texas* by TR Fehrenbach narrates the whole saga, from early Native American tribes, French colonists and Spanish missions to the birth of a republic, Civil War secession and statehood.

An alternative tour guide is *Kinky Friedman's Guide to Texas Etiquette: Or How to Get to Heaven or Hell Without Going Through Dallas-Fort Worth*, written by the part-time country musician, detective novelist and *Texas Monthly* magazine columnist. Robb Walsh's *Legends of Texas Barbecue Cookbook: Recipes and Recollections from the Pit Bosses* visits famous Lone Star smokehouses and barbecue pits, digging up anecdotal gems, tasty cookin' tips and more. Duncan McLean's *Lone Star Swing* is a thrilling and glorious romp throughout the state in search of the roots of his hero, musical legend Bob Wills. It's a great read for a long drive or bus ride.

INTERNET RESOURCES

Lonely Planet (www.lonelyplanet.com) Succinct summaries on traveling to Austin and San Antonio. Travel news and the subWWWay section with links to the most useful travel resources elsewhere on the Web.

Texas Commission on the Arts (www.arts.state.tx.us) Comprehensive calendar of arts and cultural events. Helpful links to travel bargains, general advice and activities.

Texas Historical Commission (www.thc.state.tx.us) Background on historic sites and museums, Texas heritage trails, events and traditional cultures.

Texas Monthly (www.texasmonthly.com) Excellent magazine excerpts, archives and regional travel guides. A real slice of Lone Star lifestyle.

Texas Parks & Wildlife (www.tpwd.state.tx.us) Comprehensive park and wildlife guides, conservation news, safety advice, kids' activities and downloadable brochures.

Travel Texas (www.traveltex.com) Official site of Texas Tourism. Accommodations search engine, events calendar and travel coupons. Order statewide travel guides and Texas-made products.

HOW MUCH?

Bottle of beer
$2.50

Cup of coffee
$1.25

Hotel room
$100-150

Budget motel room
$35-50

Meal at a café
$10

Movie ticket
$7.50

Museum admission
$5 on average

Parking garage
$2-3 per hour

Local phone call
25-50¢

Local bus ride
under $1

TOP TENS

OUR FAVORITE FESTIVALS & EVENTS

Yeehaw! Texans sure know how to celebrate, and there's almost always something interesting going on in the cities or around the Hill Country. The following is our Top 10, but for a comprehensive listing of festivals and events throughout the year, see the Austin and San Antonio chapters.

- San Antonio Stock Show & Rodeo (San Antonio), mid-February (p144)
- South by Southwest (SXSW) (Austin), mid-March (p34)
- Fiesta San Antonio (San Antonio), mid-April (p144)
- Eeyore's Birthday (Austin), late April (p80)
- Kerrville Folk Festival (Kerrville), late May (p182)
- Watermelon Thump (Luling), late June (p144)
- Willie Nelson's 4th of July Picnic (Luckenbach) (p32)
- Fredericksburg's Oktoberfest (Fredericksburg), early October (p176)
- Austin City Limits Music Festival (Austin), mid-September (p80)
- El Día de Los Muertos (San Antonio), early November (p145)

LANDMARK MUSICAL VENUES

Of course, most of the famous live music venues are found in Austin, but also poke your head into the Hill Country's historic dance halls, where some big names – from Bob Wills to Willie Nelson – have played. For a short history of that evolving Austin sound, see the Music chapter.

- Gruene Hall (p168) (Gruene)
- Cactus Cafe (p100) (Austin)
- Antone's (p101) (Austin)
- John T Floore Country Store (p158) (San Antonio)
- Luckenbach's old general store (p180) (Luckenbach)
- *Austin City Limits* TV studio (p100) (Austin)
- Stubb's Bar-B-Q (p101) (Austin)
- Emo's (p101) (Austin)
- Jim Cullum's Landing on the Riverwalk (p157) (San Antonio)
- Waterloo Records (p102) (Austin)

NATURAL ESCAPES

Austin and the Hill Country are meccas for outdoor recreation in Texas. Whether you're a hard-core rock climber or just want to spend a day lazily floating down the river, these spectacular green oases await. See the Outdoors chapter for the complete lowdown.

- Zilker Park (p65)
- New Braunfels (p167) and San Marcos (p169)
- Guadalupe River State Park (p188)
- Bandera (p185)
- Enchanted Rock State Natural Area (p179)
- Barton Creek Greenbelt (p72)
- Lost Maples State Natural Area (p189)
- Lady Bird Johson Wildflower Center (p72)
- Hippie Hollow & the Highland Lakes (p74)
- Hill Country State Natural Area (p186)

Itineraries

CLASSIC ROUTES

TALE OF TWO CITIES   4 days

With only four days to spend, split your time between Austin and San Antonio. Most visitors fly to Texas, then rent a car.

Start with two days around Austin, focusing on sights **downtown** (p61), around the **UT campus** (p65) and the oases of **Zilker Park** (p65); don't miss the **Bob Bullock Texas State History Museum** (p63), a splash in **Barton Springs Pool** (p73) or the **bat colony** (p64) under the Congress Ave bridge. Wacky South Austin is wonderful for people-watching, noshing and shopping. After dark, visit Austin's live music clubs.

On the third day, drive south, stopping off at **Buda** (p112), filled with **antiques stores**, or **Lockhart** (p87), the barbecue capital of Texas. Spend the rest of the day exploring San Antonio's attractions, starting with the **Alamo** (p125) and the **Mission Trail** (p128). Around sunset, stroll along the **Riverwalk** (p140) to catch live jazz at **Jim Cullum's Landing** (p157). The arts district of **Southtown** (p159), **Sunset Station** (p157) and the **St Mary's St Strip** (p157) are nightlife hot spots.

The next morning, drop by the **King William Historic District** (p133) or the **McNay Art Museum** (p138) before leaving town, then spend the afternoon exploring the natural attractions around **New Braunfels** (p167) or **San Marcos** (p169). Families may want to head to **SeaWorld** (p142) or **Six Flags Fiesta Texas** (p142) for the entire day, then drive directly back to Austin.

A whirlwind tour of Austin and San Antonio hits all of the major sights and throws in a detour to the barbecue capital of Texas, traveling 175 miles in just four days.

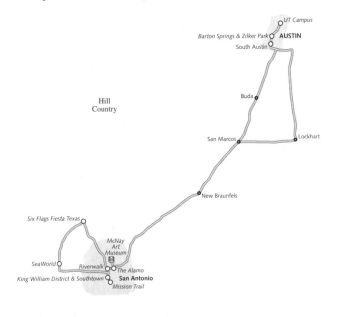

HEAD FOR THE HILLS   1 week or longer

With at least a week, you can explore south-central Texas in depth. You'll need a car. Start with two days in Austin, following the Tale of Two Cities itinerary, then strike out for the Hill Country. Be warned that life moves more slowly out there, and driving distances are longer than you might expect, so don't try to cram too much into a short vacation.

Heading west from Austin, stop first at Hippie Hollow or any of the **Highland Lakes** (p74) or go straight to **Johnson City** (p172). Spend two or three nights in **Fredericksburg** (p175) or **Kerrville** (p181). Activities around the former include a visit to the Texas **wine country** (p173), a climb up **Enchanted Rock** (p179) and a musical pilgrimage to **Luckenbach** (p179). Meanwhile, Kerrville is the place for tubing on the Guadalupe River, cowboy art and dude ranches in nearby **Bandera** (p185). On the way down to San Antonio, go hunting for antiques in **Comfort** (p180) or caving in **Boerne** (p186) or get off the beaten path on the **Waring-Welfare Rd** (p187).

In San Antonio, pick up the Tale of Two Cities itinerary again. On the last day as you make your way back to Austin, save time for stopping in **New Braunfels** (p167) or **San Marcos** (p169), or alternatively for a detour to **Lockhart** (p87) or through **Buda** (p112).

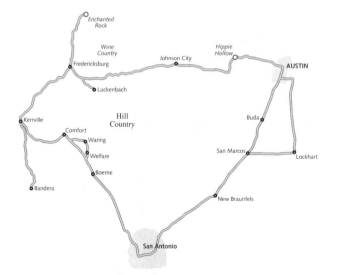

This grand loop traverses the south-central Texas region, starting in Austin and winding through the Hill Country down San Antonio way. Drive a total of 265 to 320 miles, depending on which destinations catch your eye.

TAILORED TRIPS

JUST KIDDIN' AROUND

Whether your kids gravitate toward theme parks, museums or outdoor adventures, you're in luck. Austin, San Antonio and the Hill Country are great family vacation destinations and offer lots of possibilities. For more advice on traveling with children, see p76.

In Austin, start out at the **Bob Bullock Texas State History Museum** (p63). Zip over to Zilker Park for wading in **Barton Springs Pool** (p73), **miniature train rides** (p76) and the wonders of the **Austin Nature & Science Center** (p76). Back downtown, don't miss Austin's own **bat colony** (p64). Dinosaur fun awaits at the **Texas Memorial Museum** (p70). Take a break from the urban scene with a trip out to **Pioneer Farms** (p77) or the **Austin Zoo** (p77).

On the third day, drive south. Aquatic fun awaits in **San Marcos** (p169) or **New Braunfels** (p167). In San Antonio, start by exploring **downtown** (p125), maybe taking a cruise along the **Riverwalk** (p140), then head north up to Brackenridge Park for the excellent **Witte Museum** (p142), old-fashioned **carnival rides** (p142) and more. You could easily spend a whole day at **SeaWorld** (p142) or **Six Flags Fiesta Texas** (p142).

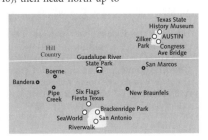

A detour from San Antonio into the Hill Country is highly recommended for giving kids a real taste of cowboy-style Texas life. Try horseback riding in **Bandera** (p185), caving around **Boerne** (p186), the horse refuge at **Pipe Creek** (p187) or **Guadalupe River State Park** (p188).

A SLACKER'S TOUR

Ah, the art of doing almost nothing! The whole 'slacker' phenomenon may be over, but not the slow-motion pace of life in south-central Texas. This tour is for those who want to perfect the art of just hangin'. Best of all, many sights and activities are absolutely free.

In Austin, take a **walking tour** (p75) of the Capitol City and visit the **Guadalupe Arts Center** (p64). Take advantage of free museums at the **University of Texas** (p65) before wandering the **Drag** (p110). Spend a lazy day in Zilker Park at the **botanical gardens** (p65), **Barton Springs Pool** (p73), **Zilker Hillside Theatre** (p109) or an outdoor **summer concert** (p80). Hang out by the Congress Ave bridge **bat colony** (p64) and do full-moon yoga on **Mt Bonnell** (p75). Hit South Austin for shopping and the no-cover 'Hippie Happy Hour' at the **Continental Club** (p103).

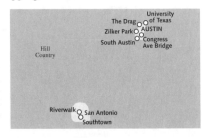

San Antonio has a graceful downtown made for rambling, where you can catch live jazz on the **Riverwalk** (p140). Hop over to the arts district of **Southtown** (p133), especially on First Friday nights. With your own car, you can explore the **Hill Country** (p171), which is loaded with places to just kick back, drink a beer, catch a live show, browse antiques shops and go swimming or inner-tubing.

The Author

SARA BENSON

Sara ('Sam') Benson first danced the two-step while teaching high school in the Rio Grande Valley, which borders Mexico deep in south Texas. In recent years she finds herself visiting the Lone Star State with surprising frequency, especially since signing on with Lonely Planet many moons ago. Her writing has also appeared in the travel pages of the *Dallas Morning News* and other nationwide publications. Already the veteran author of several Lonely Planet city guidebooks, she has previously covered the backroads of Texas and the urban Amarillo scene for Lonely Planet's *Road Trip: Route 66*.

My Austin, San Antonio & the Hill Country

With only a few days to spend, here's a wish list of my favorites. In Austin, a morning splash at Barton Springs Pool (p73), then shopping and lunch on wacky SoCo (p110) before watching the Congress Ave Bridge bat colony (p64). Afterward I'd hit the live music clubs, Waterloo Records (p102) and a midnight flick at the Alamo Drafthouse Cinema (p107). Texas-style barbecue in Lockhart (p87) fuels me for visiting San Antonio's Mission Trail (p128), perusing the arts district of Southtown (p133) and delving into the McNay Art Museum (p138). At night the Riverwalk (p157) is the place for libations and live jazz. On my drive back to Austin I'd visit the Hill Country towns of Kerrville (p181) and Fredericksburg (p175), stopping off at swimming holes, Enchanted Rock (p179), antiques stores, country dance halls and wineries along the way.

CONTRIBUTING AUTHORS:

Sam Martin wrote the Music Chapter (p30). Sam is a writer and longtime Austin resident who listens to old country, blues and jazz. Sam's writing has appeared in *Cosmopolitan UK, Budget Living, Natural Home* and the *Austin Chronicle*. His first book, *How to Mow the Lawn: The Lost Art of Being a Man*, was published in 2003.

David Goldberg MD wrote the Health Chapter (p203). Dr Goldberg completed his training in internal medicine and infectious diseases at Columbia-Presbyterian Medical Center in New York City, where he has also served as voluntary faculty. At present, he is an infectious diseases specialist in Scarsdale, New York, and the editor-in-chief of the website MDTravelHealth.com.

16

Snapshot

Texas entered the 21st century riding high, with former governor George W Bush sent to the US presidency and plenty of tech-fueled construction. But a few clouds descended soon after Bush's inauguration day, as a gyrating stock market hit the tech economy hard, causing Austin-based Dell Computers to announce its first-ever layoffs. Meanwhile, in the state capitol, the Texas legislature, realizing that a round of late-1990s tax cutting had resulted in a deep deficit, also began struggling to balance the books. These events – coupled with the 2001 terrorist attacks on the US and the nationwide scandal of wire fraud and money laundering by the Houston-based Enron Corporation – sent a sobering message statewide.

Of course, Austin's tech economy couldn't have continued on its super-heated course indefinitely. Yet there are still things to cheer about. If Texas were an independent country, it would have the 11th-largest economy in the world. Despite the dot-com bust, more than 50,000 people from other states are still packing up their homes every year to start life anew in Austin and San Antonio. What's more, those people who don't relocate do visit often. San Antonio in particular thrives on tourism, with more than eight million annual visitors feeding the River City's multibillion-dollar hospitality biz. In Austin, the South by Southwest (SXSW) music and media conference keeps growing exponentially, generating $25 million for the Capitol City each year.

Speaking of Austin, political hijinks there fueled as much entertainment as rancor during 2003. When Republican lawmakers attempted to redraw US congressional voting districts, Democrats temporarily halted the shenanigans by fleeing the state – not once, but twice. Their sojourns in Oklahoma and later New Mexico failed to produce tangible legislative results, however.

National attention turned to the Lone Star State earlier that same year when the Supreme Court struck down the state's anti-sodomy law because it unfairly discriminated against same-sex couples. It was a leap forward for gay rights, and not just in Texas. But the conservative Southern politics of President Dubya still represent the face of Texas to the nation, which tends to annoy progressive Austin residents who are passionate about some of the very things that Dubya works so hard against. One hotly debated arena of local politics is environmental protection, in which golf courses and condo developers square off against grassroots environmental groups.

When it comes to cultivating an enviable lifestyle, Texans do agree on the fundamentals of fun. This is despite any political tumult and the recent economic slowdown, which many residents are using as a chance to catch their breath. Outdoor escapes are always popular, especially on long summer weekends. Another subject of universal appeal is Austin's live music scene. In sports, everybody talks up the San Antonio Spurs basketball team, which won a second NBA championship in 2003, and Austin's Lance Armstrong, who has claimed his fifth Tour de France win. The film industry is booming, too.

FAST FACTS

Texas population: 22 million

Gross State Product (GSP): over $700 billion annually

Average personal income: $30,000

Unemployment rate as of mid-2003: 6.6%

Active concealed handgun licenses in Texas: 218,700

Average number of tornadoes per year: 130

Percentage of families who speak Spanish at home: 27%

Mexican free-tailed bats hanging under Austin's Congress Ave Bridge: up to 1 million

History

The earliest evidence of humans in what is now Texas exists in the *llano estacado* ('staked plain') section of Texas and New Mexico. Little is known about the various indigenous peoples, but by the time the first Europeans arrived in the 16th century, several distinct groups of Indians were settled in the region.

SPANISH EXPLORATION

In 1519, Alonzo Álvarez de Piñeda mapped the coast of the Gulf of Mexico from Florida to Mexico, creating the first maps of present-day Texas. He camped at the mouth of the Rio Grande (which he called the 'river of palms'). The Spanish planned a settlement along the Rio Grande, but after battles following disagreements between settlers and Coahuiltecan tribespeople, the Spanish withdrew.

History buffs should visit the Daughters of the Republic of Texas Library online at www.drtl.org.

In 1542 Luis de Moscoso led an exploration of present-day east Texas. He was frantically looking for gold – Indians would always tell him it was located somewhere else – but he never found any. What he and his men did notice was that the whole place was covered in this black stuff that was slimy, smelled bad and burned easily. It was oil, aka 'black gold.' They used the material to caulk ship seals and for other pedestrian applications, but apparently did not consider using it as fuel.

A NEW MISSION

By 1600, Spain controlled Florida and nearly all of present-day Mexico and Central America, among other lands. While the conquest of new lands was brutal, Spain's *conquistadores* considered their objectives not just economic and political but moral: winning over new Christian souls.

By the mid-17th century, the Spaniards' tack was more 'please read this pamphlet' than 'take me to the gold.' They embarked on the construction of a series of *misións* (missions) and *presidios* (forts) from Florida across the continent all the way to California in an effort to convert the Native Americans to Christianity and, not incidentally, into Spanish subjects.

The Texas State Historical Association maintains an enormous handbook of Texas history at www.tsha.utexas.edu.

More than 30 missions were constructed in Texas. The missions at their best were fully self-reliant outposts in which missionaries taught local Native Americans Spanish, as well as European building and farming techniques. During the heyday of the missions, from 1745 to 1775, they became successful enough to attract the attention of Apache and Comanche Indians, who began a series of crippling attacks.

THE FRENCH THREAT

Meanwhile, the French were also exploring North America. In the 1680s, they laid claim to the territory they called Louisiana and to a piece of Texas. This hardly amused the Spanish, and it spurred them to begin their mission-building in Texas.

In 1690, construction of Spain's first mission in east Texas, Misión San Francisco de los Tejas, began. It was completed in 1691, failing only two years later – but not before the Spaniards had taken a corruption of the Caddo Indian word for friend, which they pronounced *tejas* ('tay-has'), and used it as the name for the entire new territory.

Over the next 20 years, the Spanish continued to settle east Texas, but many of the missions designed to fortify the east Texas border fell to disease, incompetence, skirmishes with Indians and French troops and other disasters. In 1718, the Spanish began building missions and presidios in south-central Texas to reduce the distance crossed by supply trains.

Misión San Antonio de Valero, which later became known as the Alamo, and the present-day Mission Trail were constructed around this time. In 1731, the settlement of Villa de Bexar was established by Spanish colonists imported from the Canary Islands, and a civil government was established in the area.

The Spanish finally gave up control in 1821, and Texas became a state of newly independent Mexico. Under Mexican rule the missions were discontinued.

AMERICANS HORN IN

Before 1820, settlers moving to Texas from the US were mainly 'resettled' Native Americans, who were being forcibly removed from newly acquired US territories in the southeast.

The first large group of Anglo-American settlers in Texas arrived as the result of a deal brokered by Moses Austin. He negotiated for the Spanish government to allow him and 300 families from the US to move into central Texas, but he died before the actual move could begin. His son, Stephen Fuller Austin, who is credited in Texas folklore as being the 'Father of Texas,' carried out his father's plans in 1821.

Over the next several years, Austin's settlements extended to the Colorado River, the Camino Real and the Gulf Coast, attracting more than 5000 Americans and a bustling trade with Mexico. The word 'Texian' was coined to describe the region's residents, who were beginning to form a separate identity. In 1826, a short-lived attempt at a nation within Texas, the Republic of Fredonia, foreshadowed Texian demands for independence from Mexico.

The Alamo (1960) was John Wayne's paean to Texas heroism; he directed and financed the film, which left him in debt for the rest of his life. Final battle scenes redeem much of the early speechifying.

Earlier settlers in Texas called for the region to be admitted to the US. By 1830, with more than 30,000 settlers in the Texas territory, the situation was becoming, well, revolting. In that year, a Mexican decree banned further American settlement and limited the importation of slaves. By 1833, political unrest in Mexico led to the imposition of martial law in many Mexican territories, including Texas.

TEXAS' WAR FOR INDEPENDENCE

Stephen Austin traveled to Mexico City to plead the settlers' case for independence, but after being faced down by Mexican government bureaucrats, he wrote back to the Texian settlers, telling them to forget about permission and go ahead and set up an independent government. Austin was arrested and detained in Mexico until 1835. Meanwhile, William B Travis led a group of hotheaded Texians who took up arms to keep reinforcements of Mexican troops from arriving in Texas. This led to a direct confrontation with General Martín Perfecto de Cós, who would later be transferred to San Antonio.

Armed skirmishes throughout 1835 sparked the Texas War for Independence, which officially ran from September 30, 1835, to April 21, 1836. Those who died at the Alamo became heroes, and the battle itself is now considered a pivotal point in Texas – and American – history. Perhaps because of losses suffered and supplies used at the Alamo and Goliad, Mexican general Antonio López de Santa Anna's troops simply were not prepared when, on April 21, they ran into Texian troops under the command of Samuel Houston, a former major general in Tennessee's militia and 'Indian fighter' under US general Andrew Jackson. At the Battle of San Jacinto, Santa Anna's troops were routed.

THE LONE STAR REPUBLIC

While Texas declared itself an independent republic, neither the USA nor Mexico recognized it as such. In its early years the new republic's main business was maintaining its viability as a republic, forging trade and political ties with neighbors and trying very hard to establish a government-like capital city.

In 1839, the central Texas village of Waterloo was renamed Austin, in honor of Stephen F, and the capital was established there. That same year, the Republic of Texas' policy toward the Indians who lived within its borders changed drastically, and a ruthless campaign of Native American removal began. Later, President Sam Houston and the republic lobbied Washington for annexation as a territory in order to gain assistance in ridding Texas of Native Americans and to settle the border dispute with Mexico. After a state constitutional convention in 1845, Texas was annexed to the USA as a state.

This led directly to the Mexican-American War (1846–48), a total rout in which US troops captured Mexico City from indefatigable Santa Anna, who had lost and been restored to power several times since the Texas War for Independence.

DID YOU KNOW?
Texas is unique in the USA as the only state that once was a republic (1836–45) unto itself.

THE ALAMO

'You may all go to hell, and I will go to Texas.' – Davy Crockett, in 1835

It's hard to tell the story of the Battle of the Alamo – there is hot debate about almost every fact. For instance, it's difficult to verify with exact certainty the number of defenders, of Mexican troops and of casualties, among many other details. This is a volatile issue because Texans are touchy about people challenging the legends of their heroes.

Objective accounts are hard to find. Consider, for example, how the Alamo defenders are described in text reprinted in dozens of city-produced manuals and histories: '[They fought] against Santa Anna's intolerable decrees. Other [defenders] were Volunteers such as Davy Crockett and his "Tennessee Boys" who owned nothing in Texas and owed nothing to it. Theirs was a fight against tyranny wherever it might be.'

It is, however, generally agreed that on February 23, 1836, Mexican general Antonio López de Santa Anna led anywhere from 2500 to 5000 Mexican troops in an attack against the Alamo. The 160 or so men inside the fortress included James Bowie (of knife fame), who was in command of the Alamo until pneumonia rendered him too sick; William B Travis, who took command of the troops after Bowie's incapacity; and perhaps most famous of all, David Crockett, called 'Davy' by everyone. Crockett, a three-time US congressman from Tennessee with interesting taste in headgear, first gained fame as a frontiersman and then for his public arguments with President Andrew Jackson over the latter's murderous campaigns of Indian 'removal' in the southeastern USA. Less well known were Bowie's and Travis' black slaves, who fought alongside their masters during the battle and survived.

Travis dispatched a now-famous letter to other revolutionaries pleading for reinforcements, saying that his men would not stand down under any circumstances – his call was for 'Victory or Death.' Because of slow communications, the only reinforcements that arrived in time were a group of about 30 men from Gonzales, Texas, bringing the total number of Alamo defenders up to 189, according to literature from the Daughters of the Republic of Texas (DRT), which lists the names of all but one, an unidentified black man.

Santa Anna's troops pounded the Alamo for 13 days before retaking it. Mexican losses were devastating; estimates run as low as 1000 and as high as 2000. When the Alamo was finally recaptured, the advancing troops executed almost all of the surviving defenders. The few who were spared, mostly women, children and slaves, were interrogated and released.

The Battle of the Alamo was pivotal in the war because during the two weeks Santa Anna's army was distracted in San Antonio, Texas troops were gathering strength and advancing, fueled by what they called the wholesale slaughter of their brothers in arms, under the battle cry 'Remember the Alamo!'

THE CIVIL WAR & RECONSTRUCTION

The US Civil War (1861–65) was brought on by a number of issues, but a few stand in the foreground, especially the profound moral and economic debate over slavery. Settlers poured into Texas from slave-owning states in the South, but Governor Houston was firmly against the South-favored secession. Popular opinion and a referendum defeated him, and he was forced to resign as governor.

Texas seceded from the USA and joined the Confederate States of America on March 16, 1861. Aside from providing an estimated 80,000 troops, Texas' role in the Civil War was mainly one of supplying food to the Confederate war machine. There were very few battles fought on Texas soil, but the Civil War was one of the bloodiest conflicts in the history of modern warfare, and wounds ran incredibly deep for years afterward.

President Andrew Johnson, a Southerner and former slaveholder who succeeded Lincoln, devised a Reconstruction plan. While his plan granted many concessions, it was absolutely firm that the states' constitutions ratify the 13th Amendment, abolishing slavery, before readmittance. The Texas Constitution of 1866, hastily drawn up to assure readmittance to the union, granted blacks some measure of civil rights, but it did not give them the right to vote until martial law imposed it. Hyper-restrictive Black Codes, later to be expanded to what became known as Jim Crow laws, were introduced, making it illegal for blacks to be unemployed, restricting freedom of movement and segregating much of Southern life into white and black camps.

The Searchers (dir John Ford, 1956) is definitely John Wayne's finest role. A pioneer family is murdered on their Texas ranch, and their daughter Natalie Wood is kidnapped, setting off a decade-long search by her uncle, the Duke.

ON THE CATTLE TRAIL

During the Civil War, the Confederate forces' need for food had increased Texas cattle production. Ranching in Texas became an enormous business, and cattle drives – the herding of up to 200,000 head of longhorn steers northward – were born.

Of all the trails that ran through Texas, it was the Chisholm Trail – from San Antonio to Abilene, Kansas, at the western terminus of the Kansas Pacific Railroad – that really spurred the business of bringing Texas cattle to market. San Antonio boomed as a cattle town. European settlers, including vast numbers of Germans and Czechs, moved to the area, and the Germans built the city's King William District, named for Kaiser Wilhelm I of Prussia. In 1879, Fort Sam Houston was established by the US Army.

Austin also began to boom after the arrival of the Houston and Texas Central Railroad in 1871. By 1900, the city was as cosmopolitan as many in the East, with electricity, telephones, theaters, opera houses and the Moonlight Towers – 165ft streetlights, unique to Austin, that illuminated the city by night. Seventeen towers remain operational and are designated historic landmarks.

Throughout the late 19th century, cattle constituted Texas' main business (followed by agriculture, such as cotton), and ranching became a Texan way of life. However, increased settlement ended the traditional Texas ranching method of allowing cattle to graze unchecked, and the 1873 invention of barbed wire led to the fencing of the range.

By the early 1880s, fences stretched across Texas. But cowboys and ranchers would travel throughout the countryside cutting them down, and shots were fired more and more frequently. The Texas Rangers – who were established as border guards in 1835, called up for special services in the Civil War and for Indian fighting duties after it – were reinstated as a state police force. This was, effectively, the end of what most people think of as the cowboy era.

BLACK GOLD

As early as 1866, oil wells were striking in east Texas. At the time, oil was being put to a number of uses, including the sealing of dirt roads. But speculators bet that oil, found in sufficient supply, could replace coal as an energy mainstay.

Everything changed on January 10, 1901, when a drilling site at Spindletop, east of Houston in Beaumont, pierced a salt dome, setting forth a gusher of oil so powerful that it took days to bring it under control. Spindletop began producing an estimated 80,000 barrels of oil per day. As the automobile and railroads turned to the oil industry for fuel, discoveries of 'black gold' financed the construction of much of modern Texas.

San Antonio's early-20th-century growth, however, was also due to the military; Fort Sam Houston was joined by Kelly Air Force Base, now the nation's oldest air force base, in 1917, followed by Lackland, Randolph and Brooks Air Force Bases.

THE GREAT DEPRESSION

Following the end of WWI in 1918, Texas' economic machine, as well as the nation's, was humming right along. The surge in private automobiles made for an enormous Texas oil boom, and people were dancing the Charleston in the streets.

Then, on Black Thursday, October 24, 1929, the New York Stock Exchange hiccuped, and the bottom fell out. The crash, the result of unchecked Wall Street trading practices, led the country and the world into the Great Depression. Northern Texas was part of the region that became known as the 'dust bowl,' former farmland destroyed by overuse and lack of rain. Increased oil production caused a market glut that further depressed prices.

As part of Roosevelt's New Deal, the Works Progress Administration (WPA) and Civilian Conservation Corps (CCC) were created. The CCC worked to restore state and national parks, and the WPA sent armies of workers to construct buildings, roads, dams, trails and housing. For Texas, one of the most important contributions made by WPA workers was the restoration and renovation of the old Spanish missions, which had fallen into disrepair since Texas' independence from Mexico.

WWII & RECOVERY

During WWII (1939–45), Texas became a major training ground for soldiers; a dozen new military bases were created and more than 40 airfields were activated. This helped spur the local economy, which was further lifted by the unprecedented national prosperity that followed the war. For the next 15 years, the nation's economy surged, fueled by low consumer credit rates and a defense-based economy that plowed money into manufacturing military hardware, as well as ever more automobiles.

THE 1960s

Native son Lyndon Baines Johnson was from Stonewall, east of Austin, in south-central Texas. Johnson, affectionately known as LBJ, had a well-deserved reputation for being a hard-nosed Southern Democrat. He was as stubborn as a barnful of mules, as dirty a political fighter as he needed to be and fiercely loyal to Texas in the fight for pork-barrel government contracts. As majority leader of the US Senate, Johnson accepted the vice-presidential nomination in 1960.

On November 22, 1963, President John Fitzgerald Kennedy and Vice President Johnson rode in separate open limousines through downtown Dallas. At 12:30pm, JFK was shot. Texas governor John M Connally, riding in the seat in front of the president, was also injured by gunfire. The president died at 1pm; Connally survived. Later that day, as Kennedy's body was being transported to Washington, DC, Vice President Johnson took the oath of office aboard *Air Force One,* the presidential airplane, with Jacqueline Kennedy standing at his side.

LBJ defeated Barry Goldwater in the presidential election of 1964, and his administration oversaw some of the USA's most tumultuous events, from the troop buildup and invasion of North Vietnam to civil protest at home. The Johnson Administration also shepherded 'the Great Society,' an unprecedented flurry of social legislation.

THE ENERGY CRISIS

The energy crisis in the 1970s brought Sultan-of-Bruneian wealth to Texas. The crisis began when members of the Organization of Petroleum Exporting Countries (OPEC) imposed a major reduction in oil sales to the US and its allies to punish the US for its pro-Israel policy. Texans found themselves the biggest domestic suppliers of oil, and laughed all the way to the bank.

Some newly rich Texans bought British titles outright from debt-ridden members of the British aristocracy, creating legions of Lady Jane

---

YELLOW DOG DEMOCRATS

It may be hard to remember a time before George W Bush governed the state of Texas, let alone the nation. But in fact the Lone Star State has a long history of political opposition to the conservative mainstream.

The nickname 'Yellow Dog Democrats' refers to die-hard Democrats who'd vote for an old hound before voting Republican. With a stronghold in east Texas, their voter base is increasingly Latino. Among the candidates that they've managed to elect over the years is Ann Richards, who was governor from 1990 to 1994. Incidentally, when Richards was elected state treasurer in 1982, she became the first woman to hold statewide political office in Texas in more than half a century. But she was not Texas' first female governor; Miriam 'Ma' Ferguson twice successfully ran for the office in the early 20th century.

Texas' 1990 gubernatorial race was one of the messiest in state history. Richards' Republican opponent, rancher and oil millionaire Clayton Williams, started out with TV ads portraying him as a traditional Texas cowboy. Richards took up the gauntlet and painted herself as a tough-but-tender frontierswoman. Later the two candidates began muckraking – alcoholism, divorce, illegal drugs and more got thrown into the mix – but the race wasn't over until Williams made a joke about rape in front of reporters. All told, the two candidates spent $50 million on the race.

After Richards won, she spent her term as governor getting the state's finances back on track, passing stricter law enforcement measures and reforming the state's educational system in favor of local initiative. She was defeated during her 1994 reelection bid by George W Bush; mainstream voters decided they wanted a change. As Molly Ivins put it, 'The issues were God, gays and guns,' and Dubya's conservative platform won voters over.

Ann Richards' continuing presence on the national scene ensures she won't be forgotten. She also presents an alternative version of Texas politics to the Bush dynasty's. She has given keynote addresses at national Democratic conventions and still lectures around the country, having achieved renown for her folksy wit. She will also be remembered for her strong personality and flamboyance (she once posed on a motorcycle in full biker gear for a political photo-op). Meanwhile, back in the Lone Star State, the Yellow Dog Democrats continue to voice their dissent on the Texas political scene, especially in recent virulent debates over political redistricting.

Billy Bobs and Duke Zachary Jims. Ranches became practically passé in the move to bigger and better spreads for oil barons, who also built skyscrapers, hotels, casinos and pleasure domes. *Dallas,* the prime-time soap opera following the hijinks of that wacky, oil-rich Ewing clan, premiered in 1978.

At the same time, the USA was searching for new sources of oil and developing new types of energy. While OPEC nations argued, the price of oil halved; by 1986, the price was down to a paltry $10 a barrel, and Texas was hurting. Oil extraction and exploration became unprofitable.

It took another war – this time, the 1991 Persian Gulf War – to make things better and drive oil prices back up by several bucks a barrel, and not a few have speculated about whether that wasn't one of former US president George Bush's main reasons for starting the war in the first place. But that's another story.

Made in Texas: George W Bush and the Southern Takeover of American Politics by maverick Michael Lind examines the interplay of Bible Belt religion, big money and the Old South in the national political arena.

TEXAS TODAY

Today the Texas economy is based on several breadwinners, and oil is surprisingly low on the list. The state now produces the second-largest number of jobs per year in the United States.

During the 1990s the Texas economy grew strongly, and trade with Mexico has boomed since the 1994 passage of the North American Free Trade Agreement (NAFTA). Technology was another big story in the 1990s; Austin, with its highly educated populace, became a powerhouse of high-tech companies and innovation. To top it off, another Texan was elected to the White House in 2000, though many Americans feel former Texas Governor George W Bush's victory was compromised by electoral irregularities.

George W Bushisms: The Slate Book of the Accidental Wit & Wisdom of Our 43rd President is a slim collection of such classic Bush pronouncements as, 'It's clearly a budget. It's got a lot of numbers in it.'

As Texas learned with the oil business, what goes up must come down. Texas' new tech barons felt the pain as stocks started crashing in 2000. Even another energy crisis in 2001 couldn't give Texas much of a boost since, this time, its economy has become much more diversified and it is just one of many suppliers on the global energy scene. Still, the Lone Star State is unusually resilient and resourceful. If any state can get by on an inexhaustible supply of pride and moxie, Texas is the one.

THE SON ALSO RISES

In January 2001, Republican George W Bush became only the second son in American history (after John Quincy Adams in 1824) to follow his father to the White House. Bush, born in 1946, grew up in Midland and Houston, Texas, where his father was in the oil business. Despite never before having run for office, Bush won the Texas governorship in 1994. He then became the first Texas governor ever to win a second consecutive four-year term, taking 68.6% of the vote in 1998.

By then, Bush's eyes were on the US presidency. He took office in 2001 after a controversial and bitterly contested election. His first months in the White House were marked by a slowing economy, soaring energy prices and other domestic concerns. However, the terrorist attacks of September 11, 2001, thrust the once isolationist president onto the world stage.

While initially the president enjoyed wide domestic support for his 'war on terrorism,' the uncertain results of the war in Afghanistan and the increasingly drawn-out occupation of Iraq are taking a toll on his approval ratings. Even more troublesome to the president as he seeks a second term is the state of the US economy, with its 'jobless recovery' and growing deficit. As of this writing, the 2004 presidential race is heating up, with Democratic candidates challenging Bush on all these fronts. But whether voters reelect Bush or make him a one-term president like his father will most likely depend on whether the economy makes the promised turnaround.

Culture

People who have visited Dallas or Houston but never Austin, San Antonio or the Hill Country are in for a surprise. South-central Texas is an infinitely more relaxed place, with an easy-going attitude. Except at rush hour in the big cities, things may be quite a bit slower around here than you may be used to. Get into the rhythm of Texas life; smell the bluebonnets and enjoy yourself. You'll have a great time.

REGIONAL IDENTITY

Austin takes pride in its small-town feel, even since the high-tech boom turned it from sleepy college town to hip urban center. Residents long resisted the 'invasion' of their town by New Yorkers and Californians who tried to turn Austin into the next Silicon Valley. Austin is still a place where folks feel comfortable in a pair of faded jeans and a T-shirt. Anything goes here, and often it does.

www.roundtop.com is a wacky cyber-taste of the alternative Hill Country.

Politically, Austin is a left-leaning island in a conservative sea. This is partly due to Austin's university population, but also to the city's love affair with its music. Austin's rich culture, progressive thinking and geographic proximity to the Gulf of Mexico earn the city its nickname – the USA's 'Third Coast.'

San Antonio is a more conservative city. The city's attitudes are more urban and upscale overall, but there's also a vibrant arts scene. Strong ties to Texas' Mexican past are more in evidence here than in the Capitol City. Tejano and *conjunto* music draw bigger crowds than indie rock bands, and Latino cultural festivals are celebrated throughout the year.

Though the Hill Country is a tad more conservative still, you'll still find artist hamlets and quiet, friendly retreats. Many now living in the hills are expats from Austin, San Antonio and elsewhere who got tired

SLACKERS & KEEPING AUSTIN WEIRD

After Richard Linklater's movie *Slacker* came out in 1991, Austin became known as a laidback place with a 'whatever, man' attitude populated by layabouts with body piercings, long hair and an odd predilection for philosophical discourse at any hour of the day. At first the slacker spotlight was embraced: Linklater had helped define a generation and that generation's hometown became Austin. Several years later when outsiders began to discredit all of those living in the Capitol City as lazy dreamers and, well, slackers, that same spotlight began to chafe.

These days most Austinites no longer think of themselves as slackers, nor do they consider their town Slacker Central. In the 10-plus years since Linklater's movie was released, the Austin economy has boomed. High-tech companies employing software writers, web designers and computer graphics artists brought Austin a new wealth of idea-oriented individuals, who are not only creative but motivated. Even now that the dot-com bust and its economic aftermath have thinned out some of the city's high-tech businesses, Austin is defined by a new kind of creativity and progress.

That said, the change from Slacker Central to Silicon Hills has left Austin's longtime residents longing for the weirder days of yore before BMWs and Mercedes started clogging the streets and hair styles went from purple punk to purposeful. Bumper stickers and T-shirts have started appearing all over town embossed with the logo 'Keep Austin Weird' (click to www.keepaustin weird.com), a plea to locals and newcomers alike to show respect for Austin's oddities. Several local businesses have co-opted the phrase and many residents are taking note and are repatriating their freak flags with renewed vigor. It's just one more thing that makes Austin, well, Austin.

of urban stresses. So don't head to the hills expecting hillbillies; many in Austin and San Antonio consider folks out there pretty wise.

LIFESTYLE

With its bars, live music clubs and the University of Texas (UT), Austin is a fantastic place to be young and single. Because of Austin's laidback atmosphere, it's easy to meet someone and strike up a conversation, which many a stranger will do. Don't be alarmed. At the same time, Austin has enormous appeal to families due to its slower pace, low crime rate and abundant parks. Austinites spend lots of time outdoors, except when extreme summer heat keeps everyone sitting next to their air conditioners. Open-air cafés abound, and restaurants and bars often have outdoor seating year-round. Though the city isn't as racially diverse as some larger cities, there is a broad attitude of tolerance.

There is also a significant homeless population. Homeless youth hang out mainly along the Drag near UT. Many panhandle at busy intersections by holding signs, gesturing and performing for stopped cars. Most are friendly and harmless. Some, like 'Leslie,' a rail-thin bearded man dressed in drag, have become city fixtures. Leslie has been featured in city-sponsored parades, including one thrown for UT running back Ricky Williams when Williams won college football's Heisman Trophy in 1998. Leslie wore a silver prom dress and rode in a convertible Corvette. He also has run for mayor – unsuccessfully – in each of the past three elections. His platform? Keep Austin Weird.

It's out of print, but Stephen Brook's *Honkytonk Gelato: Travels Through Texas*, a collection of essays on Lone Star peccadilloes as seen through the eyes of an Englishman, is a real hoot.

San Antonio is a more racially diverse but also divided city. Although SA is subject to the same issues of urban blight as Austin, or any other big US city for that matter, most visitors are unlikely to see evidence of it, except in poorer parts of downtown or along the Mission Trail. Overall, the River City lifestyle is affluent and fast-paced. Urban, rather than

---

CONCEALED HANDGUNS

The rifle rack is as much a Texas tradition as the pickup truck. Most gun owners are law-abiding citizens, and Texans are discovering that more often than not, an armed society is a polite society. But it's also true that Texas has seen more than its share of gun-related disasters – the JFK assassination in Dallas, the shootings from the University of Texas Tower in Austin and the mass murder in Luby's chief among them.

On October 16, 1991, a madman opened fire on customers in a Luby's Cafeteria in Killeen, Texas. After the shooting, a survivor remarked that if only she'd been armed she could have stopped the carnage. This could have been the straw that broke the back of resistance to a state law granting a concealed weapons permit to any Texan never convicted of a felony who passes a course in handgun use and safety. A version of the bill was vetoed by Democratic governor Ann Richards in 1993, but a new bill was later signed by Richards' Republican successor, George W Bush.

Over 200,000 Texans (just under 1%) are now licensed and armed with concealed handguns, but the impact of the law is unclear – Texas hasn't seen an increase in random shootings, and it's likely you won't notice the situation at all. Public offices and private businesses are permitted to ban the carrying of concealed weapons on their premises, which is why you'll see signs forbidding firearms in places like post offices, restaurants, movie theaters, theme parks and at the Alamo.

Because the numbers of pistol-packin' people is unclear, you might want to take steps to avoid being introduced to the latest Colt industries product. Never argue with or make rude gestures at other motorists. And when pulled over by a police car, especially at night, keep both your hands in plain sight at all times (preferably atop the steering wheel) so the officer doesn't mistake your movements for a 'reach' (as in reaching for a weapon).

outdoor, endeavors are key. Locals aren't above strolling the Riverwalk, enjoying its outdoor cafés and bars. Most weekend activities revolve around family and cultural festivities. Gay and lesbian travelers will find a friendly, even welcoming atmosphere.

Life in the Hill Country is paced slower than in San Antonio, or even the Capitol City. On daytripper-free weekdays, shop owners casually open their doors around 10am and close around 4pm – if they open at all. It's not uncommon to find doors locked with signs that say 'Gone fishin': be back after lunch.' As in Austin, Hill Country folks are fond of the sunny skies and mild temperatures found in the fall, winter and spring. They spend plenty of time tending to ranches and yards, painting in open-air studios or just sitting on a neighbor's front porch. At night, though, you can always find a country band and a dance hall jumping with two-steppers and beer drinkers. Folks in the hills know how to have fun.

www.spanishpronto.com has a handy primer for Spanish vocabulary and grammar.

POPULATION

Because of warm weather, the technology boom and the absence of state income tax, San Antonio and Austin were two of the USA's top 10 fastest-growing cities in the 1990s. That trend won't be letting up anytime soon. Despite the current sour economy, south-central Texas still adds warm bodies at a rate of over 2% a year. That's about 30,000 people a year moving to San Antonio, only slightly less for the greater Austin area.

For the most part, the population of south-central Texas has a mix of European and Mexican heritage. The Hill Country especially is dotted with towns – Fredericksburg and New Braunfels, for example – that claim German heritage. San Antonio's Mexican flavor is bolstered by the city's Latino residents, more than half of the city's population. Austin has a large Hispanic population; about a third of its citizens claim Latin descent. Both cities have only a small percentage of African American residents.

The Last Picture Show (dir Peter Bogdanovich, 1971) is an engaging film based on a Larry McMurtry novel that traces the coming of age of two high school football players in a deader-than-dirt small Texas town in the 1950s.

SPORTS

Sports in this part of Texas don't seem to be on as high a pedestal as they are in Dallas and Houston. There's only one professional team – the NBA's San Antonio Spurs – and one big-time college program – UT Austin. But it's not uncommon to find people passionately proud of the teams they do have, and with good reason.

From October to April, everyone in the River City is aware that the NBA basketball season is underway. The Spurs won their second NBA championship in 2003, an event that brought normally sleepy San Antonio into the streets and onto the Riverwalk to celebrate. Spurs fans also inhabit the Hill Country and Austin; local newscasters report on the team as if it were their own.

UT's football, baseball and basketball teams compete with the nation's best college teams. The women's basketball program is a powerhouse; since coach Judy Conradt started in 1976, the Lady Longhorns have won an astounding 86% of their games, taking the national title in 1986 in an undefeated 34-0 season. Both women's and men's teams made it to the NCAA tournament's Final Four in 2003. (For the men, it was their first appearance since 1947.) Playing from February to May, the Longhorn baseball team has achieved a higher average winning percentage than any other college team over the past 25 years. Major-league baseball teams recruit UT players, including the New York Yankees' Roger Clemens, one of the best pitchers ever. In 2002, the Longhorns won their sixth College World Series.

The Longhorn football team is no slouch either. In 1998, Ricky Williams – now a running back for the NFL's Miami Dolphins – broke the NCAA's record for most career rushing yards in a single season. During crisp fall months in Austin, it's common to see the school colors – orange and white – in storefronts and on banners all over town. The games against Texas A&M and the University of Oklahoma are sources of home-team fervor. Games are held at the 80,000-plus Texas Memorial Stadium, with the exception of the Texas-Oklahoma game, played at Dallas' Cotton Bowl. Tickets are nearly impossible to score. Traffic snarls during the Saturday afternoon games. Cheering can be heard for miles.

Most of the rest of the sports played in south-central Texas fly under the radar. Indoor ice hockey was recently introduced to the region, bizarrely enough. In 2003, the Austin Ice Bats played the San Antonio Iguanas for the semipro Central Hockey League championship. Playing a cold-weather sport in a hot-weather market, the Iguanas promptly went out of business after losing to the Ice Bats. Austin's team continues to skate at the somewhat remote Travis County Exposition Center; the games are fast and fun to watch. Baseball has proved to have more staying power. From early April through early September, fans get their fill of baseball with the San Antonio Missions and Austin's Round Rock Express. The latter was started by Hall-of-Fame pitcher Nolan Ryan and his son in 1999.

In his raw report on Texas high school football, *Friday Night Lights*, HG Bissinger observes that in schools he visited, trophies honoring athletic achievement were on prominent display, but academic honors were absent. Surprised?

RELIGION

Known for conservative religious attitudes, Texas is part of the Bible Belt, a swath of states across the Southern USA associated with fundamentalist and Evangelical Christianity. Surprisingly, Catholicism is the largest denomination due to the region's significant Latino population, but this being the South, Baptists are certainly well represented. It's not hard to find a Methodist, Episcopalian or Presbyterian place of worship either. Traditional churchgoing is less a part of life in Austin, where for many music is the religion of choice, than in San Antonio; south of the Alamo, along the Mission Trail, mariachi mass is still celebrated every Sunday. As in politics, Austin tends to have greater tolerance than the River City when it comes to religious matters. Just north of Austin near Oak Hill, the gigantic Barsana Dham Hindu Temple has a large following. It's also not uncommon to see Buddhist meditation centers around town and the occasional flyer announcing yoga retreats or a Falun Gong gathering. If you're walking along the Drag near the UT campus, there's a good chance you'll get an earful from a member of the Church of Scientology, which established its Texas headquarters on Guadalupe St, near the corner of 22nd St, in 1967.

DID YOU KNOW?

Five-time Tour de France champion and Austin cyclist Lance Armstrong is a cancer survivor who also leads the annual Tour of Hope (www.tourofhope.org) ride from DC to LA.

ARTS

In contrast to the nationally acclaimed music scene, the arts here are produced mainly within grass-roots organizations such as San Antonio's Guadalupe Cultural Arts Center and the Austin Film Society. In both cities and the Hill Country, writers and artists can find cheap rent and lots of space to work. Many Texas artists succumb to the pull of bigger markets once they've been discovered here, though, which means that visitors will always find plenty of cutting-edge (and rough around the edges) stuff to feast their eyes on here.

Cinema & Television

Film buffs are acquainted with Richard Linklater's *Slacker*, the 1991 documentary-like manifesto for the country's meandering youth. It put the Austin film scene on the map and the word 'slacker' in the dictionary. Since that movie, filmmaking has blossomed locally into a mini-industry spearheaded by Linklater, directors Robert Rodriguez and Quentin Tarantino, and actress Sandra Bullock, all of whom either live or own property in Austin. Through their efforts, hangars at Austin's old airport have been transformed into high-tech sound stages, called Austin Studios, and the Austin Film Society (AFS) is now a resource for modest grants to indie filmmakers. Austin art house cinemas now boast a few superb film festivals, including the Austin Film Festival in October and the SXSW Film Festival in March (congruent with the SXSW music festival).

Giant (dir George Stevens, 1956) is as sprawling as the King Ranch that was the film's inspiration. Elizabeth Taylor, Rock Hudson and James Dean are superb in this big-ticket yarn tracing the life of an oil and ranching family.

Slacker wasn't the first film to spotlight central Texas, and if Austin residents are allowed to decide, it won't be the last. More than 100 movies in recent decades have been shot here, including the Coen brothers' masterpiece *Blood Simple* and the original slasher flick, *Texas Chainsaw Massacre*. John Wayne's 1960 epic film *The Alamo* brought a major piece of Texas and San Antonio history to the big screen, although most of the filming took place in Bracketville, a town 120 miles west of San Antonio, where you can still visit one of the largest sets ever built outside of Hollywood. Linklater made his sophomore effort, *Dazed and Confused*, here, and Rodriguez shot his *Spy Kids* movies in and around Austin. Sandra Bullock's *Miss Congeniality* put the state capitol in front of the camera. Also a $100-million version of San Antonio's epic battle for Texas independence, *The Alamo*, starring Dennis Quaid, Billy Bob Thornton and Jason Patric, was shot in Austin and San Antonio during 2003.

Austin has had its share of television in town as well. *Austin City Limits*, the longest-running music TV show ever, films live concerts at a studio on the UT campus. The *Ned Blessing* and *Lonesome Dove* miniseries were shot here, and both were directed by Austin resident Bill Wittliff, whose photography studio is near San Marcos.

DID YOU KNOW?

In 1997 MTV began producing a sitcom called *Austin Stories*, which received a lot of critical praise, if not popular acclaim; the show was canceled the following year.

Literature

Writing has deep roots in the region. In the 1880s, William Sidney Porter, whose pen name was O Henry, lived and wrote in a Victorian cottage in Austin that's now the O Henry Museum. During his Texas years, Porter was variously employed as a bank teller, draftsman and newspaperman. He eventually fled to Honduras to avoid being tried on charges of embezzlement, of which he was later convicted and then sent to an Ohio prison. O Henry's *Texas Stories* and *Time to Write* both contain short stories set in Austin and San Antonio.

About the same time O Henry left town, another future Pulitzer Prize winner was just reaching adolescence. Katherine Anne Porter grew up in Kyle, a little town about 20 miles south of Austin. After 1901 she attended the Thomas School, a private girl's school in San Antonio. She left the area to become a journalist, scriptwriter and teacher in New York, Mexico, Hollywood and all over the Midwest, but several of her short stories and novels are set in the Texas of her childhood. In Kyle, the Katherine Anne Porter house is now a national literary landmark. It's also the crash pad for Southwest Texas State University's writer-in-residence. An important source for fresh new voices, the university's writing program is considered to be among the top 20 in the country. National Book Award winner Tim O'Brien is a professor, as is Chicano writer and *New Yorker* contributor Dagoberto Gilb. UT Austin also has a fine arts writing program. In addition to owning one of only five complete copies of the Gutenberg Bible extant in the USA, its impressive Harry Ransom Humanities Research Center holds a vast collection of original manuscripts, letters, first editions and memorabilia from virtually every major Western author.

Important writers currently hailing from south-central Texas include Sandra Cisneros, a Chicago-born Chicana novelist, short story writer and poet who makes her home in San Antonio. Sarah Bird is another Midwestern transplant whose comic novel *The Mommy Club* takes place in San Antonio's historic King William District.

In Austin political rancor becomes colorful prose when Molly Ivins and Kinky Friedman pick up their pens. Nobody, but nobody, beats Molly Ivins on pure acerbic wit and the exposure of Texas-isms big and small. This nationally syndicated columnist for the *Fort Worth Star-Telegram* and contributor to publications such as the *New York Times* and *The Nation* was born and raised in Texas and lives in Austin. She also contributes to her hometown's political rag, the *Texas Observer*, where she worked as a young legislative reporter in the 1970s. Her books include *Molly Ivins Can't Say That, Can She?* and *Shrub: The Short but Happy Political Life of George W Bush*. Meanwhile Kinky Friedman started out playing country music in the early '70s as the frontman for Kinky Friedman & the Texas Jew Boys at Austin's Armadillo World Headquarters. From the safe haven of his trailer out in the Hill Country, he continues to write offbeat mystery novels and the columns for *Texas Monthly* magazine.

Michael Hicks' How to Be Texan has an entire section on 'How to Stay Alive in Texas.' Basically, don't try to foist your opinions on Texans, who may have rather large opinions of their own!

Visual Art

While south-central Texas' visual arts scene doesn't compare with Fort Worth or Houston, Austin and San Antonio both have productive communities of painters, photographers, printmakers and other visual artists. The Austin Museum of Art (AMOA) has for years tried unsuccessfully (so far) to establish a new facility downtown, but its beautiful AMOA Laguna Gloria campus is thriving. Smaller institutions, such as Arthouse at the Jones Center, the Guadalupe Arts Center, the Mexic-Arte Museum and UT's Blanton Museum of Art, host several excellent shows every year. Grass-roots galleries that display the efforts of Austin's creative artists include Women and Their Work and Flatbed Press.

www.arts.state.tx.us is a cyber village for Texan arts and culture.

San Antonio's visual arts are spearheaded by the city's vibrant Mexican American community. The arts district of Southtown has its heart at the Blue Star Arts Complex, while the San Antonio Art League Museum stands in the neighboring King William District. The Guadalupe Arts Center is a community gathering space and an axis for local galleries found along S Flores St. Elsewhere around SA, the McNay Art Museum is a respected institution with a research library and national touring exhibitions. In downtown, the Smithsonian-affiliated Centro Alameda (www.alameda.org) is building a new museum square dedicated solely to Chicano and Latino artwork, called the Museo Americano. It's scheduled to open next to Market Square in fall 2004.

Out in the Hill Country, Kerrville is the place for contemporary cowboy art.

Music by Sam Martin

Music is a proud tradition in this part of the state, especially in Austin, the self-proclaimed 'Live Music Capital of the World.' Visitors to south-central Texas can see any kind of musical performance on any given night, from a four-piece bluegrass band kicking out jug tunes to a lone DJ spinning the latest trance grooves. The area's unique prominence on the country's musical stage can be traced all the way back to the German settlers who immigrated to the area in the mid-1800s, as well as to the rich musical heritage Texas has always shared with Mexico. Austin's modern sound first took shape in the early 1970s at a barn-like venue known as the Armadillo World Headquarters. It was there that Nashville expat Willie Nelson turned country music on its head by combining the twang of the steel guitar with the long-hair, feel-good, pot-smokin' attitude of the hippie generation. The fresh new sound that this 'cosmic cowboy' brought to town sparked an entire movement within the music industry known as progressive or new country music, and today that trend continues as alt-country, a sound best represented by songwriters such as Lucinda Williams and bands like Wilco.

Although San Antonio can't compete with Austin's musical reputation, *conjunto* or Tejano music – a musical style born out of the German-Mexican connection – is the backbeat of any night out in the River City. In the Hill Country, you're likely to see a mix of everything – including oom-pah-pah troupes in Fredericksburg and Bob Wills cover bands at any number of creaky dance halls. But it's the Austin-based new country singer-songwriters playing in towns like Luckenbach, Kerrville or Waring that make those balmy nights in the hills so special.

TEJANO & CONJUNTO

The Spaniards may have brought the horse to Texas, but the Germans brought the squeezebox. The accordion has been a part of Texas music ever since.

In the difficult early years of the New Braunfels, Gruene and Fredericksburg settlements, entertainment was important for the weary immigrants, and the freethinking Germans, who made up most of the population in the 1840s, didn't forget to pack their instruments. True, they brought over horns and pianos, but the accordion was central to any musical entertainment. German social gatherings in central Texas were always alive with polkas, waltzes and other sounds of the homeland, to which people would dance, drink homemade beer and have rollicking fun.

Inevitably, locals in nearby San Antonio – largely Texans of Mexican descent who, as early as 1833, called themselves *Tejanos* – started to visit these German settlements and enjoy the loud and lively melody the accordion could sustain (an accordion can be played much louder than an acoustic guitar or violin, and back then – before microphones – that meant musicians were able to play to larger crowds inside bigger dance halls).

After learning to master the squeezebox along with the polkas and waltzes the Germans played, Tejanos and Tejanas (Texan-Mexican women) started creating music as influenced by traditional Mexican orchestra compositions and mariachi guitar-playing as it was by the European polka. Once the *bajo sexto*, or 12-string bass guitar, was added to the mix, along with Spanish lyrics and singing popular on the ranches of northern Mexico, *conjunto* music was born.

Narciso Martinez is known as the father of modern *conjunto*. His popular recordings in the 1930s reached larger crowds than any *conjunto* musician before him. Lydia Mendoza, Carmen and Laura Marroquin, Camilo Cantu, Tony De La Rosa, Paulino Bernal, Little Joe Hernandez y La Familia and Jaime de Anda were other pioneers of the genre. Their performances set the stage for the present-day scene, which is more diverse and popular than ever.

Literally meaning 'all together' for the collaborative quality of the music, the term *conjunto* is often dropped by musicians and fans in favor of the word *Tejano*, which is essentially the same type of accordion-driven beat. By whatever name, this music is still enormously popular in San Antonio and also most large Latino communities across the country. Like jazz and blues it's a quintessentially American creation, which has since morphed into many different styles, with some borrowing from experimental jazz and others capturing the spirit of popular rock.

Accordion Dreams, a documentary film produced and directed by Hector Galán, traces the history of *conjunto* music from its 19th-century origins in central Texas to today's vibrant, youth-driven scene.

In the early 1990s, Corpus Christi sensation Selena became pop-star famous with an enormous Latino (and non-Latino) crowd for her on-stage dancing and accordion-driven hits. Even after she was tragically shot and killed in 1995 – by the president of her own fan club, no less – her records sold millions. Today Tejano musicians like Johnny Degollado, Mingo Saldivar and Flaco Jimenez are well known and play often in San Antonio and Austin clubs.

'JANIS SANG HERE'

Soon after its birth in central Texas, Tejano music moved south to the borderlands. San Antonio held on to its German-Mexican roots but Austin started embracing country and folk music – and eventually rock and punk.

Perhaps the first popular music venue in Texas' capital city opened in 1933 under the name of Threadgill's, a converted old filling station on North Lamar Blvd that was the recipient of Travis County's first liquor license. The club's owner and namesake, Kenneth Threadgill, was at that time an aspiring country musician and yodeler who started staging performances for his Jimmy Rodgers–style band on Wednesday nights for university students and anyone else who wanted to wander in.

The state-run Texas Music Office provides an encyclopedia of the Texas music scene at www.governor .state.tx.us/music.

By the early 1960s, Threadgill's had become a regular stop for the new wave of folk musicians, including Janis Joplin, a young UT student hailing from Port Arthur. Her mix of country twang and bluesy, soulful singing turned heads almost immediately. Joplin's voice would eventually take her to San Francisco and New York as her fame grew, and her friendship with Kenneth Threadgill lasted until her death from a heroin overdose in 1970. The fire department shut down Threadgill's two years later because of fire code violations, and the building sat empty for the rest of the decade, with 'Janis sang here' spray painted on one wall. It was reopened in 1980 by Eddie Wilson, another seminal figure on the Austin music scene, and today it remains a popular Austin hangout.

Several other musical gatherings in the '60s rode the rising tide of music in Austin. The first Longhorn Jazz Festival was held in 1966 at what is now Auditorium Shores; Miles Davis, Stan Getz and Dave Brubeck were among the stellar names on the bill at that event. The first of the Austin Zilker Park KHFI-FM Summer Music festivals kicked off in 1964, and the Chequered Club on Lavaca St opened in 1967. Up-and-coming folk and country musicians such as Jerry Jeff Walker, Ray

Wylie Hubbard, Rusty Weir, Townes Van Zandt and Steven Fromholtz regularly played at both, and it was these gatherings that inspired the first Kerrville Folk Festival in 1972.

There was a burgeoning rock scene in Austin, spearheaded by the local psychedelic rock outfits 13th Floor Elevators, Conqueroo and Shiva's Head Band. With fanatical local followings made up of teeny-boppers and long-haired hippies, they weren't a great fit for either Threadgill's tiny bar or the Chequered Club's folk scene, so in 1967 a group of friends got together and opened the Vulcan Gas Company on South Congress Ave. Housed inside an old run-down office building, the mammoth Vulcan was perfect for large crowds, and it attracted all kinds of acts, including Canned Heat, Johnny Winter, Lightnin' Hopkins and Muddy Waters. Money problems and the lamentable fact that it had no air-conditioning spelled the end for the Vulcan, and the club closed its doors for good in the fall of 1969.

DID YOU KNOW?

Fifteen years before the Armadillo World Headquarters opened inside a defunct National Guard armory, the building was a boxing arena that booked touring bands, including Elvis Presley and Little Richard.

ARMADILLO WORLD HEADQUARTERS

In the wake of the Vulcan's closure, another venue immediately opened that catapulted the Austin music scene into the national spotlight it still enjoys today. Named the Armadillo World Headquarters, the club opened just down the street from the defunct Vulcan Gas Company in August of 1970 inside a former National Guard armory. The quirky name was a nod to the cosmic consciousness of the times and also to the state's official mascot. The club's owners included Eddie Wilson, former band manager for Shiva's Head Band, and Jim Franklin, a local muralist and poster artist. In the decade that the Armadillo World Headquarters stayed open, thousands of bands played there, some of whom became famous because of it and some of whom were already famous and simply wanted to experience the legendary atmosphere and new 'Austin sound.'

THE ORIGINAL COSMIC COWBOY

Perhaps no other musician has done as much for the image of Austin music as the cosmic cowboy himself, Willie Nelson. Born in 1933 on a cotton farm in Abbot, Texas, Nelson got his first guitar at age six and was in his first band by age 10. Early recognition came for the budding country musician when he lived and wrote songs in Nashville in the 1950s and '60s. 'Hello Walls,' a single performed by singer Faron Young, made it to number one on the country music charts and 'Crazy,' Patsy Cline's hit from 1961, is now a country music standard. Both were penned by Nelson.

Though he was already recording his own albums, Nelson didn't have success until he moved to Austin in 1970 and began combining blues, Tejano and conceptual rock with his traditional country roots. At the same time, instead of the clean-cut, well-shaven look he had cultivated in Nashville, Nelson grew out his hair and beard and started playing live to rednecks and hippies alike at the Armadillo World Headquarters rock palace. By the time the album *Shotgun Willie* was released in 1973, Nelson had created a niche all his own that critics were calling 'progressive' or 'new country.' In 1975, Nelson released a concept country record, *Red Headed Stranger*, thereby solidifying his unusual crossover appeal.

These days Willie – as folks around Austin call him – has recently celebrated his 70th birthday and ranks among the most successful country musicians to have ever picked up a guitar. He has performed with everyone from Bob Dylan to Neil Young to Julio Iglesias. Now in his fifth decade of playing to live audiences, he doesn't seem to have any intention of slowing down. He still tours for more than 200 days of the year, which includes an appearance at his annual 4th of July Picnic held in or near Luckenbach, an event that has become the stuff of legend since its inception in 1973. He also regularly performs at his annual Farm Aid concert, a benefit that has been raising money and awareness for US farmers since 1985.

When Wilson and Franklin took over the lease, they turned the building into a hippie haven. Franklin adorned nearly every wall with psychedelic art, depictions of musicians and, most of all, with armadillos. With the demise of the Vulcan, the Armadillo quickly became known as the new counterculture hangout, and antiestablishment hipsters from all over came to listen to local and national acts perform for a cover charge of $3 or less.

That new 'Austin sound' emerged at the Armadillo when Willie Nelson made his debut in 1972. Instead of doing straight-up country tunes, he began mixing blues, rock and Tejano influences into his songs. The result was a curious mix of styles that brought rednecks and hippies cozily together under the Armadillo's singular roof.

The music and the scene were an immediate hit, much to the shock of a lot of people who thought the combination of beer-drinkin' cowboys and pot-smokin' hippies would be a disaster. In fact, the record industry began to market Nelson's music as 'progressive country' or 'redneck rock' and the sound took off. Musicians and bands who heretofore had been hard-pressed to find an audience for their country-rock songs now began to flock to the Armadillo. Marcia Ball, Commander Cody, Doug Sahm, Joe Ely, Asleep at the Wheel and Kinky Friedman all regularly played to packed crowds.

With the success of the Armadillo, other clubs like the Hole in the Wall, near the UT campus, began drawing bigger crowds and more famous bands. *Austin City Limits*, a new television show that debuted on PBS in 1976 with Willie Nelson playing on the pilot episode, began to beam the 'Austin Sound' into homes nationwide. Big-name bands and musicians took notice of Austin's appreciative audiences and added the city to their tour lists; the Armadillo soon saw such luminaries as Frank Zappa, Bruce Springsteen, Van Morrison, Iggy Pop and the Clash.

The last show at the Armadillo World Headquarters was on New Year's Eve in 1980. The very next day Eddie Wilson reopened Kenneth Threadgill's old bar in north Austin and turned it into a home-cooking-style restaurant, as well as a music venue. Not long after, the old National Guard armory on Barton Springs Rd was demolished to make room for the office building that sits there now. In 1996, Wilson opened up Threadgill's World Headquarters in a building next door to where the Armadillo once stood, and today he continues to book live local acts five nights a week.

A TEXAS FLOOD

The closing of the Armadillo was the end of an era, but it was just the beginning of music in Austin. By the early 1980s, the town was well established, with dozens of clubs and a wide variety of music springing up in the dilapidated warehouses on E 6th St. One of the first to appear was a blues venue owned and operated by Clifford Antone, named appropriately enough Antone's (the club has moved four times since then and now resides in the Warehouse District). Along with the Victory Grill in East Austin, Antone's brought Austin's blues scene into the mainstream with the Fabulous Thunderbirds, Angela Streili and Stevie Ray Vaughan. In particular, Vaughan, with his unmatched mastery of the electric guitar and soulful voice, came to be the blues-rock face of Austin music in the '80s, much the same way Willie Nelson's country-rock was in the '70s.

Stevie Ray Vaughan recorded his first album, *Texas Flood,* in 1983 with his band Double Trouble. He then went on to win three Grammy awards in just seven years before he was tragically killed in a helicopter crash in

Willie Nelson put down his guitar long enough to write *The Facts of Life: And Other Dirty Jokes,* a funny (and at times raunchy) insight into the life of an Austin musical legend; Larry McMurtry wrote the preface.

www.threadgills.com provides a funky look at Austin's music scene and popular culture.

DID YOU KNOW?

Willie Nelson has appeared as an actor in 17 movies, including the musical vehicle *Honeysuckle Rose,* the western *Red Headed Stranger* and the political comedy *Wag the Dog.*

Stevie Ray Vaughan: Caught in the Crossfire by Austin-based journalists Joe Nick Patoski and Bill Crawford is a penetrating account of the blues guitarist's rise to fame in the Capitol City.

1990. Along with his older brother, Jimmie Vaughan, who was the lead guitarist and songwriter for the Fabulous Thunderbirds, Stevie Ray won two more Grammys after his death for the posthumously released album *Family Style*. A bronze statue of the musician was erected by the city of Austin on the south shore of Town Lake in 1993.

Also in the '80s another, totally different scene was taking root. Punk arrived in central Texas with the Sex Pistols' infamous gig at Randy's Rodeo in San Antonio during 1978. Soon after, Austin venues like Club Foot, the Cannibal Club, the Beach and the Jelly Club became legendary for their degenerate rock acts and raucous young crowds. Among the local bands that cut their teeth on this scene were the Butthole Surfers, a garage punk group that started out in San Antonio and went on to national critical acclaim.

SOUTH BY SOUTHWEST

For five nights in mid-March tens of thousands of record label reps, musicians, journalists and rabid fans from around the country descend on Austin for the **South by Southwest Music and Media Conference** (SXSW; ☎ 512-467-7979; www.sxsw.com), a musical extravaganza that attracts about a thousand groups and solo artists from around the world to 50 different Austin venues. The *San Antonio Express-News* called it 'an alt-rock, hip-hop, Tejano thing,' and as one music-loving wag put it, 'It's like a mile-long buffet where your stomach is ready to burst after just 20 feet!' In addition to the music, SXSW also hosts a film festival and an Internet conference, both of which are growing in stature.

The conference was started in 1987 by four Austin locals (including Louis Black and Nick Barbaro, respectively the editor and the publisher of the free weekly *Austin Chronicle*), who wanted to provide a showcase for the many talented but unsigned musicians in the area, in hopes that record label executives would take notice. They did. Seven hundred people showed up in 1987 and attendance has grown exponentially every year since. In 2003 over 12,000 people signed up for the various SXSW conferences and thousands more came just to see the live music.

Though SXSW started out as an opportunity for little-known bands and singers to maybe catch the eye and ear of a record label rep, it has since become more of an industry showcase for already-signed bands that need some exposure. With all the media attention it gets, the festival is also drawing bigger names into the fray: Tom Waits, Johnny Cash and Tony Bennett have all played at SXSW in recent years.

Bands and filmmakers looking to ply their creative wares at SXSW submit demo tapes and reels to the festival's board by September 1 the preceding year. Once the lineup is solidified, bands are scheduled into hour-long time slots, so that each night during the festival there are usually five or six bands booked at each venue, twice that if the venue happens to have two stages (and many do). That said, for every 'official' band and location, there's an 'unofficial' band and location, ensuring visitors and locals alike an around-the-clock music marathon on every street corner, at every coffee shop and in every park in town. During the day, when the band members are sleeping, industry buffs head to the Austin Convention Center to talk shop and pick up free earplugs, CD demos and other goodies at a trade show.

Entry to the festivities is sold in a variety of ways. The Platinum Badge ($475-775, depending how far in advance it's bought) includes a pass to the music, film and Internet trade shows, as well as access to daily conference discussions, screenings, night clubs and VIP lounges. Those interested only in the music can buy a Music Badge ($325-525), which includes the music conference, trade show and the nightly gigs, or a wrist band ($115), which is the cheapest way to get into the clubs during SXSW. Be forewarned: those who paid top dollar for a badge will get in to see the music before those with wrist bands, meaning that entry into a club is not guaranteed because of city-determined capacity limits. For the most popular acts, many people head to a venue early and sit through a couple of warm-up shows first. Hotels, of course, are booked solid for up to a year in advance, so it's essential to reserve ahead.

One other venerable club that opened its doors in the late '70s and had a huge impact on Austin music into the '80s and '90s was Liberty Lunch. For nearly 25 years, the Lunch hosted everything from local garage bands to stand-up comedy to touring rock acts. More than any other place in town, Liberty Lunch, with an outdoor beer garden and just the right-size atmosphere, took over where the Armadillo left off. In fact when the Armadillo was torn down in 1980, steel beams from the old armory roof were recycled as the Liberty Lunch's roof. Just before the turn of the 21st century, the Lunch was demolished by the city to make room for the Computer Science Corporation (CSC) building that sits there today.

Visit www.auschron.com/ music or www.austin360.com/ music to see who's performing around town.

21ST-CENTURY SCENE

The closing of Liberty Lunch at the end of the '90s was a bad omen for the live music business in Austin. The technology boom that turned Austin from a small university town into one of the fastest-growing cities in the country became a curse as well as a blessing. While there were more people to go out and see local bands (along with more cash for cover charges), property values skyrocketed. This meant that clubs either had to pay more rent, or were kicked out altogether to make room for richer tenants. Longtime venues began shutting their doors at alarming rates. In addition to Liberty Lunch, Steamboat and the Electric Lounge also called it quits. Even the Hole in the Wall, one of Austin's longest-surviving music venues, had to close down – though it opened up again under new ownership six months later, it now only occasionally books live bands.

Yet musicians still flock to Austin to make a name for themselves, and even as one club closes another opens. *Austin City Limits*, the PBS television show now in production for more than 25 years, is a well-established showcase for everyone from BB King to Beck, and South by Southwest is now the largest music-industry shmoozefest in the country.

Austin musicians continue to create an original sound with a return to the folk, country and blues roots that gave the town its musical start. Rockabilly is big here, too, with Dale Watson, Wayne Hancock and many more playing to packed crowds at places like the Continental Club. World beat, salsa and reggae bands draw big crowds at La Zona Rosa, the Flamingo Cantina and other clubs. Folk musicians like Toni Price, Alejandro Escovedo and others are always somewhere about, and of course, Willie Nelson and fellow Texan Lyle Lovett continue to pack 'em in, no matter where they happen to play.

Austin City Limits: 25 Years of American Music by John T Davis tells the story (with behind-the-scenes photos) of country music's longest-running television show; Texas troubadour Lyle Lovett penned the foreward.

Perhaps the band that is most indicative of where Austin has been and where it's going is Los Lonely Boys, a band of three brothers from San Angelo. Their bluesy, guitar-driven rock is a mix of Stevie Ray Vaughan's know-how, punk rock's stage flamboyance and Tejano's cultural flair. Plus, their biggest fan is none other than Willie Nelson himself. In south-central Texas, the beat goes on.

Environment

From the cowboy rangeland of the Hill Country to fields blanketed with wildflowers outside Austin to the cool artesian spring pools north of San Antonio, the variety of terrain in south-central Texas is a boon to visitors. Many residents are fiercely protective of it, too.

THE LAND

Texas, as everyone here will tell you, is big, but it's not the biggest. It's the second-largest state in the union, with an area of 268,600 sq miles. While that's less than half the size of Alaska, Texas is larger than all of Germany, the United Kingdom, Belgium and the Netherlands combined. Its natural boundaries are the Gulf of Mexico at the east and the Rio Grande at the west and south. Texas ranks as the ninth-largest state for total water area. Its population density ranks in the lower half of US states.

There are 11 major natural regions of Texas covering a remarkable range of terrain, from the Gulf Coastal marshes to the High Plains spreading north into America's heartland to the Trans-Pecos, an extension of the Rocky Mountains, found in the far west of the state. What is commonly known as the Hill Country of central Texas sits on the Edwards Plateau, which extends west from the Balcones Escarpment, a fault line zone running between Austin and San Antonio. Exposed outcroppings of granite like Enchanted Rock are commonly seen, and visitors can even inspect the fault line outside of San Antonio.

Instead of creating modern-day earthquakes as in California, the fault line in south-central Texas relieves its pressure by pushing artesian spring waters to the surface, notably at Barton Springs and San Marcos. These springs, and also the region's major water supply, come from underground aquifers of eroded limestone formed about 100 million years ago, which create reservoirs for water that migrates here from the

Kids love it if you carry Darwin Spearing's *Roadside Geology of Texas* in the car. Designed for driving tours, it's a beautifully yet simply written geological guide to the state.

STRIKIN' IT RICH

The most exciting geological aspect of Texas – to Texans, of course – is why there's oil underneath it. The black stuff sits beneath Texas, southern Mississippi and Alabama, and Louisiana; there are heaps of it under the Gulf of Mexico near all these states as well as the Mexican states of Tamaulipas, Veracruz and Tabasco – all areas surrounding the huge sedimentary basin that forms the Gulf of Mexico.

Evolving for more than 100 million years, the basin consists of a thick sequence of sedimentary rocks. As the sedimentary material makes its way deeper into the earth, it's subjected to a great deal of pressure and heat – enough to convert much of the organic debris (the remains of plants and animals that are always part of sediment) into petroleum.

Petroleum flows freely under the earth, but it tends to collect into large masses that migrate into traps – so named because rocks or other impermeable materials catch the oil – where it forms pools. Pools are what oil explorers are after. Under Texas, salt domes (which are just what they sound like) act as traps; when they're pierced, oil that has been trapped beneath gushes forth. Gushers, however, are rare these days, as oil exploration has become extremely sophisticated.

In 1922 prospectors found oil outside of San Antonio in Luling. The very next year a gusher was discovered beneath Austin's University of Texas (UT) campus. The 'black gold' not only floated the university through the Depression years, but also financed the building of a top-notch institution. In 1940 UT's original oil rig, Santa Rita No 1, was moved to the northwest corner of MLK Jr Blvd and San Jacinto St, but the well continued to flow for another 50 years.

Gulf of Mexico. You can learn more about the major one, the Edwards Aquifer, in Austin's Zilker Park. What nature failed to provide, humans have built. Artificial dams along major rivers have created a few bodies of water, including Town Lake in central Austin and the Highland Lakes region outside town.

WILDLIFE

Texas' sheer size and environmental diversity mean that it's home to a startling array of flora and fauna; over 5000 species of plants, 600 different birds (more than any other state) and 125 vertebrate animals are found here. The government-run **Texas Parks & Wildlife Press** (☎ 800-252-3206; www.tpwd.state.tx.us/news/press) publishes books on several subjects of interest to amateur naturalists. See 'Bird-watching' (p44) for birding tips. The conservation-minded Austin Zoo adopts native (and also exotic) animals that can't survive in the wild.

Animals

American bison, or buffalo, were hunted to the brink of extinction and today exist only in remnant populations. The two most famous Texas animals are the armadillo and longhorn steer, respectively the state's official small and large mammal.

ARMADILLOS

The nine-banded armadillo is a member of the order Xenarthra, which includes anteaters and sloths; it migrated here only relatively recently from South America. The armadillo, whose bony carapace is unique among mammals, resembles an armored vehicle. About as large as a cat, the armadillo tends to seek arid land and avoid water; when forced to cross wide streams it can ingest air and inflate into its own personal flotation device. Its diet consists mainly of insects and other invertebrates and vegetable matter. Many homeowners are annoyed when their lawns are dug up by the armadillo in its search for grubs. Speeding drivers are a hazard for the armadillo, which you may first encounter as roadkill. Otherwise, in summer they're more active in the early mornings and evenings, while winter brings them out during the warmest hours of the day.

BATS

Over two dozen species of bats call Texas home, but the state's official flying mammal is the Mexican free-tailed bat. This is a migratory subspecies of Brazilian free-tailed bats (*Tadarida brasiliensis brasiliensis*). They're in the Hill Country from spring through fall, although the exact months vary. The bats give birth during summer. Soon afterward the adult bats leave, but their offspring stays behind until cooler autumn weather jumpstarts their migratory instincts. In addition to their natural cave habitats, these bats are great recyclers of artificial constructions, including mine tunnels, wells and bridges. You can observe them hanging out under the Congress Ave Bridge in Austin and at the Old Tunnel Wildlife Management Area outside Fredericksburg.

BIRDS

The official Texas state bird is the mockingbird, a long-tailed gray bird that can mimic other birds' songs. Texas has over 600 documented bird species – more than 75% of all species reported in the US – and bird-watching is one of the state's most popular activities. Nearly two-thirds of those species found in Texas can be spotted within an hour's drive

DID YOU KNOW?

After the Civil War, about five million longhorn cattle (at least eight of 'em for every Texan) roamed the state's open rangeland.

DID YOU KNOW?

An armadillo's offspring are always quadruplets of the same sex.

Texas Parks & Wildlife (www.tpwd.state.tx.us) offers environmental news and encyclopedic outdoor activity guides.

of Austin, which is on the Central Flyway for annual migrations. The endangered golden-cheeked warbler, which exclusively nests in central Texas, is best identified by the male's distinctive song heard during late spring. Other species whose habitat is bounded by the Hill Country's Balcones Escarpment include the golden-fronted woodpecker, ruby-throated hummingbird and western scrub-jay. Nighthawks are often seen circling Austin's capitol dome, while Town Lake nearby is favored by the ringed kingfisher and other rare and migratory waterbirds.

AMPHIBIANS & REPTILES
When it comes to at-risk species, the biggest worry is over an animal that's only a few inches long: the salamander. These tiny little fellows inhabit the natural springs in south-central Texas and are threatened by pollution. The most endangered species are the Barton Springs salamander; the San Marcos salamander, which blends in with moss and algae found in rivers and lakes; and the Texas blind salamander, which lives in the underground limestone caves of the Edwards Aquifer. Only discovered a century ago, the Texas blind salamander in fact lacks eyes, an evolutionary adaptation to its habitat.

Another threatened species is the state reptile, the Texas horned lizard. Although its horn-covered head and body scales look fearsome, it's fairly gentle. When presented with danger, its typical response is to flatten and freeze (often thereby becoming roadkill), but it can squirt blood from its eyes, too. Outside of their long winter hibernation from October to April, the lizards are found in sandy soil, which they burrow inside to get warm.

Plants
To Texans, wildflowers are a way of life. Wildflower tourism is so entrenched in the state that the highway visitors centers can help you plan entire trips around watching them bloom (in spring, call ☎ 800-452-9292; www.dot.state.tx.us/wflwr/main.htm). The best time to see Texas' wide range of wildflowers is from mid-March to mid-April, when roadsides and fields throughout south-central Texas and especially the Hill Country are blanketed with explosions of color. The state flower is the bluebonnet. Other beloved wildflower species include Indian blankets, also known as fireweels, the petals of which possess a red-orange-yellow pattern that looks almost woven. Indian paintbrushes share the same palette, but are shorter and often grow in fields of bluebonnets. Mexican hats, which belong to the sunflower family, do resemble nodding sombreros, and they're easily found growing alongside highways. The pink-blossomed stalks of horsemints have a hula skirt of green leaves underneath. For a whole lot more information on Texas wildflowers, visit the Lady Bird Johnson Wildflower Center.

NATIONAL, STATE & REGIONAL PARKS
Despite over 90% of its land being privately owned, Texas maintains one of the USA's finest network of state parks. The National Park Service (www.nps.gov) manages two sites in south-central Texas, the San Antonio Missions National Historic Park and LBJ National Historic Park in Johnson City.

State Parks
More than 125 areas of natural or historical value are open to the public and maintained by the **Texas Parks & Wildlife Department** (☎ 512-389-4800, 800-

792-1112; www.tpwd.state.tx.us). These parks offer a diverse range of activities, including swimming, climbing, horseback riding, camping, biking, hiking and some ranger-led programs. Day-use fees range from $1 to $5 per person or per carload. The Texas Conservation Passport ($50) is an annual vehicle pass that gives unlimited park entry. Call ☎ 800-895-4248 or purchase it online. Texas Parks also oversees about 50 Wildlife Management Areas. These less-developed preserves are favorite spots for wildlife viewing, hunting, hiking and camping. The new Heart of Texas Wildlife Trail connects sites in and around Austin, San Antonio and the Hill Country; visit the website for details.

ENVIRONMENTAL ISSUES
Since the 1970s, a growing level of awareness about ecology and the environment, plus the value in 'green' tourism, means that many natural areas increasingly enjoy varying degrees of protection and management by local, state, federal or private government agencies. As well as providing opportunities for recreational activities, many public lands act as preserves for wildlife and offer interpretive activities and educational programs. Outside of Austin, the Lower Colorado River Authority oversees a vast conservation district that stretches from the Highland Lakes to the Gulf of Mexico. Oil drilling creates its own environmental challenges in Texas, and some highly publicized oil spills have occurred in the Gulf of Mexico, but economics dictate that oil companies are far more careful than ever before.

Greenbelts and greenways, areas of protected natural habitats within and around urban areas, are hotly debated, especially in Austin. There, as in other places, local and state government agencies are under intense pressure from developers to ease restrictions on development. Golf courses can be found everywhere, especially around San Antonio, but they waste colossal amounts of water for irrigation, and runoff from the fertilizer and pesticides used on them poisons the environment; conservationists charge that the damage to local flora and fauna is unrepairable. Golf courses also take up huge tracts of land, and the development associated with them – like condominiums and resorts – adds to the damage. Government and conservation groups have recently started to employ incentives-based programs to persuade landowners to adopt sustainable environmental practices.

Environmental Defense provides hard facts about pollution in American communities at www.scorecard.org.

Austin is environmentally progressive overall. The city has won national and international awards for its **Green Building Program** (www.ci.austin.tx.us/greenbuilder), which offers practical workshops on sustainable building practices for homeowners and developers. Habitat Suites is one of the city's exemplary 'green' hotels. The grass-roots **Save Our Springs Alliance** (☎ 512-477-2320; www.sosalliance.org) is a watchdog organization that works to protect the Edwards Aquifer zone from pollution caused by development. It monitors compliance with existing laws and ensures the protection of the endangered Barton Springs salamander.

National environmental organizations found here include the **Sierra Club** (texas.sierraclub.org), which offers environmental news, advocacy work and community events. Local Sierra Club groups in Austin (☎ 512-305-6296) and San Antonio (☎ 210-222-8195) offer organized activity outings, such as kayaking and bird-watching. The **Nature Conservancy** (☎ 210-224-8774; nature.org) is an international private nonprofit conservation organization that buys habitats to save them from threatened development or other destruction. It runs a protected reserve alongside Austin's Barton Creek, but it's open to the public only a few times per year.

Major Parks & Natural Areas	Features	Activities	Page
Brackenridge Park	a beautiful, old-fashioned city park with gardens and a zoo	jogging, cycling, boat rentals	p135
Enchanted Rock State Natural Area	the USA's second-largest granite batholith, woodlands, grasslands, armadillos	rock climbing, hiking	p179
Friedrich Wilderness Park	a small swatch of wilderness with wildflowers, rare birds	bird-watching, hiking	p139
Guadalupe River State Park	beautiful river and forest recreation, next to Honey Creek State Natural Area	canoeing, tubing, hiking, mountain biking, geology tours	p188
Highland Lakes	vast conservation district on the dammed Colorado River	swimming, boating, horseback riding, camping, hiking	p74
Hill Country State Natural Area	pristine wilderness area with 35 miles of backcountry trails	hiking, mountain biking, horseback riding	p186
Kerrville-Schreiner State Park	another beautiful spot along the Guadalupe River	canoeing, tubing, camping, cycling, hiking	p182
Lady Bird Johnson Willdfower Center	walking trails through forest, meadow and gardens, Texas flora and butterflies	plant identification, naturalist classes, activities for kids	p72
Lost Maples State Natural Area	famous fall foliage, limestone canyons and grasslands: bobcat, birds	wildlife watching, hiking, camping	p189
New Braunfels & San Marcos	water parks, caves and river recreation north of San Antonio	tubing, canoeing, kayaking, swimming	pp167-9
Old Tunnel Wildlife Management Area	an abandoned railroad tunnel, over three million Mexican free-tailed bats	wildlife watching	p176
Pedernales Falls State Park	over 5000 acres of riverside recreation and forest trails	swimming holes, mountain biking, hiking, camping	p173
San Antonio Missions Historical Park	historic Spanish colonial missions connected by a 12-mile recreational trail	sightseeing, cycling, jogging, walking	p128
Shoal Creek Greenbelt	a rambling creekside park, west of downtown Austin	disc (Frisbee) golf, cycling, jogging, walking	p74
Town Lake	an artificial lake at the south edge of downtown Austin	canoeing, kayaking, cycling, jogging, walking	p73
Zilker Park	an urban oasis with natural spring-fed pools, a nature preserve, greenbelt and trails	swimming, canoeing, kayaking, hiking, rock climbing	p72

Outdoors

Texas and the outdoors go back a long way. The cowboy custom of sleeping under the stars may not be as widespread as it was 100 years ago, but there are still plenty of ways to get out in the open. Horseback riding is very popular, and there are many opportunities to get out on the trail for a day or longer. Austin has extensive greenbelts, lakes, rivers and public swimming pools, some of which stay open year-round, while the Hill Country is full of state parks, natural areas and wilderness preserves. Kayaking, canoeing, tubing and rock climbing are all easily arranged. There are wonderful hiking and biking trails, too, as well as wildflower nature walks and birding areas.

Texas Parks & Wildlife (☎ 512-389-4800, 800-792-1112; www.tpwd.state.tx.us), a state agency, is a one-stop source for excellent information on camping, wildlife watching, outdoors activity guides, safety advice and more. Also check in with the outfitters listed in the boxed text below.

CANOEING, KAYAKING & TUBING

Austin and the Hill Country offer plenty of beautiful rivers, lakes and streams for paddling. Although wild whitewater rafting is found in other parts of the state, such as Big Bend National Park, aquatic adventures of a milder sort draw crowds, especially families, here.

Tubing is very popular on smaller streams and rivers. Generally, you rent a 'tube' – the inner tube of a truck tire – which may or may not be outfitted with luxuries such as handles or seats. Then, much like whitewater rafters, you 'put in' at a designated spot on the river and float downstream. Make sure you arrange shuttle service or a ride to pick you up at the other end – most places that rent tubes will do this for you at no extra fee.

Kayaking, canoeing and tubing are year-round activities here, weather and river conditions permitting. Equipment rental is usually not a problem – if a place has good kayaking and canoeing conditions, a savvy entrepreneur is usually around to rent you the gear. Prices tend to be around $25 to $40 a day. For inner tubes, it's generally $15 or less.

Some of the most popular places for canoeing and kayaking include Austin's **Barton Creek Greenbelt** and **Town Lake**. Near San Antonio, **New**

OUTFITTERS

Don't fret if you didn't bring along your outdoors gear! Quality outdoors outfitters include the following:

Whole Earth Provision Co (www.wholeearthprovision.com) central Austin (☎ 512-476-1414; 1014 N Lamar Blvd; 🕙 10am-9pm Mon-Fri, 10am-6pm Sat, noon-6pm Sun); near the University of Texas (UT) campus (Map pp68-9; ☎ 512-478-1577; 2410 San Antonio St; 🕙 11am-8pm Mon-Fri, 10am-6pm Sat, noon-6pm Sun); San Antonio (Map pp122-3; ☎ 210-829-8888; Alamo Quarry Market, 255 E Basse Rd; 🕙 10am-9pm Mon-Fri, 10am-7pm Sat, noon-6pm Sun) This locally owned store stocks top-brand gear, camping supplies, outdoor activity guides and topographical maps.

REI Austin (Map pp68-69); ☎ 512-343-5550; www.rei.com; Gateway Market shopping center, 9901 N Capital of Texas Hwy; 🕙 10am-9pm Mon-Fri, 10am-7pm Sat, 11am-6pm Sun) A member-owned cooperative, REI is one of the top US outdoor retailers.

Austin Outdoor Gear & Guidance Austin (☎ 512-473-2644, 877-773-2644; www.kayaktexas.com; 3411 N IH-35, off exit 236; 🕙 10am-6pm Thu-Tue) This independently owned shop rents camping gear, kayaks and canoes.

Braunfels and **San Marcos** are well-known spots to put in along the Guadalupe River. Farther out in the Hill Country, visit **Guadalupe River State Park, Kerrville** and **Bandera**.

The **Austin Paddling Club** (www.austinpaddling.org) is a great resource for information and joining trips with local enthusiasts. The **Sierra Club** (p39) has outings on the San Marcos River and evening paddles around Town Lake. **Austin Outdoor Gear & Guidance** offers instruction, advice and rentals. **Hill Country Paddlers** (www.quintanna.com/mtnsports/hcpindex.html), based in Kerrville, leads weekend trips and has an excellent online reference guide with links to get you started. Visit **Southwest Paddler** (www.canoeman.com/SWPaddler) for in-depth river descriptions. For experts, **Texas Water Safari** (☎ 512-357-6863; www.tisd.net/~txws; PO Box 686, San Marcos, TX 78667-0686) stages an annual 260-mile marathon on the San Marcos and Guadalupe Rivers.

SWIMMING HOLES

In summertime, it gets hot – real hot, in fact – starting in late May and often continuing well into September. So Texans do one of two things: either they stay indoors and crank up the air-conditioning, or they find cold water outdoors and jump in it. With all of the rivers, lakes, streams and underground springs around Austin and the Hill Country, the second is an easy option.

Ask anyone the closest place to go swimming in Austin and you'll get a knowing nod and a very quick answer: **Barton Springs** in Zilker Park. Some may point you toward tubing spots in **San Marcos** or **New Braunfels**. Others will tell you about a spot out in the Hill Country, where there are at least 100 different swimming options, ranging from secluded springs to riverside parks and roadside dams; Wimberley's **Blue Hole** is one of the best.

Or, they may share their very own secret oasis with you. But before you take a swan dive into any ole swimming hole, make sure you know how deep it is. Hidden rocks and shallow water have caused countless injuries, some of them serious. Also remember to clean up any cups, apple cores or beer bottles. Always leave the area the way you found it, or even cleaner than before. Many of the swimming holes are on private property and the owners are very proud, if not downright protective, of 'their' water. A few swimming holes are free, but many charge a small fee.

Another popular spot to get wet close to Austin is at state-run **Hamilton Pool Preserve** (☎ 512-264-2740; per vehicle $5; 🕑 9am-5:30pm daily), where a spring-fed swimming hole tucked beneath a limestone overhang is fed by a 45ft waterfall. Entry is limited to just 100 people, and too much bacteria in the water can sometimes close it down, so call first. To get there from Austin, head west on Hwy 71 for 30 miles to FM 3238 (Hamilton Pool Rd), then go left 13 miles to the entrance. Another fine choice is the spring-fed swimming pool at **Krause Springs** (☎ 830-693-4181; adult/child 4-11 $3/2.50; 🕑 9am-dusk daily), rated as one of the top 25 swimming holes in Texas. From Austin, take Hwy 71 west for about 20 miles to Hollingsworth Center (Spur 191) in Spicewood, then turn right at the four-way stop sign by the Exxon gas station. Look for the entrance a mile down on the left.

And here's a short list of more places to beat the heat:

'Devil's Hole' at Inks Lake State Park (☎ 512-793-2223; per vehicle $4; 🕑 8am-5pm daily, later in summer) Drive 9 miles west of Burnet on Hwy 29 to Park Road 4, then go left for 3 miles.

Pace Bend Park, or 'Paleface' (☎ 512-264-1482; per vehicle $5; 🕑 dawn-9pm daily) Excellent cliffs. Take Hwy 71 west of Austin 30 miles to RR 2322 (look for the sign), then go right about 5 miles.

Campbell's Hole (no ☎ ; admission free) Located in Austin, about a mile upstream from Barton Springs Pool, on Barton Creek Greenbelt; also accessible from Spyglass Rd.

Twin Falls (no ☎ ; admission free) Also on Austin's Barton Creek Greenbelt; look for the entrance off the southbound Loop 1 frontage road, just south of US 360.

Blanco State Recreation Area (☎ 830-833-4551; per vehicle $3; 🕑 8am-10pm daily) Entrance on Park Rd 23, off US 281 1 mile south of Blanco.

CLIMBING

Boulder fiends are drawn like a magnet to the limestone rocks of the vast Edwards Plateau. The Hill Country west of Austin is a popular climbing area, especially **Enchanted Rock State Natural Area**. Locals in Austin favor the **Barton Creek Greenbelt** and **McKinney Falls**, but you need to go with a guide or someone else who knows the terrain well. The climbing season runs year-round, except during the hottest summer months. Indoor climbing gyms are good places to learn the sport before attempting to climb real rock outdoors.

Climbing is a potentially hazardous activity. Don't climb if there's the threat of rain, which can also bring lightning; in dry weather, carry plenty of water. Concentrate your impact in high-use areas by using established roads, trails and routes for access; disperse in areas infrequently used to avoid the creation of new routes; refrain from creating or enhancing handholds; and eschew the placement of bolts whenever possible.

Based in Austin, **Mountain Madness** (☎ 512-329-0309; www.mtmadness.com) has a perfect safety record and offers classes, clinics and private lessons, including two-day weekend classes at Enchanted Rock ($85-150) and women's clinics. **Central Texas Mountaineers** (www.aidan.net/~ctm) is an Austin-based climbing club that works to negotiate route access. **Texas Mountaineers** (☎ 972-504-6766; www.texasmountaineers.org) has lists of climbing instructors, guides and popular climbing areas on its website.

CYCLING & MOUNTAIN BIKING

Despite this being Tour de France champ Lance Armstrong's home state, car-crazy Texas is friendly to road cyclists only in some places. Austin (Armstrong's hometown) has developed good bike trails, but in many instances road riders will be sharing space with crowded surface-street traffic, and extreme caution is necessary. Touring cyclists could plan a journey around the Hill Country, where backroads abound and it's easy to get away from traffic. For urban cycling under not-too-crowded conditions, head for **Town Lake**, the **Shoal Creek Greenbelt** or the **Veloway** around Austin. San Antonio's beautiful **Mission Trail** has a paved recreational hike/bike path.

Texas has a growing network of excellent off-road cycling trails. Mountain bikers frequent the **Barton Creek Greenbelt**, **McKinney Falls State Park** and **Emma Long Metropolitan Park**. Out in the Hill Country, there are biking trails at **Kerrville-Schreiner State Park**, the **Hill Country State Natural Area** and **Pedernales Falls State Park**.

Austin's bike shops offer rentals, sales and repairs. They are also the best places to pick up maps, events information and the free *Southwest Cycling News* newspaper published by the **Austin Cycling Association** (www.ccsi.com/~aca), which sponsors free rides for all ages and skill levels. **Austin Ridge Riders** (www.austinridgeriders.com) is the local mountain biking group; kids are welcome. Despite its name, **San Antonio Wheelmen** (www.sawheelmen.com) welcomes riders of both sexes. Check its website for a calendar of fun events, as well as technical tips. The state-wide **Texas Bicycle Coalition** (☎ 512-476-7433; www.biketexas.org) is another resource.

HIKING

There is perhaps no better way to appreciate the beauty of south-central Texas than on foot and on the trail. Short hikes and nature walks abound, and there are a few long-distance trails; many allow you to savor Texas wildlife and wildflowers. Remember to treat the backcountry like you would your own backyard – minus the barbecue pit.

In Austin, the **Barton Creek Greenbelt, Shoal Creek Greenbelt** and **Town Lake** boast recreational hike/bike paths. The **Lady Bird Johnson Wildflower Center** has gentle hiking loops. The Hill Country offers some great opportunities for hikes, especially at **Lost Maples State Natural Area, Enchanted Rock State Natural Area** and **Pedernales Falls State Park**. There are attractive walks at **Guadalupe River State Park, Kerrville-Schreiner State Park** and the **Hill Country State Natural Area**.

Fording rivers and streams is a potentially dangerous but often necessary part of being on the trail. In state and municipal parks and along maintained trails, bridges usually cross large bodies of water, but that is not always true in designated wilderness areas. Upon reaching a river, unclip all of your pack straps – your pack is expendable, but you are not. Don't enter water higher than mid-thigh; avoid crossing barefoot. Using a staff for balance is helpful, but don't rely on it to support all your weight. Remember that Texas is subject to flash floods, particularly in the Hill Country and Highland Lakes regions. Although flash floods can occur at any time of year, they are most common after heavy summer rains. Summer can also be dehydratingly hot; it's best to hike in the spring, fall or winter instead.

BIRD-WATCHING

Bird-watching is one of the state's most popular activities, and it's a great way to enjoy the trail. You can spot many species throughout the year, but peak times are the migrations in spring (late February through May) and fall (September through November).

In addition to the hiking spots mentioned above, other places to visit around Austin include **Blunn Creek Nature Reserve, McKinney Falls State Park** and **Emma Long Metropolitan Park**. Austin's premier bird-watching spot is the inauspiciously named **Hornsby Bend Biosolids Management Facility** (☎ 512-972-1960; www.hornsbybend.org; 2210 S FM 973, north of TX 71; ☺ usually 6am-8:30pm daily). Outside of town, ospreys fly around the **Highland Lakes**, and **Hamilton Pool Preserve** (see 'Swimming Holes,' p42) is an excellent place for sighting rare species, such as the golden-cheeked warbler, Acadian flycatcher and Louisiana waterthrush.

Travis Audubon Society (☎ 512-926-8751; www.travisaudubon.org) conducts field trips and birding classes. Visit the society's website for detailed information on bird-watching areas, including the society's bird sanctuary outside Austin, as well as birding checklists. **Texas Parks & Wildlife** (p41) also offers online birding checklists, species profiles, special events calendars and a guide to Austin area birding spots. *Birder's Guide to Texas* by Edward Kutac is among several state-specific guidebooks available.

HORSEBACK RIDING

Few images are more Texan than riding horseback across the open plains. The Texas Hill Country offers fine opportunities for riding year-round, with stables located everywhere from ranches to state natural areas. Many are listed in the Hill Country chapter; for others, check with local convention and visitors bureaus. Stables typically offer a range of services, from one- or two-hour trail rides to extended pack trips. Riders will be given a horse matched to their levels of riding experience, so don't be afraid to mention whether it's your first or 50th time on a horse. Usually the minimum age for aspiring cowgirls and cowboys is six years old. Rates average $20 per hour, around $75 for a half-day ride including lunch or up to $200 for an overnight trip.

Food & Drink

Texas food kicks ass. It's as simple as that. If American cooking could be summed up as combining generous portions of homegrown foods with foreign sensibilities and techniques, Texas spins this into a cuisine that is uniquely its own. If you're expecting bland, starchy American meals, you'll be shocked at the variety and quality on offer, anything from fire-engine red chili and spicy jalapeño corn bread to chilled Hill Country wine. From its humble origins in a chuckwagon's iron skillet, Texas cooking has come a long way; highlights include Texas-style barbecue, authentic Mexican fare, creative Tex-Mex cooking and down-home Southern comfort food. Vegetarians have more options than ever, too, even in this beef-loving state.

www.texascook.com is a people's encyclopedia of tried-and-true recipes.

STAPLES & SPECIALITIES

A traditional Southern dessert that you'll find everywhere is pecan pie, but fruit and meringue pies are popular. Fruit is the main ingredient of cobbler, a pudding-like pastry dessert that resembles smashed pie.

Where's the beef? The Texas Beef Council has it, and they provide recipes and more at www.txbeef.org.

Barbecue

If you're even remotely carnivorous, Texas barbecue is heavenly, and when done well (as in tiny Lockhart), it's divine. The great thing about barbecue is that it's relatively hard to screw up totally, so even the offerings of the state's chain barbecue places, like County Line, are pretty good. There are endless debates over barbecue sauces: what kind, how much or whether you need it at all. A typical barbecue sauce is sweet and tangy with clove overtones, but there are thousands of variations. In Lockhart, Kreuz Market's barbecue is served without any sauce at all, and it's so naturally juicy and tender, you'll agree it's not necessary. But sauce-heavy barbecue, like at Sam's BBQ in Austin, is equally excellent.

DID YOU KNOW?

Some say the origins of the term 'barbecue' may be French, meaning to cook an animal from *barbe* (chin) to *queue* (tail).

Mexican Staples

While Californians may disagree, some say that Texas has the best Mexican food in the USA.

Mexican staples you'll run into in Texas include the ubiquitous *burrito* made of beans, cheese, meat, chicken or seafood seasoned with salsa or *chile* and wrapped in a wheat-flour tortilla. *Enchiladas*, rolled corn tortillas stuffed with meat or cheese, then baked or partly fried, generally sit alongside the traditional side dishes – refried pinto beans, pimiento-flecked 'Spanish rice' and a cooling guacamole salad, made from avocado paste. *Chile relleno* is a mild pepper stuffed with a ground beef mixture and then fried. *Empanadas* are small pastries with savory or sweet fillings. *Tamales* are corn dough stuffed with meat, beans, chiles or nothing at all, wrapped in corn husks or banana leaves and then steamed, while *gorditas* are fried corn dough filled with refried beans and topped with sour cream, cheese and lettuce. A *tostada* is a crisp-fried, thin tortilla eaten as a nibble while you're waiting for the rest of a meal, or it can be topped with meat, cheese, tomatoes, beans and lettuce.

Cornbread Nation 1: The Best of Southern Food Writing, edited by John Egerton, is a delightful collection of essays that'll go straight to your heart and get your stomach rumblin'.

Many Mexican restaurants offer combination breakfasts for under $5, typically composed of juice, coffee, and *huevos* (eggs), which are served in a variety of ways, including *huevos fritos con jamón o tocino* (fried eggs with ham or bacon); *huevos mexicanos* (eggs scrambled with tomatoes, chilies and onions); and *huevos rancheros* (fried eggs on tortillas, covered in salsa). *Salsa* is Spanish for 'sauce,' and it's made with chopped tomatoes, onions, cilantro and chilies. Many Texans get rolling on breakfast burritos, usually eggs and either refried beans or bacon rolled in a soft tortilla. *Migas* (meaning 'crumbs') are extremely popular – they're a mishmash of eggs scrambled with broken tortilla strips and a variety of savory toppings.

THE PERFECT 'CUE *By Sam Benson & Jay Cooke*

Many Texans make seeking out the very best barbecue a lifelong hobby. It's the subject of countless newspaper and magazine articles. Regional devotees consider it not simply a dish to be enjoyed, but a culinary passion. Sliced thick onto butcher paper or slapped down on picnic plates, doused with tangy sauce or eaten naturally flavorful right out of the smokehouse barbecue pit, Texas barbecue is an experience to be savored.

Texas barbecue's cherished status is equal parts heritage, hospitality and hunger. Often just called 'cue, it can become the centerpiece of any social gathering, with guests roaming about in the backyard, knocking back lemonade, sun-brewed tea or longneck bottles of Shiner Bock. Side dishes naturally take second place to the platters of smoked meat; they typically include pinto beans, potato salad, cole slaw, pickles, white bread and, for dessert, a slice of lemon meringue pie or banana pudding with vanilla wafer cookies.

Modern aficionados trace the origins of central Texas 'cue to 19th-century Czech and German settlers, many of whom were butchers. These settlers pioneered methods of smoking meat, both to better preserve it and also to tenderize cuts that might otherwise be wasted. Credit also goes to Mexican *vaqueros* (Spanish-speaking cowboys), especially in Texas' southern and western borderland regions, who dug the first barbecue pits, then grilled spicy meats over mesquite wood. African Americans who migrated to Texas brought with them recipes for a 'wet' style of barbecue, which involved thick marinades, sweet sauces and juicier meats.

Texas' cattle ranching industry makes beef a natural choice for barbecue. Nothing beats the signature dish, beef brisket. Sliced directly from underneath the ribs of the cow, unforgivingly tough brisket has little fat content to recommend it at first. Yet barbecue pit bosses can magically turn this unappealing meat into something astonishingly succulent and fall-off-the-bone tender. Most barbecue joints have added pork chops, spicy sausage, pork loin and even chicken into their repertoire. Look out for hot links, which are sausages made up of ground pork and beef heavily seasoned with pepper.

In today's Texas, barbecue recipes are as varied as central Texas summers are long. Most folks agree on the basics: slow cooking over a low-heat fire. A cooking time of up to 12 or 16 hours isn't unheard of either. This allows the meat to be infused with a rich smoky flavor of mesquite, hickory, oak or pecan wood.

Another term you'll hear bandied about is wet or dry 'rub.' Dry rub is a mixture of salt, pepper, herbs and spices sprinkled over or painstakingly rubbed into the meat before cooking. Wet rub is created by adding liquid, which usually means oil, but also possibly vinegar, lemon juice or even mustard. Applied like a paste, wet rub seals in the meat's natural juices before cooking.

The best Texas barbecue is often found outside of major cities on rural highways and byways, where famous family dynasties have been dishing up the same crowd-pleasing recipes for generations. Telltale signs that you've located an authentic barbecue joint include zero decor, smoke-blackened ceilings and laidback table manners (silverware may be optional). At most places, you can order a combination plate or ask for specific meats to be sliced up by the pound right in front of you. Of course, there are variations on this nowadays, but in Texas, where barbecue baiting is bit of a pastime, some swear this down-home style is the only way.

Tex-Mex

Most of what the world knows about Mexican food, it learned from Texas (or to be more precise, the former Mexican territory that's now part of present-day south Texas). Based on the classic beans-and-corn combination, Tex-Mex borderlands cuisine is a hybrid of Mexican cooking dominated by hearty local ingredients that can survive in the arid conditions of the greater Rio Grande Valley. Tomatoes, chili peppers, onions and garlic accent dishes made from just about every meat, with a special emphasis on plentiful beef. Native chilies add to most Tex-Mex food the characteristic spicy kick. Jalapeños show up most often in Tex-Mex dishes, though recent years have seen a surge in the use of poblano, ancho and the deep-smoked chipotle peppers.

If you've had your fill of the usual suspects, like tacos, enchiladas and tamales, there's always more to whet the imagination and appetite. A common soup course, *caldo*, includes chunks of cabbage, carrot and the meat of the day, usually chicken or beef. *Nopalitos*, the pads of native cactus, are plucked clean, sliced thin and stuffed into tacos. Most Tex-Mex restaurants also serve *menudo*, the traditional Mexican hangover cure. It's a heady stew of jalapeños, hominy and tripe (beef stomach). According to hard-drinking experts, one bowlful will make you think twice before pounding another dozen tequila shots.

Nuevo Tex-Mex: Festive New Recipes from Just North of the Border by chef David Garrido and food critic Robb Walsh is an inspiring reinvention of the Tex-Mex genre (with creative margarita recipes, too).

Southern

Southern cuisine is heavy on fat and meats; typical specialties include buttermilk biscuits, collard greens (served with hot-pepper-infused vinegar) and black-eyed peas, which may be prepared with chunks of pork or ham. Main courses include fried chicken, roasted ham, pork in a variety of ways (including that favorite light snack, pickled pigs' feet) and gravies with cakelike corn bread. Another home-style Southern standard is chicken-fried steak, a tenderized slab of beef that's double-dipped in egg and flour batters, fried up crisp and golden-brown and served drenched in gravy, which readily explains how just one chicken-fried steak can account for almost an entire day's worth of calories. If you're here on New Year's Day, have a plate of black-eyed peas for good luck in the coming year. Every restaurant will be serving them; it's a Southern tradition. A corn-derived white glop that's peculiar to the South (though similar to German *griesbrei*), grits can be eaten as a hot cereal with cream and sugar or treated as a side dish and sprinkled with salt and pepper. Grits are often served in lieu of potatoes at breakfast.

Secrets to Cooking Tex-Mex offers what it promises at www.texmex.net.

Threadgill's: The Cookbook by Eddie Wilson is not just a compendium of homespun Texas cooking, with plenty of green vegetables to boot. It's also an entertaining trip through Austin's musical history.

DRINKS

Texas summers can be as hot as hell. Luckily, there's a lot to slake your thirst.

Nonalcoholic Drinks

The quasi-official soft drink of Texas is iced tea. It's served unsweetened and with fresh lemon slices, sometimes in exotic flavors like hibiscus or mango. If you want hot tea, specify that or you'll probably wind up with iced tea instead.

Commercially available soft drinks in Texas are the same as everywhere in the world with a few exceptions. Dr Pepper is a caffeine-heavy, sweet carbonated drink invented in Waco, just north of Austin, where there's now a quaint Dr Pepper museum. Mr Pibb is an Americanized version of the Brazilian soft drink Guaraná; that is to say, it tastes like one of those tree-shaped car air fresheners. Big Red's taste has been described as akin to liquid bubble gum.

Bottled drinking water is widely available, and you can get a gallon of filtered drinking water (bring your own jug) from dispensers at supermarkets for about 25¢. Tap water in Texas is usually fine to drink.

Alcoholic Drinks

The strictly enforced drinking age in Texas is 21, and it's illegal to drive with a blood-alcohol level over .08%. Carry a driver's license or passport as proof of age. Servers have the right to ask to see your ID and may refuse service without it. Minors are not allowed in bars and pubs, even to order nonalcoholic beverages.

BEER

Unlike many parts of the US, Texas doesn't have a big microbrew culture, though there is one excellent and widely available commercial brand, Shiner. You'll find dozens of specialty brews in the cities and around the Hill Country, where bars and pubs routinely have dozens of beers on tap. You'll encounter Witbier or Weissbier, two wheat-based beers brewed in Belgian and southern-German styles, respectively; Kölsch, a slightly dry, fermented ale; lagers, including the sweetish Helles Bier; and strong bock beer. 'Ice beer' is a brew that's been frozen, then partly drained of water to concentrate its alcohol content. You'll often hear Texans order a 'long-neck' (it's a standard 12oz beer, but the neck of the bottle is longer).

WINE

When the Spanish settled in Texas, one of the first things they did – as they did in California – was set up wine production. But at the beginning of the 20th century, only a handful of wineries were operating. Prohibition wiped out most of these, except for the few that managed to eke out a living producing sacramental wine or grape juice. Since the 1970s, Texas wine production has boomed, and there are now more than three dozen wineries in the state. Texas has two major viticultural areas, one of which is the Hill Country. Texas wines are available throughout the state in liquor stores and upscale supermarkets, but prices will generally be a few dollars higher than a corresponding vintage from California. Popular varietals are Cabernet Sauvignon, Merlot, Chardonnay and Pinot Noir.

HARD LIQUOR

Tequila, manufactured only in Mexico but available throughout the US, is something with which many travelers to this region may find themselves forced to contend. By Mexican law tequila can only be made from blue agave plants from the Mexican states of Jalisco, Guanajuato, Michoacan, Nayarit or Tamaulipas. Blue agave, a spiky succulent related to the lily, is split and cooked to produce the fermentable sugars from which tequila is made.

There are four types of tequila. Silver (*blanco*) is bottled within 60 days of distillation, gold (*joven* or *abocado*) is unaged and has color and flavor added to it, *reposado* is aged from two months to one year and *añejo* is aged for at least a year in oak barrels (by the way, the stuff that has a worm at the bottom of the bottle is *mezcal,* not tequila).

Tequila can be exquisitely expensive or extraordinarily cheap. The most popular tequila in the US is José Cuervo, though that doesn't say anything about its quality. To really taste fine tequila, ask for an excellent (and expensive) brand, such as El Tesoro de Don Felipe, Patron Añejo or Sauza Hornitos. Them's sippin' tequilas and mightily worth the extra expense.

Margaritas, the most popular tequila cocktails, are made with tequila, lime juice and triple sec, either served on the rocks or frozen and served in a glass with a salted rim. A few restaurants stake their reputations on specialty flavors, such as mango or watermelon. Don't knock 'em 'til you've downed at least one.

CELEBRATIONS

Food is celebrated here as elsewhere in the USA, but with a couple of advantages. Texas' milder climate promotes food and wine festivals happening year-round, while the region's Mexican roots bring on merry feasts with music, dancing and cultural festivities. Overseas visitors can easily find restaurants at which to sample traditional holiday meals, notably the late autumn cornucopia of Thanksgiving.

April's **Fiesta San Antonio** is the best time of year to catch a kaleidoscope of food festivities, including a Taste of New Orleans, celebrations of Mexican cooking at El Mercado (Market Square) and German fare at the Beethoven Männerchor Und Garten. The **Texas Hill Country Wine & Food Festival** (www.texaswineandfood.org) is another springtime extravaganza. About three dozen events are scheduled in Austin and around the Hill Country, mainly at vineyards, featuring demonstrations by star chefs, wine and cheese tastings, winemakers' dinners and musical concerts under the stars. Advance registration is required, except for the grand finale, a food and wine fair (same-day tickets $40).

Mary Faulk Koock's *The Texas Cookbook* (1965) was penned by the owner of Austin's Green Pastures restaurant. Her recipes and tall tales of Texan life are now decidedly retro, but still delicious.

More spring and summer celebrations include the outrageous Spamarama™ festival; the Austin Chronicle Hot Sauce Contest, which is also a microbrewers' minifestival; the Easter weekend chili cook-off in Kerrville; Zilker Park's outdoor concert series, Blues on the Green, which has top-notch food booths; and Fredericksburg's Peach JAMboree & Rodeo in June.

Oktoberfest brings German-inspired feasts of food and beer to the Hill Country, especially around Fredericksburg and Boerne. Celebrations harken back to the traditions of 19th-century European settlers who settled central Texas. October is officially Texas Wine Month, too. Celebrations include grape stomps, vineyard tours, winemakers' dinners and tastings. Wine trail weekends (www.texaswinetrail.com) occur throughout the year; see p173 for more about the Hill Country's wineries.

MEXICAN AMERICAN FESTIVALS

Mexican traditions translate with all their exuberance into Texas life, where they are accessible even to non-Spanish speakers.

On May 5, Cinco de Mayo celebrates the 1862 Battle of Puebla. In Austin, the elaborate festivities include a chili cook-off and tortilla and pepper eating contests. San Antonio's El Mercado (Market Square) is a locus of activity. During the same month, El Mercado also hosts the Return of the Chile Queens festival, a tribute to the Mexican women who once crafted their *chile con carne* and salsa in the outdoor plazas of San Antonio.

El Día de los Muertos, a ritual festival to honor the dead, actually pre-dates the arrival of the Spanish *conquistadores*. But due to the influence of Catholicism, the festival is now celebrated along with All Souls and All Saints Days on November 2. It is on this day that ancestral souls are traditionally believed to return to earth. Macabre merry-making includes ceremonial processions, feasting and sacred altars laden with food and drink. Catch some of the most colorful action along San Antonio's Mission Trail.

Cocina de la Familia by Marilyn Tausend may be out of print, but it's worth tracking down for its traditional tales and beloved recipes collected from Mexican American home kitchens.

Local families often celebrate personal events with big festive gatherings in which food, music and dancing all play vital parts. Coming-of-age parties held on a girl's 15th birthday (called *quinceanera*) involve a visit to church for the spiritual sustenance of communion, followed by a traditional feast at home where music and dancing last into the night. *Quinceanera* celebrations are so lavish that a family may go seriously into debt for years afterward. Other birthdays may be celebrated with a piñata, a papier-mâché animal filled with candy, usually suspended from a tree. Blindfolded guests take turns trying to break apart the piñata by hitting it with a long stick or baseball bat, eventually allowing the candy inside to rain down.

WHERE TO EAT & DRINK

Both major cities offer food to match any mood, even the global cuisine you'd find on the West Coast or in NYC. But you didn't come all the way to Texas to eat sushi or foie gras, did you? We've included a few ethnic eateries in each destination chapter, as long as they have a lively local scene. Otherwise, focus on authentic regional cooking. We've recommended the best neighborhoods in Austin and San Antonio for finding these kinds of restaurants and avoiding tourist traps.

The slower pace of life in the South means that service, while generally good, may not be exactly snappy. For a quick meal, shop the deli or take-out sections of grocery stores, especially Whole Foods and Central Market. Museum cafés, bakeries and caterer's outlets are great for a fast bite, as well as for solo diners. For those dining alone, some restaurants have counter stools, sometimes facing an open kitchen. At top-end restaurants, you can sometimes order a full meal at the bar, which is an especially convivial place during happy hour (usually 5pm to 7pm weekdays), when appetizers may be half price. Families and large groups are welcome almost everywhere, but if there are six or more of you, call ahead.

A few restaurants serve breakfast, usually between 6am and 10am on weekdays. Weekend brunch is typically served from 10am until 2pm. Some cafés and diners offer breakfast all day, every day. Lunch is usually served from 11:30am until 2pm on weekdays, with a few places staying open for light meals throughout the afternoon. Because lunch is the neglected family member of US meals, many fine restaurants offer drastically reduced prices at lunchtime. Also in this category are early-bird dinners, offered from around 4pm to 6pm, which try to lure customers in for early trade by offering similar discounts. Regular dinners are usually served from 5pm until 9pm, later on weekends. If restaurants take a day off, it's typically Monday.

DID YOU KNOW?

A vegetarian can save an acre of trees each year by not eating red meat. How? Grazing land is a major factor in deforestation.

VEGETARIANS & VEGANS

Vegetarianism has caught on big time in the USA, even in cattle country like Texas. Austin in particular is bursting with vegetarian- and vegan-friendly eateries. Like any major city, San Antonio also has plenty of options for vegetarians. In rural areas, though, it can be more difficult, with meat playing a key role in most Southern cooking. Ask twice if something contains meat – some people don't consider things like sausage seasoning, bacon bits or chicken to be meat! Also inquire about cooking with lard, which many restaurants do even with so-called 'vegetarian' menu items. Otherwise, salad bars are a good way to stave off hunger, and many restaurants serve large salads as main courses. Even at barbecue joints, you can often cobble together a decent meal with a number of 'sides' (side dishes) such as potato salad, beans, corn bread and banana pudding for dessert. Out in the Hill Country, look for European-style bakeries and delis serving breakfast and lunch. Throughout this book, we've mentioned good vegetarian options in restaurant reviews wherever possible.

WHINING & DINING

Families are welcome almost anywhere in Texas, especially at Mexican restaurants. Eating barbecue is another experience that kids can really dig their paws into – and it's fun! Plenty of open-air eateries (which operate year-round) and café patios are ideal places for families to dine. A few restaurants attached to bars may not accept minors, however; we've mentioned this in our restaurant reviews whenever possible. If you're unsure whether a particular establishment allows children or not, call ahead. Many restaurants in all price ranges have special kids' menus, which offer smaller portions at steeply discounted prices. Booster seats are on hand, except at cheap hole-in-the-wall joints and truly fine dining establishments. Baby food and healthy snacks are widely available at grocery stores. For more advice on traveling with children, turn to p192.

HABITS & CUSTOMS

The first thing you may notice is the incredible quantity of food served in Texas restaurants. Light eaters may do perfectly well to order an appetizer and a salad as a meal, or to share a main course (also called an entrée), for which restaurants may charge a 'split plate fee,' usually about $2. At tapas-style eateries, diners can order as many (or as few) shared dishes as they like. Many barbecue joints let you order meat by weight and skip the side dishes, if you prefer.

If you're looking for a lively meal, search out restaurants that also operate as live music venues or bars (sensibly called resto-bars in many other parts of the world), particularly in Austin's Warehouse District. In San Antonio, live entertainment often accompanies meals on the Riverwalk, at El Mercado (Market Square) and in the Southtown arts district. If food is your primary focus, however, you may find yourself going quite off the beaten path, perhaps into outlying city neighborhoods or even farther into the Hill Country. At top-notch restaurants, serious foodies may opt for the chef's tasting menu, which often comes with wine pairings for each of several courses, including dessert.

Both Austin and San Antonio have passed limited bans on smoking in public restaurants. At press time, smoking was allowed at outdoor tables and in specially enclosed indoor areas. If you need to be seated in a particular section, be sure to request it.

COOKING COURSES

Texas has its share of celebrity chefs, and most of them have published their own cookbooks. *Matt Makes a Run for the Border: Recipes and Tales from a Tex-Mex Chef* features Matt Martinez Jr, the owner of Matt's No Place in Dallas; he grew up in the kitchens of Matt's El Rancho and explores Texas' culinary frontiers. Guest chefs often appear at events organized by **Central Market** (www.centralmarket.com), an upscale chain of supermarkets; the Austin branch offers many cooking classes, food demonstrations and tasting events, particularly during summer. In April the Texas Hill Country Food & Wine Festival is an opportunity to pick up a few techniques from rising local stars and nationally renowned chefs, such as Bobby Flay.

Austin

Texas' state capital, once a charmingly overgrown university town known for the laissez-faire 'slacker' mentality portrayed in Richard Linklater's 1991 film, has become an increasingly upmarket city. Turns out that while the slackers were hanging out, drinking coffee and smoking cigarettes, University of Texas student Michael Dell (founder of Dell Computers) and others were starting companies in their dorm rooms. High tech soon rivaled state government as the engine driving the city's future. Meanwhile, many long-time Austinites found themselves struggling to maintain equilibrium amid ever-rising rents, congestion and growing materialism.

Today you'll notice a strong feeling about that the old Austin is worth fighting for, especially as the new tech-driven economy proves volatile. But some things haven't changed. Austin calls itself the 'Live Music Capital of the World,' and you won't hear any arguments. Committed fans may be tempted to visit during South by Southwest (SXSW), the annual mid-March music industry love-in. The truth, however, is that Austin is an ongoing music festival every night of the year. While the state capitol complex downtown is impressive, as are many of the city's museums, they're overshadowed by Austin's natural attractions, which include Town Lake, the magnificent natural pool at Barton Springs, Hippie Hollow (where you can git nekkid) and the almost nightly flight of a million Mexican free-tailed bats from beneath the Congress Ave bridge. Focus your attention on these areas – along with South Austin's neighborhoods, which retain a funky, live-and-let-live vibe – and you won't be disappointed.

HIGHLIGHTS

- **Wildlife** Bats under the Congress Ave bridge (p64)
- **Cooling Off** Splashing in Barton Springs Pool (p73)
- **Nightlife** Live music at legendary clubs (p99)
- **Experiencing the Past** Bob Bullock Texas State History Museum (p63)
- **Green Havens** Zilker Park (65) & Town Lake (p73)
- **Best Penny-Pinching Afternoon** Ambling UT campus & the Drag (p65)
- **Dining** Texas-style barbecue from Lockhart (p87)
- **Chill-out Spot** Anywhere in South Austin (p65)
- **Best Skinny-dipping** Hippie Hollow & the Highland Lakes (p74)
- **Offbeat Experience** Eeyore's Birthday Party (p80)

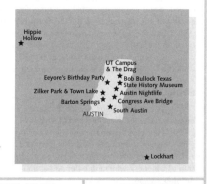

| ■ TELEPHONE CODE: **512** | ■ POPULATION: **671,900** | ■ AREA: **265 SQ MI** |

ORIENTATION

Austin is bordered by highways. I-35 runs just east of downtown, and it's the main access from the north (Dallas/Forth Worth) and south (San Antonio). The other major north-south route is Hwy 1, the MoPac Expressway (or simply 'MoPac'); the name stands for Missouri-Pacific, since the highway was constructed along the trackbeds of the old railway line.

Downtown is an orderly grid. The main north-south artery is Congress Ave, which also serves as the east-west dividing line for addresses. Most sights are within walking distance of the state capitol complex. Guadalupe (pronounced gwad-ah-loop-ee, though some Texans insist on saying guad-ah-loop) St runs three blocks west of Congress Ave. 6th St, the major westbound thoroughfare, is one-way, and so are most other downtown streets. The stretch of East 6th St between Congress Ave and Red River St has a rambunctious collection of clubs, bars and nightspots that's a tourist draw in its own right. The Warehouse District, west of Congress Ave, claims more upscale nightlife.

Downtown may be the geographical center of Austin, but the city's demographic heart has shifted elsewhere. Approaching the **West End**, art galleries, boutiques, bistros and bars radiate outward from the intersection of W 6th St and Lamar Ave, where landmark Waterloo Records stands. Directly across the bat colony bridge and Town Lake from downtown, South Congress Ave (nicknamed **'SoCo'**) is the main drag through **South Austin**, an offbeat area that recalls the city the way it was before high tech took hold. It's bordered on the north side by Riverside Dr, which goes from I-35 over to Barton Springs Rd, a winding road through Zilker Park.

Where Guadalupe St borders the University of Texas (UT) campus, it's sometimes called the **Drag**. UT cuts a huge swath of land through the area north of downtown, beyond Martin Luther King Jr Blvd and west of I-35. **Hyde Park**, a century-old enclave noted for its architecture, lies just northeast in the alphabet avenues found between Guadalupe and Red River Sts, roughly north of 38th St.

Elsewhere, sprawling **East Austin**, on the opposite side of I-35 from downtown, is comprised of historically African American and Spanish-speaking neighborhoods. Other outlying areas of the city also take commonsense geographical designations, such as **West Austin** (west of MoPac) and **Westlake** (by Lake Austin). In **Northwest Austin**, the Arboretum shopping mall, near

---

AUSTIN IN...

TWO DAYS

Start your day at the **Bob Bullock Texas State History Museum**, then stroll down to the **Texas State Capitol** or visit the art museums and galleries around downtown. Then head to South Austin's eclectic **SoCo** for lunch, people-watching and a little shopping. Spend the rest of the afternoon in **Zilker Park** splashing into **Barton Springs Pool**, rowing along the **Barton Creek Greenbelt** or cycling by **Town Lake**. Be back in time to witness the nightly flight of the **Congress Avenue bridge bats**. After dark plug into Austin's live music scene at bars and clubs along **Red River and 6th Sts** or in the **Warehouse District**. On your second day, visit the **UT Campus** for its free attractions and walk **the Drag**. Drop by the **Alamo Drafthouse Cinema** back downtown for dinner and a movie.

FOUR DAYS

Follow the two-day itinerary for the first three days, but take it nice 'n easy, y'all. While downtown, add on a side trip to the **West End and Clarksville** neighborhoods, stopping at **Waterloo Records** and, of course, **Amy's Ice Creams**. Spend the whole second day exploring **South Austin** and **Zilker Park**. On either the first or third day, save time for a rural drive out to **Lockhart**, the barbecue capital of Texas.

On the fourth day, escape the city to the **Highland Lakes** region or the **Hill Country** for a quick tour of wineries, swimming holes and antiques shops. Up for a long drive? Make a day trip to **San Antonio** instead.

the commercial axis of Research Blvd (US 183) and MoPac, is a landmark.

Austin-Bergstrom International Airport is near the junction of highways US 183 and TX 71 (E Ben White Blvd), 8 miles southeast of downtown. Heading downtown from the airport, avoid the freeway traffic by taking a right (northwest) on E Riverside Dr, which will take you right to the Congress Ave bridge, which leads into the center. The Amtrak train station is right downtown, but the bus station is far north of the center, near the I-35/US 290 junction.

Maps

The color tear sheet *Downtown Austin* map will help you get around the city center, especially since it shows CapMetro's free 'Dillo shuttle bus routes. The glossy fold-out *Austin Street Map & Guide* gives much wider coverage of the entire city and outlying districts, with a detailed street index. Pick up either for free at visitors centers (p61).

Practically a souvenir, *Tune to Austin* (www.tunetoaustin.com) is a hand-drawn color map that highlights unique Austin cafés, music venues, shops and more. *Streetwise Austin* is relatively accurate and very easy to carry in its five-fold laminated pocket-size edition. For more serious navigation, try the detailed, if unwieldy, maps from Mapsco or Rand McNally. **BookPeople** sells all of these maps.

Free road maps are available to members of the **American Automobile Association** (AAA), which has two inconvenient offices in Austin: south of downtown (☎ 512-444-4757; 4970 Hwy 290 W, ste 310; 9am-6pm Mon-Fri, 9am-1pm Sat), near Best Buy; and north (☎ 512-335-5222; 13376 Research Blvd, ste 108; same hours).

INFORMATION

The bulletin boards found outside of coffeehouses, cafés and grocery stores are a great source of news about local events, special activities and classified ads.

Bookstores

Many of Austin independent bookstores have shut their doors, but downtown museums, attractions and Texas-themed gift shops stock a variety of titles, anything from historical tomes to Old West legends to Texas barbecue cookbooks. Also visit:

Austin Books & Comics (Map pp56-7; ☎ 512-454-4197; www.austinbooks.com; 5002 N Lamar Blvd; 11am-7pm Mon-Fri, till 8pm Wed, 10am-7pm Sat, noon-6pm Sun) Comics, sci-fi books, movie posters, toys and collectible artwork, close to the UT campus.

Barnes & Noble (Map pp68-9; ☎ 512-457-0581; 2246 Guadalupe St; 9am-9pm daily)

BookPeople (Map p91; ☎ 512-472-5050, 800-853-9757; www.bookpeople.com; 603 N Lamar Blvd; 9am-11pm daily) Get your maps and 'Keep Austin Weird' T-shirts at Texas' biggest and best independent bookstore. The whiz-bang events calendar is packed with great stuff.

Book Woman (Map p91; ☎ 512-472-2785; 918 W 12th St; 10am-8pm Mon-Sat, 1-6pm Sun) Specializing in feminist and queer-friendly titles, this small bookshop also rents videos. Ask about special events.

Borders Books, Music & Cafe (☎ 512-795-9553; Great Hills Station, 10225 Research Blvd; 9am-11pm Mon-Sat, 10am-11pm Sun) Near the Arboretum mall.

Half Price Books, Records, Magazines (Map pp68-9; ☎ 512-451-4463; www.halfpricebooks.com; 3110 Guadalupe St; 10am-10pm Mon-Sat, 11am-9pm Sun, collectibles annex open 10am-6pm Mon-Sat) A broad selection of excellent new and used books, with multiple locations around town.

Ink Newsstand (☎ 512-329-5458; Barton Creek Square mall, 2901 Capital of Texas Hwy; 10am-9pm Mon-Sat, noon-6pm Sun) A division of Barnes & Noble, this newsstand stocks well-known magazines and newspapers and sells maps.

Lobo (Map pp68-9; ☎ 512-454-5406; 3204A Guadalupe St; 10am-10pm Mon-Thu, 10am-11pm Fri-Sat, noon-10pm Sun) Austin's center for gay-related merchandise stocks new and used books, videos and magazines.

Mitchie's Black Fine Art (Map pp56-7; ☎ 512-323-6901; 5706 Manor Rd; 10am-7pm Mon-Sat, 1-6pm Sun) Books, art and music from the African diaspora.

MonkeyWrench Books (Map pp56-7; ☎ 512-407-6925; 110 E North Loop Blvd; 11am-8pm Mon-Thur, 10am-9pm Fri-Sun) A radical bookstore and community events space. Punk 'zines, feminist treatises and political bumper stickers are sold by the world's friendliest anarchists.

Resistencia Bookstore (Map pp66-7; ☎ 512-416-8885; 1801 S 1st St; 11am-4pm daily) Left-of-center titles and poetry chapbooks for Spanish-speaking communities, Native Americans and women.

12th St Books (Map pp58-9; ☎ 512-499-8828; 827 W 12th St; 10am-6pm Mon-Sat) Rare, out-of-print and scholarly works.

Whole Earth Provision Co (Map pp68-9; ☎ 512-476-1414; 1014 N Lamar Blvd; 10am-9pm Mon-Fri, 10am-6pm Sat, noon-6pm Sun) This outdoors outfitter carries regional travel books, outdoor activity guides and maps.

GREATER AUSTIN

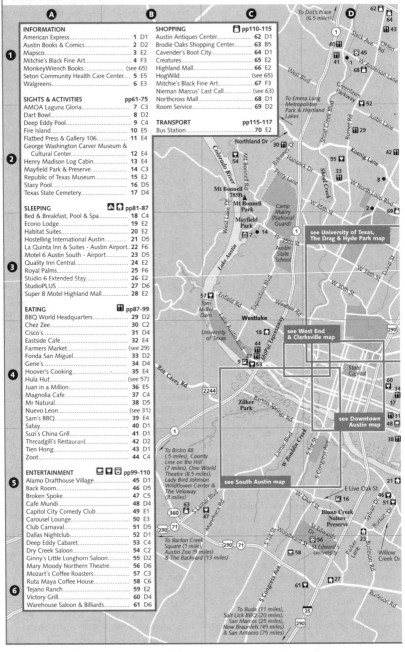

INFORMATION
American Express	**1** D1
Austin Books & Comics	**2** D2
Mapsco	**3** E2
Mitchie's Black Fine Art	**4** F3
MonkeyWrench Books	(see 65)
Seton Community Health Care Center	**5** E5
Walgreens	**6** E3

SIGHTS & ACTIVITIES   pp61-75
AMOA Laguna Gloria	**7** C3
Dart Bowl	**8** D2
Deep Eddy Pool	**9** C4
Fire Island	**10** E5
Flatbed Press & Gallery 106	**11** E4
George Washington Carver Museum & Cultural Center	**12** E4
Henry Madison Log Cabin	**13** E4
Mayfield Park & Preserve	**14** C3
Republic of Texas Museum	**15** E2
Stacy Pool	**16** D5
Texas State Cemetery	**17** D4

SLEEPING   pp81-87
Bed & Breakfast, Pool & Spa	**18** C4
Econo Lodge	**19** E2
Habitat Suites	**20** E2
Hostelling International Austin	**21** D5
La Quinta Inn & Suites - Austin Airport	**22** F6
Motel 6 Austin South - Airport	**23** D5
Quality Inn Central	**24** E2
Royal Palms	**25** F6
Studio 6 Extended Stay	**26** E2
StudioPLUS	**27** D6
Super 8 Motel Highland Mall	**28** E2

EATING   pp87-99
BBQ World Headquarters	**29** D2
Chez Zee	**30** C2
Cisco's	**31** D4
Eastside Cafe	**32** E4
Farmers Market	(see 29)
Fonda San Miguel	**33** D2
Gene's	**34** D4
Hoover's Cooking	**35** E4
Hula Hut	(see 57)
Juan in a Million	**36** E5
Magnolia Cafe	**37** C4
Mr Natural	**38** D5
Nuevo Leon	(see 31)
Sam's BBQ	**39** E4
Satay	**40** D1
Suzi's China Grill	**41** D1
Threadgill's Restaurant	**42** D2
Tien Hong	**43** D1
Zoot	**44** C4

ENTERTAINMENT   pp99-110
Alamo Drafthouse Village	**45** D1
Back Room	**46** D5
Broken Spoke	**47** C5
Cafe Mundi	**48** D4
Capitol City Comedy Club	**49** E1
Carousel Lounge	**50** E3
Club Carnaval	**51** D5
Dallas Nightclub	**52** D1
Deep Eddy Cabaret	**53** C4
Dry Creek Saloon	**54** C2
Ginny's Little Longhorn Saloon	**55** D2
Mary Moody Northern Theatre	**56** D6
Mozart's Coffee Roasters	**57** C3
Ruta Maya Coffee House	**58** C6
Tejano Ranch	**59** E2
Victory Grill	**60** D4
Warehouse Saloon & Billiards	**61** D6

SHOPPING   pp110-115
Austin Antiques Center	**62** D1
Brodie Oaks Shopping Center	**63** B5
Cavender's Boot City	**64** D1
Creatures	**65** E2
Highland Mall	**66** E2
HogWild	(see 65)
Mitchie's Black Fine Art	**67** F3
Nieman Marcus' Last Call	(see 63)
Northcross Mall	**68** D2
Room Service	**69** D2

TRANSPORT   pp115-117
Bus Station	**70** E2

AUSTIN

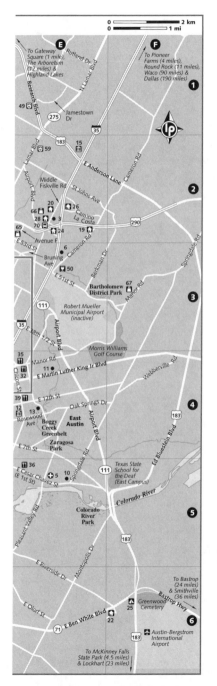

Emergency

Emergency number (☎ 911)
Police (☎ 311 or 512-974-5000)
Natural disaster (☎ 211) Statewide health and human services.
Crisis and suicide intervention (☎ 512-472-4357)
SafePlace (☎ 512-267-7233, 24-hr hotline; TTY 512-927-9616) A domestic violence and sexual assault survival center.
Emergency Animal Hospital & Clinic (☎ 512-899-0955, South Austin; ☎ 512-331-6121, Northwest Austin)

Internet Access

Free public Internet access is available at any public library branch; call ☎ 512-974-7301 for hours and locations. Bring a library card or photo ID. Sign-up procedures vary, but online time is usually limited to 30 minutes. Austin's downtown **Faulk Central Public Library** (Map pp58-9; ☎ 512-974-7400; 800 Guadalupe St; ⊙ 10am-9pm Mon-Thu, 10am-6pm Fri-Sat, noon-6pm Sun) has dozens of wired terminals.

Better hotels offer high-speed Internet access, while motel rooms at least have phones with data ports for laptop users. **Kinko's** (Map pp58-9; ☎ 512-472-4448; 327 Congress Ave; ⊙ 2pm Sun-midnight Fri) copy centers offer high-speed Internet access from 20¢ per minute. Only some branches (☎ 800-254-6567 for city-wide locations) are open 24 hours. With a toll-free or local dial-up ISP number, laptop users can use Kinko's laptop docking stations for free.

Many coffee shops are wired. Try:

Hideout Coffee House & Theatre (Map pp58-9; ☎ 512-443-3688; 617 Congress Ave; ⊙ 7am-11pm Mon-Thu, 7am-1am Fri, 8:30am-1am Sat, 10am-10pm Sun) Internet kiosks cost 15¢ per minute.
Little City (Map pp58-9; ☎ 512-476-2489; 916 Congress Ave; ⊙ 7am-midnight Mon-Fri, 9am-midnight Sat, 9am-10pm Sun; ☎ 512-467-2326; 2604 Guadalupe St; ⊙ 7am-midnight Mon-Fri, 8am-midnight Sat-Sun) Free wireless access for customers who bring their own laptops.
Mojo's Daily Grind (☎ 512-477-6656; 2714 Guadalupe St; ⊙ 24hrs) Free Wi-Fi access for laptop users. Ethernet service available for $5 per hour (one-hour minimum).
Mozart's Coffee Roasters (☎ 512-477-2900; 3825 Lake Austin Blvd; ⊙ 7am-midnight Mon-Thu, 7am-1am Fri, 8am-1am Sat, 8am-midnight Sun) Free Wi-Fi access for laptop users. It's located next to the Hula Hut .

DOWNTOWN AUSTIN

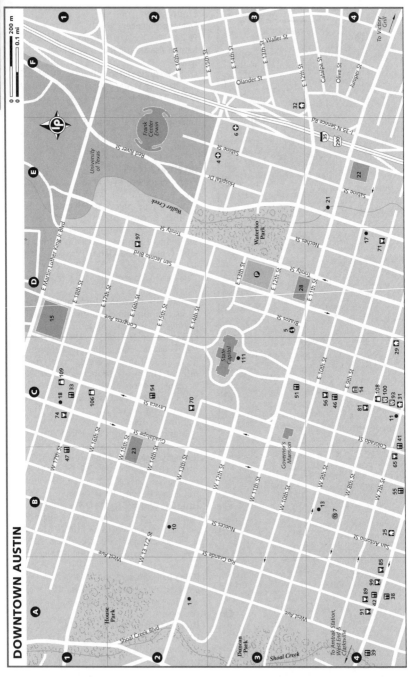

0   200 m
0   0.1 mi

University of Texas

Frank Erwin Center

E 16th St
E 15th St
E 14th St
E 13th St   Waller St
Olander St
E 12th St
Catalpa St
Olive St
Juniper St

To Victory Grill

I-35 N Service Rd
290
35

22

Sabine St
Hospital Dr
Sabine St

Waller Creek
Red River St

21

Neches St
17
71

Waterloo Park

97
San Jacinto Blvd
Trinity St

E 13th St
E 12th St
Trinity St
28
E 11th St
Brazos St
5

E Martin Luther King Jr Blvd
E 18th St
E 17th St
E 16th St
E 15th St
E 14th St
Congress Ave

15

29

State Capitol
111

18 109
33
74   106
54
70

E 10th St
E 9th St
14
108 100
93 31
51
56 46
81

11
41

W 17th St
47
W 16th St
W 15th St
23
W 14th St
W 13th St
Lavaca St
Guadalupe St

65

55

Governor's Mansion

W 12th St
W 11th St
W 10th St
W 9th St
W 8th St
W 7th St

13
7

10

West Ave
W 13-17 St
Nueces St
Rio Grande St
San Antonio St

25

85

House Park
Shoal Creek Blvd

1

89 99
42 93
38

91

Duncan Park
West Ave
Shoal Creek

To Amtrak Station,
West End &
Clarksville

39

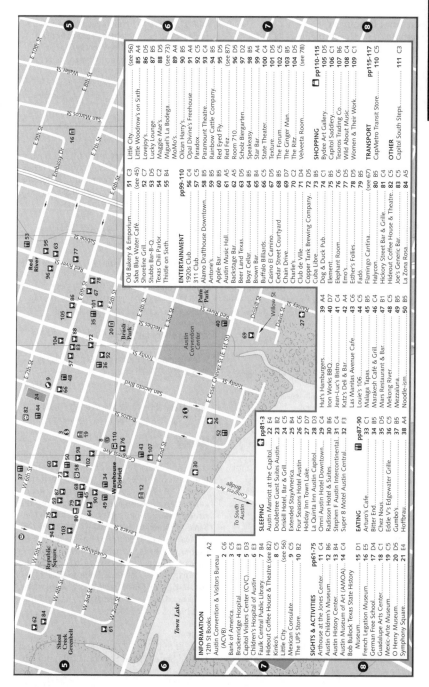

INFORMATION
12th St Books....................................1 A2
Austin Convention & Visitors Bureau
(ACVB)..2 C6
Bank of America................................3 C5
Brackenridge Hospital........................4 E3
Capitol Visitors Center (CVC)..............5 D3
Children's Hospital of Austin................6 E3
Faulk Central Public Library.................7 B4
Hideout Coffee House & Theatre (see 82)
Kinko's..8 C5
Little City.....................................(see 56)
Mexican Consulate.............................9 C5
The UPS Store................................10 B2

SIGHTS & ACTIVITIES   pp61-75
Arthouse at the Jones Center..............11 C4
Austin Children's Museum...................12 B6
Austin History Center........................13 B4
Austin Museum of Art (AMOA)............14 C4
Bob Bullock Texas State History
Museum.......................................15 D1
French Legation Museum....................16 E5
German Free School...........................17 D4
Guadalupe Arts Center.......................18 C1
Mexic-Arte Museum...........................19 D5
O Henry Museum..............................20 D5
Symphony Square.............................21 E4

SLEEPING   pp81-3
La Quinta Inn Austin Capitol...............22 E4
Austin Marriott at the Capitol.............23 B2
Doubletree Guest Suites Austin...........24 C5
Driskill Hotel, Bar & Grill...................25 B4
Extended StayAmerica........................26 C6
Four Seasons Hotel Austin...................27 D7
Holiday Inn Town Lake.......................28 D3
Omni Austin Hotel Downtown.............29 C4
Radisson Hotel & Suites......................30 B6
Stephen F Austin Intercontinental........31 C4
Super 8 Motel Austin Central..............32 F3

EATING   pp87-90
Arturo's Cafe....................................33 C1
Bitter End...34 B5
Chez Nous..35 D5
Eddie V's Edgewater Grille...................36 C5
Gumbo's...37 B5
Hofbräu..38 A4
Hut's Hamburgers..............................39 A4
Iron Works BBQ................................40 D7
Jean-Luc's Bistro...............................41 C4
Katz's Deli & Bar...............................42 A4
Las Manitas Avenue Cafe....................43 C6
Louie's 106..44 C5
Malaga Tapas....................................45 B5
Marakesh Café & Grill........................46 C4
Mars Restaurant & Bar........................47 B1
Mekong River....................................48 C5
Mezzaluna...49 B5
Noodle-ism.......................................50 A4

Old Bakery & Emporium.....................51 C3
Saba Blue Water Café.....................(see 45)
Shoreline Grill...................................52 C7
Stubbs Bar-B-Q.................................53 D5
Texas Chili Parlor..............................54 C2
Thistle on Sixth.................................55 B4

ENTERTAINMENT   pp99-110
1920s Club.......................................56 C4
311 Club...57 C5
Alamo Drafthouse Downtown.............58 B5
Antone's..59 B5
Apple Bar..60 B5
Austin Music Hall...............................61 A5
Backstage Bar....................................62 A5
Beer Land Texas.................................63 C5
Boyz Cellar..64 B5
Brown Bar...65 B4
Buffalo Billiards..................................66 C5
Casino El Camino...............................67 D5
Cedar Street Courtyard.......................68 B5
Chain Drive.......................................69 D7
Charlie's..70 C2
Club de Ville......................................71 D4
Copper Tank Brewing Company...........72 D5
Cuba Libre...73 B5
Dog & Duck Pub...............................74 C1
Element...75 B5
Esther's Follies...................................76 C6
Fado...77 D5
Flamingo Cantina...............................78 B5
Halcyon...(see 67)
Hickory Street Bar & Grille..................79 B5
Hideout Coffee House & Theatre..........80 B5
Joe's Generic Bar...............................81 C4
La Zona Rosa.....................................82 C5
Little City..83 C5
Little Woodrow's on Sixth..................84 A5
Lovejoy's...85 A4
Lucky Lounge....................................86 D5
Maggie Mae's....................................87 D5
Miguel's La Bodega.........................(see 73)
MoMo's..88 D5
Oilcan Harry's...................................89 A4
Opal Divine's Freehouse.....................90 B5
Paradox...91 A4
Paramount Theatre............................92 C4
Rainbow Cattle Company....................93 C4
Red Eyed Fly......................................94 D5
Red Fez..(see 87)
Room 710...95 D5
Scholz Biergarten...............................96 D5
Speakeasy..97 D2
Star Bar...98 B5
State Theater.....................................99 A4
Texture...100 C5
The Forum..101 D5
The Ginger Man.................................102 C5
The Ritz..103 B5
Velveeta Room..............................(see 78)

SHOPPING   pp110-115
Bydee Art Gallery.............................104 C4
Capitol Saddlery...............................105 D5
Tesoros Trading Co............................106 C1
Wild About Music.............................107 C4
Women & Their Work........................108 C4

TRANSPORT   pp115-117
CapMetro Transit Store......................109 C1

OTHER
Capitol South Steps...........................110 C5
....111 C3

Internet Resources

Austin360 (www.austin360.com) Inside the *Austin American-Statesman*'s encyclopedic city guide, search for absolutely anything Austin-related (watch out for occasionally obsolete information).

Austin Chronicle (www.austinchronicle.com) Austin's local alternative weekly newspaper archives news and articles online, including comprehensive guides to live music venues, restaurants, outdoor activities and the arts.

Austin Citysearch (www.austin.citysearch.com) Citysearch's Austin site has a few snapshots of city entertainment, shopping and attractions.

Austin City Links (www.austinlinks.com) The motherlode of Austin-related links covers everything from honky-tonk dance halls to Shakespearean theater festivals.

Laundry

Predictably, the UT campus area is a good place to look for self-serve laundries. **Ecomat** (Map pp68-9; ☎ 512-236-8645; 2915 Guadalupe St; ⏰ 7am-8pm Mon-Fri, 9am-8pm Sat) also offers environmentally friendly dry-cleaning services. **Kwik-Wash Coin Laundry** is the big chain around town; check the yellow pages for its over two dozen locations.

Media

NEWSPAPERS & MAGAZINES

Austin American-Statesman (www.statesman.com) The respected daily newspaper; publishes *XLent*, a supplemental what's-on guide with restaurant and entertainment reviews, every Thursday.

Austin Chronicle (www.austinchronicle.com) Free alternative weekly with independent coverage of local politics and the lowdown on the Austin music, food and performing arts scenes.

Daily Texan (www.dailytexanonline.com) Free UT campus paper, published weekdays when school is in session.

AustinMonthly (www.austinmonthly.com) A monthly magazine catering to affluent socialites, but may be worth buying for its restaurant reviews alone.

RADIO

Most of the following stations do live streaming broadcasts online, so that you can virtually visit Austin before you arrive.

KGSR 107.1 FM (www.kgsr.com) 'Radio Austin' is an eclectic station that airs lots of local talent; check out the 'Lone Star State of Mind' broadcasts from 10pm until midnight every Friday.

KVRX 91.7 FM (www.kvrx.org) The UT student radio station; shares its bandwidth and sensibilities with KOOP.

KOOP 91.7 FM (www.koop.org) Austin's community radio station has excellent local flavor and multicultural programming; Jay Robillard's ever-popular 'The Lounge Show' spins 'Hi-Fi kitschy fun' from 10am until noon on Saturday.

KUT 90.5 FM (www.kut.org) Local NPR affiliate; 'Eklektikos,' with music and performing arts, is on from 9am to 2pm weekdays.

KLBJ 590 AM Local news, talk and traffic.

Medical Services

Check the yellow pages for dentists offering emergency care; some keep extended office hours or stay on-call overnight. **Walgreens** (Map pp56-7; ☎ 512-452-9452; 5429 N IH-35, at Cameron Rd; ⏰ 24hrs) has a 24-hour pharmacy.

Brackenridge Hospital (Map pp58-9; ☎ 512-324-7000; 601 E 15th St) Downtown Austin's central emergency room.

Children's Hospital of Austin (Map pp58-9; ☎ 512-324-8000; 1400 N IH-35)

People's Community Clinic (Map pp68-9; ☎ 512-478-4939, 512-478-8924; 2909 N IH-35) Nonemergency health care for families who lack adequate health insurance.

St David's Hospital (Map pp68-9; ☎ 512-397-4240; 919 E 32nd St)

Seton Community Health Care Centers (Map pp56-7; ☎ 512-324-4930; 2811 E 2nd St; ☎ 512-324-4940; 3706 S 1st St) Both of Seton's nonemergency clinics charge sliding-scale fees.

Seton Medical Center (Map pp68-9; ☎ 512-324-1000; 1201 W 38th St) A major hospital near the UT campus.

Money

ATMs accepting most network and credit cards are easily found, except in the most popular nightlife areas, where privately owned ATMs (look for them inside convenience stores or often right on the street) charge exorbitant transaction fees. **Bank of America** (Map pp58-9; ☎ 512-397-2200; 501 Congress Ave; ⏰ 9am-4pm Mon-Thu, 9am-5pm Fri) exchanges foreign currency and traveler's checks. There are exchange booths at the airport, too. **American Express** (Map pp56-7; ☎ 512-452-8166; Hillside Center, 2943 W Anderson Lane, cnr Rockwood Lane; ⏰ 9am-6pm Mon-Fri) has an office two blocks east of MoPac.

Post

Call ☎ 800-275-8777 to locate the closest United States Postal Service (USPS) branch.

Austin's central **post office** (510 Guadalupe St; ⊗ 8:30am-6:30pm Mon-Fri) holds general delivery mail for up to 30 days. Address poste restante to:

YOUR FAMILY NAME, First Name
General Delivery
Austin, TX 78701-9999

The UPS Store (Map pp58-9; ☎ 512-478-2917, 888-346-3623; www.theupsstore.com; 603 W 13th St; ⊗ 9am-7pm Mon-Fri, 9am-5pm Sat) offers shipping and specialty mail services. Its many Austin-area locations include one near the University of Texas (Map pp68-9; ☎ 512-478-2334, 2002-A Guadalupe St; ⊗ 9am-6pm Mon-Fri, 10am-2pm Sat).

Tourist Offices

Austin Convention & Visitors Bureau (CVB; map pp58-9; ☎ 512-583-7203, 800-926-2282; www.austintexas.org; 201 E 2nd St; ⊗ 8:30am-5pm Mon-Fri, 9am-5pm Sat-Sun) Nearby the convention center, the Austin CVB has helpful staff, free maps, extensive racks of informational brochures and a sampling of local souvenirs for sale.

Capitol Visitors Center (CVC; map pp58-9; ☎ 512-305-8400; www.texascapitolvisitorscenter.com; 112 E 11th St; ⊗ 9am-5pm Mon-Sat, noon-5pm Sun) At the southeast corner of the capitol grounds, the CVC is also an official Texas Travel Information Center (☎ 512-463-8586) offering free brochures and maps.

Travel Agencies

STA Travel (Map pp68-9; ☎ 512-472-2900; 2116 Guadalupe St; ⊗ 10am-6pm Mon-Sat, 11am-6pm Sun) This well-known budget and student travel specialist is convenient to the UT campus.

DANGERS & ANNOYANCES

Common sense and awareness usually ensure problem-free travel in Austin. Some folks may tell you that anywhere east of I-35 is dangerous, and while there is some truth to that, overt or covert racism – this is a predominantly African American and Latino part of town – may exaggerate claims of danger.

One major complaint is drunken college students letting it all hang out on E 6th St. It's a party atmosphere (imagine a small-scale Mardi Gras happening every weekend), and if you're drunkenly counting your cash and appraising your jewelry in an alley at 2am, you're as likely to encounter interest here as anywhere else. Generally speaking, Red River St is as far east as most people go after dark.

Transients and panhandlers congregate downtown near Congress Ave, especially from 4th through 7th Sts. Keep your wits about you when returning to your car at night, or hail a taxi (or a pedicab).

Austin natives claim they live in the allergy capital of America, and at any time of year visitors are likely to sneeze and wheeze along with the rest of the city's denizens. If you're at all susceptible, especially to pollen or mold, bring proper medication. Local TV news weather segments on KVUE, Austin's ABC affiliate, include allergy forecasts, or get them instantly at www.austin360.com by clicking on the allergy report link.

SIGHTS

Most of Austin major sights are around downtown, Zilker Park and the UT campus area. Many sights are accessible via CapMetro's free 'Dillo shuttle buses and, on weekends, the No 470 'Tour the Town' bus (p117). For advice on finding parking around the city, see p116.

Downtown

The Texas Capitol Complex is made up of more than two dozen state government office buildings, bounded by Lavaca St and San Jacinto Blvd on the west and east and 14th and 11th Sts on the north and south. Many downtown sights are within reasonable walking distance of the capitol grounds. For our recommended downtown walking tour, see p75. Other guided walking tours (p78) depart from the south capitol steps. Free two-hour parking is available inside the Capitol Visitors Parking garage, entered from either 12th St or 13th St.

CAPITOL VISITORS CENTER

Get oriented at the **Capitol Visitors Center** (CVC; map pp58-9; ☎ 512-305-8400; www.texascapitol visitorscenter.com; 112 E 11th St; ⊗ 9am-5pm Mon-Sat, noon-5pm Sun), housed in the 1850s mock-medieval General Land Office building. William Sydney Porter, whose pen name was O Henry, once worked here as a draftsman. The short story writer, famous for his surprise twist endings, lived in both Austin p63 and San Antonio (the O Henry House Museum, p133), and the rise and fall of his Texas fortunes are chronicled well here.

Second-floor **historical exhibits** explore the role of land – who owned it, who fenced it off and who ranched it – in Texas history, with displays that are a cartographer's dream. High-definition TVs showcase 'secret spots' in and around the state capitol that can't normally be viewed by the public. More interesting are documentaries about the XIT ranch deal, whereby four men from Chicago agreed to finance Texas' state capitol in exchange for a land grant, which they built into the world's largest fenced-in ranch. It was another death knell for the free-rangin' cowboy lifestyle.

Downstairs the travel information office provides self-guided tour booklets for the state capitol and grounds, as well as Austin information and maps of the entire state. The Texas-themed **gift shop** (☎ 512-305-8406, 888-678-5556; www.texascapitolgiftshop.com; ☺ 9am-5pm Mon-Fri, 10am-5pm Sat, noon-5pm Sun) sells books of all kinds and enough Lone Star State paraphernalia to outfit an army.

TEXAS STATE CAPITOL

The Renaissance revival **state capitol** (Map pp58-9; ☎ 512-463-0063; admission & tours free; ☺ 7am-10pm Mon-Fri, 9am-8pm Sat-Sun, tours 8:30am-4:30pm Mon-Fri, 9:30am-3:30pm Sat, noon-3:30pm Sun) of sunset red Texas granite is Austin's most distinctive landmark and the largest state capitol in the US. Completed in 1888 after years of construction, the capitol was built to replace the original limestone structure (erected 1852-53), which was destroyed by fire. Incidentally, ruins of an older temporary capitol can be seen at 11th St and Congress Ave.

Self-guiding brochures of the capitol building and grounds are available inside the tour guide office on the ground floor. From here you can also take one of the interesting guided tours. In the **lobby** look for the painting of Davy Crockett, hero of the Alamo, and Elisabet Ney's life-size sculptures of key figures Stephen Austin and Sam Houston. Her marble bust of Miriam 'Ma' Ferguson, Texas' first woman governor, is oft overlooked. To see more of Ney's work, visit her studio museum in Hyde Park (p70).

The capitol **rotunda** features terrazzo seals of the six nations whose flags have flown over Texas – Spain, France, Mexico, the Republic of Texas, the Confederate States of America and the USA – centered on the Lone Star of the Texas republic.

You can see government in action from a seat in the third-floor **visitors balconies** overlooking the House of Representatives and Senate chamber galleries, which are open to the public when the state legislature is in session (from the 2nd Tuesday of January through May or June, but only of every odd-numbered year). Texans like to brag that the gold star held by the **Goddess of Liberty** atop their capitol dome is several feet higher than the US Capitol in Washington, DC, but no one has ever proven this.

The green sprawl of the **capitol grounds** and its **monuments** are worth a stroll before or after your tour. The Great Walk leading up to the capitol steps is 25ft wide and 500ft long, ending by two memorials. One is dedicated to the heroes of the Alamo and the other to the legendary Texas Rangers who kept law and order in the Old West. Nearby is a vibrant sculpture honoring the Texas cowboy. If you continue around to the capitol's northwest side, a replica Statue of Liberty stands near the rose garden and close by another monument to Texas' pioneer

---

SOME OF THE BEST THINGS IN AUSTIN ARE FREE

Watch the bats fly out from under the **Congress Ave bridge** (p64). Tune into **Radio Austin** (p60). Take a **historical walking tour** of downtown (p69). See the legislature in action at the **state capitol** (p62). Visit with artists at the **Guadalupe Arts Center** (p64). Catch a live show at **Waterloo Records** (p102). Score tickets to an **Austin City Limits** taping (p100). Play disc golf along the **Shoal Creek Greenbelt** (p74). Travel back in time at the **Hartman Prehistoric Garden** (p77). Be awed by the **Harry Ransom Humanities Research Center** (p69), **Blanton Museum of Art** (p70) and **LBJ Library & Museum** (p65). Swing by SoCo on **First Thursday** evenings (p110). Celebrate summer at **Blues on the Green** (p80) or the **Zilker Hillside Theater** (p109). Do yoga under a full moon atop **Mt Bonnell** (p71).

women. The capitol buildings and grounds are especially pretty at night.

BOB BULLOCK TEXAS STATE HISTORY MUSEUM

Named for an influential Texas lieutenant governor who died in 1999, this impressive **museum** (The Story of Texas; map pp58-9; ☎ 512-936-8746, 866-369-7108; www.thestoryoftexas.com; 1800 Congress Ave; adult/senior/youth under 18 $5.50/4.50/free, including both theaters $13.50/10.50/6.50; ❤ 9am-6pm Mon-Sat, noon-6pm Sun) is still practically brand-new. It features exhibits tracing Texas history from pre-European contact to the present. What's surprising is how despite an obvious enthusiasm for all things Lone Star, the museum manages to take an honest look at the state's history, celebrating both its triumphs and travails. Audio tours ($2) are available, and parking is only $3 with museum validation.

Allow at least a few hours for your visit. Ground-floor exhibits re-imagine the Native American experience and later arrival of French Jesuits, Spanish *conquistadores* and other frontier settlers. Upstairs, visitors trace the revolutionary years of the Republic of Texas, its rise to statehood and economic expansion into oil drilling and space exploration, even Western movies and home-grown music from Bob Wills to Buddy Holly to the Big Bopper.

The museum also houses Austin's first **IMAX theater** (p108) and the **Texas Spirit Theater**, a three-screen multimedia venue featuring *The Star of Destiny*, a 15-minute special-effects film showcasing such Texas events as the 1900 Galveston hurricane, a Saturn V rocket liftoff and the eruption of a gushing oil well. Nearby the **Story of Texas Cafe** (most items $3-6; ❤ 10am-5pm Mon-Sat, noon-5pm Sun) has creative Tex-Mex and Cajun offerings like spicy chicken tortilla wraps and catfish po' boy sandwiches; after 3pm only snacks and drinks are available. Downstairs, the gift shop carries even more Texas-made products than the CVC, as well as travel and history books on topics ranging from ghost towns to pioneer women to buffalo soldiers.

GOVERNOR'S MANSION

The lovely Greek revival **Governor's Mansion** (Map pp58-9; ☎ 512-463-5516; www.txfgm.org; 1010 Colorado St; admission free; ❤ tours every 20 minutes 10am-11:40am Mon-Thur) is a national historic landmark dating from 1856. The building is closed during state holidays, official functions and at the governor's whim like if he's eating a late breakfast. The mansion is getting a lot more traffic these days since it was home to former Texas governor and now US President George W Bush. Each governor has left something behind for posterity, from Stephen F Austin's writing desk to Sam Houston's mahogany four-poster bed. Former governor James Stephen Hogg put nails in the banister so his kids wouldn't slide down it. Altogether too brief tours whisk visitors through the impressive interior and gardens, with many starry-eyed Texans eager for a glimpse of any artifact of Lone Star political royalty. A quirky free handout, *The Governor's Mansion Historical Gazette*, contains more amusing and obscure factoids.

AUSTIN MUSEUM OF ART

The museum's main **downtown gallery** (AMOA; map pp58-9; ☎ 512-495-9224; www.amoa.org; 823 Congress Ave; adult/student & senior/child under 12 $5/4/free, Tues $1; ❤ 10am-6pm Tues-Sat, till 8pm Thu, noon-5pm Sun; Ⓟ $2.50 with validation) has changing exhibitions as wells as a small permanent collection of 20th-century paintings, sculpture, photographs, prints, and drawings. The museum expects to build a more spacious downtown headquarters – eventually, that is, since plans have been held up by a lack of funding for many years now.

But expansion is almost complete at the museum's secondary facility, the **AMOA Laguna Gloria** (Map pp56-7; ☎ 512-458-8191; 3809 W 35th St; bus No 9-Enfield on Sat only; admission free; ❤ 9am-5pm Mon-Sat, 1-5pm Sun), situated on 12 acres overlooking the Colorado River and Lake Austin. Although the Driscoll Villa is still being restored (with parts of it slated to reopen by 2004), the art school remains open and visitors are welcome to view the monumental sculptures on its riverside grounds.

MEXIC-ARTE MUSEUM

This downtown **museum** (Map pp58-9; ☎ 512-480-9373; 419 Congress Ave; adult/senior & student/child under 12 $5/2/free; ❤ 10am-6pm Mon-Thu, 10am-5pm Fri-Sat, noon-5pm Sun) is a wonderful, eclectic

AUSTIN

gallery featuring works from Mexican and Mexican American artists in exhibitions that rotate every two months. The museum's holdings include carved wooden masks, modern Latin American paintings, historical photographs and contemporary art. Don't miss the back gallery where new and experimental talent is shown. The museum's gift shop is another draw, with killer Mexican stuff that's pricey if you're heading south of the border but reasonable if you're not. Ask about special events, like the Taste of Mexico festival or El D a de Los Muertos celebrations in early November.

ARTHOUSE AT THE JONES CENTER
Run by the Texas Fine Arts Association, **Arthouse at the Jones Center** (Map pp58-9; ☎ 512-453-5312; www.tfaa.org; 700 Congress Ave; admission free; ☺ 11am-7pm Tues-Fri, till 9pm Thu, 10am-5pm Sat, 1-5pm Sun) presents the best of Texas' regional contemporary art in the heart of downtown Austin. Temporary exhibitions spotlight emerging talent. In May look for 'Five by Seven,' where small works are sold anonymously for $100 each, after which the artist's name is revealed; you could end up with an original painting, photograph or collage by the next Picasso of the Hill Country!

GUADALUPE ARTS CENTER
On the far north side of downtown, but just a couple of blocks from the Bob Bullock Museum, this working artists' studio and **gallery space** (Map pp58-9; ☎ 512-473-3775; www.guadalupearts.com; 1705 Guadalupe St; admission free; ☺ 10am-6pm Tues-Sat) brings you face to face with art and its makers. After browsing the cutting-edge downstairs gallery, go upstairs and wander the halls, stopping to look at works-in-progress or chat with some of the artists-in-residence (only if their doors are open, please).

O HENRY MUSEUM
Austin resident and writer, lyricist, punster, ladies' man and convicted embezzler William Sydney Porter (O Henry) lived in this cottage, now a simple **museum** (Map pp58-9; ☎ 512-472-1903; www.ohenryfriends.com; 409 E 5th St; admission free; ☺ noon-5pm Wed-Sun) adjacent to Brush Park. It's tiny and there's not much to see, but interior holdings include a few genuine Porter family articles from the 1890s and other period pieces, plus an amusing gift shop that's practically out on the back porch. You can view the museum's collection of historical photos and take a virtual tour online.

GOING BATTY
Austin isn't just the live music capital of the world; it's also home to the largest urban bat population in North America. The reconstruction of the Congress Ave bridge in the 1980s created platforms and crevices beneath the span. These caught the attention of some apparently homeless Mexican free-tailed bats that fly each spring from central Mexico to the southwestern US. Initially fearful of the bats, Austinites have since embraced the winged mammals, who are typically in town from mid-March through early November. Every June, the females each give birth to one pup, and moms and kids set out each night in search of food. It's a serious spectacle – up to a million bats streaming out from beneath a bridge! It's become an Austin tradition to bring a six-pack of beer to Town Lake and watch as, around sunset, the bats head out to feed on an estimated 10,000lb to 30,000lb of insects.

Bat Conservation International (BCI; ☎ 512-327-9721; www.batcon.org) holds programs throughout the bat season and often has volunteers on duty at the bat observation center by the *Austin American-Statesmen*'s parking lot (free after 6pm daily), located on the east side of the bridge off South Congress Ave. Check in the *Austin American-Statesman* for a bat calendar of events, or call its **Bat Hotline** (☎ 512-416-5700 ext 3636) for an update. The TGI Friday's restaurant by the Radisson Hotel (p82) on Town Lake is an especially popular perch for bat-watching. Also try the Lone Star Riverboat or Capital Cruises (pp77-8) for bat-watching tours.

Do not pick up grounded bats or touch bat droppings; some bats carry rabies, and even if they don't, they don't need folks picking them up, okay? Bat-watchers also are asked not to shine flashlights under the bridge, since that may delay the bats' emergence.

It was in Austin that O Henry began publishing the weekly newspaper *The Rolling Stone*, one of the first to take political satire seriously. Watch out for the annual **O Henry Pun-Off**, a pun-making contest each May that attracts thousands of potential punsters vying for 'Punniest of Show.' Although the outdoor venue is subject to change, last year downtown's Woolridge Park was the scene of the antics, which included live music, food and drinks.

GERMAN FREE SCHOOL

The **German-Texan Heritage Society** (Map pp58-9; ☎ 512-482-0927; www.gths.net; 507 E 10th St; admission free; ⓨ tours 1-4pm Thu) is headquartered in this beautiful cream-colored brick building, which German immigrants constructed in 1857. Today, it's a meeting place and cultural center promoting German-Texan connections, with special events, language classes, slide shows and guest lecturers. Call for more information.

South Austin

Most of the what's going on in South Austin centers on **Zilker Park**, a mecca for outdoors activities (p72) and kids of all ages (p76).

ZILKER BOTANICAL GARDENS

These lush **gardens** (Map pp66-7; ☎ 512-477-8672; www.zilkergarden.org; 2220 Barton Springs Rd; admission free; ⓨ 7am-dusk daily, garden center & gift shop 8:30am-4:30pm Mon-Fri, 10am-5pm Sat, 1-5pm Sun) cover 31 acres on the south bank of the Colorado River, with displays including natural grottoes, a Japanese garden, a xeriscape demonstration garden and a fragrant herb garden. A 19th-century pioneer cabin, blacksmith shop and schoolhouse are also on the grounds, giving the garden its nickname, 'The Attic of Austin.'

UMLAUF SCULPTURE GARDEN

Near Zilker Park, these **open-air gardens and indoor museum** (Map pp66-7; ☎ 512-445-5582; www.umlaufsculpture.org; 605 Robert E Lee Rd; adult/senior/student $3.50/2.50/1, child under 6 free; ⓨ 10am-4:30pm Wed-Fri, 1-4:30pm Sat-Sun) show off over 100 works by 20th-century American sculptor Charles Umlauf, who was an art professor at UT for 40 years. His works in varied materials, which range in subject

from mythology to realism to abstract art, are also on display at NYC's Metropolitan Museum of Art and the Smithsonian in Washington, DC. Artists workshops, lectures by contemporary sculptors and other special events are held on an ongoing basis.

UT Campus Area

The **University of Texas at Austin** (UT; www .utexas.edu) is the main campus of Texas' higher education system. Established in 1883, UT has about 50,000 students in schools that include architecture, business, communication, education, fine arts, law, liberal arts, public affairs and social work. Students are drawn here from all over Texas, the rest of the USA and over 100 foreign countries. The sprawling 350-acre main campus is bounded by Guadalupe St at the west, Martin Luther King Jr Blvd at the south and stretches east up to I-35. The UT campus is also well-served by Austin's public transit system (p116).

There are several notable buildings on campus, including **Texas Memorial Stadium**, home of the Longhorns football team (p70), as well as the LBJ Library and UT Tower. The **Texas Union** (Map p68-9; ☎ 512-475-6636, 24hr events hotline 512-475-6666; 24th & Guadalupe Sts), west of the tower, is a good place to get oriented; the front desk sells tickets for the tower tours, and there's also the Cactus Cafe (p100), a few places to eat and an underground bowling alley (p108).

LYNDON BAINES JOHNSON (LBJ) LIBRARY & MUSEUM

History buffs and political junkies won't want to miss the **LBJ Library & Museum** (Map pp68-9; ☎ 512-721-0200; www.lbjlib.utexas.edu; 2313 Red River St; admission free; ⓨ 9am-5pm daily) on the east side of the UT campus. The LBJ Museum does a fascinating, well-balanced job of explaining Johnson's life and times. As the 36th US president (1963–69), Johnson presided over one of the most exciting, angst-filled decades in US history. It's all here: the Cuban Missile Crisis; the assassinations of President Kennedy, Martin Luther King Jr and Robert Kennedy; the groovy music; the Vietnam War. But there's also plenty of material on Johnson's early life, his rise to political power, and his successes as

AUSTIN

the architect of the 'Great Society,' the most far-reaching social legislation passed since Franklin Roosevelt's New Deal in the 1930s.

On the second floor, a spooky animatronic LBJ regales museum visitors with the kind of humorous anecdotes the ol' Texan himself liked to tell. Don't miss an elevator trip to the eighth floor for a look at a near-actual-size replica of Johnson's Oval Office in the White House and an exhibit on Lady Bird Johnson, the president's wife, who found success on her own promoting environmental causes. Back downstairs the gift shop sells vintage US political buttons, White House china patterns and '60s rock star paper dolls.

THE UT TOWER

Standing 307ft high, with a clock more than 12ft in diameter, the **UT Tower** (Map pp68-9; ☎ 512-475-6633 or 877-475-6633 for tour reservations; tour $3; ⏰ tour schedules vary) looms large in campus and Austin history. In a classic case of Texan 'mine's bigger than yours,' the UT Tower can also claim to be

---

CHARLES WHITMAN, THE TEXAS TOWER SNIPER

The UT Tower is possibly best known as the place where, on August 1, 1966, 25-year-old Charles Whitman holed up with a backpack containing several rifles, handguns and ammunition, plus food, water, gasoline, deodorant and a roll of toilet paper, and opened fire on passersby. During the 96 minutes he was in the tower, Whitman killed over a dozen people and wounded 31 before being shot after two Austin policemen and a retired Air Force gunner stormed the tower. Click to www.crimelibrary.com for controversial theories of Whitman's motivations for such a heinous killing spree.

Whitman lore is rife among students, who will cheerfully point out holes in the sidewalk and tell tourists that they're bullet holes from the fateful day. Tower tour guides may be reluctant to talk about it, though they will point out the chunk of the observation deck that was removed as forensic evidence, since the bullet that killed Whitman lodged there.

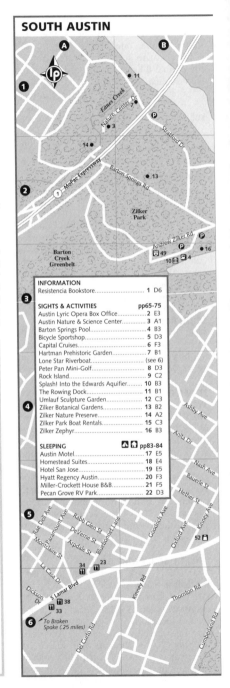

SOUTH AUSTIN

INFORMATION
Resistencia Bookstore.............................. 1 D6

SIGHTS & ACTIVITIES   pp65-75
Austin Lyric Opera Box Office................... 2 E3
Austin Nature & Science Center............... 3 A1
Barton Springs Pool................................ 4 B3
Bicycle Sportshop.................................... 5 D3
Capital Cruises.. 6 F3
Hartman Prehistoric Garden..................... 7 B1
Lone Star Riverboat............................ (see 6)
Peter Pan Mini-Golf................................. 8 D3
Rock Island.. 9 C2
Splash! Into the Edwards Aquifier........... 10 B3
The Rowing Dock..................................... 11 B1
Umlauf Sculpture Garden....................... 12 C3
Zilker Botanical Gardens........................ 13 B2
Zilker Nature Preserve............................ 14 A2
Zilker Park Boat Rentals......................... 15 C3
Zilker Zephyr... 16 B3

SLEEPING   pp83-84
Austin Motel... 17 E5
Homestead Suites................................... 18 E4
Hotel San Jose.. 19 E5
Hyatt Regency Austin.............................. 20 F3
Miller-Crockett House B&B...................... 21 F5
Pecan Grove RV Park.............................. 22 D3

0 ━━━━━━ 400 m
0 ━━━━━━ 0.2 mi

EATING 🍴 pp92-94
Artz Rib House.................................**23** A5
Bouldin Creek Coffee House..........**24** E5
Casa de Luz...................................**25** D3
Chuy's...**26** C3
El Sol y La Luna.............................**27** E5
Green Mesquite BBQ & More.........**28** D3
Güero's Taco Bar...........................**29** E5
Jo's..**30** E5
Lambert's.......................................**31** E6
Magnolia Cafe South.....................**32** E6
Matt's El Rancho............................**33** A6
Mr Natural.....................................**34** A6

Sandy's..**35** E4
Shady Grove Restaurant..................**36** D3
South Congress Cafe.......................**37** E5
Taco Xpress...................................**38** A6
Threadgill's World Headquarters.......**39** F4
Uchi...**40** D4
Vespaio..**41** E5

ENTERTAINMENT 🖥️🎭🎬 pp99-110
Continental Club.............................**42** E5
Dougherty Arts Center.....................**43** D3
Ego's..**44** F4
Flipnotics..**45** D3
Jovita's...**46** E5
Saxon Pub......................................**47** C4
Zachary Scott Theatre Center...........**48** D3
Zilker Hillside Theater......................**49** B3

SHOPPING 🛍️🎁 pp110-115
Allen's Boots..................................**50** E5
Amelia's Retrovogue & Relics..........**51** C5
Austin Found..................................**52** B5
Blackmail..**53** E5
Creatures..**54** D6
Dragonsnaps...................................**55** E6
Eco-wise..**56** E5
Electric Ladyland............................**57** E5
Flipnotics..**58** D3
Gomi..**59** F5
New Bohemia..............................(see 41)
Off the Wall................................(see 55)
Pink...(see 53)
Roadhouse Relics............................**60** D5
Rue's Antiques.............................(see 55)
SoCo Center...................................**61** F5
Terra Toys.......................................**62** E6
Uncommon Objects.....................(see 57)

UNIVERSITY OF TEXAS, THE DRAG & HYDE PARK

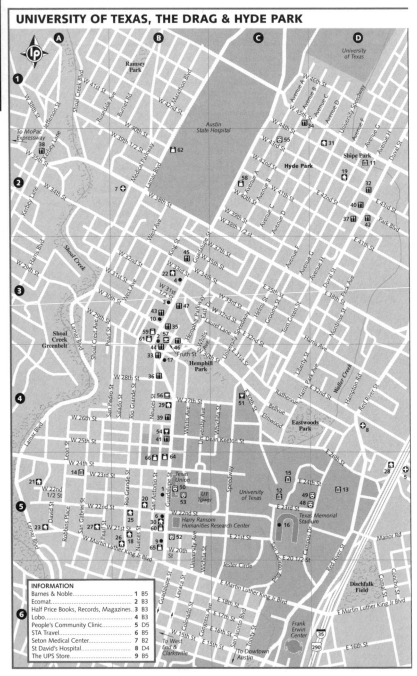

taller than the state capitol. Despite it being illegal to construct anything in Austin higher than the seat of Texas government, UT architects slyly placed the tower on a small rise, which effectively places it above the capitol by several feet.

Completed in 1937, the tower is sometimes lit orange to celebrate UT athletic victories or other achievements. For the last few decades, Tom Anderson (who was once a graduate student in music here) has been playing carillon bell concerts at 12:50pm on Mondays, Wednesdays and Fridays. The tower belfry is reached through a trap door up a winding stairway of over 50 steps, but is off-limits to visitors.

The tower's recently renovated observation deck is accessible by guided tours; you'll have to pass through a metal detector first, and no backpacks or 'oversized' bags are allowed (locker rental $1). Tours are usually offered both weekday evenings and all day Saturday during the summer, but only on weekends during the academic year. Always call ahead to check schedules, then try to time your visit around sunset, since otherwise the tours can seem way too long. Advance reservations, which are recommended, are accepted with a credit card. Same-day, standby tickets may be available. To get on the waiting list, stop by the Texas Union's front desk.

HARRY RANSOM HUMANITIES RESEARCH CENTER

The fascinating **Ransom Center** (Map pp68-9; ☎ 512-471-8944; 21st & Guadalupe Sts; admission free; ☑ 10am-5pm Tues-Fri, till 7pm Thu, noon-5pm Sat-Sun) is a major repository of historic manuscripts, photography, books, film, TV, music and more. Highlights include a complete copy of the Gutenberg Bible and what is thought to be the first photograph ever taken, 'View from the Window at Le Gras,' dating from 1826. Other rare and first editions are equally impressive, ranging from Dante's Divine Comedy to books of Dylan Thomas poetry. Some of the most visually entertaining pieces, such as movie posters for *The Texas Chainsaw Massacre* and Al Hirschfield caricatures, are drawn from the innovative performing arts collections. Recent acquisitions include the Watergate papers by Bob Woodward and Carl Bernstein that eventually brought down the presidency of Richard Nixon. Check the website for special online-only exhibitions and the center's busy events calendar of author readings, live music, lectures and more. All in all, this jewel of a place should be a must-see on anyone's itinerary.

JACK S BLANTON MUSEUM OF ART

The **Blanton** (Map pp68-9; ☎ 512-471-7324; www .blantonmuseum.org; Art Building, 23rd St & San Jacinto Blvd; admission free; ⊗ 9am-5pm Mon-Fri, 1-5pm Sat-Sun, sometimes later Thu evenings) ranks among the best university art collections in the US, though only a small portion of it has ever been on public view. Selections from the permanent collection are showcased in the campus Art Building. The Blanton is best known for its modernist, social realist and abstract expressionist art, including works by Thomas Hart Benton, Arshile Gorky and Max Weber. Other strengths include both Renaissance and Baroque paintings and drawings; the CR Smith Collection of Art of the American West; and an outstanding collection of 20th-century modern and contemporary Latin American art.

TEXAS MEMORIAL MUSEUM

In a huge art deco building on the UT campus, this kid-oriented **museum** (Map pp68-9; ☎ 512-471-1604; 2400 Trinity St; admission free; ⊗ 9am-5pm Mon-Fri, 10am-5pm Sat, 1-5pm Sun) explores Texas' natural and social history, with exhibits on paleontology, anthropology, natural history, geology and biodiversity. Outside, don't miss seeing the dinosaur tracks found in Glen Rose, Texas. Inside, the museum owns the skeleton of a pterosaur (a Cretaceous-era flying reptile with a wingspan of 40ft) recovered at Big Bend in 1971. There's also an interactive exhibit tracing geologic time. Upstairs, you can glimpse taxidermic examples of a Texas softshell turtle, Mexican beaded lizard and other critters, but most of the exhibits are like something you'd find in the dusty attic of an eccentric great aunt. Downstairs, the gift shop has a king's ransom of educational toys, such as create-a-fossil kits and diorama stuff, plus books and field guides for naturalists of all ages.

NEIL-COCHRAN MUSEUM HOUSE

On a side street a few blocks west of the Drag, this impressive **Greek revival home** (Map pp68-9; ☎ 512-478-2335; 2310 San Gabriel St; tour $2; ⊗ 2-5pm Wed-Sun) was built by Abner Cook, the same architect who designed the downtown Governor's Mansion (p63). Today, this stately Austin home, filled with paintings and fine Victorian antique furnishings, is open for tours. Buy tickets at the gift shop around back, where you'll find a few modest historical displays (admission free).

Hyde Park

Held during Father's Day weekend, the annual **Historic Hyde Park Homes Tour** (www .hydepark-na.org; same-day tickets $12.50) is a rare chance to peek inside some of the city's most impressive 19th- and 20th-century homes and wander around their lovingly tended gardens. But at any time of year, you can still amble around the neighborhood, either on foot or bicycle, with a free self-guided tour brochure available at the Austin CVB (p61) or Austin History Center (p78).

ELISABET NEY MUSEUM

The reconstructed studio of Elisabet Ney, this **museum** (Map pp68-9; ☎ 512-458-2255; 304 E 44th St at Ave H; bus No 7-Duval; donations welcome;

TIPS FOR ESCAPING THE CROWDS

▪ Rest under the shade of the 500-year-old **Treaty Oak** (Map p91).

▪ Wander around the **Umlauf Sculpture Garden** (p65).

▪ Row or hike along the **Barton Creek Greenbelt** (p73) on a weekday, not a weekend.

▪ Take a deep breath inside the studio at the **Elisabet Ney Museum** (p70).

▪ Sun yourself on a garden bench at the **French Legation Museum** (p71).

▪ Visit Austin's offbeat neighborhoods, such as **North Loop Blvd** and anywhere (except busy SoCo) in **South Austin**.

☻ 10am-5pm Wed-Sat, noon-5pm Sun) contains more than a hundred of the vivacious German-born sculptor's busts and statues of political figures, heads of state and royalty in Texas, other parts of the USA and Europe. It's an untrammeled oasis, and interesting not only to art lovers. Three of Ney's better-known works reside in the state capitol, but the artist herself considered her greatest legacy to be a sculpture of Lady Macbeth; the original is owned by the Smithsonian in Washington, DC, but a replica can be see here. Surrounded by lovely gardens, this exceptional little museum also contains classically inspired statues, historical photos and interesting biographical exhibits on Ney's life. Incidentally, Ney and her husband devoted much of their time to cultivating the arts in Texas, especially among students.

East Austin

Although it sees few visitors, East Austin has some rich history. Traditionally, it's an African American neighborhood, with roots stretching back to the 19th century. The **Henry Madison log cabin** (Map pp56-7; 2300 Rosewood Ave) built by an African American homesteader in 1863, stands in Rosewood Park near the auditorium.

FRENCH LEGATION MUSEUM

France was one of the few countries to recognize the Republic of Texas, and the **French Legation Museum** (Map pp58-9; ☎ 512-472-8180; www.frenchlegationmuseum.org; 802 San Marcos St; bus No 4-Montopolis; tour adult/senior/student $4/3/2; ☻ 1-5pm Tues-Sun) was built in 1840–41 to house the French charg d'affaires, Monsieur Dubois, who falsely styled himself as a member of the French royal family. Dubois was quite the rabble-rouser during his brief sojourn in Austin (ask your tour guide about the infamous 'Pig Wars'), and he may not have even stayed in this stately house for very long.

Nevertheless, it has been wonderfully restored and contains a meticulous reconstruction of the first Creole kitchen in Texas (with lots of quirky gadgets and implements) and the republic's first wine cellar. The museum comes alive for **Bastille Day** (p80), but awe-inspiring views of the state capitol, as seen from the front porch of the house, are alone worth the trip. Insightful tours start at the old carriage house, now a gift shop selling books and replicas of the house's more fascinating period pieces, including courting candles and glass flycatchers.

TEXAS STATE CEMETERY

Revitalized in the 1990s, the state's **official cemetery** (Map pp56-7; ☎ 512-463-0605; 909 Navasota St, just north of E 7th St; bus No 4-Montopolis; ☻ 8am-5pm daily, visitor center 8am-5pm Mon-Fri) is just what it sounds like – the final resting place of key figures in the history of Texas. Interred here are luminaries such as Stephen F Austin, Alamo survivor Susanna Dickinson, Miriam 'Ma' Ferguson (the state's first female governor), writers James Michener and Fred Gipson (author of *Old Yeller*) and Lone Star State flag designer Joanna Troutman, along with thousands of soldiers who died in the Civil War and their spouses, plus more than 100 leaders of the Republic of Texas who were exhumed from other sites and reburied here. According to local soothsayers, those families who objected to the reinterring of their ancestors were simply outwaited (until they died as well) by the state. How macabre! Self-guided tour brochures are usually available from the visitor center, as well as at the Austin CVB (p61) and Austin History Center (p78).

HIGH POINTS

Just across from Mayfield Park, Mt Bonnell Rd climbs to the *tostada grande* of Austin overlooks, the much-heralded **Mt Bonnell**. At 785ft above sea level, the mountain offers a panoramic view of the Colorado River all the way back to downtown after you climb the 99-odd steps to the observation level. It's best to go around sunset, though that's when it's most crowded, too. Mt Bonnell is just about the highest point in Austin, but you can also get a bird's-eye perspective atop the **UT Tower** (p65), **Speakeasy's** rooftop terrace (p104) and at the **Dry Creek Saloon** (p105).

**GEORGE WASHINGTON CARVER
MUSEUM & CULTURAL CENTER**
In Austin's first public library building, dating from 1926, this neighborhood **museum** (Map pp56-7; ☎ 512-472-4809; 1165 Angelina St; bus No 2-Rosewood; admission free; ☺ 10am-6pm Tues-Thu, noon-5pm Fri-Sat) was the first in the state dedicated to African American culture. Displays focus on Texas' unique Juneteenth holiday (p80) and historic photographs, archival documents and videos concerning early African American pioneers, scientists and inventors. Temporary exhibitions rotate throughout the year.

Greater Austin
Run by the Daughters of the Republic of Texas (DRT), the small **Republic of Texas Museum** (Map pp56-7; ☎ 512-339-1997; 510 E Anderson Lane; adult/child $2/50¢; ☺ 10am-4pm Mon-Fri) mostly caters to visiting school groups, but special exhibitions may be of interest to history buffs; call ahead.

LADY BIRD JOHNSON WILDFLOWER CENTER
Anyone with an interest in Texas' flora and fauna should make the 20-minute drive to these wonderful **gardens** (Map pp56-7; ☎ 512-292-4100; www.wildflower.org; 4801 La Crosse Ave; adult/student & senior/child 5-12 $5/$4/2, higher during peak spring flowering season; ☺ 9am-5:30pm Tues-Sun, open daily mid-Mar through Apr), southwest of downtown Austin. The center, founded in 1982 with the assistance of Texas' beloved former first lady, has a display garden featuring every type of wildflower and plant that grows in Texas, separated by geographical region, with an emphasis on Hill Country flora.

Incidentally, the aqueducts and cistern system here are part of the largest rainwater harvesting system in North America. Other notable features include several short nature trails through forest and meadow, a butterfly garden, wetland pond and a 'Little House' where activities for kids are offered. Call the center or go online for a schedule of family programs, lectures, workshops and adult education classes, too.

The best time to come is during spring (especially National Wildflower Week in May), but there's something in bloom all year. There's an **orientation gallery** on native landscaping that might have you ready to rip out your water-sucking bluegrass lawn by the time you've seen all its exhibits. The pleasant **Wildflower Cafe** (lunch $5-8; ☺ 10am-4pm Tues-Sat, 1-4pm Sun) does a nice daily special, besides selling snacks and drinks.

To get here by car, take MoPac straight south for over three-quarters of a mile past Slaughter Lane. Turn left at the next stoplight for La Crosse Ave, following the signs for a half mile east to the entrance. There's no bus service from Austin.

ACTIVITIES
If there's an epicenter to outdoor recreation in Austin, it's **Zilker Park** (Map pp66-7; ☎ 512-478-0905; Barton Springs Rd; admission free; ☺ 5am-10pm daily), just south of the Colorado River about a mile west of I-35. This 350-acre park is a heavenly slice of green, lined with hiking and biking trails and home to a **nature center** (p65), **botanical gardens** (p65) and **sculpture gardens** (p65). The park also provides access to the famed Barton Springs natural swimming pool and Barton Creek Greenbelt.

Austin has quite a few other places to play outside, including Town Lake, Lake Austin and creekside parks, riverine nature preserves and spreading greenbelts throughout the city. You can get just about any information you might need from the **City of Austin Parks & Recreation Department** (☎ 512-974-6700; www.ci.austin.tx.us/parks; ☺ 8am-5pm Mon-Fri). The department oversees six municipal golf courses and four tennis complexes (call ☎ 512-480-3020), as well as neighborhood recreation centers offering fitness classes and more.

See the boxed text 'Detour: The Highland Lakes' (p74) for information on visiting the nearby Highland Lakes and clothing-optional Hippie Hollow. Outdoor activity guides are sold at Whole Earth Provision Co and BookPeople, both in central Austin ('Bookstores,' p55). Women can find activity buddies through the **Texas Outdoors Woman Network** (townaustin.homestead.com/files/index.htm), which organizes weekly events and classes in the Austin area.

Swimming & Boating
When the weather's hot, Austinites are not. Find out why at the following aquatic oases.

BARTON SPRINGS POOL

This 1000ft-long **natural spring pool** (Map pp66-7; ☎ 512-476-9044, 24hr hotline 512-867-3080; 2101 Barton Springs Rd; adult weekdays/weekends $2.50/2.75, youth/child under 12 anytime $1/50¢; ⏰ 5am-10pm year-round, closed 9am-7pm Thu for cleaning) is simply the bee's knees when it comes to year-round swimming fun. Austin natives and newcomers hold this place dear in their hearts, and after one visit you'll see why. The Edwards Aquifer pumps 32 million gallons of very cold but very clear water into the pool, which is a constant 68°F year-round. Draped with century-old pecan trees, the area around the pool is a social scene in itself, and the place gets packed on a hot summer day. In winter, admission is free.

BARTON CREEK GREENBELT

Paddling along the waterways in the Barton Creek Greenbelt – an environmentally sensitive area constantly under pressure from developers who firmly believe that Austin needs more condos and golf courses – is one of the highlights of a trip to the city.

There's access to the waterways at several spots along the creek. Waterbirds are commonly spotted, and it's amazing how quickly you can be immersed in nature in what's essentially the city's center. Check out the *Austin Chronicle's* **Barton Creek Guide** (www.auschron.com/guides/bartoncreek) for more information.

Zilker Park Boat Rentals (Map pp66-7; ☎ 512-478-3852; www.zilkerboats.com; ⏰ 11am-dusk Mon-Fri, from 9am Sat-Sun, Mar-Oct; closed weekends in winter), just downstream from Barton Springs Pool, rents 17ft canoes and open-deck ocean kayaks. The price is $10/40 per hour/day, including paddles and life jackets. They also have maps and will describe the best routes. Arrive early on the weekends before the boats are all gone. To find the boathouse, walk to the east end of the upper parking lot, then down the steps. Check the website for two-for-one coupons.

TOWN LAKE

Town Lake is actually a dammed-off section of the Colorado River just south of downtown. It's a very nice area – as you'll notice if you're staying in the youth hostel, whose windows overlook it. You can rent kayaks from the hostel. **The Rowing Dock** (Map pp66-7; ☎ 512-459-0999; www.rowingdock.com; 2418 Stratford Dr; ⏰ call for hours), conveniently near the Austin Nature & Science Center (p76), rents kayaks for $10 to $20 per hour and water cycles for slightly more.

DEEP EDDY POOL

With its vintage 1930s bathhouse, Texas' oldest **swimming pool** (Map pp56-7; ☎ 512-472-8546; www.deepeddy.org; usually admission free; ⏰ usually 8am-8pm daily) is fed by cold springs and surrounded by cottonwood trees. There are separate areas for waders and lap swimmers. This historic swimming hole is especially popular with families on Splash Movie nights (adult/child $2/50¢), when films are shown on an outdoor screen by the pool in summer.

AROUND AUSTIN

Besides the waterfront at Emma Long Metropolitan Park (p86), the city also manages several neighborhood swimming and wading pools. **Stacy Pool** (Map pp56-7; ☎ 512-445-0304; 800 E Live Oak St; admission free; ⏰ hours vary) is one of the best. See the boxed text 'Swimming Holes' (p42) for an insider's guide to local swimming holes.

Disc Golf

The **Shoal Creek Greenbelt** is complete with a very cool Frisbee (okay, flying disc) course, which runs from Pease Park around Enfield Rd, north and parallel to the west side of Lamar St through the greenbelt to just past 24th St. On any warm day, dozens of beer-toting devotees can be seen maneuvering the course, using a variety of discs, in hopes of ultimately tossing their 'putting discs' into metal cages.

There's also a nine-hole disc golf course in **Zilker Park**, but it's nothing to write home about. For true fanatics, the city has full 18-hole disc golf courses at:

Mary Moore Searight Metropolitan Park (907 Slaughter Lane) This South Austin fave is just over a mile west of I-35 (exit Slaughter Lane).

Bartholomew District Park (5201 Berkman Rd) It's a hilly course near the old airport; from downtown, take I-35 north to exit 237B, then head east on 51st St for less than a mile.

Circle C Ranch Metropolitan Park (507 W Slaughter Lane) On Slaughter Creek, this tree-filled course presents plenty of obstacles. It's west of MoPac, off FM 1826.

Cycling & Hiking

See p116 for bicycle rental, sales and repair shops. Keep in mind that some of the recreation paths described here also allow in-line skating; check www.austininline.com for ideas of where to go and special skating events.

Town Lake, lined with over 10 miles of hiking and biking trails, is the most popular spot. For most of its way, it runs along the lake's northern side, which is the south edge of downtown Austin. There's another recreational path running for more than 4 miles through the **Shoal Creek Greenbelt** (Disc Golf above). You can also hike or mountain bike for almost 8 miles along the **Barton Creek Greenbelt**, which can be entered near Barton Springs Pool (p73).

ZILKER NATURE PRESERVE

At the west end of Zilker Park, the 60-acre **Zilker Nature Preserve** (Map pXXX; ☎ 512-327-7723; 302 Nature Center Dr; ☾ dawn-dusk daily) has footpaths that lead through a wilderness made up of meadows, streams and a high cliff with caves. There is a good view of downtown Austin from the rock-walled *ramada* (shelter). Access is off Barton Springs Rd by the MoPac bridge.

BLUNN CREEK NATURE PRESERVE

Hidden in South Austin, this quiet **place** (Map pp66-7; 1101 St Edwards Dr) has a 1-mile trail that passes by woodland streams. The real draw is the **overlook,** where interpretive signboards point out features from Texas' Cretaceous-era history: a coral reef, a volcanic cone and multiple ash deposits. The overlook is also accessible from a driveway on the west side of Travis High School, but it's best to visit outside of regular school hours.

THE VELOWAY

If you head out to the Lady Bird Johnson Wildflower Center, plan some extra time to ride or skate the great 3.2-mile **Veloway track** (☎ 512-440-5150; admission free; ☾ dawn-dusk daily) nearby. The track runs clockwise, and no walking or running is permitted.

MAYFIELD PARK & PRESERVE

On a bluff above the Colorado River sits this **20-acre preserve** (Map pp56-7; ☎ 512-372-7723; 3508 W 35th St; bus No 9-Enfield on Sat only; admission free; ☾ 8am-5pm daily), an idyllic spot settled at the turn of the 20th century. The whole kit and caboodle is now run by the city's parks department. The formal gardens, featuring peacocks, lily ponds, a gazebo overlooking the Colorado and a flower garden, are very peaceful. A tame walking trail leads less than a mile down by the creek. Solo travelers are advised to use caution, as the place can be deserted. Don't leave any valuables in your car, either.

DETOUR: THE HIGHLAND LAKES

With a conservation district stretching from central Texas to the Gulf of Mexico, the **Lower Colorado River Authority** (LCRA; ☎ 800-776-5272; www.lcra.org; ☾ office 8am-5pm Mon-Fri) manages a fabulous string of parks northwest of Austin. These parks front 'lakes' created by the damming of the Colorado River in the 1930s.

The main recreation area northwest of the city is along Lake Travis and Lake Austin, which are divided by Mansfield Dam. The most popular destination in the Highland Lakes, Lake Travis offers heaps of opportunities for swimming, sailing and camping. Farther northwest, Lake Buchanan is a bit more serene, as it's just that much farther from the crowds that descend on Lake Travis every summer weekend.

Hippie Hollow (Macgregor Park; day-use per vehicle $5; ☾ 9am-6pm, until 9pm in summer) is Texas' only official clothing-optional beach. There are views of Lake Travis, opportunities for swimming and wonderful primitive hiking trails through the hills. By car, take FM 2222 west of Loop 360, then turn left onto Hwy 620. Drive 1¼ miles south to the first traffic light, then turn right onto Comanche Trail Rd. The entrance is 2 miles ahead on the left.

Pace Bend Park (☎ 512-264-1482; day-use per vehicle $5; ☾ sunrise-9pm), with swimming-only coves, boat launches and hiking and biking trails, is looped with a 7-mile roadway connecting piers, campsites and swimming beaches. The interior of the park is a wildlife preserve and can be reached only by hiking, biking or horseback. You are also allowed to camp on the beach. By car, take Hwy 71 over 10 miles west of Hwy 620, then turn right on RM 2322 and go another 4½ miles.

There are more than three dozen other Highland Lakes-area campgrounds; call the LCRA for a brochure listing all the parks, admission fees, camping fees and facilities, or visit the website.

AUSTIN

DOWNTOWN AUSTIN WALKING TOUR

Start off your tour at the **Capitol Visitors Center (1)**, then walk west on 11th St. Turn right at the gates, stroll up the south steps of the **Texas state capitol (2)** and peek inside. After ambling the lawns of the capitol grounds, walk back down to the gates and cross the street.

Continue on the west side of Congress Ave, passing the ruins of a temporary state capitol, which burned to the ground in 1899. Further on is the **Old Bakery & Emporium (3)**, housed in an 1876 limestone building.

Briefly detour west on 10th St to the **Governor's Mansion (4)**, then retrace your steps. Stop in at **Little City (5)** for an espresso if you like before crossing over to the east side of Congress Ave.

Continue walking south past the **Austin Museum of Art (6)** and on the next block, the **Wild About Music (7)** store. Beyond the **State Theater (8)** stands the art deco **Paramount Theatre (9)**, which opened as the Majestic Theater in 1915; notice the carved gargoyles eyeing passersby from the second story.

Keep going south, past the **Hideout Coffee House & Theatre (10)**, then walk one block east along 6th St to see the historic **Driskill Hotel (11)**, a Romanesque structure dating from the late 19th century.

Back on Congress Ave, turn south again past the **Mexic-Arte Museum (12)**. Note the subterranean **Elephant Room (13)** for later if you're a jazz fan.

Hungry yet? Drop by **Las Manitas Avenue Cafe (14)**, next door to the funky folk art at **Tesoros Trading Co (15)**.

By now it's probably late afternoon, so conclude your tour by walking down to the **Congress Ave bridge (16)**, home to Austin's **bat colony**.

Otherwise, retrace your steps for a night of live music along **E 6th & Red River Sts** or in the **Warehouse District**; see 'Entertainment' (p99).

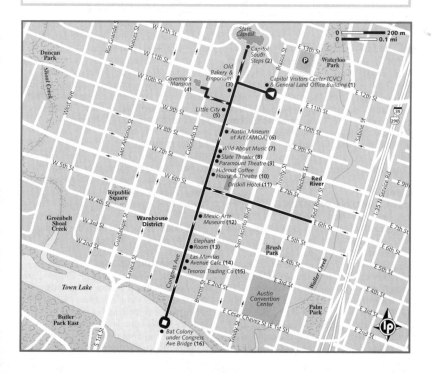

Rock Climbing

While most of the rock-climbing opportunities are out in the Hill Country, visitors can practice their skills (or learn) at the **Austin Rock Gym** (☎ 512-416-9299; www.austinrockgym.com; SouthPark Commerce Center, 4401 Friedrich Lane; day pass $10-13, gear rental $4-7), near the I-35/US 290 intersection. There's a second location in **North Austin** (☎ 512-416-9299; 8300 N Lamar Blvd), north of US 183. Hours vary, depending on the season.

Yoga

An oasis north of Barton Springs Rd, **Casa de Luz** (Map pp66-7; ☎ 512-476-2535; www.casadeluz.org; 1701 Toomey Rd) is an alternative community center that hosts various yoga, tai chi, Middle Eastern dance and other holistic fitness classes. The on-site cafe serves fresh vegan meals (p93).

Meditative **Full Moon Yoga** takes place at night atop Mt Bonnell (p71). Led by local yoga teacher Charles MacInerney (www.yogateacher.com), it's free and good for hatha practitioners of all levels. Check the monthly schedules online. Bring along a thick blanket, too, since the mountainside can be rocky.

AUSTIN FOR CHILDREN

Austin is absolutely kid-friendly, thanks to the casual south-central Texas lifestyle. **Zilker Park** is a wonderland of family-oriented fun; turn to p72 for more information on outdoor activities. Think about visiting the **Texas Memorial Museum** (p70) on the UT campus, too. See also individual reviews of Austin restaurants and hotels for some great family options. For practical information, see p192.

Downtown

AUSTIN CHILDREN'S MUSEUM

This **museum** (Map pp58-9; ☎ 512-472-2499; www.austinkids.org; 201 Colorado St; adult & youth/child under 2 $4.50/2.50, free 5-8pm Wed & 4-5pm Sun; ☑ 10am-5pm Tues-Sat, till 8pm Wed, noon-5pm Sun) offers lots of interactive and educational fun. Kids can try their hands at running a ranch, order a meal at the Global Diner and hang upside down beneath a bridge, just like the real Austin bats. There are special areas for preschool-aged children. Call the museum or check the website for schedules of family events held throughout the year, including storytelling festivals, science-o-rama days and especially 'Austin Kiddie Limits' musical concerts. Traveling exhibitions can be a hit-or-miss proposition, though. The museum gift shop is full of puzzles, mind-bending games and bat-mania books.

CHILDREN'S ART DAY PARK

This vibrant **event** (Map pp58-9; ☎ 512-476-6064; www.austinsymphony.org; Symphony Square, 1101 Red River St; admission 50¢) usually takes place on Wednesday mornings during the summer. Local musicians, magicians, storytellers, dancers and artisans create an all-day art immersion camp for little 'uns. Touch a tuba in the Instrument Petting Zoo, listen to live country-and-western music or learn to make crafts. Best of all, lemonade costs just 10¢ a cup. Bring a blanket and a sack lunch for picnicking by Waller Creek.

Zilker Park

SPLASH! INTO THE EDWARDS AQUIFER

Located in the old Barton Springs Pool bathhouse, this neat little **interpretive center** (Map pp66-7; ☎ 512-478-3170; 2201 Barton Springs Rd; admission free; ☑ 10am-5pm Tues-Sat, noon-5pm Sun) tells the aquifer's story through interactive and multimedia displays and explains why it's so important to protect central Texas' groundwater source. Here children can also spy on the endangered Barton Springs salamander, a salt-and-pepper fellow that's only a couple of inches long. The gift shop sells snorkels and other water toys.

ZILKER ZEPHYR

Trains on the Zilker Zephyr **miniature railroad** (Map pp66-7; adult/senior & child under 12 $2.75/1.75; ☑ 10am-5pm Mon-Fri, 10am-dusk Sat-Sun) make the 25-minute, 2-mile ride along Barton Creek and Town Lake year-round. They leave the depot near the playground every hour on the hour weekdays and every 30 to 40 minutes on weekends.

AUSTIN NATURE & SCIENCE CENTER

In the northwestern area of Zilker Park, the **Austin Nature & Science Center** (Map pp66-7; ☎ 512-327-8181; www.ci.austin.tx.us/nature-science; 301 Nature Center Dr; donations requested; ☑ 9am-5pm Mon-Sat, noon-5pm Sun) has exhibitions of native Texan mammals, birds, reptiles, amphibians and arthropods that have been injured and nursed back to health at the center. The center also has outdoor nature trails lined with native plants, where you'll see bats, butterflies and birds. There's a hands-on discovery area inside the main building aimed at visiting school groups. Summer camps, family programs and naturalist classes for adults are just a few of the activities offered; pick up the 'Natural Selections' brochure or download it online. The gift shop sells nature-related toys, bird feeders and practical outdoor stuff, like hats and bug juice. Free parking is available off Stratford Dr, underneath the MoPac bridge, from where it's a short walk uphill to the center.

HARTMAN PREHISTORIC GARDEN
Before the turn-off to the Austin Nature & Science Center is this fascinating **garden** (Map pp66-7; back entrance off Stratford Dr, main entrance through Zilker Botanical Gardens; admission free), managed by the **Zilker Botanical Gardens** (p65). Here the bones of a prehistoric turtle and what scientists think are the tracks of ornithomimus, an ostrich-like dinosaur, were found in the early 1990s. Today the garden contains reproductions of the dino tracks and a Cretaceous-era-type habitat that does its best to imitate the natural growing conditions of Texas 100 million years ago. It's a place to dream, and a good chance to see rare flora, too.

Greater Austin
Both of these rural sights are a pleasant . drive outside of downtown Austin.

PIONEER FARMS
On the banks of Walnut Creek is a **living history museum** (Map pp56-7; ☎ 512-474-5198 ext 14; www.ci.austin.tx.us/pioneerfarm, www.heritage societyaustin.org/pioneerfarm.html; 11418 Sprinkle Cut Off Rd; adult/child $5/4, special events $3-10; ☉ 9:30am-1pm Mon-Wed, 1-5pm Sun) of 19th-century Texas pioneer life. Many restored post–Civil War era buildings have moved to this site and costumed interpreters make it come alive. There's also an old-fashioned general store that sells reproductions of antique toys and books.

Time your visit carefully. Sundays are usually your best bet for family fun. Pioneer Farms hosts other special events, such as leathercraft and toy-making

workshops (☎ 512-837-1215 for reservations) year-round. From June to October, watch out for **Mo-o-ovies Under the Moon** (☎ 512-416-5700 ext 1539; admission free, parking $2). Gates open around 5pm for a food, arts and crafts fair, maybe along with historical reenactments or storytelling by Texas authors, until the movie starts after dark. Bring blankets for sitting on the grass.

The farm is a 25-minute drive northeast of downtown. Take I-35 north, exit Braker Lane and head east. Where it dead ends into Dessau Lane, turn left and go about another half mile. After the bridge, there's a righthand turn lane for Sprinkle Cut Off Rd, about a mile from the farm's entrance.

AUSTIN ZOO
Out where the Hill Country begins, this conservation-minded **zoo**; (☎ 512-288-1490, 800-291-1140; www.austinzoo.com; 10807 Rawhide Trail; adult/student/senior & child 2-12 $6/5/4, train rides $2; ☉ 10am-6pm daily) is a sanctuary for rescued, abandoned or donated animals. Although it has been open for over a decade, even many locals haven't yet heard of it. Today the zoo harbors more than 250 animals drawn from over 100 domestic and exotic species. There's a picnic area, petting zoo and miniature train ride along a 2-mile track with glorious Hill Country views. You can buy snacks for feeding the animals.

From South Austin, follow US 290 west past the intersection with Hwy 71 about 2½miles, then turn right onto Circle Dr for another 1½ miles. At Rawhide Dr, turn right and drive another 1½ miles to the zoo entrance.

TOURS
The **Austin CVB** (p61) downtown has information and brochures for many of the following city tours.

Boat Tours
With a dock on the south shore of Town Lake near the Hyatt, **Lone Star Riverboat** (Map pp66-7; ☎ 512-327-1388; lonestar.austin.citysearch .com) runs 90-minute cruises on its double-decked paddle wheel riverboat at 3pm each Saturday and Sunday, March through October. The cost is $9/7/6 per adult/senior/child under 12; no reservations are necessary. The company also offers nightly sunset bat-watching trips for $8/6/5 on its 32ft electric

AUSTIN

cruiser from April through October. Times vary; call ahead for reservations.

Between March and November, **Capital Cruises** (☎ 512-480-9264; www.capitalcruises.com) offers competitively priced lake excursions and bat-watching trips that depart from the Hyatt's dock. Dinner cruises (featuring fajitas!) cost $30/20 per adult/child and depart at 6pm on Friday, Saturday and Sunday evenings.

Austin Duck Adventures (☎ 512-477-5274; www.austinducks.com; adult/senior & student/child 3-12 $18/16.50/13) utilize amphibious British Alvis Stalwarts, which parade around the state capitol, roll down Congress Ave and 6th St, then splash into Lake Austin; tour guides provide a few entertaining historical tidbits along the way. Schedules are subject to change, but tours depart at least daily (more frequently on weekends). Advance reservations are only taken for large groups. Buy tickets at the Austin CVB (p61).

Driving Tours

For an interesting alternative to stereotypical bus and van tours, trust **Texpert Tours** (☎ 512-383-8989; www.io.com/ ~zow), led by an affable public radio host, Howie Richie (aka the 'Texas Back Roads Scholar'). Historical anecdotes, natural history and environmental tips are all part of the educational experience. A three-hour tour of central Austin takes visitors to the state capitol, Governor's Mansion and up to the top of Mt Bonnell. Tailored trips of either Austin or the Hill Country can be arranged. Advance reservations are required for all tours. The cost is $75 per adult (two-person minimum), including door-to-door service.

Train Tours

The **Austin Steam Train Association** (☎ 512-477-8468; www.austinsteamtrain.org) runs seasonal weekend day trips aboard the *Hill Country Flyer* steam train from Cedar Park north of Austin into the Texas Hill Country. Between June and November, there are also 90-minute jaunts aboard the *River City Local* through historic neighborhoods and parks in Austin along the old Southern Pacific railroad tracks. Special *Twilight Flyer* runs into the Hill Country have themed entertainment, perhaps bedtime stories for kids or a little murder mystery

game. Call the association directly or check the website for tour details, schedules of year-round departures and a map to the depot. Short tours start at $12/11/8 per adult/senior/child under 13; coach seats for the longer trips cost $25/22/15. Lounge car seating costs more.

For a shorter, cheaper miniature train ride, check out the **Zilker Zephyr** (p76) in Zilker Park.

Walking Tours

One of the best deals around is the free walking tour of downtown Austin, which leaves from the capitol's south steps at 9am Thursday, Friday and Saturday and at 2pm Sunday, weather permitting. The tour, led by very informative and sometimes funny guides, takes in the major sights around the Capitol Complex and then heads south down Congress Ave, covering the history and architecture of many central Austin landmarks. Other free walking tours concentrate on the capitol grounds (9am Saturday and 2pm Sunday) or the historic Bremond Block (11am Saturday and Sunday). Tours last between 60 and 90 minutes and are available March through November. For more information, call the Austin CVB at ☎ 800-926-2282 ext 7226.

Self-guided walking tours are possible through a comprehensive series of free brochures put out by the city. They are available from the Austin CVB (p61) and the **Austin History Center** (Map pp58-9; ☎ 512-974-7480; www.ci.austin.tx.us/library/ahc; 810 Guadalupe St; ☽ 10am-9pm Mon-Thu, 10am-6pm Fri-Sat, noon-6pm Sun). These remarkably detailed pamphlets cover Congress Ave and E 6th St, the Bremond Block, West Austin, Hyde Park neighborhoods, the Texas State Cemetery and other historic places.

Austin Ghost Tours (☎ 512-695-7297; www.austinghosttours.com) take visitors on haunted pub crawls, graveyard tours and along the route of 19th-century serial killings perpetrated by Austin's 'Servant Girl Annihilator.' Downtown ghost tours last 90 minutes, usually departing at 8pm every other Saturday night from the **Hideout Coffee House & Theatre** (Map pp58-9; 617 Congress Ave). Tours cost $15 or less per person, but reservations are required. Check the website or call for tour details, current schedules and reservations.

AUSTIN

Most **UT campus tours** (www.utexas.edu/tours) are aimed at prospective students and nostalgic alumni. In addition to the **UT Tower tour** (p65), visitors may also enjoy an after-dark 'Moonlight Prowl' across campus, complete with amusing anecdotes, hair-raising tales and a UT trivia quiz. Prowls start at 8pm and last about 90 minutes. They're also free, and are consequently so popular that tours often fill up weeks in advance. Check the website for schedules, advance reservations and instructions for how to get on the waiting list.

FESTIVALS & EVENTS

Following are some special events worth planning a trip around. For a complete list, check with the **Austin CVB** (p61).

JANUARY
Red-Eye Regatta (☎ 512-266-1336; www.austinyacht club.org; Jan 1) An annual New Year's Day race of 50 first-class keel boats held on Lake Travis and sponsored by the Austin Yacht Club.

FEBRUARY
Carnival Brasileiro (☎ 512-452-6832; www.sambaparty.com; date & venue vary) Started by Brazilian foreign-exchange students in 1975, this euphoric

one-night bash features samba, carnival drumming and bare skin galore. Buy tickets early.
Mardi Gras (date varies) Celebrate downtown on E 6th St, Austin's own version of Bourbon St, where the revelry has gotten quite rowdy in recent years. Expect Cajun food, a masquerade ball, parades and beads for exhibitionists.

MARCH
Zilker Park Kite Festival (☎ 512-647-7488; www .zilkerkitefestival.com; early Mar) This 75-year-old festival sometimes changes its date to take advantage of the best winds. It's a free rite of spring.
South by Southwest (SXSW; see p34; mid-Mar) Among the world's top music-industry gatherings, SXSW features dozens of venues packed with record company execs, gaggles of critics and wannabe critics, producers and hundreds of bands. The town goes absolutely nuts.
Jerry Jeff Walker's Birthday Weekend (☎ 512-477-0036, 800-966-7469 for tickets; www.jerryjeff.com; late Mar) This 1970s outlaw country icon's birthday party covers a series of live shows and dances in Austin clubs and the Hill Country.
Capital 10K Road Race (☎ 512-472-3254; one Sun in late Mar/early Apr) This road race is Texas' largest, attracting about 10,000 runners, many attired in creative, wacky costumes.
Star of Texas Fair & Rodeo (☎ 512-919-3000; www.staroftexas.org; 7331 Decker Lane, off US 290 E; 15 days in late Mar/early Apr) For two weeks, Austin goes yee-haw! with professional rodeo competitions, country

---

A UNIQUELY WEIRD AUSTIN TOUR

Locals treasure the wild, wacky and wonderful things that set Austin apart, not only from the rest of Texas, but from the rest of the country. A quick tour of some of our faves (dig deeper on your own, and magically more will appear) includes:

- The bats under the Congress Ave bridge (p64)
- Jay Robillard's 'The Lounge Show' on Saturday mornings (p60) and Radio Austin (p60) anytime
- Wacky festivals like Spamarama™ (p80), Eeyore's Birthday Party (p80) and the O Henry Pun-Off (p65)
- SXSW (p34) and the *Austin City Limits* TV show (p100) and music festival (p80)
- Barton Springs Pool (p73), Hippie Hollow (p74) and Splash Movie nights at Deep Eddy Pool (p73)
- Playing disc golf on the Shoal Creek Greenbelt (p73)

- Eccentric storefronts on SoCo and North Loop Blvd
- *Mr Sinus Theatre 3000* or any other offbeat event at the downtown Alamo Drafthouse Cinema (p107)
- Live shows at Waterloo Records (p102) and afterward Amy's Ice Creams (p90)
- Dive bars like the Carousel Lounge (p106), Saxon Pub (p103), Deep Eddy Cabaret (p105), Ginny's Little Longhorn Saloon (p105), Ego's (p105) or Dry Creek Saloon (p105)
- Peter Pan Mini-Golf (p108) and rockin' Glow Bowl at the Union Underground (p108)
- Yoga under a full moon on Mt Bonnell (p75)

and western music, a chuck wagon cook-off and a livestock fair at the Travis County Exposition Center, which is about 10 miles northeast of downtown Austin.

Spamarama™ (☎ 512-791-4676; www.spamarama .com; Auditorium Shores, 920 W Riverside Dr; late Mar, Apr or May) The pre-fab luncheon meat's hometown is Austin, Minnesota. But its Texas counterpart gets into the act with this silly festival. It's a trip. Celebrity judges preside over a Spam cook-off, local lounge acts play and the 'Spamalympics' host the Spam cram, the Spam toss and more things to turn any athlete's stomach. Carnival rides for kiddies add to the county fair atmosphere.

APRIL

Texas Hill Country Wine & Food Festival (www .texaswineandfood.org; first week in Apr) Headquartered at Austin's Four Seasons Hotel, celebrations include a wine auction, free wine and food tastings, cooking classes and many more events scattered at venues around Austin, the Highland Lakes and the Hill Country.

Austin Fine Arts Festival (☎ 512-458-6073; www .austinfineartsfestival.org; Republic Square, 5th & Guadalupe Sts; early Apr) This two-day event has a juried showcase for watercolors, sculpture, ceramics, blown glass and more works by over 200 artists. Get into the spirit with hands-on kids' art activities and gourmet culinary treats, and sing along to zydeco and Western swing bands.

Old Settler's Music Festival (☎ 512-370-4630; www.bluegrassfestival.com; mid-Apr) This homegrown bluegrass and acoustic American music festival happens at Salt Lick BBQ Pavilion and Camp Ben McCulloch in Driftwood, a short drive southwest of Austin.

Eeyore's Birthday (☎ 512-448-5160; www.sexton.com /eeyore; Pease Park, 1100 Kingsbury St; late Apr) Started by UT students during the hippie-dippie 1960s, perhaps no other annual event proves Austin's offbeat flavor so completely, with Maypole dancing, live music and even a birthday cake for the namesake melancholy Winnie-the-Pooh character. Proceeds benefit nonprofit groups, and you'll feel silly if you *don't* wear a costume.

MAY

O Henry Pun-Off (early May) See p65.

Old Pecan Street Spring Arts Festival (☎ 512-441-9015; www.roadstarproductions.com; early May) A downtown arts-and-crafts street fair with live rock, country, Latin and world music and kids' carnival rides along E 6th St.

Cinco de Mayo Festival (☎ 512-867-1999; www.austin-cincodemayo.com; Fiesta Gardens, 1901 Bergman Ave; admission $5-10; May 5) On the days leading up to May 5th, this event celebrates the Mexican cavalry victory at the Battle of Puebla in 1862. It's also an excuse to dance to the over 40 music acts (including country, Tejano, Noreteño and mariachi) at Fiesta Gardens,

on the north side of Town Lake, with ballet folklorico, a chili cook-off, mechanical bull-riding and cumbia dance contests. Kids under 12 get in free, and there are plenty of family events.

JUNE

Austin Pride Parade (www.austinprideparade.org; early Jun) Austin's gay pride celebration is one of Texas' largest (but that's not saying a whole lot). Still, there's a whole of partyin' goin' down, from gay men's choral performances to women-only raves to interfaith prayer services.

Blues on the Green (www.kgsr.com; mid-Jun through mid-Aug) Free summertime gigs by big-name musicians, usually held every other Wednesday night, at Rock Island in Zilker Park. Visit the website for schedules.

Juneteenth (Jun 19) Remembering the arrival in Texas of the news of the Emancipation Proclamation freeing slaves, the city bursts with carnival rides, sports tournaments, dances, a fine arts show and a pageant, all celebrating African American freedom. Many events held in East Austin.

JULY

4th of July Celebration (☎ 512-476-6064; www.austinsymphony.org; Jul 4) Nearly 100,000 people come out to watch the Austin Symphony perform a free one-hour concert in Zilker Park, followed by fireworks over Town Lake. Don't miss hearing Howitzer cannons fired off by the Texas National Guard.

Bastille Day (☎ 512-451-1704; www.alliance -francaise.austin.tx.us; admission $6; mid-Jul) The Alliance Française d'Austin celebrates at the French Legation Museum with lots of French food, wine and music, including Cajun, zydeco and accordion-inspired Musette tunes.

AUGUST

Austin Chronicle Hot Sauce Contest (☎ 512-454-5766; www.austinchronicle.com; date varies) Currently held in Waterloo Park, this summer contest has been going strong since 1990. Beer, music and all sorts of spicy delights accompany an enthusiastically judged hot sauce competition.

SEPTEMBER

Austin Museum Day (Sep 14) Special events, celebrations and discount admission at museums and attractions around town.

Austin City Limits Music Festival (☎ 512-389-0315; www.aclfestival.com; mid-Sep) Everyone from REM to the Reverend Al Green to the String Cheese Incident turns out at Zilker Park for this festival, named after the acclaimed public television show. Fast becoming the locals' fave alternative to SXSW madness, the festival also features food and art shows. Three-day passes cost $70, but cheaper single-day tickets are available. Waterloo Records also sells tickets.

Old Pecan Street Fall Arts Festival (late Sep) A repeat of E 6th St's May shindig.

OCTOBER

Austin Film Festival (☎ 512-478-4795, 800-310-3378; www.austinfilmfestival.com; mid-Oct) Hollywood and independent filmmakers and screenwriters flock to this multiday event held at various venues. Keep an eye out for weird upstarts, like 2003's *Raiders of the Lost Ark: The Adaptation*, a homage to the Spielberg classic made by a couple of teenagers with video cameras.

Halloween (Oct 31) Downtown's E 6th St is the scene of a huge bash that attracts as many as 60,000 costumed partygoers.

NOVEMBER

El Día de los Muertos (Nov 2) Fanfare surrounding the Day of the Dead may include a parade and special exhibitions at the Mexic-Arte Museum (p63).

Thanksgiving Day (4th Thu of Nov) The annual football game between UT and Texas A&M makes this traditional holiday an even bigger event.

Victorian Christmas on 6th St (☎ 512-441-9015; www.roadstarproductions.com; late Nov or early Dec) Carolers and bell ringers, falconry, clog dancing, banjo music, parades and a wooden carousel – yes, everything and anything typical of Austin weirdness happens, along with an arts-and-crafts show on E 6th St.

DECEMBER

Christmas Lights (after Thanksgiving) All of Austin gets decked out in holiday lighting, with Zilker Park among the most scenic spots.

SLEEPING

Chain motels and hotels dominate accommodations in Austin; only the most noteworthy are included here. Hotel prices tend to be high in and near downtown, though a few bargains can be found. There's no shortage of rooms until major events, such as the Thanksgiving Day football game between UT and Texas A&M and especially during SXSW. At these peak times, prices skyrocket, and rooms are booked up months in advance. At other times, choose accommodations as close to downtown as you can afford. If you're staying at least a week, many outlying motels and all-suite hotels offer discounted rates; some extended-stay options offer a large suite (bedroom with a living area, bathroom and kitchen) starting at $25 per

night. Many hotels and r   deals via their own wel www.orbitz.com and ot discounters.

Downtown

Hotel prices are highest in downtown Austin, though a few bargains can be found near the interstate. Public transport is easy with free 'Dillo shuttle buses (p116). Motels usually provide guest parking for free; hotels charge at least $10 for self-parking and $15 for valet service (which may or may not include in-and-out privileges). Expensive hotels provide in-room Internet access either directly via WebTV or with high-speed connections for laptop users.

MID-RANGE

Extended StayAmerica (Map pp58-9; ☎ 512-457-9994, 800-398-7829; www.exstay.com; 600 Guadalupe St; s/d from $75/80, weekly $350/370; **P**) This extended-stay hotel has an excellent downtown location near the Warehouse District. Rooms are typically bland, but include a kitchenette stocked with utensils. There's a 24-hour coin-op guest laundry and bike racks outside.

   Holiday Inn Town Lake (Map pp58-9; ☎ 512-472-8211, 800-273-0077; www.holiday-inn.com; 20 N IH-35, exit 233; s & d from $75; **P** **🏊**) It's not as classy as some of the other hotels fronting Town Lake, but not as pricey either. Lakeside trails and a children's playground are right out the back door. Guests enjoy complimentary on-site parking and an above-average breakfast. Executive rooms have more amenities for business travelers. German and Spanish are spoken.

   La Quinta Inn Austin Capitol (Map pp58-9; ☎ 512-476-1166, 800-531-5900; www.laquinta.com; 300 E 11th St; s/d from $80/100; **🏊**) Just a block from the state capitol complex, La Quinta is a solid downtown value, with clean, comfortable rooms. The daily continental breakfast features coffee, pastries, yogurt, fresh fruit, juices and milk. The hotel is also pet-friendly. Kids stay free.

   Doubletree Guest Suites Austin (Map pp58-9; ☎ 512-478-7000, 800-222-8733; www.doubletree hotelaustin.com; 303 W 15th St; ste from $95; **🏊**) Just northwest of the capitol and within walking distance of UT, the all-suites Doubletree has accommodations featuring a separate bedroom, sleeper sofa, full kitchen, dining and balcony. Some even have views the Hill Country or the state capitol. There's a pool and fitness center. Small pets are allowed.

Super 8 Motel Austin Central (Map pp58-9; ☎ 512-472-8331, 800-800-8000; www.super8.com; 1201 N IH-35; s/d from $55/60, ste $75; P ☒) Although it can get noisy, Super 8 has reasonable rates. It's just a 15-minute walk or short bus ride (No 6, at the door) from downtown. There's a small outdoor pool, and coffee, juice and doughnuts are served each morning. All rooms have refrigerators and microwaves.

TOP END

Perks at Austin's top-tier hotels include fitness centers and business traveler services. Check hotel websites for special packages and weekend getaway deals, as well as discounts for seniors, executives and others.

Four Seasons Hotel Austin (Map pp58-9; ☎ 512-478-4500, 800-819-5053; www.fourseasons.com/austin; 98 San Jacinto Blvd; d from $200, ste from $350; ☐ ☒) A blend of urban high-rise and lakefront resort, the Four Seasons is Austin's finest hotel, with sublime service and prices to match. Its grand common areas and oversized guest rooms (you'll pay more for views) are all done up in Southwest style, and the swimming pool and grounds are just beautiful. Guests can borrow anything from a bicycle to headphones for jogging to children's games; spa services are available.

Stephen F Austin Intercontinental (Map pp58-9; ☎ 512-457-8800, 866-932-4118; www.austin.intercontinental.com; 701 Congress Ave; d from $160, ste from $200; ☐ ☒) Originally built in 1924, this downtown landmark was extensively renovated after standing empty for many years. Not as historic as the Driskill Hotel, but it's nicely done, with a Lone Star motif in much of the décor. Spring for the slightly more expensive deluxe rooms, which are worth the extra $40. A daily breakfast buffet is complimentary. There's also an indoor pool, whirlpool and sauna, plus fitness facilities. Staffers speak French, German, Spanish and Japanese.

Radisson Hotel & Suites (Map pp58-9; ☎ 512-478-9611, 800-333-3333; www.radisson.com/austintx; 111 E Cesar Chavez St; d from $100, ste from $130; ☐ ☒) The Radisson has a great Town Lake location. A big outdoor pool and fitness center with views make it one of the best-value upscale choices downtown. Suites have high-speed Internet access. The onsite TGI Friday's restaurant is a great place to watch the nightly flight of bats from beneath the Congress Ave bridge.

Hyatt Regency Austin (Map pp66-7; ☎ 512-477-1234, 888-591-1234; www.austin.hyatt.com; 208 Barton Springs Rd; d from $140; ☐ ☒) With nearly 450 rooms on the south shore of Town Lake, the Hyatt is central Austin's largest hotel. There's a neat sunken pool and hot tub area and easy access to lakeside trails, plus a fully equipped fitness center. Rooms with a shoreline view cost slightly more. Business rooms have high-speed Internet access.

Austin Marriott at the Capitol (Map pp58-9; ☎ 512-478-1111, 800-228-9290; www.marriott.com; 701 E 11th St; d from $100; ☐ ☒) This standard Marriott is east of the capitol and fairly close to everything downtown – including the interstate, unfortunately. All rooms have high-speed Internet access. Naturally, rooms with good views cost a bit more. On-site amenities include a restaurant,

---

AUTHOR'S CHOICE

Driskill Hotel (Map pp58-9; ☎ 512-474-5911, 800-252-9367; www.driskillhotel.com; 604 Brazos St; d from $175, ste from $400; ☐) Built by cattle baron Colonel Driskill in 1886, this national trust historic hotel exudes old-style Texas elegance. The Driskill is where LBJ and Lady Bird had their first date and where they later watched 1964 presidential returns. The public areas are fabulously hospitable (with milk and cookies or peanut-butter-and-jelly sandwiches served nightly in the lobby), and the corridors are stuffed with books and art. A recent multimillion-dollar restoration has resulted in guest rooms that are charmingly Romanesque, some with window seats, all with original artwork and striking bathrooms. Modern conveniences include high-speed Internet access, WebTV and European-style bath amenities. You can't go wrong splurging here, especially on the four-room Cattle Baron's Suite or the Governor's Suite apartment once exclusively reserved for LBJ. The top-rated **Driskill Bar & Grill** (p89) downstairs is icing on the cake.

lounge, indoor/outdoor pools and fitness and business centers. Small pets are allowed.

Omni Austin Hotel Downtown (Map pp58-9; ☎ 512-476-3700, 800-843-6664; www.omnihotels.com; 700 San Jacinto Blvd; d from $120, ste from $190; 🖳 💺) The Omni's soaring, open-air glass lobby sets the stage for an upscale experience. Posh but somewhat pedestrian rooms have all the amenities; special 'Get Fit' rooms are furnished with treadmills and healthy snacks. The 20th-floor rooftop boasts a lap pool, hot tub and plenty of *chaise longues* for baking in the Texas sun.

West End & Clarksville

Brava House (Map p91; ☎ 512-478-5034, 888-545-8200; www.bravahouse.com; 1108 Blanco St; d from $90, ste from $130; 🅿) One of the only nonhotel options in the city center, this boutique bed-and-breakfast has lovely rooms and suites, with a canopy bed in the Moroccan-style Casablanca Room, a clawfoot bathtub in the Garbo Suite and a parlor stove in the art deco Fitzgerald Suite. Each room has its own private bath, telephone, cable TV and Wi-Fi Internet access. In keeping with a motto of 'urban serenity,' the innkeepers provide aromatherapy oils and bath salts. There's a breakfast buffet, gardens and two-night minimum stay on most weekends. Business travelers are welcome.

South Austin

If want to see the kind of weirdness that makes Austin unique, base yourself here. South Austin's proximity to Zilker Park and Town Lake is another draw. Some of these accommodations are within walking distance of free 'Dillo shuttle bus routes. Off-street parking for guests may be limited, so ask ahead of time.

BUDGET

Pecan Grove RV Park (Map pp66-7; ☎ 512-472-1067, fax 512-472-2946; 1518 Barton Springs Rd; RV sites with full hookups $20; 🅿 🖳) Pecan Grove has very pleasant RV sites available right near Zilker Park and just steps away from Shady Grove Restaurant. The RV park also offers showers, laundry and Internet access.

Hostelling International Austin (Map pp56-7; ☎ 512-444-2294, 800-725-2331; www.hiaustin.org; 2200 S Lakeshore Blvd; dm members/nonmembers $16.50/19.50,

additional child 6-12 $8.25; ☑ office 8-11am & 5-10pm daily; 🅿 🖳) Austin's only official hostel is off the beaten path from downtown, but it's smack dab on Town Lake. The hostel rents canoes, kayaks and bicycles ($10 per day). Other amenities include a well-equipped communal kitchen, lockers, laundry, bike storage, Internet kiosk and TV room. There's live music many nights, and plenty of spontaneous jamming, too. Bedding is provided. There's no curfew, but everyone's expected to be out of the dormitory area between 11am and 5pm. No alcohol is allowed, and smoking is permitted outside only.

The hostel is about a 35-minute walk or 10-minute bus ride from downtown. From the Greyhound bus station, take bus No 7-Duval south. From the Amtrak train station, walk a block north to 5th St and take bus No 22 east to Congress Ave; cross the street and change to southbound bus No 26 or No 27. From the airport, take bus No 350 to Austin Community College, where you transfer to bus No 26. In all cases, get off at the intersection of Burton and Riverside Drs, then walk two blocks north on Tinnin Ford Rd.

MID-RANGE & TOP END

Austin Motel (Map pp66-7; ☎ 512-441-1157; www.austinmotel.com; 1220 S Congress Ave; s/d from $55/80, ste $125-135; 🅿 💺) For more than 65 years, the family-run Austin Motel has been a favorite among musicians, artists and other individualists. There's a wide range of rooms, some with wall murals, and a few boast '50s-style carports. Some of the rooms could be in better repair, but with funky decor and a small pool, this remains a fun and offbeat place to stay on lively SoCo.

The Miller-Crockett House Bed & Breakfast (Map pp66-7; ☎ 512-441-1600, 888-441-1641; www .millercrockett.com; 112 Academy Drive; d $120-160; 🅿) This New Orleans Victorian-style house (circa 1888) has become a favorite among music and film-industry folks. The huge grounds feature a 300-year-old live oak tree, a hammock for lazing about and a deck with views of downtown Austin. Out back are two private bungalows with kitchens and sitting rooms, perfect for honeymooners or small families. All accommodations have cable TV, VCR and high-speed Internet access. Rates include a weekday continental breakfast or on weekends, gourmet brunch.

Homestead Suites (Map pp66-7; ☎ 512-476-1818, 888-782-9473; www.homesteadhotels.com; 507 S 1st St; s/d from $70/75, weekly $315/350; P) This extended-stay hotel chain is ideally fixed between SoCo and Zilker Park, and only a short walk from Threadgill's World Headquarters (p93). Each room has its own full kitchen, bathroom and spacious living area. Guest parking is free; high-speed Internet access is available for laptop users. Check the website for online discounts.

Lazy Oak Bed and Breakfast (Map pp66-7; ☎ 512-447-8873, 877-947-8873; www.lazyoakbandb.com; 211 W Live Oak St; d $85-125; P) Relax at this early 1900s plantation-style house while soaking in the outdoor hot tub or reading the *New York Times* on the porch. Home-baked goodies magically appear on the breakfast table and other sweets are available throughout the day. Rooms have phones, TVs and upon request, VCRs.

UT Area & Hyde Park

Although the university area doesn't have as much to recommend itself to travelers as South Austin, there are some goods rates on offer. It's also conveniently reached via CapMetro's free 'Dillo buses and other UT shuttles. Free on-street parking is usually available in the residential areas west of Guadalupe St.

BUDGET

The Goodall Wooten (Map pp68-9; ☎ 512-472-1343; www.goodallwooten.com; 2112 Guadalupe St; s & d $30-40, stay 6 nights, get seventh free) A private dorm near the University of Texas, 'the Woo' generally has rooms available mid-May to mid-August, and sometimes has space

for travelers at other times of the year. Each room has a small refrigerator and private bathroom, cable TV and Internet access. Common-area amenities include a community kitchen and computer lab.

If the Woo is full, try other student housing organized through **College Houses Cooperatives** (www.collegehouses.org). They include **Taos Hall** (Map pp68-9; ☎ 512-474-6905; 2612 Guadalupe St), **Pearl St Co-Op** (Map pp68-9; ☎ 512-476-5678; 2000 Pearl St) and the **21st St Co-op** (Map pp68-9; ☎ 512-476-5678; 707 W 21st St). Doubles cost $10 to $20 per night and include three meals a day (vegetarian options available). These co-op dormitories may only have room for visitors during summer.

MID-RANGE

Adams House (Map pp68-9; www.theadamshouse .com; 4300 Avenue G; d $80-90, ste $125; P) On a quiet corner in historic Hyde Park, this B&B has many restored early-20th-century architectural features. All of the rooms are furnished with antiques, and the William T Adams Suite has a separate sun porch with a sleeper sofa. Continental breakfast is served on weekdays, and weekend guests enjoy a full hot gourmet breakfast.

Austin Folk House (Map pp68-9; ☎ 512-472-6700, 866-472-6700; www.austinfolkhouse.com; 506 W 22nd; d $95-145; P ⌨) A charming blue-and-white house near the Drag, this B&B's cheerful interiors include Southern folk art on the walls. Each room has its own cable TV/VCR and private bathroom stocked with bubble bath and robes. The honeymooner's choice, Room Seven, has a canopied bed, while Room One has its own private entrance. The innkeeper's breakfast buffet is impressive: expect the likes of

---

AUTHOR'S CHOICE

Hotel San Jose (Map pp66-7; ☎ 512-444-7322, 800-574-8897; www.sanjosehotel.com; 1316 S Congress Ave; rooms with shared bath from $75, d from $120, ste $170-250; P ⌨) A major renovation has transformed this once-marginal motel into a sleek spot with award-winning interior design (possibly too Zen minimalist for some tastes) and ultra-hip amenities, including complimentary DSL and Wi-Fi Internet access. Rooms have CD and DVD players, and the front desk has tons of great discs to lend (free) and movies to rent ($2). A boxed breakfast is delivered right to your door, after which you can splash about in the courtyard swimming pool, or get inspired after borrowing a manual Remington typewriter or Polaroid camera from reception. Tranquil common areas are planted with native Texas vegetation and connected by crushed granite pathways. A cocktail lounge under the stars strikes the right mood for twilight drinks. Hungry? **Jo's** (p92) is right next door.

raspberry pancakes, green chile casserole or banana enchiladas. Ask about special midweek rates.

Governor's Inn B&B (Map pp68-9; ☎ 512-477-0711, 800-871-8908; governorsinn@earthlink.net; 611 W 22nd St; d $90-130; (P)) This buttercup-colored neoclassical Victorian inn dates from the turn of the 20th century. Wraparound porches have rockers and swings; there are antique clawfoot bathtubs inside many rooms. The atmosphere is decidedly romantic, but with modem conveniences like cable TV, private phones and an Internet-ready office. Blue Bell ice cream is complimentary anytime you fancy.

Austin's Wildflower Inn (Map pp68-9; ☎ 512-477-9639; www.austinswildflowerinn.com; 1200 W 22nd St; d from $80, ste from $110; (P)) This low-key inn resides in a colonial two-story house surrounded by well-kept gardens. Each of the three rooms has a private bath, telephone and antique furnishings; the Texas Country Suite, which can accommodate three people, has a sleeper sofa and private entrance. Breakfast is often served in the backyard garden.

Brook House (Map pp68-9; ☎ 512-459-0534, 800-871-8908; brookhouse@earthlink.net; 609 W 33rd St; d $90-130; (P)) A stately old place dating from 1922, this B&B has six charming rooms, each with private bath, cable TV and phone with voice messaging. Delia's Cottage in the back has its own kitchenette and can sleep up to four people. Special touches include ice cream or cookies in the evening. A buffet breakfast is served on the veranda in nice weather.

Carrington's Bluff B&B (Map pp68-9; ☎ 479-0638, 888-290-6090; www.carringtonsbluff.com; 1900 David St; d $80-160; (P)) Near the Shoal Creek Greenbelt, this shady property was an original Republic of Texas homestead. The house itself dates from 1877, and a 500-year-old oak tree presides over the porch. Each flowery room has a telephone and cable TV; out back, the two-bedroom carriage house also has a full kitchen. A VCR and video library are available to guests.

Days Inn Austin University (Map pp68-9; ☎ 512-478-1631, 800-329-7466; www.daysinn.com; 3105 N IH-35; s & d from $55; (P)(🛁)) Be sure to ask for a room toward the back of this motel, since the freeway traffic noise can be bad up front. Amenities include a fridge and microwave in each room, a tiny pool and free parking.

Next door is Star Seeds (p97), an all-night diner.

Rodeway Inn University/Downtown (Map pp68-9; ☎ 512-477-6395, 877-424-6423; www.rodewayinn.com; 2900 N IH-35; s & d from $60; (P)(🛁)(🛁)) In the shadow of I-35, this multilevel motel has better soundproofing than the Days Inn nearby. There's a microwave, fridge and high-speed Internet access in each room, a small outdoor pool and free parking. Furnishings are a bit worn, but the continental breakfast is complimentary. Kids stay free.

TOP END

Woodburn House (Map pp68-9; ☎ 512-458-4335, 888-690-9763; www.woodburnhouse.com; 4401 Avenue D; d $100-110, ste $140; (P)) This gracious Hyde Park hostelry is well removed from the bustle of the Drag. The house itself is nearly a century old, and its unique mix of architectural styles places it on the National Register of Historic Places. Each of the four rooms and also the two-bedroom suite are furnished with antiques, but no TV. Spanish is spoken.

Mansion at Judge's Hill (Map pp68-9; ☎ 512-495-1800, 800-311-1619; www.mansionatjudgeshill.com; 1900 Rio Grande St; d $130-300; (P)) This brand-new boutique hotel epitomizes luxury. The staff's attitude can be snooty, but the property itself is lovely, with shady grounds that invite dreaming, strolling and, of course, wedding parties. Inside, the authentic turn-of-the-20th-century mansion exhibits vibrant textures and rich colors, appearing both timeless and modern. Each room has all the amenities, including CD and DVD players, high-speed Internet access and plush bathrobes. The hotel's ambitious American-French restaurant (closed Monday) is also worthy of attention.

Greater Austin
BUDGET
Super 8 Motel Highland Mall (Map pp56-7; ☎ 512-467-8163, 800-800-8000; www.super8.com; 6000 Middle Fiskville Rd; s/d from $40/45; (P)) A short walk from the bus station and near plenty of shopping, rooms here have small balconies or patios and access to the pool and fitness room at the Hilton next door. There's also guest laundry, free parking for oversized vehicles and complimentary continental breakfast. Children under 12 stay free.

Studio 6 Extended Stay (Map pp56-7; ☎ 512-458-5453, 888-897-0202; www.motel6.com; 6603 N IH-35; s/d from $40/45, weekly $200/225; **P**) Motel 6's extended-stay business branch has several south-central Texas locations, including this one just northeast of the I-35/Hwy 290 junction. Rooms may not be as spacious as those at other extended-stay hotels, but each has a dining nook, full kitchen and atdoor parking. Kids stay free.

Motel 6 Austin South-Airport (Map pp56-7; ☎ 512-444-5882, 800-466-8356; www.motel6.com; 2707 S IH-35, at Oltorf St; s/d from $45/50; **P** 🐾) Motel 6 has four outposts in the Austin area, plus two Studio 6 extended-stay locations. This motel near the airport and convenient to South Austin has basic comforts, including an outdoor pool and free morning coffee. Kids stay free. Small pets are welcome.

There are a few **campgrounds** on the outskirts of Austin, and also around the Highland Lakes.

McKinney Falls State Park (Map pp56-7; ☎ 512-243-1643, reservations 512-389-8900, fax 512-243-0536; www.tpwd.state.tx.us; 5808 McKinney Falls Pkwy; primitive 4-person campsite $10, 8-person campsite with hookup $14, plus per person entrance fee $2; 🕑 gates open 7am-10pm daily; **P**) So close to the city, and yet so far away in spirit, this is a fantastic bet for camping. Just south of the airport, McKinney Falls State Park has primitive walk-in tent sites that are set a couple of hundred yards apart from the rest of the camping areas. Take US 183 south about 1-1/2 miles past Hwy 71, then look for the turn-off to the park on your right and drive 3 miles to the park entrance.

Emma Long Metropolitan Park (Map pp56-7; ☎ 512-346-1831; 1600 City Park Rd; tent/RV site with hookup $6/15, plus per car entrance fee Mon-Thu/Fri-Sun $5/8; 🕑 gates open 7am-10pm daily; **P** 🐾) The only Austin city park with overnight camping, 1000-acre Emma Long Metropolitan Park (aka 'City Park') on Lake Austin has good swimming, sunbathing, fishing and boating. Get there early as it fills up quickly (no reservations). It's 16 miles northwest of downtown. Take MoPac north to RR 2222, then drive west for 4 miles. Past the intersection with Loop 360 (Capital of Texas Hwy), take a left at the first light, which is City Park Rd, and follow this (it's winding, but just keep going) until it dead-ends at the park after 5 miles.

Royal Palms (Map pp56-7; ☎ 512-385-2211; www.royalpalms.net; 7901 E Ben White Blvd; RV site with hookup $32, weekly/monthly $170/325; 🕑 office 9am-6pm Mon-Fri, 8am-noon Sat; **P** 💻 🐾) An RV-only park, Royal Palms is less than a mile from Austin's airport. Guests enjoy coin laundry, Wi-Fi Internet access, cable TV hookups and limited showers. There's a swimming pool, barbecue grills, picnic tables, a clubhouse with a TV lounge and library, and tennis and volleyball courts. Self-registration after office hours is subject to space availability.

MID-RANGE & TOP END
There are many chain motels near the I-35/US 290 junction, northeast of downtown and close to Austin's former airport. We've listed a few, but keep in mind most of these places are quite far from downtown. Still, if you've got your own transport, the best deals may be found here. A few more places are nearby Austin-Bergstrom International Airport, southeast of downtown.

Bed & Breakfast, Pool & Spa (Map pp56-7; ☎ 512-499-0081; www.bnbspa.com; 1309 Meridien Lane; d Mon-Thu/Fri-Sun $125/175, ste $150/200; **P** 💻 🐾) This luxury garden B&B may be a bit out of the way, but it's all about indulgence. Take your pick of rooms and suites, some with breakfast nooks, cathedral ceilings, an antique bed or leather couch, fireplaces, skylights and an entertainment center. Relax in a massage chair while you wait your turn for the indoor pool and sauna. A continental breakfast is served and high-speed Internet access is available. To get here from central Austin, take 15th St west onto Enfield Rd, then turn left a few blocks west of MoPac onto Meridien Lane. A free UT shuttle bus stops nearby.

Habitat Suites (Map pp56-7; ☎ 512-467-6000, 800-535-4663; www.habitatsuites.com; 500 E Highland Mall Blvd; d Fri-Sat/Sun-Thu from $80/140; **P** 🐾) This eco-conscious, low-rise hotel is a convivial place, and the complimentary breakfast buffet (featuring macrobiotic selections) and happy hour are lively. Spacious suites have full kitchens and there's an outdoor courtyard pool. Guests enjoy discounted entry to a nearby health club. Most of the clientele are business travelers or families.

StudioPLUS (Map pp56-7; ☎ 512-452-0880, 888-788-3467; www.exstay.com; 6300 E US 290; s/d $55/60, weekly $270/290; **P**) Extended Stay America's deluxe studio lodgings near Austin's airport are more spacious than the norm, each with a full kitchen, a sleeper sofa and living area.

La Quinta Inn & Suites – Austin Airport (Map pp56-7; ☎ 512-386-6800, 800-531-5900; www .laquinta.com; 7625 E Ben White Blvd; s & d from $65, ste from $120; (P) (≊)) Another chain near the airport, La Quinta has a green courtyard, fitness room, laundry and heated outdoor pool. Ask about their airport shuttle. Rates include a complimentary breakfast of coffee, pastries, yogurt, milk, juices and fresh fruit. Small pets are allowed.

Also recommended are:

Econo Lodge (Map pp56-7; ☎ 512-458-4759, 877-424-6423; www.econolodge.com; 6201 E US 290; s &d from $60; (P) (≊))

Quality Inn Central (Map pp56-7; ☎ 512-452-4200, 877-424-6423; www.qualityinn.com; 909 E Koenig Lane; s & d from $65; (P) (≊))

Lake Austin Spa Resort (☎ 512-372-7300, 800-847-5637; www.lakeaustin.com; 1705 S Quinlan Park Rd, near Bee Cave; all-inclusive packages from $450 per night; (P) (≊))

EATING

Barbecue and Tex-Mex are the mainstays, but Austin also has many fine-dining restaurants and a broadening array of world cuisines; for a proper introduction to Texas cuisine, turn to the Food & Drink chapter (p45). For hot tips on new restaurants, pick up the free alternative weekly *Austin Chronicle* or *Xlent*, both published on Thursday. Foodies should pick up the latest issue of *Austin Monthly* magazine, which has a directory of restaurant reviews at the back and often interviews the city's up-and-coming chefs.

Downtown eateries are a real mixed bag, serving tourists, business folks, politicians, artists and night-owl clubbers. Over the bridge in individualist South Austin, there are some long-running favorites that justify any trip. Other neighborhoods, such as West End and Hyde Park, also boast a few eclectic and gourmet restaurants. Around the UT campus area, prices drop – but often so does food quality. Although the Drag is all about students filling their belly for less, some decent international and Tex-Mex food can be found. Soul food and authentic Mexican joints will justify the detour to East Austin, while various restaurants in all categories make a drive to the outskirts of the city worthwhile.

DETOUR: LOCKHART

The reason to come to this little town, about a 40-minute drive south of Austin on US 183, is to indulge – we don't mean to eat, we mean to stuff yourself silly. In 1999, the Texas Legislature adopted a resolution naming Lockhart the barbecue capital of Texas. Of course, that means it's the barbecue capital of the *world*.

You can eat very well for under $10 at:

Black's Barbecue (☎ 512-398-2712; 208 N Main St; ☺ 10am-8pm Sun-Thu, 10am-8:30pm Fri-Sat) A longtime Lockhart favorite (since 1932), with sausage so good Lyndon Johnson had the establishment cater a party at the nation's capital. There's a great selection of side salads, veggies and desserts. A family pack includes your choice of a pound of meat, five sausages or a chicken-and-a-half plus sides ($14).

Kreuz Market (☎ 512-398-2361; 619 N Colorado St; ☺ 9am-6pm Mon-Fri, 9am-6:30pm Sun) They pack 'em in at Kreuz (pronounced 'Krites') Market, a Lockhart institution since 1900. Line up by the open pits to buy your choice of succulent beef shoulder, ribs, sausage, brisket or pork chops, all priced by the pound (but order as little as you like) and wrapped in butcher paper. Don't ask for sauce; they don't serve it, and the meat is so tender, moist and flavorful it doesn't need it.

Chisholm Trail Bar-B-Q (☎ 512-398-6027; 1323 S Colorado St; ☺ 11am-8:30pm Mon-Sat) Like Black's and Kreuz, Chisholm Trail has been named one of the top 10 barbecue restaurants in the state by *Texas Monthly* magazine. It serves up a good selection of ribs, brisket, chicken and sausage and (on Monday, Wednesday and Friday) fried catfish.

Smitty's Market (☎ 512-398-9344; 208 S Commerce St; ☺ 7am-6pm Mon-Fri, 7am-6:30pm Sat, 9am-3pm Sun) In the former Kreuz Market location, Smitty's is owned by a branch of the same family (the Schmidts) who run Kreuz.

AUSTIN

Downtown

Most restaurants are found by the state capitol complex, the city's convention center and nightlife areas around the upscale Warehouse District and 6th St.

A **farmer's market** (Map pp58-9; ☎ 512-236-0074; 422 Guadalupe St; ⊗ 8am-noon Sat May-Nov) sets up shop at Republic Park, with local farm produce, chef demonstrations, live music and fun for kids.

BUDGET

Las Manitas Avenue Cafe (Map pp58-9; ☎ 512-472-9357; 211 Congress Ave; meals $4-8; ⊗ 7am-4pm Mon-Fri, 7am-2pm Sat-Sun) This is Austin at its best: unpretentious, multiracial and politically astute. The food is good, too. For breakfast, have the *migas especiales con hongos* (tortilla strips, mushrooms and garlic scrambled with eggs, topped with cheese and ranchero sauce), perhaps with a glass of fresh hibiscus teas. Look for folk art on the walls, and enjoy the back patio.

Hut's Hamburgers (Map pp58-9; ☎ 512-472-0693; 807 W 6th St; burgers $4-7; ⊗ 11am-10pm Mon-Sat, 11:30am-10pm Sun) A sports bar inside a converted 1930s drive-in, Hut's burgers (in beef, chicken, buffalo and veggie varieties) are justifiably famous, especially served with a dollop of hickory sauce or melted blue cheese. As for the daily blue plate specials, be forewarned the catfish quickly sells out quickly on Friday.

Texas Chili Parlor (Map pp58-9; ☎ 512-472-2828; 1409 Lavaca St; meals $5-11; ⊗ 11am-2am) A typical Tex-Mex menu becomes exceptional when it features firebrand red bean chili (order it X 'mild', XX 'spicy' or XXX 'hot, hot, hot!'), habanero-pinto bean chili and frito chili pie. It all tastes the way your grandfather would've made it, if he'd been lucky enough to be born in the Hill Country.

Arturo's Cafe (Map pp58-9; ☎ 512-469-0380; 314 W 17th St; meals around $5; ⊗ 7am-2:30pm Mon-Fri) By the Guadalupe Arts Center, this basement-level café wins awards for its bewildering variety of Southwest-style quesadillas, stuffed with anything from chipotle-sauced chicken to a garden's worth of vegetables. Organic juices, espresso and home-baked desserts are great for refueling.

Old Bakery & Emporium (Map pp58-9; ☎ 512-477-5961; 1006 Congress Ave; snacks & sandwiches $2-6; ⊗ 9am-4pm Mon-Fri, confectionery 11am-1:30pm) In a historic building that housed a Swedish bakery until the 1930s, this downtown institution serves sandwiches, cookies and coffee in its confectionery. A hospitality information desk at the front is staffed by senior citizen volunteers.

MID-RANGE

Stubb's Bar-B-Q (Map pp58-9; ☎ 512-480-8341; 801 Red River St; mains $8-12, Sun gospel brunch $15; ⊗ 11am-10pm Tues-Thu, 11am-11pm Fri-Sat, 11am-9pm Sun) Good ol' Stubb's is more apt to draw people for its live music shows (p101), but it's got decent food, too. Request (or reserve) a table downstairs near the stage for the Sunday gospel brunch, which features an all-you-can-eat Southern-style buffet and a Bloody Mary bar.

Iron Works BBQ (Map pp58-9; ☎ 512-478-4855; 100 Red River St; meals $6-12; ⊗ 11am-9pm Mon-Sat) On Waller Creek by the convention center, the Iron Works draws a downtown business crowd with smoked pork loin, huge beef ribs and an all-you-can-eat salad bar. It's inside an old ironsmith's shop, and there's even a pot-bellied stove in the cozy dining room.

Noodle-ism (Map pp58-9; ☎ 512-275-9988; 107 W 5th St; meals $7-10; ⊗ 11am-10pm Mon-Thu, 11am-11pm Fri, noon-11pm Sat, noon-9pm Sun) A respite from the Warehouse District, this pan-Asian noodle shop achieves an urban Zen atmosphere with its clean and modern interior design. The cooking is worthy of any Bangkok market stall or back-alley Tokyo noodle shop, and the iced green tea flows endlessly.

Hoffbrau (Map pp58-9; ☎ 512-472-0822; 613 W 6th St; mains $10-18; ⊗ lunch 11am-2pm Mon-Fri, dinner 5-9pm Mon-Sat) A venerable old steakhouse that has little fanfare and even fewer frills (air-conditioning is the exception), the Hoffbrau has been going strong for decades. Here, servers heft platters of butter-grilled chicken, steaks and glorious desserts.

Katz's Deli & Bar (Map pp58-9; ☎ 512-472-2037; 618 W 6th St; mains $6-12; ⊗ 24 hrs) Katz's is a NYC-style eatery that's part bar, part deli. The high-priced menu can claim some authenticity, even if it's a bit lackluster; try the egg-white omelettes with Nova Scotia salmon, corned beef hash or a kosher-style hot dog with sauerkraut. It's a good place to nosh after music at MoMo's (p102).

Marakesh Café & Grill (Map pp58-9; ☎ 512-476-7735; 906 Congress Ave; meals $7-11; ⊗ 11am-10pm

Mon-Fri, noon-10pm Sat) Marakesh is an oasis of greenery, with murals on the walls, lazily whirling fans and hardwood floors. It serves delicious and cheap Mediterranean food, including daily specials like Moroccan chicken or vegetable tajin in a tomato curry-coriander sauce. Wines are sold by the glass, and there's honey-sweet baklava for dessert.

Mekong River (Map pp58-9; ☎ 512-236-8878; 215 E 6th St; mains $7-10; ☒ 10:30am-10pm daily, till11pm Fri-Sat) On the main drag of 6th St, slim pickin's are the norm for hungry club-hoppers. But not at this spacious Vietnamese/Thai restaurant, where the kitchen staff prepares respectable (and occasionally inventive) bowls of noodles, curries, soups and more.

TOP END

Reservations are advisable for these restaurants, except for those in the Warehouse District that are also bars.

Eddie V's Edgewater Grille (Map pp58-9; ☎ 512-472-1860; 301 E 5th St; mains $20-45; ☒ 5-11pm Mon-Sat, 5-10pm Sun) Deep Southern influence, live jazz after 7pm nightly and a menu of oceanic cuisine that rivals a small dictionary – it's no wonder this is rated Austin's top seafood restaurant. Chefs turn out Gulf Coast cooking and oysters cost just 35¢ during happy hour. Steaks and sumptuous desserts are also above par.

Gumbo's (Map pp58-9; ☎ 512-480-8053; 710 Colorado St; mains $15-30; ☒ lunch 11am-2pm Mon-Fri, dinner 5:30-10pm Mon-Thu, 5:30-11pm Fri-Sat) Louisiana is in fact a neighbor of the Lone Star state, and Cajun cooking comes alive here with the likes of shrimp and crawfish etoufée, homemade custards and even steaks. Have

an after-dinner drink at Brown Bar (p104), also found in the historic Brown Building.

Malaga Tapas (Map pp58-9; ☎ 512-236-8020; 208 W 4th St; small plates $5-12; ☒ dinner from 5pm Mon-Sat) This is so close to the Cedar Street Courtyard (p102) that you can hear the live jazz. Yet inside it's a traditional cut of Spain, from the dark wooden bar to a classic tapas menu that changes every few months. Over 50 wines are sold by the glass.

Saba Blue Water Café (Map pp58-9; ☎ 512-478-7222; 208 W 4th St; small plates $6-10, mains $10-20; ☒ dinner from 4pm Mon-Fri & 5pm Sat) A soothing place to go for happy hour in the Warehouse District, this ocean-themed café serves up Pacific Rim and Caribbean tapas and also specialty drinks. Menu offerings include cilantro pork and shrimp potstickers, Creole spiced calamari and seafood ceviche in jicama and watermelon juices.

Jean-Luc's Bistro (Map pp58-9; ☎ 512-494-0033; 705 Colorado St; lunch $8-12, dinner mains $15-40; ☒ lunch 11:30am-2:30pm Mon-Fri, dinner from 5:30pm Mon-Sat) A French bistro with a twist: here the young chef-owner utilizes farm fresh produce and other locally grown ingredients in a style that's almost Californian. The wine list and pastry chef's creations are equally impressive. Make reservations far in advance.

Driskill Bar & Grill (Map pp58-9; ☎ 512-391-7162; 604 Brazos St; breakfast $6-12, lunch $10-18, dinner mains $18-38; ☒ 6.30am-10:30pm daily) The Driskill Hotel (p82) is a superb place to dine any time of day. Here, top chefs marry 21st-century culinary trends with classic American fare. At breakfast, the gingersnap blueberry pancakes are scrumptious. Dinner

---

MORNING MEALS

Start off with a sugar rush at **Crescent City Beignets** (p91) any day of the week. Vegetarian-friendly **Mother's Cafe & Garden** (p95) serves breakfast on weekdays and brunch until 3pm Saturday and Sunday. Buttermilk-blueberry pancakes, Thai-style crab cakes and cocktails are on the Sunday brunch menu at **Starlite** (p96).

Also on Sunday, there's live gospel music at **Stubb's** (p88; brunch buffet $15; ☒ seatings 11am & 1pm) and also at **Threadgill's World Headquarters** (p96; brunch buffet $10; ☒ brunch 10am-1pm Sun, music from 11am). Reservations are advised at Stubb's.

Farther afield **Chez Zee** (p99; meals $10-16; ☒ brunch 9am-3pm Sat & Sun) delights weekend diners with its savory Southwest crab cakes benedict and famous bakery desserts. **Fonda San Miguel** (p99; buffet from $30; ☒ brunch 11am-2pm Sun) is another top choice.

selections feature steaks, fish and wild game dishes. It's expensive, but worth it.

Thistle on Sixth (Map pp58-9; ☎ 512-275-9777; 300 W 6th St; breakfast $5, lunch $8-13, dinner mains $18-26; ☺ 7am-10pm Mon-Thu, 7am-11pm Fri, 5-11pm Sat) Thistle has a gorgeous interior design, from its soaring ceilings down to the soft white glow that permeates the hyper-modern bar, with its plasma TVs and Wi-Fi access. Downtown suits, artists and foodies crowd around the counter for lunch, but dinner is more inventive, offering confetti crab cakes, lollipop lamb chops and white chocolate cherry bread pudding.

Bitter End (Map pp58-9; ☎ 512-478-2337; 311 Colorado St; mains $12-20; ☺ kitchen open 11:30am-10: 30pm Mon-Thu, 11:30am-11pm Fri, 5-11pm Sat, 5-10pm Sun) It's a laid-back brewpub with a bistro. In fact, some people come here more for the upmarket translations of traditional bar fare than the beer. Try the brick oven-fired pizzas, spinach salads and artfully grilled tuna. Or duck across the street to its sister establishment, **Mezzaluna** (Map pp58-9; ☎ 512-472-6770; 310 Colorado St), for similarly priced contemporary Italian cuisine.

Mars Restaurant & Bar (Map pp58-9; ☎ 512-472-3901; 1610 San Antonio St; mains $10-25; ☺ dinner from 5:30pm) Housed inside what was once Austin's first head shop, here the deep red hues, golden stars and eclectic cuisine influenced by the Pacific Rim and Southeast Asia are like a siren's call. Creative dishes may not always hit the mark, but service is finely tuned and vegetarians have oodles of choices. There's an out-of-this-world wine list and Texas microbrews are on hand.

Chez Nous (Map pp58-9; ☎ 512-473-2413; 510 Neches St; lunch $8-15, three-course dinner $22; ☺ lunch 11:45am-2pm Tues-Fri, dinner 6-10: 30pm Tues-Sun) This classic Parisian-style bistro's three-course *prix fixe* dinner will leave you celebrating. Close to the 6th St scene, sophisticated Chez Nous is made cozy by fresh flowers on the table and its homemade desserts. Fittingly, there's a great wine and aperitifs list.

Shoreline Grill (Map pp58-9; ☎ 512-477-3300; 98 San Jacinto Blvd; lunch $10-15, dinner mains $18-30; ☺ 11am-10pm Mon-Sat, 11am-9pm Sun) Overlooking Town Lake next to the Four Seasons hotel, the Shoreline Grill has outdoor balcony tables with views of the Congress Ave bat bridge. The house specialty is seafood, anything from sea scallops over polenta to crab cakes with chipotle-mango sauce – all satisfying, with imaginative Southwestern twists.

Louie's 106 (Map pp58-9; ☎ 512-476-1997; 106 E 6th St; lunch $8.50-13, dinner mains $15-23; ☺ lunch 11:15am-5pm Mon-Fri, dinner from 5pm nightly) A longstanding Austin favorite, Louie's turns out fine Spanish, Provençal and Italian food. Look for the *paella valencia*, Mediterranean grilled meats and a wide array of Spanish tapas. The atmosphere is Old World, with a cigar lounge, hundreds of wine labels in the cellar and valet parking.

West End & Clarksville

Starting from the intersection of 6th St and Lamar Blvd, there are a few good hunting grounds lying west and north, including around the intersection of West Lynn and 12th Sts.

SWEET ENDINGS

Around the corner from Waterloo Records, **Amy's Ice Creams** (Map p91; ☎ 512-480-0673; 1012 W 6th St; scoops from $2; ☺ 11:30am-midnight daily, till 1am Fri-Sat) is an Austin classic. With spades a-flyin', Amy's staff members bash and flatten huge portions of solidly frozen, delicious, full-fat ice cream, then mush in 'crush-ins' before grinding it all into cups, cones and bowls. Excellent Mexican vanilla, key-lime cheesecake, Belgian and dark chocolate flavors just scratch the surface at half a dozen locations.

Hyde Park's **La Dolce Vita** (Map pp58-9; ☎ 512-323-2686; 4220 Duval St; desserts $3-5; ☺ 9am-midnight) is aptly named. This little Italian bar and café not only makes tarts, tortes, profiteroles and cheesecakes, but also mixes up Austin's best gelato in a rainbow of flavors, from chocolate sprinkle to mango-kiwi. The espresso is Sicilian in its strength, and there's a full bar of wines, liqueurs and mixed drinks.

If your sweet tooth craves more, stop by the **Chez Zee** bakery (p99) or the heavenly dessert case at **Mozart's Coffee Roaster's** (p98).

BUDGET

Portabla (Map p91; ☎ 512-481-8646; 1200 W 6th St; mains $5-8.50, daily special $6; ⊙ 10am-8pm Mon-Sat) Italian meatloaf with succulent tomato sauce, Moroccan chicken or deli salads, all made by an esteemed caterer, are sold here. Enjoy the wholesome goodness (including top-drawer desserts) at chic outdoor tables, or swing by for easy take-out meals.

Austin Java Company (Map p91; ☎ 512-476-1829; 1206 Parkway; burgers & meals $5-8; ⊙ 7am-midnight Mon-Fri, 8am-midnight Sat, 8am-11pm Sun) On a side street near Pease Park, this uniquely Austin coffeehouse has a tantalizing menu – offering everything from crawfish quesadillas to Thai sesame noodle salads – that takes far too long to read. Happily, the lemon pucker cookies are instantly available.

Crescent City Beignets (Map p91; ☎ 512-472-9622; 1211 W 6th St; beignets $2, meals $6; ⊙ 7am-10pm daily) Fresh, made-to-order beignets with a 'dusting' (which is the world's biggest understatement) of powdered sugar and cups of steaming café au lait let patrons imagine for themselves a misty

New Orleans morning. Substantial daily specials include jambalaya and chicken-sausage gumbo.

Whole Foods Market (Map p91; ☎ 512-476-1206; 601 N Lamar Ave; ⊙ 8am-10pm daily) An Austin original that now has more than 140 stores nationwide, Whole Foods Market focuses on fresh, healthy, natural and organic groceries. There's a great selection of take-out, maybe the best in the city, with delicious wraps, burgers, sandwiches and salads to go. Whole Foods also stocks quirky body care products, fine wine and beer.

Cipollina (Map p91; ☎ 512-477-5211; 1213 W Lynn St; $2-12; ⊙ 7am-9pm Mon-Thu, till 9:30pm Fri-Sat, till 8pm Sun, happy hour 3:30-5:30pm Mon-Sat) Run by the same folks as Jeffrey's (p92), this gourmet Italian deli's happy hour practically gives away small thin-crust pizzas for just $5. Wines are sold by the glass, and it's a social scene.

Nau's Enfield Drug (Map p91; ☎ 512-476-1221; 1115 West Lynn St; $2-4.50; ⊙ 7:30am-4pm Mon-Fri, 8am-2:30pm Sat) A time capsule all its own, this 1950s neighborhood pharmacy

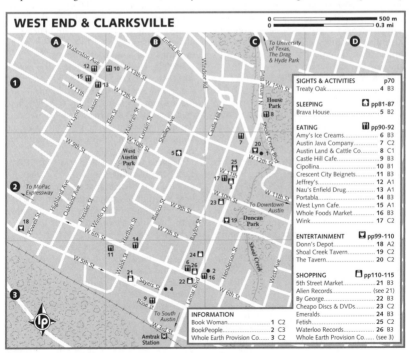

AUSTIN

maintains a quaint soda fountain and grill counter at the back. Milkshakes are made with Blue Bell ice cream, and there are breakfast tacos, too. Things get really busy at lunchtime.

MID-RANGE & TOP END

Reservations are recommended for all of the following.

West Lynn Cafe (Map p91; ☎ 512-482-0950; 1110 W Lynn St; mains $6-12.50; ☾ 11:30am-10pm Tues-Thu, 11:30am-10:30pm Fri, 11am-10:30pm Sat, 11am-9:30pm Sun) A swanky steel-and-glass building is the setting for upscale and wildly creative fresh vegetarian fare like Caribbean stir-fry or enchiladas draped in pumpkin-adobo sauce. It's an interior designer's dream, with local artwork, a divine crowd and a colorful menu that travels around the globe.

Castle Hill Cafe (Map p91; ☎ 512-476-0728; 1101 W 5th St; lunch $8-10, dinner mains $10-15; ☾ lunch 11:30am-2:30pm Mon-Fri, dinner 6-10pm Mon-Sat) Applauded by Austin foodies for its creative combinations that really reach, Castle Hill Cafe delivers a reasonably priced wine list and consistent quality. A tasteful interior compliments the seasonally inspired menu, which changes every few weeks. Look for inventive Southwest creations, like serrano-lime roasted chicken enchiladas with smoked tomato purée.

Wink (Map p91; ☎ 512-482-8868; 1014 N Lamar Blvd; mains $15-30; ☾ 6-10:30pm Mon-Sat) At this gem hidden behind Whole Earth Provision Co, diners are ushered to tables underneath windows screened with Japanese *washi* (rice paper), then presented with an exceptional wine list. The chef-inspired fare takes on a nouveau fusion attitude that's equal parts modern French and Asian.

Jeffrey's (Map p91; ☎ 512-477-5584; 1204 W Lynn St; mains $18-35; ☾ 6-10pm Mon-Thu, 5:30-10:30pm Fri-Sat, 6-9:30pm Sun) This high-end restaurant is small (perhaps too small, seeing as tables are packed together) but nevertheless popular for romantic dining. Service is exceptional, the wine list is luxuriantly long, and the New American menu stretches from Texas to the Pacific Northwest. Pick the chai tea crème brulée for dessert.

Austin Land & Cattle Co (Map p91; ☎ 512-472-1813; 1205 N Lamar Blvd; steak & seafood $15-35; ☾ 5:30-10pm daily, till 11pm Fri-Sat) One of the city's most pleasant steakhouses, this low-key establishment possesses the grace of a Spanish hacienda. Every steak is cut right here on the premises, and each entrée comes with two (count 'em) complimentary desserts.

South Austin

With more variety than any other neighborhood in the city, South Austin is a sure-fire choice for any appetite.

BUDGET

Jo's (Map pp66-7; ☎ 512-444-3800; 1300 S Congress Ave; sandwiches $5; ☾ 7am-9pm Tues-Fri, 7am-10pm Sat, 7am-6pm Sun-Mon) A portable picnic on SoCo, complete with prime people-watching from the outdoors-only tables, this mint-green coffee shack serves gourmet deli sandwiches off its chalkboard menus. Pulled pork is a local fave, but there are vegetarian varieties.

Taco Xpress (Map pp66-7; ☎ 512-444-0261; 2529 S Lamar Blvd; tacos $1-3, meals $5.50; ☾ 7am-3pm Mon, 7am-9pm Tues-Fri, 8am-9pm Sat, 9am-2pm Sun) This place is run by totally hyperactive guys – don't get in line if you don't already know exactly what you want! There's a congenial courtyard for scarfing down the tasty stuffed gorditas, crispy tacos and enchilada plates. Musicians play live here on many evenings and Sunday afternoons.

Bouldin Creek Coffee House (Map pp66-7; ☎ 512-416-1601; 1501 S 1st St; $3-6; ☾ 7am-midnight Mon-Fri, from 9am Sat-Sun) Vegetarian meals are made from scratch right in their kitchen, and breakfast is served all day. A 'Slacker's Banquet' of beans over rice and 'Cosmic Sloppy Joes' should clue you in about the clientele. See also p98.

Magnolia Cafe South (Map pp66-7; ☎ 512-445-0000; 1920 S Congress Ave; meals $4-8; ☾ 24hrs) An outpost of the original Westlake café (p97), here the mix of artists, surfers and bleary-eyed clubhoppers is something to groove with, but lines are excruciatingly long.

Sandy's (Map pp66-7; ☎ 512-478-6322; 603 Barton Springs Rd; $1.50-4; ☾ 10:30am-10:30pm) A drive-in with better-than-average burgers and fries, old-fashioned Sandy's serves frozen custard, shakes and malts, too. It's a perfect place for a bite after running around Zilker Park, and kids love it. Check out that retro neon sign.

Mr Natural (Map pp66-7; ☎ 512-916-9223; 2414-A S Lamar Blvd; breakfast/lunch specials $4.50/6.50;

⟨♥ 9am-9pm) has a branch in East Austin. See p96 for a full review.

MID-RANGE

Threadgill's World Headquarters (Map pp66-7; ☎ 512-472-9304; 301 W Riverside Dr; meals $6-18; ⟨♥ 11am-10pm Mon-Thu, 11am-10:30pm Fri-Sat, 11am-9: 30pm Sun) Fittingly, Eddie Wilson established Threadgill's World Headquarters next to the original Armadillo World Headquarters (the Music chapter, p30) site on Riverside Dr, and it's positively packed with Austin music memorabilia. Both locations, including the original Threadgill's on North Lamar (p97), offer Southern-style food (meatloaf, chicken-fried steak and glazed ham) and wonderful sides, including garlic cheese grits and Texas caviar (a marinated black-eyed pea salad).

Güero's Taco Bar (Map pp66-7; ☎ 512-447-7688; 1412 S Congress Ave; mains $5-13; ⟨♥ 11am-11pm daily, from 8am Sat-Sun) Across the street from the Continental Club, you'll find this prime Tex-Mex restaurant inside a century-old feed-and-seed company building. It's a SoCo scene (Bill Clinton once ate here, ya know) with an inventive garden-meets-garage type of atmosphere, plus plenty of Mexican beer and margaritas.

Shady Grove Restaurant (Map pp66-7; ☎ 512-474-9991; 1624 Barton Springs Rd; mains $6-12; ⟨♥ 11am-10:30pm daily, till 11pm Fri-Sat) Ah, you can dine outdoors under the pecan trees. The comfort food is American/Tex-Mex, with vegetarian choices (order the 'Hippie Sandwich'). On Thursday nights in summer, 'Austin Unplugged' concerts by well-known musicians take place (no cover); catch an old Western movie in their Starlight Theater on other nights.

El Sol y La Luna (Map pp66-7; ☎ 512-444-7770; 1224 S Congress Ave; meals $6-10; ⟨♥ 7am-3pm Sun-Tues, 7am-10pm Wed-Sat) It's a great spot for huevos rancheros, weekend *pozole* (a whole-kernel corn hominy soup with chile and lime) or fried plantain to start your day (actually, breakfast is served all day). The funky sun-and-moon décor and laid-back patio hit just the right notes, especially when Latin music happens on weekends.

Green Mesquite BBQ & More (Map pp66-7; ☎ 512-479-0485; 1400 Barton Springs Rd; meals $4-8, kids menu $3; ⟨♥ 11am-10pm) An old-fashioned spot with Southern charm, Green Mesquite is another good bet for families. A Texas-size

menu includes barbecue plates, catfish po' boy sandwiches, ooey-gooey pecan pie and cold draft beer. There's usually live music on Friday, Saturday and Sunday evenings.

Matt's El Rancho (Map pp66-7; ☎ 512-462-9333; 2613 S Lamar Ave; meals $6-12; ⟨♥ 11am-10pm Sun-Mon & Wed-Thu, 11am-11pm Fri-Sat) Open since 1952, Matt's has a wide menu with every sort of Mexican specialty; the fajitas and chile relleno are standards. Some Austin families have been coming here every Sunday night for decades. If there's a wait for a patio table, sip one of their knock-out margaritas by the bar.

Artz Rib House (Map pp66-7; ☎ 512-442-8283; 2330 S Lamar Blvd; meals $6-13; ⟨♥ 11am-10pm) This is *the* place for barbecue in South Austin. Especially good are the baby-back ribs; vegetarians aren't left entirely out in the cold either. There's live music, mostly folk and bluegrass, almost nightly (except Wednesday).

Casa de Luz (Map pp66-7; ☎ 512-476-2535; 1701 Toomey Rd; meals $8-12; ⟨♥ 11.30am-2pm & 6-8pm) This macrobiotic haven is hidden by greenery off Barton Springs Rd. Vegan meals here are 98% organic and entirely delicious; the farm-fresh seasonal ingredients are often home-grown. Relax with an herbal tea after taking one of their yoga classes (p75).

Chuy's (Map pp66-7; ☎ 512-474-4452; 1728 Barton Springs Rd; mains $6-12; ⟨♥ 11am-10:30pm daily, till 11:30pm Fri-Sat) Known for its fun, kitschy décor with a special penchant for Elvis memorabilia, Chuy's really packs 'em in. The Tex-Mex food may not be special, but

---

TOP 10 FEASTS FOR LESS

- Las Manitas Avenue Cafe (p88)
- Noodle-ism (p88)
- Portabla (p91)
- Austin Java Company (p91)
- Jo's (p92)
- Taco Xpress (p92)
- Chango's Taqueria (p94)
- Mother's Cafe & Garden (p95)
- Sam's BBQ (p96)
- Kerbey Lane Café (p95)

when New Mexico-style green chile sauce appears on the menu in late August and early September, it's the real thing.

TOP END

Reservations are recommended for these restaurants.

Uchi (Map pp66-7; ☎ 512-916-4808; 801 S Lamar Blvd; sushi from $3, appetizers & mains $5-18; ⊙ 5-10pm Mon-Thu, 5-11pm Fri-Sat) When East meets West, they collide beautifully at this top-notch South Austin sushi haunt. *Uchi* means 'house' in Japanese, and somehow smiling staff make this sleek LA-style interior design seem homelike. Seat yourself by the sushi bar or linger at tables over creative appetizers, like duck *yakitori* skewers or brie tempura with apple chutney.

Lambert's (Map pp66-7; ☎ 512-383-8877; 1716 S Congress Ave; mains $12-25; ⊙ 5:30-10pm Tue-Thu, 5:30-10:30pm Fri-Sat) Renowned for its intelligent updates of American comfort food classics, this modest-looking dining room is owned and run by Austin chef Lou Lambert. A bottle of robust wine, a plate of roast chicken and a slice of coconut cream pie are heavenly.

South Congress Cafe (Map pp66-7; ☎ 512-447-3905; 1600 S Congress Ave; mains $12-18; ⊙ 5:30pm-10ish) A culinary newcomer, this restaurant evinces strong, eclectic American flavors. Inside are cathedral ceilings, hewn rock walls and panoramic windows overlooking the SoCo scene. Burgeoning crowds throng the curled cocktail bar by the entryway.

Vespaio (Map pp66-7; ☎ 512-441-6100; 1610 S Congress Ave; pasta & pizza $13-18, mains $20-26; ⊙ dinner from 5:30pm) Vespaio has the feel of a country manor library or a gentleman's club; a crowd of swanky suits and cocktail dresses are in attendance. The Italian restaurant gets high marks for authentic seasonal menus, including wood oven-fired pizzas; smoked duck with port-soaked figs remains the critical fave. Dining at the bar is an option if the tables are full.

UT Area & The Drag

There are some spicy exceptions to the generally bland, student-oriented fare that crowds Guadalupe St (aka the Drag).

BUDGET

Chango's Taqueria (Map pp68-9; ⊙ 512-480-8226; 3023 Guadalupe St; $3-6; ⊙ 11am-10pm) Local

Tex-Mex devotees know this place is one of Austin's best. The sleek dining room serves fresh-pressed tortillas, grilled mahi mahi burritos, tacos filled with succulent pork and more. They even encourage folks to drop by in their pajamas!

Austin's Tamale House (Map pp68-9; ☎ 512-472-0487; 2825 Guadalupe St; tacos & tamales from $1.35; ⊙ 7am-4pm Mon-Fri, 7am-2:30pm Sat-Sun) A little shack at the intersection of Guadalupe and 29th Sts just north of UT, this no-frills spot has decent carry-out food. Students feast on tacos and tamales on the tiny streetside patio.

Madam Mam's (Map pp68-9; ☎ 512-472-8306; 2514 Guadalupe St; meals $5-8; ⊙ 11am-9:30pm daily, from noon Sat-Sun) Madam Mam's is an authentic noodle house run by Thai expats and culinary fiends. Enjoy eavesdropping on foreign-language conversations at nearby tables while waiting for your steaming bowl of noodles, curries, savory salads and more. Be sure you ask for the food prepared as spicy as it should be.

Wheatsville Food Co-op (Map pp68-9; ☎ 512-478-2667; 3101 Guadalupe St; ⊙ 9am-11pm, deli closes 9pm) This wonderful grocery store is open to nonmembers (though with a 7% surcharge) and offers organic and imported foods and coffees. The deli section is a ready-made picnic, very vegetarian-friendly (but not exclusively so). Shop on Wednesday, when 1% of profits go to community groups. An

---

GOOD GREEN GRAZIN'

Tired of Texas barbecue? Austin's many great escapes for vegetarians, vegans and others starved for healthy options include the following:

■ Noodle-ism (p88)

■ Mars Restaurant & Bar (p90)

■ Whole Foods Market (p91)

■ Austin Java Company (p91)

■ Portabla (p91)

■ West Lynn Cafe (p92)

■ Bouldin Creek Coffeehouse (p92)

■ Mother's Cafe & Garden (p95)

■ Eastside Cafe (p96)

■ Kerbey Lane Café (p95)

onsite chair massage therapist is available some days.

Central Market (Map pp68-9; ☎ 512-206-1000, events 512-458-3068; 4001 N Lamar Ave; 🕙 9am-9pm, coffee & smoothie bar open from 8am) It's snobby, but this recommended grocery store is filled with mind-bogglingly good fresh and packaged foods. You can buy a heat-and-serve take-away feast. The Central Market also hosts wine and cheese seminars, chef lectures and cooking classes.

Dirty Martin's Kum-Bak Hamburgers (Map pp68-9; ☎ 512-478-0413; 2808 Guadalupe St; $2-5; 🕙 11am-11pm) At this classic hamburger shack from the 1920s, the waitstaff are snappy, and both tator tots and limeades are on the menu. Locals like to chew the fat at picnic tables outside.

MID-RANGE & TOP END

Kerbey Lane Café (Map pp68-9; ☎ 512-451-1436; 3704 Kerbey Lane; breakfast $4-8, lunch & dinner $6-11; 🕙 24hrs) The original Kerbey Lane Café is a huge Austin favorite, especially for breakfast (gingerbread pancakes, anyone?), fulsome salads and fresh seasonal specials. The café grows much of its food at its own farm. Vegetarians are well catered to here. There's another **branch** closer to campus (Map pp68-9; ☎ 512-477-5717; 2606 Guadalupe St).

Trudy's Texas Star (Map pp68-9; ☎ 512-477-2935; 409 W 30th; meals $6-10; 🕙 7am-midnight Mon-Thu, 7am-2am Fri, 8am-2am Sat, 8am-midnight Sun, bar until 2am daily) Trudy's hot sauces and salsas are famous. The food is typical Tex-Mex, but with a healthy twist, including many options for vegetarians. Drop by for a sunset margarita on the tree-shaded deck; relax and see what all the fuss is about.

Ruby's BBQ (Map pp68-9; ☎ 512-477-1651; 512 W 29th St; meals $7-12; 🕙 11am-midnight) A down-home spot with a bluesy Southern soundtrack, Ruby's is a gem. They smoke hormone-free, locally ranched meats in brick pits, then serve them up doused in tangy sauces with a selection of sides. Even vegetarians are well catered to, with delicious black bean tacos and salads.

Ray's Steakhouse (Map pp68-9; ☎ 512-478-0000; 3010 Guadalupe St; lunch $10-30, dinner $18-36; 🕙 11:30am-2pm Mon-Fri, dinner from 5:30pm daily) In a former Ruth's Chris location, ivy-covered Ray's is a locally favored steakhouse known for its old-fashioned cowboy chic, large fireplace and ample portions. All of the

wild animal decor – from rawhide leather seat covers to the antlers mounted on the wall – is real. The Nova Scotia lobster is extravagantly priced, but very fresh. Reservations recommended.

Hyde Park

Beyond the UT campus, but close to many of the city's B&Bs, Hyde Park has a few striking choices.

BUDGET

Mother's Cafe & Garden (Map pp68-9; ☎ 512-451-3994; 4215 Duval St; meals $6-9; 🕙 11:30am-10pm daily, from 10am Sat-Sun) The vegetarian and vegan menu (of always satisfying pastas, enchiladas, Asian stir-frys and more) rarely changes, and the devoted clientele keeps Mother's busy. There's a lovely fern-filled covered patio; everyone wants to sit there, so expect a wait. If time is precious, seat yourself at the front counter instead.

Avenue B Grocery (Map pp68-9; ☎ 512-453-3921; 4403 Avenue B; 🕙 8am-6pm Mon-Sat) This old-timey grocery store is the quirkiest of its kind in Austin. They mainly make deli sandwiches and sell cold drinks, but also vend old-fashioned candy, balsa-wood airplanes and vintage stuff to beat the band.

MID-RANGE & TOP END

Asti (Map pp68-9; ☎ 512-451-1218; 408C E 43rd St; lunch $8-10, dinner mains $8-16; 🕙 11am-10pm Mon-Thu, 5-11pm Fri-Sat) A pan-Italian trattoria

---

WORTH A SPECIAL TRIP

Out-of-the-way places we adore include the following:

- West Lynn Cafe (p92)
- Wink (p92)
- Lambert's (p94)
- Uchi (p94)
- Asti (p95)
- Eastside Cafe (p96)
- Threadgill's Restaurant (p97)
- Manny Hattan's (p97)
- Chez Zee (p99)
- Fonda San Miguel (p99)
- Zoot (p99)

AUSTIN

with modern industrial chic decor, this warmhearted place is chef-owned. They may even try to tempt you inside with a free sample of the awesome array of Italian foodstuffs made here, anything from focaccia to Italian sausages. The counter fronts an open kitchen, where the creative and attentive staff turn out baked trout, robust risotto and more delights. Reservations are helpful.

Starlite (Map pp68-9; ☎ 512-374-9012; 624 W 34th St; brunch $7-11, dinner $25-45; ⏰ 6-11pm Wed-Sat, 11am-3pm Sun) Except for the glittering star sign, it's hard to tell that this modest house is actually a chichi restaurant. Starlite's adventurous New American menu is short, but it's enough to satisfy any appetite. Service can be absent-minded, however. Tables on the front porch are ideal for Sunday brunch. Reservations are essential.

Hyde Park Bar & Grill (Map pp68-9; ☎ 512-458-3168; 4206 Duval St; mains $5-16; ⏰ 11am-late) A reliable standby for comfort food, this darkly lit neighborhood haunt serves the likes of yellowfin tuna sandwiches, chicken-fried steaks and peach puddings. Look for the eye-popping gigantic metal fork stuck upright into the ground outside.

East Austin

East Austin's ethnic eateries are worthy of notice, especially if you're already sightseeing in the neighborhood.

BUDGET

Sam's BBQ (Map pp56-7; ☎ 512-478-0378; 2000 E 12th St; $2-8; ⏰ 10am-2am daily, till 3am Fri-Sat) Plenty of people say Sam's serves Austin's best barbecue. The walls are covered with photos and notes from grateful clients, who form long lines in the wee hours on weekends and after church on Sunday. Savory mixed plates (two meats, beans, bread, onions, pickles and potato salad) are about $6.

Juan in a Million (Map pp56-7; 512-472-3872; 2300 E Cesar Chavez St; meals $4.50-7; 7am-3pm daily, till 8pm Thu-Sat) Everyone loves the name and the food, too. Huge breakfast tacos (around $2) will keep you filled up way past lunch. These days Juan's even has its own private-label salsa for sale.

Mr Natural (Map pp56-7; ☎ 512-477-5228; 1901 E Cesar Chavez St; breakfast/lunch specials $4.50/6.50; ⏰ 8am-7pm Mon-Sat) This small health food store attracts vegans and vegetarians with its hot food bar (the flavors are vaguely Tex-Mex) and fresh juices, smoothies and wheatgrass shots. It's tiny, but a real community hang-out.

MID-RANGE

Eastside Cafe (Map pp56-7; ☎ 512-476-5858; 2113 Manor Rd; meals $8-16; ⏰ 11:30am-9:30pm daily, till 10pm Fri-Sun) East Austin's most elegant café inhabits an old-fashioned house with a garden out back. Sold at the gift shop next door, cookbooks drawn from the café's own menu reveal the secrets of artichoke manicotti, sesame-encrusted catfish, wild mushroom crepes and apple-almond waffles. Service is personable without being stuffy. Reservations are advised.

Hoover's Cooking (Map pp56-7; ☎ 512-479-5006; 2002 Manor Rd; meals $6-13, kids menu $3-5; ⏰ 11am-10pm Mon-Fri, 9am-10pm Sat-Sun) Another eastside institution, Hoover's dishes up true Southern-style cooking (cheese grits, candied yams and fried green tomatoes) alongside Jamaican jerk chicken and ribs, jalapeño creamed spinach and other unusual items. Don't miss out on the fruit cobblers, banana pudding cheesecake or homemade lemonade. Butcher paper covers the tables, and there's a small bar.

Cisco's (Map pp56-7; ☎ 512-478-2420; 1511 E 6th St; meals $5-9; ⏰ 7am-2:30pm) One of Austin's beloved long-running places for Tex-Mex cuisine, this family-owned bakery and restaurant serves *migas* and *huevos rancheros* every morning. By the way, LBJ used to eat here, too.

Nuevo Leon (Map pp56-7; ☎ 512-479-0097; 1501 E 6th St; meals $6-13; ⏰ 11am-10pm daily, till 11pm Fri-Sat) You'll find consistently excellent Tex-Mex fare and margaritas nearly big enough to drown in here. The decor is bright, with neon signs and Christmas lights, and the servers cheerfully seat big families.

Gene's (Map pp56-7; ☎ 512-477-6600; 1209 E 11th St; meals $6-10; ⏰ 6:30am-7pm Mon-Sat) Gene's is a simple place, with a tiny porch outdoors in the heart of East Austin. Come for New Orleans-style po' boys and plates of catfish, fried chicken or red beans and rice. Expect a longish wait at lunchtime.

Greater Austin

BUDGET

Magnolia Cafe (Map pp56-7; ☎ 512-478-8645; 2304 Lake Austin Blvd; meals $4-9; ☯ 24hrs) In Westlake opposite Deep Eddy Cabaret (p105), this all-night caf 's menu can be hit-or-miss, but always filling, with American/Tex-Mex standbys like *migas*, enchiladas, pancakes and potato scrambles. It gets absurdly crowded on weekends.

Rudy's Country Store & BBQ (Map pp56-7; ☎ 512-418-9898; 11570 Research Blvd; sides $1-2, mains $4.50-7; ☯ 6:30am-9:30pm Mon-Thu, 6:30am-10:30pm Fri-Sat, 7am-9:30pm Sun) Slyly calling itself the 'worst barbecue in Texas,' Rudy's ain't half bad. It's a barn-size place, conveniently near the Arboretum mall.

Dot's Place (Map pp56-7; ☎ 512-255-7288; 13805 Orchid Lane; meals $5-8; ☯ lunch 11am-2pm Mon-Fri, dinner 6-8pm Fri) Dot starts cooking around 4am to prepare for the daily cafeteria-style lines of blue-collar folks who show up around noon for her fried catfish, meat loaf and chicken and dumplings. Add a side of stewed okra or collard greens. Save room for the blackberry cobbler or the sweet-potato pie, the latter of which can bring about world peace. Dot's is out of the way, but it's worth a stop if you're heading north at lunchtime (or for the Friday evening all-you-can-eat catfish fry, $8). Take the Howard Lane exit off I-35 and head west, or go east from MoPac.

MID-RANGE

Threadgill's Restaurant (Map pp56-7; ☎ 512-451-5440; 6416 N Lamar Blvd; meals $6-18; ☯ 11am-10pm Mon-Sat, 11am-9pm Sun) Kenneth Threadgill's original restaurant and hootenanny palace in North Austin is where Janis Joplin once performed. See Threadgrill's World Headquarters (p93) for a full review.

Salt Lick BBQ (Map pp56-7; ☎ 512-894-3117; 18300 FM 1826, Driftwood; meals $7-15, kids menu $5; ☯ 11am-10pm) Many people say the Salt Lick is well worth the drive for the vast Hill Country horizons as seen from its rustic outdoor tables. The family-style meal includes all-you-can-eat beef, sausage, pork ribs and sides. There's also live music on weekends. To get here, take I-35 south to Slaughter Lane, head west to FM 1826, then turn left (south) and go about 10 miles.

BBQ World Headquarters (Map pp56-7; ☎ 512-323-9112; 6710 Burnet Rd; plates $6-10; ☯ 10am-4pm Mon-Sat) At the Austin Farmer's Market, this down-home, family-owned barbecue shack lets its smoky goodness waft over nearby produce stands. On hot days, a tall lemonade with banana pudding for dessert are just perfect.

County Line on the Hill (Map pp56-7; ☎ 512-327-1742; 6500 Bee Caves Rd, west of Loop 360; meals $9-15, all-you-can-eat dinners $15-20; ☯ 5-9pm daily, till 10pm Fri-Sat) Although County Line has since gone nationwide, it all started here. The Hill Country views are quite good and the food is adequate, but serious barbecue junkies will head to Lockhart.

Manny Hattan's (☎ 512-794-0088; Gateway Square, 9503 Research Blvd; dishes $5-11; ☯ 11am-9pm Mon-Thu, 11am-midnight Fri, 10am-midnight Sat, 9am-9pm Sun) It's worth the drive (and paying through the nose) for true NYC deli fare. Overstuffed Reuben sandwiches could easily qualify as two whole meals, and the cheesecake from Carnegie's deli ($6 for a heavenly slice) and fresh H&H bagels are flown in from the Big Apple.

Satay (Map pp56-7; ☎ 512-467-6731; Shoal Creek shopping plaza, 3202 W Anderson Lane; mains $8-12, lunch specials $5-6; ☯ lunch 11am-2:30pm Mon-Sat, 12:30-3pm Sun, dinner 5-10pm daily) Austin's most authentic Thai cuisine is served in this tropically inspired dining room, where fabric hung from the rafters resembles the sails of boats on the Chao Phraya River. Trust the chef, even with Singaporean, Malaysian and Indonesian items on the

---

MIDNIGHT MUNCHIES

Both **Kerbey Lane Café** (p95) and **Magnolia Cafe** (p92 and p97) stay open around the clock. At the west end of 6th St downtown, **Katz's** deli (p98) never closes.

But the king of weird late-night diners, **Star Seeds** (Map pp68-9; 3101 N IH-35; meals $5-8; ☯ 24hrs) is the kind of place where you'll see scruffy musicians hanging out after a late-night gig, bikers and maybe even a movie star or two. Greasy grill fare is exactly what you'd expect, but it's cheap – and a classic Austin experience.

menu. For dessert, there's chocolate tofu pie and 'Cassava Delight.'

Suzi's China Grill (Map pp56-7; ☎ 512-302-4600; 7858 Shoal Creek Blvd; mains $7-11; ☺ 11am-10pm Mon-Thu, 11am-11pm Fri-Sat, 11:30am-10pm Sun) Suzi's serves a modish version of Chinese and pan-Asian cuisine, such as firecracker prawns, lemon scallops and plates of bok choy and eggplant. The ultra-modern atmosphere is sleek, but laid-back, and there's a full bar.

Tien Hong (Map pp56-7; ☎ 512-458-2263; 8301 Burnet Rd; dim sum from $3; ☺ 11:30am-2pm & 5-10pm Mon-Fri, 11am-10pm Sat-Sun) In North Austin, this is the place for Cantonese-style dim sum on Sunday mornings. During the week, lobster dinners go for $20.

JAVA JIVIN' AROUND AUSTIN

In Austin, you've got to perfect the art of doing almost nothing. Hangin' out, sipping a cup o' joe and eavesdropping is the perfect way to do just that, since Austin has a good coffeehouse scene, with most places offering light meals in addition to caffeine libations. Their bulletin boards with ads for yoga retreats, musicians wanted and motocross bikes for sale are added insights into the south Texas lifestyle.

Once at the center of Austin's alternative universe, **Ruta Maya Coffee House** (Map pp56-7; ☎ 512-707-9637; www.rutamaya.net; Bldg D, Penn Field Complex, 3601 S Congress Ave; ☺ 7am-1am daily, till 2am Thu-Sat) has moved, retreating deep into South Austin under the watertower. It's loud as hell when they're roasting fair-trade coffee, but otherwise it's excellent for early morning yoga, open-mic poetry, live music and DJs (p103). All ages are welcome.

Bouldin Creek Coffee House (p92) is pretty darn representative of the entire South Austin scene: outdoor tables by creaky old fans, punk music playing, vegetarian food and everybody's got a tattoo.

Flipnotics (Map pp66-7; ☎ 512-322-9750; www.flipnotics.com; 1601 Barton Springs Rd; ☺ 7am-7pm Mon, 7am-midnight Tue-Fri, 7am-1am Sat, 8am-11pm Sun) is a good place to nurse a hangover or just chill with a cigarette on the back porch. Caffeine brews are served in bowls reminiscent of witches' cauldrons. There's music, too (p103).

Cafe Mundi (Map pp56-7; ☎ 512-236-8634; www.cafemundi.com; 1704 E 5th St, ☺ 8am-10pm daily, till midnight Fri-Sat) inhabits a vintage adobe building down by the railroad tracks in East Austin. This oasis is packed with artists, slackers and other neighborhood types. The café also has a full calendar of acoustic and jazz music, belly dancing, film screenings and open-mic poetry – the works.

Near Pease Park, **Austin Java Company** (p91) is great little café for hanging out on a Saturday afternoon after playing disc golf along the Shoal Creek Greenbelt. Huge breakfasts and other healthy meals are served all day long.

Looking for 21st-century ambience? **Little City** (Map pp58-9; ☎ 512-476-2489; 916 Congress Ave; ☺ 7am-midnight Mon-Fri, 9am-midnight Sat, 9am-10pm Sun) is a mod place with strong espresso and free Wi-Fi access. This downtown location is where they do roasting. Its other **branch** (Map pp68-9; ☎ 512-467-2326; 2604 Guadalupe St; ☺ same hrs) has outdoor tables.

Ramshackle **Mojo's Daily Grind** (Map pp68-9; ☎ 512-477-6656; www.mojosdailygrind.com; 2714 Guadalupe St; ☺ 24hrs) is Austin's most political coffeehouse. It's definitely part of the 'Keep Austin Weird' contingent with its anti-Starbucks campaign (take a look at the website). Day and night, UT students crowd around the comfy tables.

Flower-bedecked **Spider House** (Map pp68-9; ☎ 512-480-9562; 2908 Fruth St; ☺ 8am-2am) is another UT-area coffeehouse, which also serves beer and wine. Its deck is made for lazy lounging, and there's oddball stuff in the garden such as decapitated religious statues and even an antique bathtub.

On Lake Austin, **Mozart's Coffee Roasters** (Map pp56-7; ☎ 512-477-2900; 3825 Lake Austin Blvd; ☺ 7am-midnight Mon-Thu, 7am-1am Fri, 8am-1am Sat, 8am-midnight Sun) offers free Wi-Fi access, and a sinful dessert case holds more cheesecakes, mousses and tarts than you ever could have imagined. Listen for live music Thursday to Sunday nights.

Back in the Warehouse District, upstart **Halcyon** (Map pp58-9; ☎ 512-472-9637; 218 W 4th St; ☺ at least 11am-1am) is a hybrid coffeehouse-bar. Although the vibe is definitely not old-school Austin, you'll still find a few musicians hanging out here. With luxurious couches like these and free air-conditioning, it's hard to complain.

TOP END

Reservations are essential at the following places.

Fonda San Miguel (Map pp56-7; ☎ 512-459-4121; 2330 W North Loop Blvd; mains $13-29; 🕓 5:30-9:30pm Mon-Thu, 5:30-10:30pm Fri-Sat, brunch 11am-2pm Sun) When Austinites are asked to recommend a special occasion restaurant, Fonda San Miguel is often the answer. Drenched in the atmosphere of old Mexico with folk-inspired art, it has been serving up regional Mexican cooking for over 25 years. Especially recommended are the seafood dishes, Yucatan-style pork and almond-flavored flan. Indulge in a renowned lime, mango or watermelon margarita while you're here.

Zoot (Map pp56-7; ☎ 512-477-6535; 509 Hearn St; mains $17-25; 🕓 6-10pm Tue-Thu, 5:30-10pm Fri-Sun) In a charming early-20th-century bungalow off Lake Austin Blvd, this unpretentious New American bistro turns out some of Austin's finest cuisine, as it has for many years, despite many changes in ownership. Expect surprisingly good New American fare, perhaps halibut with grilled mango relish. A French influence is also apparent, not least of all in the wine list.

Chez Zee (Map pp56-7; ☎ 512-454-2666; 5406 Balcones Dr; lunch $6-14, dinner mains $12-16; 🕓 11am-10:30pm Mon-Thu, 11am-midnight Fri, 9am-midnight Sat, 9am-10pm Sun) At this intimate honey-colored house in North Austin, local artwork adorns the walls and the expert staff are welcoming. Sophisticated American bistro food is accompanied by piano jazz on Friday and Saturday evenings and during Sunday brunch ($10-16). Stop by for fabulous desserts made at Chez Zee's on-site bakery.

Bistro 88 (Map pp56-7; ☎ 512-328-8888; 2712 Bee Caves Rd; lunch $9-15, dinner mains $13-40; 🕓 lunch 11am-2pm Mon-Fri, dinner 5:30-9:30pm daily, till 10pm Fri-Sat, till 9pm Sun) If you quickly blink while heading west of town on Bee Caves Rd, you'll miss this Eurasian favorite. It's chef-owned, with impressive wines available by the glass or half bottle. On the menu Kobe beef stands beside more whimsical creations, like wonton shooters or '100 Corners' shrimp and crab cakes.

ENTERTAINMENT

Austin's contention that it's the 'Live Music Capital of the World' may very well be true. Music is the town's leading nighttime attraction, and a major industry as well, with several thousand bands and performers from all over the world plying their trade in the city's clubs and bars. On a given Friday night, there are several hundred acts playing in the town's 200 or so venues. Even on an off night (Monday and Tuesday are usually the slowest), you'll typically have your pick of more than two dozen performances. Most bars stay open till 2am (p192 for a description of standard bar and pub hours), while a few clubs stay hoppin' until 4am. See the Music chapter (p30) for a short history of the evolving Austin sound.

You can get heaps of information on the city's whole entertainment scene in the *Austin Chronicle* or the *Austin American-Statesman*'s *XLent* section, both out on Thursday. *XLent* has an ultra-streamlined 'Club Listings' chart that lets your plan you evening's entertainment at a glance, but the *Chronicle*'s night-by-night encyclopedia of listings often includes set times (handy if you'd like to hit several venues in one night), plus music critics' picks and local gossip to really plug you into the scene. On weekdays at 3:30pm, Radio Austin (107.1FM) DJs play unreleased demo tapes, then check back around 7:30pm for the 'Live Music Spotlight' on that day's best shows around town.

Advance tickets (which may be cheaper) for major venues are sold through **Star Tickets** (☎ 512-469-7469, 888-597-7827; www.startickets.com), which has outlets in **Waterloo Records** (Map p91; 600 N Lamar Blvd), the **Paramount Theatre** (Map pp58-9; 713 Congress Ave; 🕓 noon-5:30pm Mon-Sat) and Albertsons grocery stores. Star Tickets also handles some performing arts and sports events. **AusTIX** (☎ 512-472-8497; www.austix.com) sells tickets mainly for theater, but also music, dance and special events. Half-price discount tickets are available only for same-day shows and only if you buy them in person (cash or check only; no credit cards) at AusTIX outlets, such as the **Austin CVB** (Map pp58-9; 201 E 2nd St; 🕓 noon-5pm Wed-Sun). Call ahead to check availability.

Live Music

Most live-music bars and clubs have a mix of local and touring bands. Generally there are two to three bands per venue each night.

Cover charges cost from $3 (for local bands) to $15 or more (for touring acts). Music shows often start late, with the headliner starting anywhere from 9pm to midnight, though a few clubs offer music as early as 4pm, and doors almost always open a half hour to an hour before showtime. Showing up at the last minute or fashionably late may result in not getting in. If you want to get started early, most places have a happy hour (4-7pm).

Many of the venues we recommend are longtime Austin institutions. If you want to experience Austin's music scene but aren't sure where to start, any of these are good bets. Then again, you don't have to leave your motel to catch local music on cable channel 15, the Austin Music Network. But remember – it's always better live.

Major places to catch live touring acts include the following:

Austin Music Hall (Map pp58-9; ☎ 512-263-4146; www.austinmusichall.com; 208 Nueces St) A grown-up venue at the edge of downtown, with a capacity of 3000 people.

The Backyard (Map pp56-7; ☎ 512-263-4146; www.thebackyard.net; 13101 W Hwy 71, just west of RM620) An open-air amphitheater shaded by trees, a half-hour drive west of town. Seats up to 5000 people.

Cactus Cafe (Map pp68-9; ☎ 512-475-6515; www.utexas.edu/student/txunion; Texas Union, 24th & Guadalupe Sts) This small nonsmoking bar in the UT student union is where a stellar array of performers, such as Lyle Lovett and Shawn Colvin, have performed since it opened in the 1970s. Seating starts 45 minutes before showtime (usually 9pm). People start lining up even earlier, though. The focus is on the music, mostly acoustic.

Frank Erwin Center (Map pp68-9; ☎ 512-477-6060; www.uterwincenter.com; 1701 Red River St) What is that vaguely spaceship-shaped thing near I-35? A major concert and UT sports venue that can hold up to 17,000 screaming fans.

La Zona Rosa (Map pp58-9; ☎ 512-263-4146; www.lazonarosa.com; 612 W 4th St) Hosts an eclectic range of bands, both local and national. There's free parking in the garage opposite the venue; the Backstage Bar around the corner is open daily.

AUSTIN CITY LIMITS

For many public television viewers in North America, *Austin City Limits* is the best live music showcase on the air. This long-running series from Austin PBS affiliate KLRU started in 1975 and has featured hundreds of top acts – everyone from the well-known (Willie Nelson has been on more than a dozen times) to upstart performers deserving wider acclaim. Many have at least a bit of country music appeal, but plenty veer off into folk, rock, Latin, blues or alternative directions.

How do you score tickets for a taping? The answer: It ain't easy. 'Don't plan a trip to Austin solely to see *Austin City Limits*,' say the show's publicists. The studio has only 400 seats, and the byzantine ticket distribution method favors locals who know the drill. There's no pattern to the tapings; sometimes weeks will go by without one, then there'll be three in 10 days. Moreover, there may not be information on a taping until a few days before the gig.

Still, if you're in town for a week or so – especially September through October, when the tapings usually reach their peak – you can call the **KLRU hotline** (☎ 512-475-9077) to learn if any tapings are planned (there are usually none from April to late June). If there are, there will be an announcement one or two days before the show listing the artist, taping date, time and which radio station(s) will air the ticket distribution announcement. Then one or two working days before the show, you'll need to listen to that station to hear when tickets will be given away – usually in the morning, and typically within an hour of the station's announcement. Tickets are distributed by KLRU staff at the specified location. They go quickly, usually within five minutes, and they don't guarantee admission, though most ticket holders will get in. (It's smart to arrive early on taping night.) Tickets are free, but there's a two-per-person limit.

If you land in town during a time with no tapings, you can still take KLRU's free *Austin City Limits* tour, held at 10:30am each Friday, year-round. It's a good way to gain some backstage insight into the show. No reservations are necessary; just show up (though you can call ☎ 512-471-4811 if you have any questions). Used for both tours and tapings, the KLRU studio is located in Communications Building B at the corner of 26th and Guadalupe Sts on the University of Texas campus. For more information on the show, see the Austin Cyber Limits website (www.pbs.org/klru/austin). The world-class Austin City Limits music festival (p80) happens every autumn in Zilker Park.

One World Theatre (Map pp56-7; ☎ 512-329-6753; www.oneworldtheatre.org; 7701 Bee Caves Rd, west of Capital of Texas Hwy) An intimate venue with stucco Italianate villa-style architecture and Hill Country views. Blues, rock, ballet, classical, jazz, acoustic – and no liquor. Seats up to 300 people.

Paramount Theatre (Map pp58-9; ☎ 512-472-5470; 713 Congress Ave) An early 20th-century art deco theater that stages a little bit of everything, from alt-country to comedy to choral music.

Stubb's Bar-B-Q ('Downtown' below) A small indoor stage looks out onto the main backyard concert venue, which rocks the Red River scene. Excellent acoustics.

DOWNTOWN

Red River Street has an emerging music scene.

Stubb's Bar-B-Q (Map pp58-9; ☎ 512-480-8341; www.stubbsaustin.com; 801 Red River St) Stubb's has live music almost every night, with a great mix of premier local and touring acts from across the musical spectrum. Many warm-weather shows are held out back along Waller Creek. There are two stages, a smaller stage indoors (where the Sunday gospel brunch takes place – see p88) and a larger backyard venue from where raucous sounds spill over onto Red River St.

Emo's (Map pp58-9; ☎ 512-477-3667; www.emos austin.com; 603 Red River St) Long one of Austin's great punk rock clubs, the expanded Emo's still has some of the cheapest covers in town. Alternative bands rule here, including quite a few touring acts. There are at least three or four bands nearly every night with punk, alternative rock and heavy-metal tendencies, and two stages along with outdoor tables. Show are all ages unless explicitly stated otherwise.

Red Eyed Fly (Map pp58-9; ☎ 512-474-1084; www.redeyedfly.com; 715 Red River St) On Waller Creek near Stubb's, it has rock music nightly (plus pool tables and a jukebox), and bands sometimes play outdoors in fine weather. The neon is extreme. It's an anchor on the Red River scene. Free happy-hour appetizers and no cover for bands on the local lounge stage Sunday to Tuesday.

Beer Land Texas (Map pp58-9; ☎ 512-479-7625; 711 Red River St) This is another punk and indie rock club on Red River St, not a brewpub (sorry, folks). But inside this converted garage (and one-time brothel), they do have pool, 25¢ pinball and retro arcade video games. Even better, the place is owned by musicians. DJs spin at 'Disco Hospital' on Sunday nights.

Room 710 (Map pp58-9; ☎ 512-476-0997; 710 Red River St) Wear black and arrive ready for great grunge, hardcore and other alternative tunes, mostly harsh local sounds. The likes of new bluegrass, reggae or funk sounds might magically appear during happy hour. The Monday night 'Gong Show' also has quite a rep.

Although **6th Street** generally has become more of a frat-boy-and-tourist scene, there are still a few venues for dependably great live shows.

Flamingo Cantina (Map pp58-9; ☎ 512-494-9336; www.flamingocantina.com; 515 E 6th St) Called 'the last place with soul on Sixth,' Austin's premier reggae joint prides itself on its good rasta vibes and bouncy dance floor. Seat yourself on the carpeted bleachers for good views of the stage. There's almost always a line, but hangin' with the chill folks outside ain't a waste of time neither.

Joe's Generic Bar (Map pp58-9; ☎ 512-480-0171; 315 E 6th St) Modestly named, this long-running blues venue on 6th St hasn't yet changed its stripes. Beer is cheap and a virtual museum of neon bar signs covering the club is worthy of collectors. Never a cover. Bikers always welcome.

311 Club (Map pp58-9; ☎ 512-477-1630; 311 E 6th St) A good club right on 6th St, with a steady stream of blues and R&B acts. The 311's low-key, cool attitude is a welcome relief from all the 6th St shot bars. Jam sessions are not unheard of here.

The **Warehouse District** is more about sexy salsa spots and swinger's drinks, but you'll also find a couple of decent live music venues.

Antone's (Map pp58-9; ☎ 512-320-8424; www.antones .net; 213 W 5th St) It's the 'Home of the Blues,' though many styles of music are represented here. At the earlier Guadalupe St incarnation, Stevie Ray Vaughn launched his career. Another local icon is the owner, who is now back at the club after some time spent in the federal pen on charges of marijuana dealing, among other things. There's something on almost every night, and the bar is excellent. All ages, all the time.

Lucky Lounge (Map pp58-9; ☎ 512-479-7700; 209A W 5th St) Head for this no-pretense

Warehouse District spot for early shows (usually starting around 8pm) with no cover charge. And check out that neon sign and mod '60s decor. It's hip, but not as tricked out as Red Fez next door (p104).

Cedar Street Courtyard (Map pp58-9; ☎ 512-495-9669; 208 W 4th St) This outdoor courtyard a few steps below street level showcases jazz, swing and other cocktail-hour tunes. An alluringly beautiful, well-heeled (and by that we often mean very high-heeled) crowd often kicks off its night here with a martini or two.

On **Congress Avenue**, the dividing line between E 6th St and the Warehouse District, live music spots are few and far between – literally.

Elephant Room (Map pp58-9; ☎ 512-473-2279; 315 Congress Ave) Probably the city's consistently best place for jazz, this subterranean bar has live music just about every night; occasionally infusions of world music and other trends are heard. Happy-hour shows start at 6pm on weekdays. Mondays are jam session nights. The cover charge stays low, mostly free except on weekends.

Hickory Street Bar & Grille (Map pp58-9; ☎ 512-477-8968; 800 Congress Ave) On a beautiful Congress Ave patio near the state capitol, live Dixieland jazz bands play almost nightly and during Sunday brunch. Beers are $2 anytime – what could be better than that?

What people refer to as 6th St generally means that thoroughfare's eastern end, found between Congress Ave and I-35.

However, there's life over on the **west side**, too.

Waterloo Records (Map pp91, see p110) This music store anchors the throbbing intersection of 6th St and Lamar Blvd. It often hosts live shows by sought-after local bands. Afterward you can adjourn for drinks at the adjacent Waterloo Ice House.

MoMo's (Map p58-9; ☎ 512-479-8848; www.momos club.com; 618 W 6th St) Named after a very different Las Vegas club, MoMo's has a great rooftop patio and eclectic mix of bands, making it a casual, fun place to hear music (alt-country, jazz, acoustic guitar or a psychedelic drum jam, anyone?). Often there's no cover before the end of happy hour.

Donn's Depot (Map p91; ☎ 512-478-0336; 1600 W 5th St; closed Sun) Step inside this old railway car, and it's as if you've stepped back in time. Why not try a Great Train Wreck cocktail while you're at it? Piano cabaret, oldies from the '50s and country music are the predominant themes. It's oddly romantic after all.

SOUTH AUSTIN

Unmistakably weird (in a good way!), South Austin hides a few musical gems.

Threadgill's World Headquarters (Map pp66-7; ☎ 512-472-9304; www.threadgills.com; 301 W Riverside Dr) See the Music chapter (p30) for a short history of this Austin musical landmark. It's also a fantastic restaurant (see p93) with a Sunday gospel brunch. Live bands take to the stage five nights a week, and sometimes there's no cover.

AUSTIN AFTER DARK: A BEGINNER'S GUIDE

Austin's encyclopedic array of live music venues for punks, alt-country types, indie rock fans, bluegrass freaks, latter-day folkies and other music auteurs, plus other places where plain ol' barflies can pull up a chair, is a roller coaster. It's thrilling, yes, but can be intimidating.

On your maiden voyage to the Third Coast, here's some advice:

▪ Catch a well-known touring act at a renowned Austin-only venue, such as the backyard stage at **Stubb's Bar-B-Q** (p101), the **Austin Music Hall** (p100) or **La Zona Rosa** (p100) in the Warehouse District, or even the jewel-like **Paramount Theatre** (p109) downtown.

▪ Make a pilgrimage to landmarks in Austin's musical history, perhaps the **Cactus Cafe** (p100), **Antone's** (p101), the **Continental Club** (p103) **Emo's** (p101) or the **Victory Grill** (p103).

▪ Venture into at least one of Austin's beloved dive bars, like **Deep Eddy Cabaret** (p105), the **Carousel Lounge** (p106), **Ego's** (p105) or **Ginny's Little Longhorn Saloon** (p105).

▪ Feeling lucky? Chase after free tickets to an **Austin City Limits** taping (warning: winning a million dollars on a reality TV show may be easier, but that's just our opinion; see p100).

Continental Club (Map pp66-7; ☎ 512-441-2444; www.continentalclub.com; 1315 S Congress Ave) The Continental is essential Austin – and little has changed since it opened in 1957. Even the classic cars parked outside look the same. A mixed roots rock, country and latter-day hippie crowd gravitates here. People line up around the block each Tuesday night for the no-cover 6:30pm show with blues goddess Toni Price.

Saxon Pub (Map pp66-7; ☎ 512-448-2552; www.thesaxonpub.com; 1320 S Lamar Blvd) The Saxon has music every night, mostly Texas performers in the blues-rock vein; even Willie Nelson has played here. Free weekday happy-hour shows see established names hailing from Nashville and beyond. Shiner Bock is on draft, and there's a pool table, big-screen TVs and darts. Look for 'Rusty,' the huge knight out front.

Jovita's (Map pp66-7; ☎ 512-447-7825; 1619 S 1st St) This Tex-Mex restaurant secreted way down in South Austin is best known for being able to book top-notch local talent. Ice cold beer, outdoor patio seats and a congenial rabble-rousing atmosphere are a bonus.

Ruta Maya Coffee House (Map pp56-7; ☎ 512-707-9637; www.rutamaya.net; 3601 S Congress Ave, Bldg D) In new digs, Ruta Maya (also p98) still manages to schedule a jam-packed calendar of events, including down-to-earth live shows, CD release parties, salsa nights and DJ-driven dance parties. Cover charges are usually low or nonexistent.

Flipnotics (Map pp66-7; ☎ 512-322-9750; 1601 Barton Springs Rd) This funky, alternative coffeehouse (p98) close to Zilker Park also books local acts. Most shows start about 8pm or 9pm, usually going on nightly except Monday.

AROUND AUSTIN
If you're already in the neighborhood, any of these places might have live music, depending on the night. Call ahead to check.

Hole in the Wall (Map pp68-9; ☎ 512-477-4747; 2538 Guadalupe St) Up on the Drag near UT is this bar with cheap beer and occasionally no-frills rock. On nights when no bands are booked, it's really just what it says, a hole in the wall.

Victory Grill (Map pp56-7; ☎ 512-474-8669; 1104 E 11th St) There may or may not be something

going on, so call ahead. This legendary east side joint recalls what a really cool jazz room would have been like in St Louis during the '40s. Ike and Tina Turner even once played at this national historic site.

Back Room (Map pp56-7; ☎ 512-441-4677; 2015 E Riverside Dr) Heavy rock and metal predominates, with some touring shows by the likes of Dio and Henry Rollins. Bikers call loudly for beer while they all crowd around over a dozen pool tables.

Reed's Jazz & Supper Club (Map pp56-7; ☎ 512-342-7977; Gateway shopping center, 9901 N Capital of Texas Hwy; closed Sun) Admittedly, it's a long way to drive. But the luxuriant surroundings, top-tier cuisine (with appetizers served from the bar until midnight) make for a night out that's both classy and convivial. The acoustics need some work, though.

Bars & Pubs

There are bejillions of bars in Austin, so what follows is only a very short list.

DOWNTOWN
The legendary **6th Street** bar scene has spilled over onto nearby thoroughfares, especially Red River St. Many of the new places on 6th St are shot bars aimed at party-hardy college students and tourists, while the Red River establishments retain a harder local edge.

Club de Ville (Map pp58-9; ☎ 512-457-0900; 900 Red River St) With its unmistakably royal neon sign, Club De Ville is a great place to go out to get a drink before going out to get drinks. It's a low-key spot, but with plenty of beautiful hipsters and a leafy outdoor patio.

Casino El Camino (Map pp58-9; ☎ 512-469-9330; 517 E 6th St) With a legendary jukebox and even better burgers, this is the spot for serious drinking and late-night carousing. If it's too dark inside, head for the back patio.

Lovejoy's (Map pp58-9; ☎ 512-477-1268; 604 Neches St) Basically a bar with an artsy coffeehouse vibe, it's a comfortable yet cool place to hang out. They've got a pool table, jukebox and draft beers brewed on site. Set 'em up on the coffin-shaped table if you're so inclined.

Copper Tank Brewing Company (Map pp58-9; ☎ 512-478-8444; 504 Trinity St) Hello, foosball. This Austin brewpub is a frat-boy hangout and boomingly loud sports bar that's a blast if that's the sort of thing you're after; good happy hours.

Maggie Mae's (Map pp58-9; ☎ 512-478-8541; 323-325 E 6th St) This is a very touristy spot, albeit with a wonderful beer selection and live music many weekend nights. Expect mostly cover bands doing tunes from decades you might rather forget.

Drawing a somewhat older and more moneyed crowd than E 6th St, the **Warehouse District** lies west of Congress Ave, mostly along 4th and 5th Sts. Here the **Bitter End** (p90) also makes its own beer, so stop by for a brew or two.

Red Fez (Map pp58-9; ☎ 512-478-5120; 209B W 5th St) Red Fez has a part-Manhattan, part-Middle East milieu and an updated 1960s vibe. There's almost always a line, as it trades on its trendiness with belly dancing, Arabian grooves and more. DJs may spin on the weekends.

Cuba Libre (Map pp58-9; ☎ 512-472-2822; 409 Colorado St) Next to the Alamo Drafthouse Cinema (p107), this tapas bar is definitely a place to see and be seen. Low-lit table lamps, leather seats and a sexy crowd at the door are fixtures. Beware the kitchen closes before 11pm.

Speakeasy (Map pp58-9; ☎ 512-476-8086; 412D Congress Ave) Once the hottest venue in town, this tri-level bar and nightclub has a rooftop terrace (and a side alley entrance). Enjoy a little bit of everything here: sunset happy hours (weekdays before 7pm) with a free food buffet, pool tables, plush booths, free salsa lessons and DJ dance nights.

Brown Bar (Map pp58-9; ☎ 512-480-8330; 201 W 8th St; ☺ 4pm-midnight Mon-Tue, 4pm-2am Wed-Fri, 5:30pm-2am Sat) Wait, is this LA? A total aberration in Austin, this upmarket bar serves premium martinis (how about one made with Godiva chocolate?). Most of the clientele are big-wig politicos, thirtysomethings who didn't lose their stocks in the dot-com bust or occasionally folks waiting for a table at Gumbo's restaurant (p89).

Apple Bar (Map pp58-9; ☎ 512-322-9291; 120 W 5th St; closed Mon) A swingin' newcomer, the Apple Bar will satiate all of those Adams and Eves who are tempted by luscious martinis and ambient DJ grooves. Still hungry? Across the street is Noodle-ism (p89).

The Ginger Man (Map pp58-9; ☎ 512-473-8801; 304 W 4th St) It's one of those increasingly rare long-runners in the Warehouse District, but still deservedly popular and not only for its world-class beer selection. It also has an outdoor beer garden.

Fadó (Map pp58-9; ☎ 512-457-0172; 214 W 4th St) An Irish-style pub chain, but there's nothing wrong with that when they've got boxties (stuffed, seasoned potato pancakes) on the menu and the rugby and footie games on satellite TV. Look for live music during the week, except on Monday's Quiz Night.

Opal Divine's Freehouse (Map pp58-9; ☎ 512-477-3308; 700 W 6th St) Named for the owner's grandmother, a woman who supposedly enjoyed 'good drink and a good card game,' this breezy and spacious pub is worth a detour to the happening 6th St and Lamar Blvd intersection. Microbrews, import lagers and almost 20 types of tequila are on hand.

And there are more spots elsewhere around downtown.

1920s Club (Map pp58-9; ☎ 512-479-7979; 918 Congress Ave) Drawing sophisticates to a largely down-at-the-heels area of north Congress Ave, this cavernous bar manages to create an intimate, even romantic mood. Occasionally there's live jazz or blues. The crowd tends to be predominantly but not exclusively gay.

Scholz Biergarten (Map pp58-9; ☎ 512-474-1958; 1607 San Jacinto Blvd) Near the capitol complex, this enormous 19th-century German pub was one of O Henry's hangouts back in the day. It's a low-key spot, and equally popular with politicians, UT students and European expats.

Dog & Duck Pub (Map pp58-9; ☎ 512-479-0598; 406 W 17th St) When you graduate from the Crown & Anchor (p105), you start hitting this Britishy place for its UK draft beers, single-malt scotch and pub grub like bangers and mash. They brag their jukebox plays anything from Frank Sinatra to heavy metal. The picnic tables out front always have a few folks hanging about, even early in the afternoon. Pints are all $2.50 on Tuesday. No mixed drinks.

For idiosyncratic and otherwise neighborly places, search out the second-floor outdoor terrace at the **Stephen F Austin Intercontinental** (p82); the classy bar at the romantic **Driskill Hotel** (p82); the glass atrium lounge at the **Omni Hotel** (p83); **Little Woodrow's on Sixth** (Map pp58-9; ☎ 512-477-2337; 520 W 6th St), an outpost of the Houston bar chain; and the stylish

Star Bar (Map pp58-9; ☎ 512-477-8550; 600 W 6th St), a good place to unwind.

AROUND AUSTIN

Most locals have a strange (and often inexplicable) attachment to dive bars that seem as if they've been around since before the Cold War. Inside, these scruffy places are too dark to even find your way around, let alone figure out just exactly what that sticky spot on the floor might be. Maybe that's a good thing, though. Wherever these dive bars are found, they're likely to be local institutions. Check out the following watering holes, which are arranged in order of their distance from downtown.

Shoal Creek Saloon (Map p91; ☎ 512-474-0805; 909 N Lamar Blvd) True to its name, this sports bar sits right on the Shoal Creek Greenbelt. If the breezy shoreline views aren't enough to draw you inside, consider the Cajun cooking and fried catfish, too.

The Tavern (Map p91; ☎ 512-474-7496; 922 W 12th St) A landmark that dates from the 1930s, the Tavern was recently renovated but still has its sign advertising 'Air Conditioned.' Ah, the conveniences of modern life. Look for a mountain chalet-style building standing at the corner of 12th St.

Ego's (Map p66-7; ☎ 512-474-7091; 510 S Congress Ave) In an apartment complex just south of the Congress Ave bridge, Ego's is a very mid-1970s lounge with live music and pool tables. It's dark as hell inside. Punk bands sometimes play for charity; the weekly poetry slam is on Wednesday night. Ask the bartender if you can borrow finger paints for the walls.

Crown & Anchor (Map pp68-9; ☎ 512-322-9168; 2911 San Jacinto Blvd) Gotta love this pub, with cheap beer and good, dirt-cheap hamburgers. It's a big UT undergrad scene. The bartenders have absolute authority over which CDs get played, so make any requests nicely.

Deep Eddy Cabaret (Map pp56-7; ☎ 512-472-0961; 2315 Lake Austin Blvd) In the wealthy Westlake neighborhood, it comes as a relief that this dive bar (originally a bait shop) has stuck around for over half a century. Crank up the jukebox, loaded with almost a thousand tunes in all genres. Across the road, the Magnolia Cafe (p97) is open 24 hours.

Dry Creek Saloon (Map pp56-7; ☎ 512-453-9244; 4812 Mt Bonnell Rd; closed Sun) It's a roadhouse survivor, and the sunset views of Lake Austin from the rooftop deck are just perfect. It's tricky to find, though; take 35th St west of MoPac, turn right on Balcones Rd, then left on Mt Bonnell Rd. Follow the road by turning right soon after, and after less than a mile, look for the saloon on your left. Cash only.

Hula Hut (Map pp56-7; ☎ 512-476-4852; 3826 Lake Austin Blvd) Way over in Westlake, this surf-style restaurant and bar has a capacious deck stretching out over Lake Austin. Too crowded? Step next door and get the same views at Mozart's Coffee Roasters (p98).

Ginny's Little Longhorn Saloon (Map pp56-7; ☎ 512-458-1813; 5434 Burnet Rd; closed Sun) This is one of those honky-tonk dive bars that Austinites love so very much. Live country

---

AND THE WINNERS ARE...

Obviously not everyone in Austin shares the same tastes. But many folks would agree with us about the following:

- Best Place to Hear More Bands than You Can Stand in One Night: Emo's (p101)
- Coolest Neon Sign: Red Eyed Fly (p101) and Club de Ville (p103)
- Most Likely Place for a Rastafarian Pride Parade: Flamingo Cantina (p103)
- Best Biker Bar with Live Blues: Joe's Generic Bar (p101)
- Best Carnivores' Hang-out on 6th St: Casino El Camino (p103)
- Best Recycling of a Musical Landmark Site: Threadgill's World Headquarters (p102)
- Most Historic Venue in the Warehouse District: Antone's (p101)
- Hottest Salsa and Merengue Bands: Miguel's La Bodega (p106)
- Coolest Underground Jazz Sessions: The Elephant Room (p102)
- Best Outdoor Spot for Dinner and a Live Show: Shady Grove Restaurant (p93)
- Most Authentic Country-and-Western Dance Hall: Broken Spoke (p106)
- Best Place to be on Tuesday Night: Hippie Happy Hour at the Continental Club (p103)
- Best Jukebox: Deep Eddy Cabaret (p105)

music is an occasional thing, but not to be missed when it does happen, especially local legend Dale Watson.

Carousel Lounge (Map pp56-7; ☎ 512-452-6790; 1110 E 52nd St) Almost in the middle of nowhere, this bar draws a whimsical mixture of rednecks, college kids, Elk and Moose lodge members and slackers. Everyone cavorts happily amid the circus-inspired décor, and there's frequently live music. If you're lucky, the bartender will do magic tricks. Local flavor? You bet.

Dance Clubs

Austin's dance-club scene isn't as developed as you'd think, probably because most of the potential clientele are out at live-music shows. There's incredibly high turnover in dance clubs – don't be surprised if some of these are gone or replaced with new ones when you visit. DJs can be fickle. The main areas to groove are the Warehouse District and 6th St. Pick up the free *Austin Chronicle* weekly for new listings. Dance divas should also check out Austin's gay and lesbian venues (pp58-9).

Texture (Map pp58-9; ☎ 512-480-8921; www.texture austin.com; 505 Neches St; ☽ 10pm-4am Thu-Sat, 9pm-1am Sun) After the 6th St scene winds down, head to Neches St. DJs from around Austin and both coasts spin here, with couches for lounging about and grooves you can't hear anywhere else, especially electronica. Queer-friendly.

Miguel's La Bodega (Map pp58-9; ☎ 512-472-2369; 415 Colorado St; ☽ 5pm-2am Wed-Sat) One of the most svelte spots in town, Miguel's has live salsa and merengue music. Chances are, you'll hear the band from outside before you can even find the place. Call to ask about free dance lessons. Wednesday is hip-hop night.

Element (Map pp58-9; ☎ 512-480-9888; 301 W 5th St; ☽ 9pm-3am Thu-Sat) One of the most urban dance clubs in town, this gargantuan space once throbbed with the beats of some of Austin's best DJs. The crowd is mostly young club kids these days, but you can still belly up to three (count 'em) bars.

Paradox (Map pp58-9; ☎ 512-469-7615; 311 E 5th St; ☽ 9pm-4am Wed-Sun) Slightly out-of-date, but with a big dance floor, Paradox does live radio broadcasts on local hip-hop and R&B stations. The crowd is mainly under 21 years old.

Of course, this *is* still Texas. Elsewhere around Austin you'll find a few country music and Tejano dance halls, but not nearly as many as in San Antonio.

Broken Spoke (Map pp56-7; ☎ 512-442-6189; 3201 S Lamar Blvd; ☽ live music Tues-Sat evenings) The Broken Spoke is country-and-western nirvana – a smallish but nonetheless totally authentic (down to the pitchers of Pearl) Texas dance hall that's been in business since 1964. The restaurant also serves barbecue and chicken-fried steaks. Look for the big ol' oak tree out front.

Dallas Nightclub (Map pp56-7; ☎ 512-452-2801; 7113 Burnet Rd; ☽ 5pm-2am Tues-Sun) Austin's mainstream country-and-western dance destination can be a very social place, especially on Wednesday nights when longneck beers and well drinks are just 69¢. There are free dance lessons nightly at 7pm, and no cover for ladies on Saturday nights.

Austin's major Tejano scene can often be tracked down at **Club Carnaval** (Map pp56-7; ☎ 512-444-6396; 2237 E Riverside Dr, cnr Willow Creek Dr; ☽ 7pm-2am Fri-Sun) and the **Tejano Ranch** (Map pp56-7; ☎ 512-453-6615; 7601 N Lamar Blvd; ☽ closed Mon).

Gay & Lesbian Venues

Austin's gay and lesbian club scene is mainly in the Warehouse District, though there are outposts elsewhere. **Texture** and other dance clubs are gay-friendly, as are a few bars and pubs such as the **1920s Club** (p104)

Rainbow Cattle Company (Map pp58-9; ☎ 512-472-5288; www.rainbowcattleco.com; 305 W 5th St; ☽ 3pm-2am daily, from 2pm Sun) Yee-haw! This place has country-and-western music, shirtless bartenders, lots of cowboy hats and an enormous dance floor. At presstime, Thursday was ladies' night from 10pm onward. Show up on Tuesday for beginners' dance lessons or Sunday for advanced classes. There's often Tejano, salsa and merengue music on weekends.

Oilcan Harry's (Map pp58-9; ☎ 512-320-8823; www.oilcanharrys.com; 211 W 4th St; ☽ 2pm-late) With a garden-esque patio out back and the Momma's Boyz strippers on stage every weekend, this place wins many votes for the best gay bar award. Inside, things sometimes resemble a mosh pit – so crowded that you can't move – but with beautiful boys. Unwind at the bar with drink specials all week long.

AUSTIN

Boyz Cellar (Map pp58-9; ☎ 512-479-8482; 213 W 4th St; ✹ 3pm-late) This is another male bastion, as the name implies, and there's rarely a cover charge. Almost any excuse for a party will do here – midnight drag shows, midweek bi/curious parties and amateur strip contests that walk that fine line between outrageous and merely campy. Gurlz Cellar, a lesbian lounge, is usually on Tuesday nights.

The Forum (Map pp58-9; ☎ 512-476-2900; 408 Congress Ave; ✹ 4pm-2am) The Forum changes, but keeps up with the times. A mostly male, upscale crowd always has plenty of fun on the tropical rooftop patio. Wednesday's Lipstick Lounge is for amateur drag shows and special guest appearances. Call to check if women still take over the joint on '80s-themed Monday nights.

Club Skirt (www.austinclubskirt.org; suggested donation $10-15) Although lesbians don't have any bars in Austin to call their own, Club Skirt nights happen about once a month, usually at Fiesta Gardens or the Zilker Park Clubhouse, with dance-driven DJs, crazy themes and all profits to benefit local community and activist organizations. No, you don't have to wear a skirt.

Charlie's (Map pp58-9; ☎ 512-474-6481; 1301 Lavaca St; ✹ 2pm-2am) Up near the state capitol, Charlie's is the oldest gay bar in town. Friendly staff, a laid-back atmosphere, pool tables, $5 steak nights and free parking are just some of the perks. On some nights DJs spin progressive house music. There's a moon-view patio, too.

Chain Drive (Map pp58-9; ☎ 512-480-9017; 504 Willow St; ✹ until 2am) Hidden away on a side street by Town Lake, the Chain Drive isn't nearly as menacing as it sounds, guys. Austin's tame leather and Levis scene relies on this bar.

Comedy Clubs

Esther's Follies (Map pp58-9; ☎ 512-320-0553; www.esthersfollies.com; 525 E 6th St; tickets $16-18; ✹ shows Thu-Sat) It's run for over 25 years now, and everyone in town says this is funny and worth seeing – it's mainly a satire of current events, movies and the like. They call it 'all the news that's fit to parody.' On-site Esther's Pool showcases local and national touring acts, from magicians to hip-hop comedy shows.

Velveeta Room (Map pp58-9; ☎ 512-469-9116; www.thevelveetaroom.com; 521 E 6th St; cover varies) Next door to Esther's Follies, in what was formerly a cheesy (Velveeta, get it?) topless bar, this 6th St storefront space books stand-up comics, improv teams and other acts. Late on Thursday night Notorious Open Mic is a cut-throat competition of local talent. The website makes for amusing reading.

Hideout Coffee House & Theatre (Map pp58-9 ☎ 512-443-3688; www.heroescomedy.com; 617 Congress Ave; tickets $5-10; ✹ shows usually Thu-Sat) The hipsters' Hideout is a small coffeehouse/ theater space that rubs shoulders with the big theaters on Congress Ave. Shows here features live improv with plenty of audience participation. Performances by the National Comedy Theatre (www.comedy7.com) are

---

AUTHOR'S CHOICE

Ah, to enjoy a cold brewski, turkey sandwich and some jalapeño-cheese poppers during a flick. Is it only a dream? Not when Austinites enjoy the divine **Alamo Drafthouse Cinemas** (☎ 512-476-1320; www.drafthouse.com). These movie houses show mostly independent and classic film fare and serve lots of great food and drinks. Waitstaff inside the theater take your order, then deliver it right to your seat. (After the house lights go down, you'll need to write down your order on the white piece of paper provided, fold it up and then wave it around a bit to get the staff's attention.) Before the movie ends, they'll drop off your check; you can pay by cash or credit card.

Catch movies rarely seen anywhere else at the original **Alamo Drafthouse Downtown** (Map pp58-9; 409 Colorado St; tickets around $6). Its dizzying film schedule constantly changes, sometimes at the speed of blink-and-you-miss-it. Most popular screenings, like midnight movies, old silent films (with a live sound effects crew!) or *Mr Sinus Theater 3000*, where improv comics poke fun at bad B-movies, sell out days beforehand. Advance tickets are only available for purchase online. More mainstream new releases are screened at the **Alamo Drafthouse Village** (Map pp56-7; Village Shopping Center, 2700 W Anderson Lane; adult/student & senior $7/5, before 6pm and all day Mon $5).

clean enough for kids. The box office usually opens a half hour before showtime.

Capitol City Comedy Club (Map pp56-7; ☎ 512-467-2333; www.capcitycomedy.com; 8120 Research Blvd, ste 100; ticket prices vary; shows 8pm Sun-Thu, 8pm & 10:30pm Fri & Sat) Far from downtown, Capitol City hosts national headliner comics. Mondays are often reserved for local talent. Check the website for discount coupons and details about half-price admission nights.

Cinema

Check the free *Austin Chronicle* weekly for movie reviews and cinema showtimes. The **Austin Film Society** (AFS; ☎ 512-322-0145; www.austinfilm.org) has frequent classic and independent film screenings (often free for members) at venues around town. *Slacker* director Richard Linklater was an early promoter and Quentin Tarantino is now on the board of directors. During the summer, **CinemaTexas** (☎ 512-471-6497; www.cinematexasorg), an international short film festival, features a competition for movies made of live music performances from around the world. Also look for the **Austin Film Festival** (p81) in the fall.

IMAX Theatre (Map pp58-9; ☎ schedule 512-936-8746 , 866-369-7108 ext 4, advance tickets 512-936-4649; 1800 Congress Ave; adult/child $9/4.50) Housed at the Bob Bullock Texas State History Museum, this state-of-the-art IMAX cinema is only a few years old. Combined discounts with museum entry are offered if you want to make an entire day of it. There's no surcharge for purchasing advance tickets by phone.

Dobie Theatre (Map pp68-9; ☎ 512-472-3456; www.landmarktheatre.com; Dobie Mall, 2025 Guadalupe St; 5-ticket discount card $28) Part of the Landmark chain, the Dobie is a four-screen venue for independent, foreign language and other off-beat films. First takes for *Slacker* were shown here, as was the premier of Linklater's next effort, *Dazed and Confused*. Each theater has its own unique decor, from faux-French to Gothic gargoyle. There's free parking in the Dobie Garage at Whitis and 20th Sts, just east of the mall.

Regal Westgate Stadium 11 (☎ 512-899-2717; 4477 S Lamar Blvd, cnr E Ben White Blvd; tickets $5.50-8) Most of the city's shopping malls have cinemas with the usual Hollywood offerings, but Regal sets itself apart with a mix of mainstream and arthouse films shown on nearly a dozen screens.

Texas Union (Map pp68-9; ☎ 24hr events hotline 512-475-6666; 24th & Guadalupe Sts) On the UT campus, the student union occasionally schedules free movies. Expect anything from French film retrospectives to blast-from-the-past '80s flicks like *Ghostbusters*.

Billiards, Bowling & Mini-Golf

Plenty of other bars and pubs have a few pool tables, too.

Buffalo Billiards (Map pp58-9; ☎ 512-479-7665; 201 E 6th St; ⊙ until 2am) Calling itself an 'atomic cowboy lounge,' this 19th-century boarding house (and presumably ex-brothel) is now an always busy bar. There are pool and billiards tables, darts, foosball, cigars, beers and wine, all on a prime stretch of 6th St.

The Ritz (Map pp58-9; ☎ 512-474-2270; 320 E 6th St; ⊙ until 2am) In an old movie theater, this punk, skater and all-around slacker hangout is one of the cheapest places for pool, foosball, air hockey and pinball (plus a jukebox), along with occasional live music or indie film screenings in the upstairs lounge.

Union Underground (Map pp68-9; ☎ 512-475-6670; Texas Union, 24th & Guadalupe Sts; bowling per person from $2.50; ⊙ 10am-midnight daily, till 2am Fri-Sat, from 11:30am Sun) On the UT campus, this family-friendly underground bowling alley has a dozen lanes and pool tables. Students and even professors show up for 'Glow Bowl' – blacklight, lasers and rockin' tunes – usually held on Thursday to Saturday nights and also Sunday afternoons. Look for video arcade games, air hockey and pinball, too.

Peter Pan Mini-Golf (Map pp66-7; ☎ 512-472-1033; 1207 Barton Springs Rd; 18/36 holes $5/7; ⊙ 11am-11pm Mon-Sat, 9am-10pm Sun) At this wacky Austin landmark, giant dinosaurs and other concrete-and-fiberglass characters loom large (including Peter Pan himself) over the aging greens of both 18-hole courses. It's close to Zilker Park.

Dart Bowl (Map pp56-7; ☎ 512-452-2518; 5700 Grover Lane; bowling per person from $3; 9:30am-11:30pm daily, till 1:30am Fri-Sat) This classic Austin bowling alley belongs to a different era (the shag-carpeted 1970s, to be precise). A steakhouse at the back serves seriously good hangover fare, and even bakes its own bread. Look for retro bowling memorabilia in the lobby display cases. Kids are always welcome.

Warehouse Saloon & Billiards (Map pp56-7; ☎ 512-443-8799; 509 E Ben White Blvd; discounted table rental $3 11am-4pm weekdays, ladies play free Mon; ☺ 11am-2am) A sports bar and pool hall on Austin's outskirts is where you'll find Brunswick Gold Crown tables, plus weekly pool and foosball tournaments. They've even got phones at every table hooked straight to the bar, for ordering drinks while you play. There's a free happy hour buffet some nights.

Performing Arts

Austin's performing arts scene doesn't rival other US cities, but the number of national and touring troupes that stop off in the Capitol City is astonishing. Some of the venues are historic, like the downtown Paramount Theatre, or merely beautiful, like the outdoor theatre in Zilker Park. Thanks to the region's mild climate, performances often run year-round.

CLASSICAL MUSIC, DANCE & OPERA

The outdoor **Zilker Hillside Theater** hosts Mexican *ballet folklorico*, classical symphony and orchestral concerts, too. All performances are free, but event parking costs $2.

Austin Symphony (Map pp58-9; ☎ 512-476-6064, 888-462-3787; www.austinsymphony.org; Jeremiah Hamilton Bldg, Symphony Square, 1101 Red River St; tickets $20-35; ☺ box office 9am-5pm Mon-Fri, also noon-5pm Sat on performance days) Founded in the early 20th century, the city's oldest performing arts group plays classical and pops music at numerous venues throughout the city. The main performance season runs from September to April. There's a July 4th concert at Zilker Park, a free outdoor summer concert series and a Halloween Children's Concert at the Paramount Theatre.

Performing Arts Center (Map pp68-9; ☎ 512-477-6060; www.utpac.org; E 23rd St & Robert Dedman Dr; tickets $10-55; ☺ box office noon-6pm Mon-Fri) The UT campus arts center plays host to a sweeping array of music, opera and dance touring events each year. Venues include Bass Concert Hall and Bates Recital Hall on the east side of campus and Hogg Auditorium near the UT Tower.

Ballet Austin (Map pp68-9; ☎ information 512-476-2163; www.balletaustin.org; 3004 Guadalupe St; ☺ box office 10am-6pm Mon-Fri, noon-3pm Sat) Performing at Bass Concert Hall on the UT campus and the Paramount Theatre downtown,

the city's ballet company is especially beloved for its Nutcracker recitals during the Christmas holidays.

Austin Lyric Opera (☎ 512-472-5992, 800-316-7372; www.austinlyricopera.org; 901 Barton Springs Rd; tickets from $25; ☺ box office 9am-5pm Mon-Fri) This fledging opera company performs mostly at Bass Concert Hall on the UT campus. Expect international operas and a few foreign singers, too.

THEATER

Austin has a small, but active theater scene at venues all over town. Check the *Austin Chronicle* or *XLent* for performance schedules. Some of the best theaters include:

Paramount Theatre (Map pp58-9; ☎ 512-472-2901; www.austintheatrealliance.org; 713 Congress Ave; ☺ box office noon-5:30pm Mon-Sat) Dating from 1915, this old vaudevillian house has staged everything from the Ziegfeld Follies to splashy Broadway shows.

State Theater (Map pp58-9; ☎ 512-472-2901; www.austintheatrealliance.org; 719 Congress Ave) On the same block as the Paramount, this is a major venue for classic and contemporary plays. Tickets are sold through the Paramount Theatre's box office.

Zilker Hillside Theater (Map pp66-7; ☎ 512-479-9491; www.ci.austin.tx.us/dougherty/hillside.htm; off Barton Springs Rd; sliding-scale admission, event parking $2) Having celebrated its 45th anniversary season, the nonprofit **Zilker Theatre Productions** (www.zilker.org) performs popular musicals on some summer evenings starting around 8pm. Show up early and bring a picnic; people start reserving spots with blankets from 6pm onward.

Zachary Scott Theatre Center (Map pp66-7; ☎ 512-476-0541 www.zachscott.com; 1510 Toomey Rd; ☺ box office noon-7pm Mon-Sat) Named after an Austin movie star, the center produces classical and classic dramas along with contemporary experimental works at two locations – the **Arena Stage** (1510 Toomey Rd) and the **Kleberg Stage** (1421 W Riverside Drive).

Dougherty Arts Center (Map pp66-7; ☎ 512-397-1471; www.ci.austin.tx.us/dougherty/theater.htm; 1110 Barton Springs Rd) The 150-seat theater is home to many small visual and performing arts groups, including Naughty Austin Productions and Different Stages Inc.

Mary Moody Northern Theatre (Map pp56-7; MMNT; ☎ 512-448-8484; www.stedwards.edu/hum/thtr/mmnt.html; 3001 S Congress Ave) St Edward's University has the country's only undergraduate Actor's Equity program, with a variety of contemporary works and modern classics performed on its stage.

Hyde Park Theatre (Map pp68-9; ☎ 512-479-7529; 511 W 43rd St) This diversified community theater often premieres new plays, and it also puts on Fronterafest, an annual fringe theater competition with over 800 participants.

Spectator Sports

Athletic events at the **University of Texas** are the big games in town, especially the football season, which lasts from about September to November. For tickets to any university-sponsored sporting event, contact the **UT ticket office** (Map pp68-9; ☎ 512-471-3333, 800-982-2386) in the first-floor lobby of Belmont Hall. Tickets for 2003 Longhorns football games ranged from $35 to $75; see www.hookem.com for complete coverage. Held in early April the **Texas Relays** is a high-profile track-and-field event (it's also a major excuse for UT students and out-of-town visitors to get together and party all weekend long). To be one of the event's 50,000 attendees, buy an all-session pass for $15 or scramble for one-day tickets (some are free). Also keep an eye out around campus for the H2hos, a feminist synchronized swimming team. Visit www.texassports.com for information about all UT athletics.

Catch minor league baseball action with the **Round Rock Express** (☎ 512-255-2255; www.roundrockexpress.com; Dell Diamond, 3400 E Palm Valley, Round Rock; tickets $5-9; regular season Apr-Aug). Started only a few years ago by baseball legend Nolan Ryan's son, this Texas League team has already broken AA attendance records. Half-price cold beer every Thursday and fireworks on Friday nights must be at least partly responsible. Save a little cash by bringing a blanket and sitting on the grass. To get here, take I-35 north to exit 253, then drive 3-1/2½miles east on US 79.

Ice hockey in Texas? You'd better believe it. The minor league **Austin Ice Bats** (☎ 512-927-7825; www.icebats.com; 7311 Decker Lane, off US 290 E; tickets $10-30; regular season Oct-Mar) play at the Travis Country Exposition Center, just a 10-mile drive northeast of downtown Austin.

One of Texas' oldest racetracks, **Manor Downs** (☎ 512-272-5581; www.manordowns.com; 9211 Hill Lane, off US 290 E; admission $1-5) hosts live quarterhorse and thoroughbred racing a few times in the spring. It's about a half-hour's drive from central Austin to Manor, the town where the track is located.

SHOPPING

Not many folks visit Austin just to shop. That said, music, of course, is a huge industry here, and if it's alt-country, indie rock, punk or anything else you crave, you'll find heaps of it – and priced much less than you'd expect – in Austin's record stores. Vintage is a lifestyle, and the city's best hunting grounds for retro fashions and furnishings are South Austin and Guadalupe St near the UT campus. Up-and-coming clothes designers have storefronts around the West End and also in South Austin. This being Texas, cowboy hats and western wear are tempting buys everywhere. Antiques and art galleries are stashed in various offbeat spots around town. On the first Thursday of the month, South Congress Ave (SoCo) is definitely the place to be, when stores stay open until 10pm and there's live entertainment, maybe punk bands or skateboarding competitions; visit www.firstthursday.info for upcoming events. For a list of bookshops, see p55.

Music

Music is tops on the list of things to buy in Austin, and record-shop employees are as knowledgeable, if not more so, than most you'll find in other cities. The best stores let you listen to just about anything before you buy; they also sell CDs or cassettes recorded by many of the same bands you'll see around town, including at free in-store shows.

Waterloo Records (Map p91; ☎ 512-474-2500; www.waterloorecords.com; 600A N Lamar Blvd; 10am-11pm Mon-Sat, 11am-11pm Sun) Waterloo is a landmark and the best music store in town, with a huge selection and low prices on new and used CDs and vinyl. There are sections reserved just for local bands and listening stations featuring Texas, indie and alt-country acts. In-store live shows send lines around the block, even past Amy's Ice Creams (p90).

Antone's Records (Map pp68-9; ☎ 512-322-0660; www.antones.com; 2928 Guadalupe St; 11am-10pm Mon-Sat, noon-5pm Sun) North of UT, legendary Antone's was founded in 1972 and has a well-respected selection of Austin, Texas and American blues music (with plenty of rare vinyl), plus a bulletin board for musicians and vintage concert posters for sale.

Jupiter Records (Map pp68-9; ☎ 512-454-5678; Hancock Center, 1000 E 41st St; until midnight) This musical galaxy east of campus is populated by every genre, from alt-country to ska to electronica, in both CD and vinyl form. Super-friendly staff are eager to make recommendations, and even Bob Dylan approved of the stock found here. Listening stations have lounge chairs, and there are free live shows (and beer!) on most Friday nights.

33° Records (Map pp68-9; ☎ 512-302-5233; 4017 Guadalupe St; www.thirtythreedegrees.com; ☉ 11am-10pm Mon-Sat, noon-5pm Sun) Punk, funk, '60s psychedelia, experimental music, garage, goth and that elusive Austin sound are all found at this anticorporate music haven north of the Drag. There's plenty of rare vinyl, indie music collectibles and 'zines, too.

Cheapo Discs & DVDs (Map p91; ☎ 512-477-4499; 914 N Lamar Blvd; ☉ 9am-midnight) Though not as much of a bargain as the name suggests, it does have racks of used CDs, including Texas and alt-country music. Free in-store performances are often scheduled for the first Friday of the month.

Alien Records (Map p91; ☎ 512-477-3909; 5th Street Market, 1114 W 5th St; ☉ noon-9pm Mon-Sat) Alien is a DJ's nirvana for esoteric vinyl and CDs, both new and used. Various shades of trance, jungle, drum 'n bass, trip-hop and hip-hop are enough to satisfy any auteur. Flyers for raves and DJ events can be picked up by the entrance.

Clothing & Shoes
FASHION

By George (Map p91; ☎ 512-472-5951; 524 N Lamar Blvd; ☉ 10am-8pm Mon-Sat, noon-6pm Sun) For both men and women, this is *the* place for hip new designs without the fussy attitude of ultra-exclusive boutiques. By George also sells shoes, jewelry and handbags. Prices can be sky-high, so try to hit the semi-annual sales, usually held in January and July.

Emeralds (Map p91; ☎ 512-476-4496; 624 N Lamar Blvd; ☉ 10am-9pm Mon-Sat, noon-7pm Sun) Almost a mini-department store for trendy women, Emeralds sells racks of spirited clothes that instead of being separated by designer are grouped together by color. You'll also find jewelry by Texas artisans, handbags and oh, the shoes.

Fetish (Map p91; ☎ 512-457-1007; 1112 N Lamar Blvd; ☉ 10am-7pm Mon-Sat, noon-5pm Sun) Look no further for those svelte skirts, jeweled heels and other romantic fashion confections. Ignore the snooty staff (they'll probably ignore you first) and concentrate instead on catching that great find, maybe something in silk or scarlet.

Blackmail (Map pp66-7; ☎ 512-376-7670; 1202 S Congress Ave; ☉ 10:30am-6pm Tue-Sat) It's an unabashed celebration of the color that unites goth, punks and urban sophisticates. That means gorgeous black dresses and *guayabera* shirts, black-and-silver jewelry, black beaded handbags, black shoes and even minimalist black-and-white home decor.

Pink (Map pp66-7; ☎ 512-447-2888; 1204 S Congress Ave; ☉ 10am-6pm Tue-Fri, 10am-5pm Sat) Right next door but at the opposite end of the color spectrum is Pink, an inspired combination of a beauty parlor and a clothing shop. There's a small boutique with fashions by local designers up front, and chairs for an up-do at the back.

Flipnotics (Map pp66-7; ☎ 512-322-9011; 1603 Barton Springs Rd; ☉ 11am-8pm Mon-Sat, noon-6pm Sun) Downstairs from Flipnotics coffeehouse (pXXX), this 'clothespad' even employs aspiring designers, who may be seen behind the counter whipping up their newest creations. Sassy, faux-vintage wear is the order of the day. They also sell handbags, jewelry and – it's bizarre, but true – barista action figures.

Gomi (Map pp66-7; ☎ 512-442-9977; 1313 Congress Ave; ☉ call for hours) The name means 'trash' in Japanese, but the clothes are anything but at this ultra-hip South Austin shop. Gomi's motto ('the cure for mundane living') says it all. Urban styles play up the sex kitten side of life, with daring dresses, faux fur coats and spiky heels.

Creatures (Map pp66-7; ☎ 512-707-2500; 1905B S 1st St; ☉ 10am-6pm) One of the many off-beat boutiques on this stretch of 1st St, Creatures carries bath products from California, shoes made by John Fluevog, artisan handbags and clothes wispy enough to keep you cool on a Texas-hot summer day. Its other branch is in the unique North Loop neighborhood (Map pp56-7; ☎ 512-453-6505; 106 E North Loop Blvd; ☉ same hours).

Pangaea Trading Company (Map pp68-9; ☎ 512-472-3533; 2712 Guadalupe St; ☉ 11am-6pm) Good clothes can be hard to find on the Drag, but one stop that's sure to warm your heart is Pangaea. Unique and affordable

AUSTIN

clothing, shoes and jewelry designs from around the world find their way here. Staff are very personable.

Legs Diamond (Map pp68-9; ☎ 512-477-1559; 2430 Guadalupe St; ☺ 11am-9pm Mon-Sat, noon-6pm Sun) Named after a movie star gangster, this off-kilter store carries clothing, but the main squeeze is shoes of all kinds, from big brands like Doc Martens and Sketchers to dainty little Cinderella-esque heels.

Cutting-edge boutiques lease storefront space at South Austin's **SoCo Center** (Map pp66-7; 1113 S Congress Ave).

VINTAGE, USED & DISCOUNT
Some of South Austin's antiques stores, including **Uncommon Objects** (p113) and **New Bohemia** (p113), also sell vintage clothing.

Electric Ladyland (Map pp66-7; ☎ 512-444-2002; 1506 S Congress Ave; ☺ 11am-7pm Mon-Sat, noon-5pm Sun) It's a legendary place to find zebra lounge pants, rhinestone jewels, swing-dancing jackets or anything else you could think of. Although most of the high-priced vintage duds are rented out as costumes and movie props, it's OK to just browse and marvel.

Amelia's Retrovogue & Relics (Map pp66-7; ☎ 512-442-4446; 2024 S Lamar Blvd; ☺ 11am-5pm Tues-Sat) Austin's queen of vintage high fashion, Amelia's brings together *Vogue*-worthy dresses, retro '50s bathing suits and other old-school glamour for both men and women. It's a favorite with film industry folks.

Although it's no longer a bargain-priced nirvana, the Drag is still a decent place to find good vintage wear and used clothing.

Blue Velvet (Map pp68-9; ☎ 512-472-9399; 2100 Guadalupe St; ☺ 11:30am-8pm Mon-Sat, noon-5pm Sun) Western wear, vintage T-shirts and even oddities like all-American bowling wear hang on the racks at Blue Velvet, where you'll find an equal number of men and women eyeing the goods. Summer fashions are stocked year-round.

Buffalo Exchange (Map pp68-9; 512-480-9922; 2904 Guadalupe St; ☺ 11am-8pm Mon-Sat, noon-6pm Sun) The Austin branch of this nationwide used clothing store chain has an impressive selection of vintage clothes and shoes for both men and women, including Texas styles and Western wear. A retro T-shirt matched with a simple skirt or jeans will instantly achieve that alternative Austin look, y'all.

Nieman Marcus' Last Call (Map pp56-7; ☎ 512-447-0701; Brodie Oaks Shopping Center, 4115 S Capital of Texas Hwy; ☺ 10am-6pm Mon-Tues, 10am-7:30pm Wed-Sat, noon-6pm Sun) Austinites flock to this discount store run by the famous Nieman Marcus department store chain. Top designer fashions for men, women and children are sometimes marked 75% off.

Bargain shoppers may also want to visit the **factory outlets** at San Marcos and New Braunfels.

WESTERN WEAR
Capitol Saddlery (Map pp58-9; ☎ 512-478-9309; 1614 Lavaca St; ☺ open Mon-Sat) With its modest exterior, this family-owned business is almost an anachronism in the downtown arts district, but it's where true Texas spirit shines. They make custom leather boots and sell belt buckles and horse blankets.

DETOUR: BUDA
Twenty minutes outside the city lies the antiques mecca of Buda, just a blip on the map. It's best visited on a Saturday morning or afternoon. From Austin, take I-35 south over a dozen miles to exit 221 (Loop 4), then drive west over the railroad tracks into town. At the intersection with Buda's only stoplight, the **1898 Store** (☺ 11am-6pm Sat-Sun) is an old-fashioned general store selling kitchen goods, hardware and other curiosities. Inside the town's original drugstore, **Memory Lane Antiques** (300 N Main St; ☺ 10am-5pm Mon-Sat, noon-5pm Sun) is known for American folk art, quilts and collectibles. For lunch, stop by the old **Buda Grocery** (☎ 512-295-2151; 100 N Main St; ☺ open daily) for fried chicken ($5) or **Yogi's Bar-B-Que** (☎ 512-750-7300; 306 S Main St; meals from $5), where they claim Elvis once ate. Head back to I-35, then drive south to exit 220. Turn left, cross over the interstate and on the east frontage road look for legendary **Texas Hatters** (☎ 512-295-4287; www.texashatters.com; 5003 Overpass Rd; ☺ 9:30am-5:30am Tues-Sat). Their hand-blocked cowboy hats have been worn by the likes of Stevie Ray Vaughan and Willie Nelson; custom designs start at $60.

AUSTIN

Allen's Boots (Map pp66-7; ☎ 512-447-1413; 1522 S Congress Ave; ⏱ 9am-8pm Mon-Sat, noon-6pm Sun) Another aberration, this time in hip South Austin, family-owned Allen's sells rows upon rows of traditional cowboy boots for ladies, gents and kids. A basic pair costs from $50, while somethin' fancy runs a few hundred dollars.

Vertigo (Map pp68-9; ☎ 512-476-1203; 2002 Guadalupe St; ⏱ 11:30am-6pm Mon-Thu, 11:30am-7pm Fri-Sat, 1-6pm Sun) It's an institution for cowboy hats on the Drag. Let the owner help you find your own personal style, then customize the hat: paint it purple, tattoo it or add a wild brim, it's all up to you.

In North Austin, **Shepler's** ☎ 512-454-3000; 6001 Middle Fiskville Rd, just south of Highland Mall) and **Cavender's Boot City** (Map pp56-7; ☎ 512-451-7474; 8809 Burnet Rd) are giant chains for western wear of all kinds.

Art & Antiques

For a complete list of art galleries and happenings around town, visit www.inthegalleriesaustin.com, or pick up an 'In the Galleries' fold-out brochure at any gallery. Many evening events are scheduled for the 'First Saturday' of the month.

Women & Their Work (Map pp58-9; ☎ 512-477-1064; 1710 Lavaca St; ⏱ 9am-5pm Mon-Fri, noon-4pm Sat) Around the corner from the Guadalupe Arts Center, this art gallery and artisan gift shop spotlights new and emerging female artists. It's a delight just to wander through, and exhibitions change frequently.

In South Austin, **SoCo** has its share of folk and fine arts galleries. But it's also known for vintage antiques shops, which sell all sorts of 20th-century collectibles and odds and ends.

Uncommon Objects (Map pp66-7; ☎ 512-442-4000; 1512 S Congress Ave; ⏱ 11am-6pm daily, till 7pm Fri-Sat) 'Curious oddities' is what they advertise. A variety of individual stalls inside reveal vintage cowboy duds, art nouveau baubles, estate jewelry and quirky 1950's nostalgia items. If you can't find it here, you won't find it anywhere else.

New Bohemia (Map pp66-7; ☎ 512-326-1238; 1606 S Congress Ave; ⏱ noon-10pm) What they like to call 'funky junk from all eras' is sold here. It's really a cosmic garage sale of clothing, toys and kitschy décor aimed at a younger crowd. Get your 'Someone in Austin *&£!ing Hates Me' T-shirts here.

Off the Wall (Map pp66-7; ☎ 512-445-4701; 1704 S Congress Ave; ⏱ 10am-6:30pm Mon-Sat, noon-6pm Sun) Stocking both flea market-type stuff and very good vintage wares, this antiques shop charges less than the SoCo norm. The low-key owner is quite knowledgeable.

Rue's Antiques (Map pp66-7; ☎ 512-442-1775; 1500 S Congress Ave; ⏱ 10am-6pm daily, from noon Sun) Rue's has an odd mixture of antiques and reproductions, along with folkcraft from around the Southwest and Mexico. The ever-changing inventory may include vintage political buttons, rustic pottery or art deco lamps.

Roadhouse Relics (Map pp66-7; ☎ 512-442-6636; 1720 S 1st St; ⏱ call for hours) This studio re-creates vintage neon and metal sign art, the type you'd see along Route 66 or at a dusty old roadhouse on the Texas plains. The walk-through gallery is like being transported back to the 1930s and '40s.

Austin Found (Map pp66-7; ⏱ 512-383-1234; 2050 S Lamar Blvd; ⏱ 10am-6pm Tue-Sun) The real genius of this house is that its cluttered front yard lures shoppers inside, where they'll find Texas antiques and off-beat vintage galore. There are more secondhand shops nearby on South Lamar Blvd.

Room Service (Map pp56-7; ☎ 512-451-1057; 107 E North Loop Blvd; ⏱ 11am-5:30pm Mon-Sat, noon-5pm Sun) Whether your style is '70s moon chairs or art nouveau fainting couches, it's the most fabulous place in the city for vintage furnishings. Plenty of smaller (and more

---

MUSEUM MARKETPLACES

Many of Austin's museums (big and small) have gift shops that are gold mines, whether you're on the hunt for Lone Star-emblazoned souvenirs, Mexican folk art or rare reproductions of 19th-century antiques for your grandmother's kitchen. The **Capitol Visitors Center** (p62) and **Bob Bullock Texas State History Museum** (p63) have Texas-themed gift shops right downtown. Now if only they could figure out a way to box up that lip-smackin' Texas barbecue, we'd be in heaven! For distinctive gifts, try browsing at the **Mexic-Arte Museum** (p63) and **French Legation Museum** (p63). Meanwhile, science geeks of all ages will be tempted to spend some dough at the **Texas Memorial Museum** (p70).

portable) stuff is for sale, like gobstopping ashtrays, silk kimonos and more.

Flatbed Press & Gallery 106 (Map pp56-7; ☎ 512-477-9328; 2830 E MLK Jr Blvd; ⏰ 10am-6pm Tues-Fri, 10am-5pm Sat) The main gallery space belongs to Flatbed Press, which sells stimulating original prints by local artists. Wonderful but small, Gallery 106 (☎ 512-472-1219) gives free exhibition space to Cuban artists, promoting international arts and cultural exchange.

Fire Island (Map pp56-7; ☎ 512-389-1100; 3401 E 4th St; ⏰ 9am-4pm Tue-Sat) This East Austin studio opens its doors for glass-blowing demonstrations on Saturday mornings from March until May and again from September through January. Its gallery shop is open year-round.

Austin Antiques Center (Map pp56-7; ☎ 512-459-5900; 8822 McCann Rd; ⏰ 10am-6pm) Several dozen vendors deal in just about everything at this mini-mall, including Mexican antiques, kitschy collectibles, old Texas license plates and even jewelry and hats in the style of Lady Bird Johnson circa 1965.

Gifts
Pick up Texas wildflower seeds, gardening gear or naturalist guides from the gift shops at the **Zilker Botanical Gardens** (p65) and the **Lady Bird Johnson Wildflower Center** (p72). There's also a gift gallery at **Mitchie's Black Fine Art** (p55).

Bydee Art Gallery (Map pp58-9; ☎ 512-474-4343; 412 E 6th St; ⏰ 11am-10pm Tue-Thu, 11am-11pm Fri-Sat, noon-6pm Sun) Here, amid the shot bars and tattoo parlors of 6th St, is a small shop that sells cool stuff promoting racial unity, literacy, drug abuse prevention and other worthy aims.

Tesoros Trading Co (Map pp58-9; ☎ 512-479-8377; 209 Congress Ave; ⏰ 10am-6pm) This store stocks a fun mother lode of kitsch and iconographic crap-a-roonie, like evil-eye key chains, risqué greeting cards and Chairman Mao hats. They also sell high-quality Central American folkcraft like El Día de Los Muertos dolls, jewelry and hand-painted kites. At the back they hide an exceptional selection of art books.

Wild About Music (Map pp58-9; ☎ 512-708-1700; 721 Congress Ave; ⏰ 11am-7pm Mon-Sat, noon-6pm Sun) Found in the downtown theater block, this store features art and gifts inspired by music and musicians, everything from caps,

T-shirts and bumper stickers to Elvis cookie jars and handcrafted CD racks.

Especially for Kids
Traveling with kids? Or only a child at heart yourself? Start shopping at the stores mentioned in the special 'Austin for Children' section (p76). Then try these:

Dragonsnaps (Map pp66-7; ☎ 512-445-4497; 1700 S Congress Ave; ⏰ 10am-6pm daily, from noon Sun) Presided over by a jolly green dragon, this kids' clothing store is perfect for comfortably outfitting your young 'uns with a dash of panache. Prices may be high, but most of this well-made clothing will last a long time.

Eco-wise (Map pp66-7; ☎ 512-326-4474; 112 W Elizabeth St; ⏰ 11am-7pm Mon-Fri, 10am-6pm Sat) Specializing in hemp, organic cotton and nontoxic goods, this store aimed at adults also carries a wealth of eco-friendly baby products, as well as cooperative games and outdoor gear for older kids.

Terra Toys (Map pp66-7; ☎ 512-445-4489; 1708 S Congress Ave; ⏰ 10am-7pm Mon-Sat, noon-6pm Sun) Meant for zany adults almost as much as it is for kids, this toy store sells puzzles and puppets, Mad Libs books, Nunzilla wind-up dolls, bouncy balls and even kites to fly in nearby Zilker Park.

Toy Joy (Map pp68-9; 512-320-0090; 2900 N Guadalupe St; ⏰ 10am-11pm daily, till midnight Fri-Sat) Popular with UT students, this repository of eye-catching toys nearly bursts at the seams. Whether it's a glow-in-the-dark Frisbee, plastic pig catapults, Tiki ware, a Japanese *anime* T-shirt or bags of vintage marbles, all ages will find something their heart desires.

Hogwild (Map pp56-7; 512-467-9453; 100A E North Loop Blvd; ⏰ 11am-7pm Mon-Fri, noon-6pm Sat-Sun) Wow! Vintage '80s board games still in their original cellophane, action figures from cartoons past and more nostalgia toys line the shelves here. You'll also find a few Hawaiian shirts and retro lunchboxes.

Malls
These malls are handy to outlying accommodations.

The Arboretum ☎ 512-338-4437; 10000 Research Blvd; ⏰ 10am-6pm Mon-Sat, till 8pm Thu, Sun hours vary) Northwest of downtown at the busy junction of Loop 360, MoPac and Hwy 183, the Arboretum is a park-like collection of high end stores, including Sharper Image and Restoration Hardware.

Northcross Mall (Map pp56-7; ☎ 512-451-7466; 2525 W Anderson Lane at Burnet Rd; ⏰ 10am-9pm Mon-Fri, 10am-7pm Sat, noon-6pm Sun) Northeast of downtown off I-35 near the old Austin airport, Northcross is one of the city's smallest malls, but it's the only one with an ice skating rink.

GETTING THERE & AWAY

See the Transport chapter (p199) for toll-free numbers, transportation company contact information and further details about service to and from Austin.

Air

Opened in 1999, **Austin-Bergstrom International Airport** (AUS; ☎ 512-530-2242; www.ci .austin.tx.us/austinairport; 3600 Presidential Blvd) is about 10 miles southeast of downtown. It's served by America West, American Airlines, Continental Airlines, Delta, Frontier, Mexicana, Northwest-KLM, Southwest and United-Lufthansa.

Garage parking is free for the first 30 minutes, then costs $2 per hour or $18 per day. Outdoor parking lots cost less than $10 per day. The airport features free live music by local acts on some evenings; performers play by the Highland Lakes Bar near the center of the departures level. You can also sample food from Austin-based restaurants, including Amy's Ice Creams and the Salt Lick barbecue, or buy some last-minute CDs from the Austin City Limits store. The airport's only big drawback is its lack of lockers, so plan to keep your carry-on bags with you.

Bus

Served by **Greyhound** (☎ 512-458-4463) and the **Kerrville Bus Co** (☎ 512-458-3823), the main bus station (Map pp57-7; 916 E Koenig Lane) is far north of downtown (reached by Capital Metro bus No 7-Duval) and convenient to nothing but itself, a couple of hotels and the Highland Mall. Buses leave from here for other major Texas cities frequently; there's also some rather pricey service to the nearby Hill Country.

This table details bus services from Austin, and sample standard fares charged for same-day tickets:

to/from	frequency (per day)	duration	one-way/ roundtrip
Dallas	15	3 to 5 hrs	$26/48
El Paso	3	12 to 14 hrs	$113/200
Fredericksburg	3	3 to 5 hrs	$32/54
Kerrville	6	3 to 5 hrs	$29/48
Laredo	13	4 to 5 hrs	$33/55
Lubbock	3	11 to 15 hrs	$76/130
San Antonio	14	1 to 2 hrs	$14/22
Waco	4	1¾ to 2 hrs	$15/21

Car & Motorcycle

Austin spreads alongside I-35, which runs north from San Antonio past Waco toward Dallas-Fort Worth. For the Texas Hill Country, you can take US 290 west to Johnson City and Fredericksburg.

All of the major rental car agencies have outlets at Austin-Bergstrom International Airport. See p201 for details about renting a car.

Train

The downtown Amtrak station (Map p91; ☎ 512-476-5684; 250 N Lamar Blvd) is served by the *Texas Eagle*. There's free parking and an enclosed waiting area, but no staff. Fares vary wildly.

GETTING AROUND
To/From the Airport

Ground transportation from Austin-Bergstrom International Airport can be found on the lower level near baggage claim. **Capital Metro** (p116) runs limited-stop Airport Flyer (bus No 100) service between the airport and downtown and the University of Texas area, with departures every 40 minutes from approximately 5:30am until 11:15pm on weekdays, 6:30am to 10:30pm on Saturday and 8am to 10pm on Sunday. Check with Capital Metro for exact schedules. It takes at least 20 minutes to get downtown from the airport, and 35 minutes to reach the UT campus. Capital Metro's Route 350 takes just over an hour to reach Highland Mall, the North Lamar Transit Center and finally Northcross Mall, which is also a bus transfer center. The fare for either route is 50¢.

SuperShuttle (☎ 512-258-3826, 800-258-3826; www .supershuttle.com) offers shared van service from the airport to downtown hotels for about $10 one-way, or a few dollars more to accommodations along north I-35 and near the

Arboretum mall. A taxi between the airport and downtown costs about $25 to $30.

Bicycle

A grand bicycle tour of greater Austin isn't feasible, due to interstate highways and the like, but cycling around downtown, parts of South Austin, around the UT campus and Hyde Park is a good plan if you're reasonably fit. There are also miles of recreational paths around the city that are ideal for cruisin'.

The cool thing about **Bicycle Sportshop** (Map pp66-7; ☎ 512-477-3472; www.bicyclesportshop.com; 1426 Toomey Rd; ☯ 10am-7pm Mon-Fri, 9am-6pm Sat, 11am-5pm Sun) is its proximity to Zilker Park, Barton Springs and the Town Lake bike paths, all of which are within a few blocks. Rentals range from $10 for a two-hour cruise on a standard bike to $50 a day for top-end full-suspension models. On weekends and holidays, advance reservations are advised.

You can also rent bikes from **Waterloo Cycles** (Map pp68-9; ☎ 512-472-9253; waterloocycles.com; 2815 Fruth St; ☯ 10am-7pm Mon-Sat, till 8pm Thu, noon-5pm Sun), just off Guadalupe St, from $10 per day for a single-speed cruiser to over $60 per day for an ass-kickin' front-suspension whatchamacallit. They also sell used bikes and show free movies at their quirky 'Bike-in Theatre.' Both shops are good places to inquire about local biking groups, such as the **Austin Ridge Riders** (www.austinridgeriders.com), and also to pick up copies of the free *Southwest Cycling News* and Austin bicycle maps (from $1).

The **Yellow Bike Project** (☎ 512-457-9880; www.austinyellowbike.org; 2013 W 51st St) repairs old bicycles (classes are available), paints them yellow and makes them available free for public use. When you see a yellow bike, you can pick it up, ride where you're going and leave it standing against a wall or lamppost for the next rider. The **Wheatsville Food Co-op** (p94) usually has a bike sale on the last Saturday of each month and a bike swap in May.

Car & Motorcycle

During the day, parking at the **Capitol Visitors Parking Garage** (Map p58-9) is free for the first two hours. Other downtown garages and lots are fairly abundant. They usually charge $1 to $2 per hour, with a daily maximum of $8 to $10. On-street parking meters cost 25¢ for 15 to 20 minutes. Free park-and-ride lots on the outskirts of downtown sponsored by Capitol Metro (below) let you connect with free 'Dillo shuttle buses into downtown.

In the evening, on-street metered parking downtown is free. The state-operated parking garage at 4th and San Antonio Sts is free after 6pm, and it fills up quickly. Other downtown garages and parking lots typically charge a flat fee of around $6 or so after dark. People also park for free under I-35 at the east end of 6th St, but you can't depend on it being available (or legal).

Day or night, finding a spot around the UT campus can take a while. Free visitor parking is available outside the LBJ Library, but from there it's a long, hot walk across campus to the UT Tower and other sights. Campus parking lots are usually free for general use after 5pm and all weekend long, but read the restricted permit parking signs carefully first. Campus parking garages are free for the first 30 minutes. Parking spots on Guadalupe St are both timed and metered. Otherwise, your best bet is to search for free parking in the residential streets west of Guadalupe St.

Elsewhere around Austin, on-street parking is usually available for free, but pay careful attention to posted permit parking and time limits. Meters are usually free after 6pm and anytime on Sunday.

Public Transport

Austin's handy public transit system is run by **Capital Metro** (CapMetro; ☎ 512-474-1200, 800-474-1201; www.capmetro.org). Call for directions to anywhere or stop into the downtown customer information center, now officially called the **Capital Metro Transit Store** (Map pp58-9; 323 Congress Ave; ☯ 7:30am-5pm Mon-Fri).

Many visitor attractions are accessible via CapMetro's free **'Dillo shuttle buses** that circulate through central Austin, connecting downtown with South Austin and the UT campus area. The **Silver 'Dillo** runs east-west along 5th and 6th Sts, providing easy access to the 6th St and Warehouse District entertainment meccas, as well as out to some East Austin sights. The **Gold 'Dillo** also circulates around downtown, up to the UT campus and along Barton Springs Rd into Zilker Park.

The **Orange 'Dillo** is good for reaching the South Congress (SoCo) area, while the **Red 'Dillo** runs along 'the Drag' (Guadalupe St) near the UT campus. Both the Red and Silver 'Dillos head west across the MoPac Expressway onto Lake Austin Blvd.

On weekends visitors can ride the No 470 **'Tour the Town'** bus route, which runs every 45 minutes from 10am to 6pm on Saturday, 11am to 6pm Sunday, and conveniently connects sights around UT, downtown and Zilker Park. City buses (other than the free 'Dillo) cost 50¢ per ride; express bus routes (numbered in the 900s) cost $1. A 20-ride coupon booklet costs $5. A bus pass good for one calendar month costs $10. There are bicycle racks (where you can hitch your bike for free) on the front of almost all CapMetro buses, including over a dozen UT shuttle routes.

Taxi

You'll usually need to call for a cab instead of just flagging one down on the street, except at the airport, major hotels, around the state capitol and also major entertainment areas. The flag drops at $1.75, then it's $1.75 for each additional mile. Larger companies include **American Yellow** (☎ 512-452-9999), **Austin Cab** (☎ 512-478-2222), **Checker Cab** (☎ 512-472-1111) and **Roy's Taxi** (☎ 512-482-0000), or check the yellow pages.

Human-powered bicycle taxis, or **pedicabs**, are available downtown on 6th St and around the Warehouse District, usually from about 9pm until after 2am from Wednesday to Saturday evenings. The drivers, who are typically young students or musicians, work entirely for tips, so please be generous.

San Antonio

CONTENTS

Orientation	120
Information	121
Dangers & Annoyances	124
Sights	125
Activities	139
Downtown San Antonio Walking Tour	140
San Antonio For Children	141
Tours	143
Festivals & Events	143
Sleeping	145
Eating	151
Entertainment	157
Shopping	163
Getting There & Away	165
Getting Around	166
Around San Antonio	**167**
New Braunfels	167
Gruene	168
San Marcos	169

One of Texas' most walkable downtowns graces San Antonio, and the city's Texan roots and Spanish origins are readily apparent. It is the only city in the country that contains five original Spanish colonial missions; the missions' churches still function, and their aqueducts still carry water to local farmers. And, San Antonio has the be-all and end-all of monuments to courage, the Alamo.

The River City is a major melting pot of American and Mexican residents and cultures. Locals joke about San Antonio's laidback feel – the 'mañana syndrome' is considered rife. The downtown is laid out in the sort of discombobulated grid system one associates with colonial-era cow paths. But don't be fooled by the 'jes' folks' breeziness. San Antonio, or SA as locals call it, is the nation's ninth-largest city. Its quaintness neatly distracts attention from the fact that it's a major export zone, a biotechnology and technology sector and a town with a whole lot of firepower – five military bases call the region their home.

The Riverwalk, touristy as it may be, is a pleasant strolling ground, and no matter how hard-boiled you are, you'll probably still enjoy a river cruise along it. The nightlife may not match Austin's, but there's enough to keep visitors entertained. For families, SeaWorld and Six Flags Fiesta Texas are both big draws, too. And the food – Tex-Mex and authentic Mexican at its finest – is worth the trip all by itself.

SAN ANTONIO

HIGHLIGHTS

- **Touching History** The Alamo (p125) and the Mission Trail (p128)
- **Cooling Off** Splashing around New Braunfels (p167)
- **Wet & Wild Life** Creatures and coasters at SeaWorld (p142)
- **Urban Oasis** Strolling or cruising the Riverwalk (p140)
- **Dining** Authentic Mexican and Tex-Mex eateries (p151)
- **Art Appreciation** McNay Art Museum (p138) and SAMA (p135)
- **Green Haven** Brackenridge Park (p135)
- **Best Free Night Out** First Fridays in Southtown (p133)
- **Sweet Sleeps** Historic King William District (p149)
- **Offbeat Experience** Buckhorn Saloon & Museum (p131)

| TELEPHONE CODE: **210** | POPULATION: **1.1 MILLION** | AREA: **350 SQ MI** |

ORIENTATION

San Antonio is daunting for drivers, and parking is no treat either. Yet the city is laid out in a grid system (albeit a little skewed at times), making navigation easier on the nerves. Pay close attention to highway signs, especially when they indicate a lefthand exit – miss one of these in San Antonio, and you're in for a nickel tour of the surrounding suburbs.

Central SA is enclosed by two concentric rings of highways. The ring closest to downtown is formed by I-35 in the west and north, Hwys 87 and 90 and I-10 in the south and west (they run along I-35 for a while), and I-37 and US 281 in the east. All these highways feed out to I-410, locally called Loop 410, which circles the city. Note I-10, which usually runs east-west across Texas, runs north-south in most of San Antonio; directions to take I-10 west from downtown to Six Flags Fiesta Texas (which is almost due north of downtown) are accurate.

Downtown has a complex system of one-way streets, as well as streets that change direction at will and at once. Major north-south arteries include Broadway and Main Ave, which runs into San Pedro Ave north of downtown. East-west thoroughfares include Commerce St, Market St and Houston St. The intersection of Commerce and Losoya Sts is the very heart of downtown and below street level is the Riverwalk. The main Riverwalk area is a developed canal loop off the San Antonio River, extending east like the curvy part of a lowercase 'b.' Signs both above and below direct pedestrian traffic to and from the Riverwalk. The Alamo is a few blocks east and north of the Commerce-Losoya intersection.

The historic King William District lies directly south of downtown across Durango Blvd. The mainly residential district is bordered on the east by S Alamo St, which is the main drag through Southtown, an arts district of galleries, cafés and restaurants. North of downtown, the Brackenridge Park area is bounded by Broadway on the east, while Hwy 281 winds through the area, generally north-south. Other major roads are N St Mary's St, which curves northeast into the park, and Mulberry Ave, a shortcut across the park between Broadway and N St Mary's

---

SAN ANTONIO IN...

ONE DAY

Start your day off with a leisurely breakfast on the **Riverwalk**, then pay your respects to the **Alamo** and any other downtown sight that tickles your fancy, perhaps the **Buckhorn Saloon & Museum**, the **Southwest School of Art & Craft** or **Market Square**. Stop in the **King William District & Southtown** for a quick lunch before hitting the historic **Mission Trail**. Return to Southtown or the Riverwalk for sunset margaritas and dinner, then indulge in a good night's sleep at any of SA's historic downtown hotels.

TWO DAYS

Those traveling with kids may want to spend the whole day visiting **SeaWorld** or **Six Flags Fiesta Texas**. Otherwise, on your second day, head north to **Brackenridge Park**. Have lunch at **Earl Abel's** diner, then spend the afternoon at the **San Antonio Botanical Gardens**, while art lovers should visit the divine **McNay Museum** or the **San Antonio Museum of Art**. Have dinner on eclectic **Josephine St**, then meander over to **St Mary's St** (aka 'the Strip') to catch a live show. Alternatively, head back to **Southtown** for drinks, a fine Mexican meal and dancing.

THREE DAYS

On your third day escape to the **Hill Country** to visit cowboy ranches, art museums and country dance halls. Or visit **New Braunfels** or **San Marcos**, towns that offer aquatic fun-in-the-sun and factory outlet shopping. Feeling ambitious? Consider taking a day trip north to **Austin** instead.

St. The military bases Fort Sam Houston, Brooks Air Force Base, Randolph Air Force Base and Lackland Air Force base are, respectively, northeast, southeast, east and southwest of downtown.

In optimal traffic conditions, San Antonio International Airport is only a 15-minute drive north of downtown on US 281, past the intersection with Loop 410. Long-distance buses arrive at the central downtown terminal, a short walk north of the Riverwalk. The Amtrak station is east of downtown, near the Alamodome.

Maps

Procuring a good map of the city can be a challenge, as those handed out by the **San Antonio CVB** (p124) are far too general for a city of this size. Gousha's *San Antonio City Map* is comprehensive but cumbersome. *Streetwise San Antonio* is relatively accurate and very easy to carry in its fivefold laminated pocket-size edition; it's available at bookstores. For more extensive navigation, try the detailed, if unwieldy, maps from Mapsco or Rand McNally.

Free road maps are available to members of the **American Automobile Association** (AAA; p194). There are two offices on the outskirts of town: north of the airport (☎ 210-499-0222; 13415 San Pedro Ave; ☼ 9am-6pm Mon-Fri, 9am-1pm Sat), off US 281; and west of the airport (Map pp122-3; ☎ 210-877-2222; 11075 W I-10, exit 560; ☼ same hours).

INFORMATION
Bookstores

Many museums, attractions and Texas-themed gift shops, including souvenir stores inside the Alamo and along the Mission Trail, stock a variety of regional-interest titles. For used and rare books of all kinds, head north of downtown to the Brackenridge Park area.

Borders Books, Music & Cafe (Map pp122-3; ☎ 210-828-9496; Alamo Quarry Market, 255 E Basse Rd; ☼ 9am-11pm Mon-Sat, 10am-9pm Sun) Multiple locations with an extensive offering of travel books and maps.

Brentano's (Map pp126-7; ☎ 210-223-3938; river level, Rivercenter Mall, 849 E Commerce St; ☼ 10am-9pm Mon-Sat, noon-6pm Sun) Next to the Marriott's lower entrance, this central bookshop has a small selection of travel guides, Texana titles and Spanish-language books.

Broadway News (Map pp136-7; ☎ 210-223-2034; 2202 N Broadway; ☼ 9am-1am) True, half of this indoor newsstand is marked 'adults only.' Up front there's an encyclopedic selection of magazines and newspapers, though.

Cheever Books (Map pp136-7; ☎ 210-824-2665; 3613 Broadway; ☼ 10am-7pm Mon-Sat, noon-7pm Sun) Fine used and out-of-print titles, specializing in Texas and Western Americana, as well as art, architecture and the classics.

Half Price Books, Records, Magazines (Map pp136-7; ☎ 210-822-4597; www.halfpricebooks.com; 3207 Broadway; ☼ 9:30am-9pm Mon-Sat, 11:30am-7pm Sun) A broad selection of excellent new and used books. Multiple locations.

The History Shop (Map pp126-7; ☎ 210-229-9855; 713 E Houston St; ☼ 10am-6pm) Sells antiquarian Texana books, maps and documents near the Alamo. Call to confirm hours.

Remember the Alibi Bookstore (Map pp122-3; ☎ 210-344-7776; Castle Oaks Village, 8055 West Ave; ☼ 10am-6pm Mon-Fri, 10am-5pm Sat) A mystery bookseller on the outskirts of town.

The Twig Bookshop (Map pp136-7; ☎ 210-826-6411; http://thetwig.booksense.com; 5005 Broadway; ☼ 10am-8pm Mon-Thu, 10am-6pm Fri-Sat) This neighborhood bookshop has Texana titles, other regional-interest books, and the Red Balloon, with children's books. Call for in-store events.

Unlimited Thought Bookstore (Map pp122-3; ☎ 210-525-0693; www.unlimited-thought.com; Town Square shopping center, 5525 Blanco Rd; ☼ 10am-9pm Mon-Fri, 10am-6pm Sat, noon-6pm Sun) Alternative spirituality, health and lifestyle books fill this quirky bookshop. Look for in-store astrologers, intuitive counselors and a monthly psychic fair.

Whole Earth Provision Company (Map pp122-3; ☎ 210-829-8888; Alamo Quarry Market, 255 E Basse Rd; ☼ 10am-9pm Mon-Sat, noon-6pm Sun) This outdoors outfitter is a decent source of travel guides and maps, especially for activities around Texas.

Emergency

Emergency number (☎ 911)
Police (☎ 210-207-7273, TTY 210-224-1411)
Downtown Foot/Bike Patrol (☎ 210-207-7764; 240 E Houston St; ☼ 10am-2am)
Natural disaster (☎ 211) Statewide health and human services.
San Antonio Rape Crisis Center (24hr hotline ☎ 210-349-7273; www.rapecrisis.com)
United Way (☎ 210-227-4357) General crisis intervention and various social services.
Animal Emergency Room (Map pp122-3; ☎ 210-737-7380; 4315 Fredericksburg Rd)

SAN ANTONIO

GREATER SAN ANTONIO

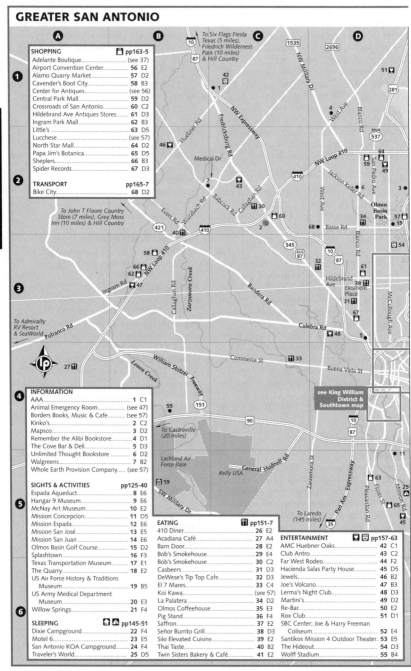

SHOPPING pp163-5
Adelante Boutique...........................(see 37)
Airport Convention Center...........**56** E2
Alamo Quarry Market....................**57** D2
Cavender's Boot City.....................**58** B3
Center for Antiques.....................(see 56)
Central Park Mall..........................**59** D2
Crossroads of San Antonio...........**60** C2
Hildebrand Ave Antiques Stores......**61** D3
Ingram Park Mall..........................**62** B3
Little's..**63** D5
Lucchese....................................(see 57)
North Star Mall............................**64** D2
Papa Jim's Botanica......................**65** D5
Sheplers......................................**66** B3
Spider Records.............................**67** D3

TRANSPORT pp165-7
Bike City......................................**68** D2

INFORMATION
AAA...**1** C1
Animal Emergency Room................(see 47)
Borders Books, Music & Cafe.........(see 57)
Kinko's...**2** C2
Mapsco..**3** D2
Remember the Alibi Bookstore........**4** D1
The Cove Bar & Deli......................**5** D3
Unlimited Thought Bookstore.........**6** D2
Walgreens.....................................**7** B2
Whole Earth Provision Company.....(see 57)

SIGHTS & ACTIVITIES pp125-40
Espada Aqueduct...........................**8** E6
Hangar 9 Museum.........................**9** E6
McNay Art Museum.......................**10** E2
Mission Concepción.......................**11** D5
Mission Espada............................**12** E6
Mission San José..........................**13** E5
Mission San Juan.........................**14** E6
Olmos Basin Golf Course...............**15** D2
Splashtown...................................**16** F3
Texas Transportation Museum........**17** E1
The Quarry...................................**18** E2
US Air Force History & Traditions
 Museum....................................**19** B5
US Army Medical Department
 Museum....................................**20** E3
Willow Springs.............................**21** F4

SLEEPING pp145-51
Dixie Campground.........................**22** F4
Motel 6.......................................**23** E5
San Antonio KOA Campground.......**24** F4
Traveler's World...........................**25** D5

EATING pp151-7
410 Diner.....................................**26** E2
Acadiana Café...............................**27** A4
Barn Door.....................................**28** E2
Bob's Smokehouse.........................**29** E4
Bob's Smokehouse.........................**30** C2
Casbeers.......................................**31** D3
DeWese's Tip Top Cafe..................**32** D3
El 7 Mares....................................**33** C4
Koi Kawa.....................................(see 57)
La Palatera...................................**34** D2
Olmos Coffeehouse.......................**35** E3
Pig Stand......................................**36** F4
Saffron...**37** E2
Señor Burrito Grill.........................**38** D3
Silo Elevated Cuisine.....................**39** E2
Thai Taste....................................**40** B2
Twin Sisters Bakery & Café............**41** E2

ENTERTAINMENT pp157-63
AMC Huebner Oaks........................**42** C1
Club Antro....................................**43** C2
Far West Rodeo.............................**44** F2
Hacienda Salas Party House............**45** D5
Jewels..**46** B2
Joe's Volcano................................**47** B3
Lerma's Night Club........................**48** D3
Martini's.......................................**49** D2
Re-Bar..**50** E2
Rox Club.......................................**51** D1
SBC Center; Joe & Harry Freeman
 Coliseum...................................**52** E4
Santikos Mission 4 Outdoor Theater.**53** E5
The Hideout..................................**54** D3
Wolff Stadium...............................**55** B4

see King William District & Southtown map

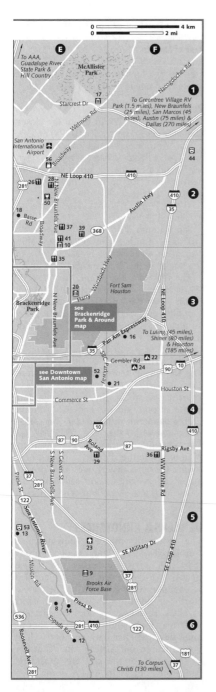

Internet Access

SA's public library system provides free Internet access, but time online may be limited to 30 minutes. You must sign up in-person (no phone reservations) for the next available terminal. Bring a library card or photo ID. The central **San Antonio Public Library** (Map pp126-7; ☎ 210-207-2500; www.sanantonio.gov/library; 600 Soledad St; 9am-9pm Mon-Thu, 9am-5pm Fri-Sat, 11am-5pm Sun) is a first-rate multimedia facility with children's programs and helpful staff. Validated parking at the library garage is free for one hour.

You can check your email for $2.50 per 20 minutes at **Espuma** (p154) coffeehouse. Otherwise **Kinko's** (Map pp136-7; ☎ 210-821-6911; 4418 Broadway; 24hrs; also map pp122-3; ☎ 210-731-4400; 3740 NW Loop 410, west of Fredericksburg Rd; 6am-11pm Mon-Fri, 9am-5pm Sat-Sun) offers high-speed Internet access from 20¢ to 30¢ per minute. Only some copy center branches (☎ 800-254-6567 for city wide locations) are open 24 hours. Laptop users with a toll-free or local dial-up ISP number can use Kinko's laptop docking stations for free.

Internet Resources

The **San Antonio Convention and Visitors Bureau** site (www.sanantoniocvb.com) has plenty of general information on the city, but for something more in-depth, check these out:

Digital City San Antonio (www.digitalcity.com/sanantonio) Coverage of restaurants, nightlife and events around town.
My San Antonio (www.mysanantonio.com) This up-to-date website from the *San Antonio Express-News* covers local news, entertainment and a calendar of events.
San Antonio Current (www.sacurrent.com) SA's alternative weekly has thumbnail entertainment listings, restaurant reviews, news and classified ads.

Laundry

The **Cove Bar & Deli** (Map pp122-3; ☎ 210-227-2683; 606 W Cypress St; at least 7:30am-10pm) has an attached coin laundry (and a car wash!); serves Blue Bell ice cream, cold beer and margaritas, and frequently has live music on its outdoor porch. **E-Z Wash Laundry** (Map pp136-7; ☎ 210-444-0208; 2402 Broadway; open daily) has a multitude of washers. **Kwik-Wash Coin Laundry** is the big chain around town; check the yellow pages for its over four dozen locations.

Media

NEWSPAPERS & MAGAZINES

San Antonio Express-News (www.express-news.com)
The major daily newspaper; publishes Friday 'Weekender'
and Wednesday food sections; Jim Beal's 'Night Lights'
column is a good guide to live music.

San Antonio Current (www.sacurrent.com) The free
alternative weekly is not nearly comprehensive enough,
but it's still the best local what's-on guide.

La Prensa (www.laprensa.com) A bilingual Spanish-
language weekly.

San Antonio Observer (www.saobserver.com) A weekly
that focuses on SA's African American community.

Lowrider Magazine (www.lowridermagazine.com)
Interesting if you're curious about those peculiar low-
clearance trucks around San Antonio.

RADIO

KSTX 89.1FM (www.tpr.org) Local NPR affiliate; 12:30pm
Friday is 'Texas Matters,' with local news and events; 7pm
Saturday is an hour of live jazz from Jim Cullum's Landing
(see p157), and after 10pm, Voz Latina, a two-hour Latin
world beat show.

KRTU 91.7FM (www.krtu.org) The Trinity University
station plays jazz during the day and alternative rock all
night; 'Live from Studio A' performances by San Antonio
bands broadcast at 10pm Thursday.

KCYY 100.3FM Country music.

KLEY 94.1FM & KEDA 1540AM Tejano music.

KROM 92.9FM Regional Mexican music.

KCOR 95.1FM Spanish-language pop.

KPAC 88.3FM Classical music.

Medical Services

Check the yellow pages for dentists offering
emergency care; some keep extended office
hours or stay on-call at night.

Walgreens (Map pp122-3; ☎ 210-614-3590; 5282
Medical Dr, cnr Babcock Rd; ☼ 24hrs) A 24-hour pharmacy
north of Loop 410, near the major hospitals and medical
complexes.

Baptist Medical Center (Map pp126-7; ☎ 210-297-
7000; 111 Dallas St) A central hospital, just east of Navarro
and Soledad Sts.

Santa Rosa Hospital (Map pp126-7; ☎ 210-704-2011;
333 N Santa Rosa St) Another central facility, with an
emergency room and children's services.

Money

There are ATMs that accept most network
and credit cards throughout the city,
including in malls, major theme parks
and in the gift shop at the Alamo. You
can change foreign currency and traveler's

checks at **Frost Bank** (Map pp126-7; ☎ 210-220-4011;
100 W Houston St; ☼ 9am-4pm Mon-Thu, 9am-5pm Fri) or
Bank of America (Map pp126-7; ☎ 210-270-5540; 300
Convent St; ☼ 9am-4pm Mon-Thu, 9am-5pm Fri). There
are also two foreign-exchange desks at the
airport and one in Six Flags Fiesta Texas.

Post

Call ☎ 800-275-8777 to locate the closest
United States Postal Service (USPS) branch.

San Antonio's central **post office** (Map
pp126-7; 615 E Houston St, enter off Alamo St; ☼ 9am-
5pm Mon-Fri), near the Alamo, holds general
delivery mail for up to 30 days. Address
poste restante to:

YOUR FAMILY NAME, First Name
General Delivery
San Antonio, TX 78205-9998

There's another convenient **post office**
(Map pp136-7; 4801 Broadway; ☼ 8am-5:30pm Mon-Fri,
8am-1pm Sat) in the Brackenridge Park area.

The **UPS Store** (Map pp126-7; ☎ 210-258-8950,
888-346-3623; www.theupsstore.com; 200 E Market St;
☼ 8am-6:30pm Mon-Sat) offers shipping and
specialty mail services. Call its toll-free
number or visit its website to find its city-
wide locations.

Tourist Offices

The **San Antonio Convention & Visitors Bureau**
(CVB; ☎ 210-207-6700, 800-447-3372; www.san
antoniocvb.com) stocks the brochure stands
at the airport kiosks. The San Antonio
CVB's **downtown visitors center** (Map pp126-7;
☎ 210-207-6748; 317 Alamo Plaza; ☼ 8:30am-6:30pm
daily in summer, shorter hrs in winter) is opposite the
Alamo. While the staff do not book hotel
rooms, they can answer questions, provide
maps and brochures and sell tickets for
tours and also VIA bus and streetcar
passes.

DANGERS & ANNOYANCES

The swarming-with-cops downtown is
considered safe. East and west of downtown
(basically, anywhere across the railway
tracks) is by no means as well-patrolled,
so common sense is needed in these areas.
North of downtown, Avenue B, which
parallels Broadway beside Brackenridge
Park, may look handy for parking, but it's
often deserted after dark and not well-lit.
Poorer Latino and African American areas
to the south of the city are considered
dangerous, but as in Austin, some latent

racism may play a part in exaggerating the actual danger.

The San Antonio River is not a toy, as there are several drownings a year. Be especially careful in areas near the Riverwalk that don't have fences. It's easy to see how people are accidentally knocked into the muddy waters. Other hazards for first-time visitors, especially during summer, are dehydration, heat exhaustion or even heat stroke; sweating combined with inadequate fluid intake are the commonest causes. To avoid passing out in front of the Alamo (as a few tourists each year inevitably do), always maintain a good fluid intake – a minimum of 3L a day is recommended. For more advice, see the Health chapter.

SIGHTS

Most of San Antonio's sights are along the San Antonio River downtown, in the historic King William District and in the Brackenridge Park area. VIA streetcars circulate around downtown and also run south into the King William residential area and Southtown arts district. For outlying sights around San Antonio, it's quicker and easier to drive than to take the bus; however, all bus routes detailed below originate in downtown SA. For parking advice in the city's most congested areas, see p166.

The Alamo

The story of the Battle of the Alamo, when Davy Crockett, Jim Bowie and other Texas revolutionaries valiantly tried to hold out against all odds and thousands of Mexican troops, is an enduring legend. The famous **fort** (Map pp126-7; ☎ 210-225-1391; www.thealamo.org; 300 Alamo Plaza; admission free, donations encouraged; ☼ 9am-5:30pm daily, from 10am Sun) is a former Spanish *presidio* (military prison), now a shrine to those who died defending it in the Texas War for Independence. What is surprising is both its size (it's much smaller than many people think) and its beauty. An ornately decorated portal leads to a typical Spanish colonial church that has a distinctly Moorish flavor. (Muslims ruled Spain from the 8th to the 15th centuries and had a great influence over Spanish architecture.)

The Alamo was originally constructed in 1724 in this location as the Misión San Antonio de Valero, though the Valero mission had had an unsuccessful start in 1720 on the banks of the San Antonio River. After its destruction by a storm, construction on the present compound began. Throughout the 18th century, the mission was operated along much the same lines as the others along San Antonio's Mission Trail; it was a relatively self-supporting home for Spanish missionaries and Native American converts who worked the fields. The missions were secularized in 1793, but after the turn of the 19th century, Spanish colonial troops reoccupied the mission, expanded on its buildings, added defenses and renamed it Misión del Alamo del Parras, after the troops' hometown (some say it was in honor of the cottonwood trees that grow along the banks of the old missions' aqueduct – in Spanish, álamo means 'poplar').

Today, the former fort and mission is one of the premier tourist attractions in Texas. It occupies the entire area between Houston St at the north, Bonham St at the east, Crockett St at the south and Alamo Plaza at the west. The main entrance sits on Alamo Plaza.

It's managed by the rather persnickety Daughters of the Republic of Texas (DRT), a group of women who can document their lineage directly to the Texas Republican period prior to 1846. The DRT insists that all visitors behave in a manner due such a monument – keep a respectful tongue in your head, wear a shirt and shoes at all times and don't make any jokes, please.

The DRT has been in charge of the Alamo since 1905, and it runs all areas of the monument, including its (armed) police force, and the organization is the beneficiary of the donations. Frequent free talks given by docents on the outdoor lawn patio provide the DRT's history of the battle and a highly colorful description of pre-revolutionary life in San Antonio.

In the main chapel building is the **shrine**, with an exhibit on the battle and the defenders of the Alamo. Informative free brochures describing the Alamo and the battle in a number of languages are available as you enter from the desk to the right at the center. As you exit the shrine, to your right is the gift shop; to your left is
Continued on page 128

DOWNTOWN SAN ANTONIO

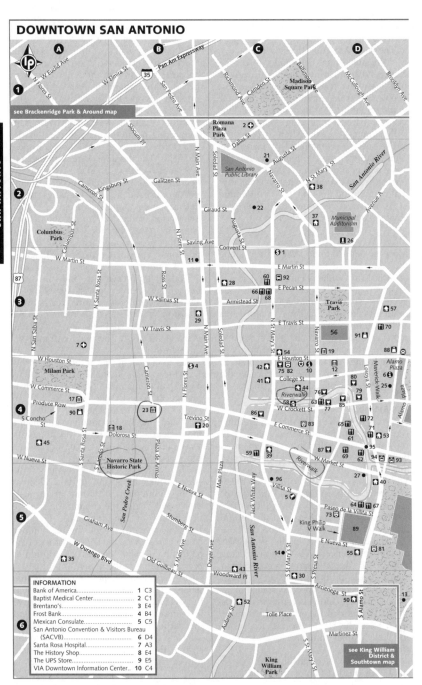

see Brackenridge Park & Around map

see King William District & Southtown map

INFORMATION		
Bank of America	1	C3
Baptist Medical Center	2	C1
Brentano's	3	E4
Frost Bank	4	B4
Mexican Consulate	5	C5
San Antonio Convention & Visitors Bureau (SACVB)	6	D4
Santa Rosa Hospital	7	A3
The History Shop	8	E4
The UPS Store	9	E5
VIA Downtown Information Center	10	C4

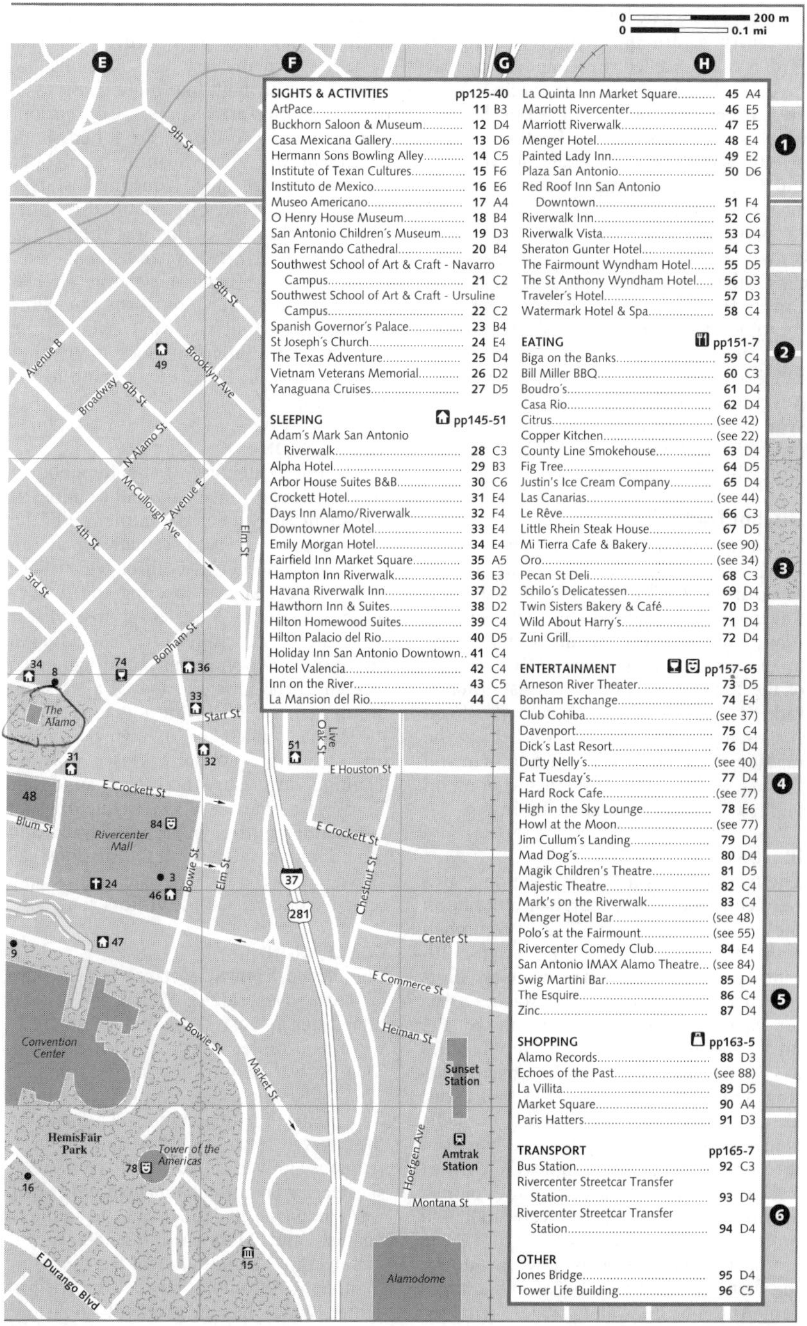

SAN ANTONIO

0 —————— 200 m
0 —————— 0.1 mi

SIGHTS & ACTIVITIES	pp125-40
ArtPace	11 B3
Buckhorn Saloon & Museum	12 D4
Casa Mexicana Gallery	13 D6
Hermann Sons Bowling Alley	14 C5
Institute of Texan Cultures	15 F6
Instituto de Mexico	16 E6
Museo Americano	17 A4
O Henry House Museum	18 B4
San Antonio Children's Museum	19 D3
San Fernando Cathedral	20 B4
Southwest School of Art & Craft - Navarro Campus	21 C2
Southwest School of Art & Craft - Ursuline Campus	22 C2
Spanish Governor's Palace	23 B4
St Joseph's Church	24 E4
The Texas Adventure	25 D4
Vietnam Veterans Memorial	26 D2
Yanaguana Cruises	27 D5

SLEEPING	pp145-51
Adam's Mark San Antonio Riverwalk	28 C3
Alpha Hotel	29 B3
Arbor House Suites B&B	30 C6
Crockett Hotel	31 E4
Days Inn Alamo/Riverwalk	32 F4
Downtowner Motel	33 E4
Emily Morgan Hotel	34 E4
Fairfield Inn Market Square	35 A5
Hampton Inn Riverwalk	36 E3
Havana Riverwalk Inn	37 D2
Hawthorn Inn & Suites	38 D2
Hilton Homewood Suites	39 C4
Hilton Palacio del Rio	40 D5
Holiday Inn San Antonio Downtown	41 C4
Hotel Valencia	42 C4
Inn on the River	43 C5
La Mansion del Rio	44 C4

La Quinta Inn Market Square	45 A4
Marriott Rivercenter	46 E5
Marriott Riverwalk	47 E5
Menger Hotel	48 E4
Painted Lady Inn	49 E2
Plaza San Antonio	50 D6
Red Roof Inn San Antonio Downtown	51 F4
Riverwalk Inn	52 C6
Riverwalk Vista	53 D4
Sheraton Gunter Hotel	54 C3
The Fairmount Wyndham Hotel	55 D5
The St Anthony Wyndham Hotel	56 D3
Traveler's Hotel	57 D3
Watermark Hotel & Spa	58 C4

EATING	pp151-7
Biga on the Banks	59 C4
Bill Miller BBQ	60 C3
Boudro's	61 D4
Casa Rio	62 D4
Citrus	(see 42)
Copper Kitchen	(see 22)
County Line Smokehouse	63 D4
Fig Tree	64 D5
Justin's Ice Cream Company	65 D4
Las Canarias	(see 44)
Le Rêve	66 C3
Little Rhein Steak House	67 D5
Mi Tierra Cafe & Bakery	(see 90)
Oro	(see 34)
Pecan St Deli	68 C3
Schilo's Delicatessen	69 D4
Twin Sisters Bakery & Café	70 D3
Wild About Harry's	71 D4
Zuni Grill	72 D4

ENTERTAINMENT	pp157-65
Arneson River Theater	73 D5
Bonham Exchange	74 E4
Club Cohiba	(see 37)
Davenport	75 C4
Dick's Last Resort	76 D4
Durty Nelly's	(see 40)
Fat Tuesday's	77 D4
Hard Rock Cafe	(see 77)
High in the Sky Lounge	78 E6
Howl at the Moon	(see 77)
Jim Cullum's Landing	79 D4
Mad Dog's	80 D4
Magik Children's Theatre	81 D5
Majestic Theatre	82 C4
Mark's on the Riverwalk	83 C4
Menger Hotel Bar	(see 48)
Polo's at the Fairmount	(see 55)
Rivercenter Comedy Club	84 E4
San Antonio IMAX Alamo Theatre	(see 84)
Swig Martini Bar	85 D4
The Esquire	86 C4
Zinc	87 D4

SHOPPING	pp163-5
Alamo Records	88 D3
Echoes of the Past	(see 88)
La Villita	89 D5
Market Square	90 A4
Paris Hatters	91 D3

TRANSPORT	pp165-7
Bus Station	92 C3
Rivercenter Streetcar Transfer Station	93 D4
Rivercenter Streetcar Transfer Station	94 D4

OTHER	
Jones Bridge	95 D4
Tower Life Building	96 C5

Map labels: 9th St, 8th St, Avenue B, Broadway, 6th St, Brooklyn Ave, N Alamo St, McCullough Avenue E, Elm St, 4th St, 3rd St, Bonham St, The Alamo, Starr St, Live Oak St, E Houston St, E Crockett St, Blum St, Rivercenter Mall, Bowie St, Elm St, E Crockett St, Chestnut St, Center St, E Commerce St, Heiman St, Convention Center, S Bowie St, Market St, Sunset Station, HemisFair Park, Tower of the Americas, Hoefgen Ave, Amtrak Station, Montana St, E Durango Blvd, Alamodome

Continued from page 125
the **convent garden** and wishing well. In the garden is an excellent timeline history that covers the Spanish missionary period to the present day. Farther on is the **Long Barrack**, which served as residence for the Spanish priests and later a hospital for Mexican and Texan troops. Today this museum has displays on the history of the Republic of Texas. Finally, the Alamo's busy gift shop contains a fine collection of guns, coonskin caps (the preferred headgear of Davy Crockett), a nice diorama of the battle, a very good selection of books for sale and some fun crapola.

See 'Cinema' (p161) for reviews of Texas Adventure, a multimedia show on the Texas War for Independence, and *Alamo: The Price of Freedom*, an IMAX film showing in nearby Rivercenter Mall.

Mission Trail

If you do only one thing in San Antonio after visiting the Alamo, make it the Mission Trail. This 12-mile marked path traversing roads and fields between the Alamo and Mission Espada is maintained by the National Park Service (NPS) as part of the **San Antonio Missions National Historical Park** (Map pp122-3; ☎ 210-932-1001; www.nps.gov/saan). Religious services are still held in the mission churches of San José, San Juan and Espada, and the mariachi mass at noon on Sunday is a San Antonio tradition.

HISTORY

The five missions in the San Antonio area were constructed in a flurry of building in the early 18th century. These, combined with others constructed in the late 17th century elsewhere in Texas, were an effort to provide way-stations and staging areas for Spanish colonial expansion to the north and to maintain tight supply lines as French forces began encroachments from Louisiana. The native Coahuiltecans, already under pressure from other nomadic Native American tribes pushing down from the north, showed a willingness to convert to Christianity, and labored for the colonial Spanish priests in order to receive food and protection at the missions.

Constructed in what is now downtown, the first and most impressive mission was San Antonio de Valero, later renamed Misión del Alamo del Parras, since shortened to the Alamo. With the destruction by war or disease of many east Texas missions, the Spanish quickly built four more missions in the San Antonio area: San José, Concepción, San Juan and Espada. All are found south of downtown. The Spanish also built an extensive acequia (aqueduct) system throughout the region around this time. The largest section of this was the Espada Dam, which diverted water from the San Antonio River through an elaborate, arched aqueduct that still functions – you can follow the waterway (but you can't swim in the aqueduct, even though it looks so inviting) from the dam in Espada Park south to the Misión Espada.

INFORMATION

While the Daughters of the Republic of Texas maintain control and police duties at the Alamo, park rangers run the rest of the show. The main visitor centers are at San José and Concepción, both of which have interpretive displays covering the history of the missions. A series of free visitor information brochures are chockful of interesting data on architectural highlights of each of the missions as well as mission life in general. All of the missions except the Alamo (which sets its own hours) are open 9am to 5pm daily, closed only on Thanksgiving, Christmas Day and New Year's Day. Park rangers frequently run fascinating and free interpretive walks and other programs at many of the missions; call ahead, check the NPS website or pick up a schedule of events at the visitors centers.

CONCEPCIÓN

The **Misión Nuestra Señora de la Concepción de Acuña** (Map pp122-3; 807 Mission Rd) was established in east Texas in 1716 to try to serve as a buffer against French invasion. That it was moved to San Antonio in 1731 tells you exactly how successful it was in its first incarnation. The mission then served as the center of the colonists' religious universe. Today it contains a spectacular Spanish colonial church (which was completed in 1755), and the southern Spanish and Moorish influences in the architecture remind one of Seville more than San Antonio. Outside the visitors center, which has an excellent bookstore, you can pick up a brochure explaining the mission's frescoes.

SAN JOSÉ

In 1720, Franciscan missionary Antonio Margil de Jesús founded **Misión San José y San Miguel de Aguayo** (Map pp122-3; 6539 San Jose Dr). Known in its time as the Queen of the Missions, it's certainly the largest and possibly the most beautiful of all on the trail. By the time the entire mission – stone walls, granary, church and bastions – was finished in 1782, it had become quite a place, and area Apache and Comanche raiders were not slow to pick up on this fact. The mission was attacked repeatedly and often looted quite successfully until the converted Indians and missionaries starting using firearms.

While the mission was allowed to deteriorate terribly beginning in the 19th century, the Depression-era reconstruction by the Works Progress Administration (WPA) was spectacular, and today it's one of the busiest places on the trail. Ranger-led tours, which usually leave the visitors center and museum before noon, cover life in the mission and show up close the magnificent

---

FIESTA SAN ANTONIO

Late in April, hundreds of thousands of partygoers throng the streets – and that's how you know Fiesta San Antonio has arrived. A nine-day series of riotous events makes for the city's biggest celebration, with general mayhem, fairs, feeds, rodeos, races and a whole lot of music and dancing. Going strong after more than 110 years, the festival (☎ 210-227-5191, 877-723-4378; www.fiesta-sa.org; box office & festival store: 2611 Broadway) is the high point of the River City's year.

Fiesta San Antonio dates back to 1891, when local women paraded on horseback in front of the Alamo and threw flowers at each other, all meant to honor the heroes of the Alamo and the Battle of San Jacinto. Today's **Battle of the Flowers** (www.battleofflowers.org) is only a small piece of the fiesta, which has grown into an enormous party involving 75,000 volunteers, millions of spectators and over 150 events. To attend any of the major parades, either purchase reserved bleacher seats in advance or show up two hours before the scheduled start time to rent street chairs from on-site vendors. At the beginning of Fiesta week, the **Texas Cavaliers' River Parade** kicks off with decorated floats drifting along the San Antonio River and a pilgrimage to the Alamo. On the final Saturday night, **Fiesta Flambeau** claims to be the largest lighted parade in the USA, with marchers carrying candles, sparklers, flashlights, torches and anything else handy.

Speaking of pyrotechnics, the Battle of the Flowers' **marching band competition** at the Alamodome finishes off with a fireworks display midweek. Hosted by St Mary's University, the **Fiesta Oyster Bake** is a major food fair and live music extravaganza, usually on the first Friday and Saturday nights of the festival. In Southtown, the **Gartenfest** at the Beethoven Männerchor Und Garten (p160) is *the* place for beer and polka. El Mercado is usually bustling on any given night. But locals' top pick of Fiesta week is **A Night Out in Old San Antonio**, which actually runs for four nights, during which a small army of women volunteers transforms La Villita into a multiethnic bazaar of food, music, dancing, arts and much, much more.

Apart from these major events, keep a sharp eye out for a kaleidoscope of neighborhood parades, food fairs, art exhibitions, sports competitions, fashion shows and yes, a beauty pageant. Many Tejano, mariachi and country-and-western bands also perform throughout Fiesta week, providing a constant festive soundtrack around the city. Of course, any festival of this size also engenders its own **fringe festival events**, including art happenings, live music shows, parodies and vibrant gay and lesbian events, from carnivalesque dance parties to charity fundraisers. Check local newspapers for listings.

Book your accommodations as far in advance as possible, even as much as a year beforehand. Tickets for major events, such as parades, masked balls, galas and the oyster bake, go on sale in March; most tickets cost $6 to $22 per person and sell out quickly. During some events, it's possible to pay at the gate (or for the smallest happenings, admission may be free). *A Century of Fiesta in San Antonio* by Jack Maguire is the book to search out if you want to know more about the history of the festival, while SA's tourist office also has a good handout on Fiesta week and all of the attendant hoopla. *Viva la fiesta!*

church and its famous rose window, a stunningly carved masterpiece attached to the sacristy. The best time to visit is on Sunday during church services, when a locally famous mariachi band plays at noon. More serene services are held in Spanish at 7:45am, and in English at 9am and 10:30am.

SAN JUAN
The most somber of the missions, **Misión San Juan Capistrano** (Map pp122-3; 9102 Graf Rd) was moved in 1731 to the east bank of the San Antonio, in the middle of what's now Espada Park. There were attempts to enlarge it, but the church itself was never finished. By the mid-18th century, however, the mission's rich farmlands and vast herds of sheep and cattle became an important source of necessary supplies and income for the entire mission chain. Today the surviving church is open, as is a small visitors center and a quarter-mile nature trail along the river.

ESPADA
Southernmost of the missions, **Misión San Francisco de la Espada** (Map pp122-3; 10040 Espada Rd) was the oldest mission in the east Texas chain. Like San Juan, it was moved to its current location in 1731. Two decades later it was a training ground for artisans studying weaving, blacksmithing and other skills. Today, Mission Espada has interesting displays on weaving cotton and on the Spanish colonists.

The main irrigation system for the mission is still in use. It was part of a 15-mile network that began at the **Espada Dam**, which diverted water from the San Antonio River into the Espada Aqueduct after 1745. It's the only functioning aqueduct in the USA from the Spanish colonial period, and it still carries water over Piedras Creek to the mission. The entire area between the mission and the dam is set aside as **Espada Park**, and the marked paths through it allow access by foot, bicycle or car. There are picnic tables and barbecue pits at various places. However, at times it can be dangerously deserted, so it's best to visit only on a busy weekend.

GETTING THERE & AWAY
From downtown, VIA transit bus No 42 goes to San José (see p166 for transit details). The Texas Trolley tours (p143) visit San José and Concepción. Otherwise, rent a bicycle or drive. From downtown, take St Mary's St south until it becomes Mission Rd, then follow the brown signs indicating the direction to the missions.

Around Downtown
Like the Alamo, other sights worth seeing downtown keep an eye on the city's history, as well as its arts and culture.

SOUTHWEST SCHOOL OF ART & CRAFT
With two adjacent campuses, the **Southwest School of Art & Craft** (Map pp126-7; ☎ 210-224-1848; www.swschool.org; 300 Augusta St; admission free; ❧ most galleries 9am-5pm Mon-Sat, 11am-4pm Sun), on the north bank of the San Antonio River, should be a required stopping point. The center offers the largest art curriculum in south Texas, with free workshops, classes and lectures on work in many media, including ceramics, photography, painting and sculpture. Visiting artists make installations, and regularly scheduled workshops invite the public into the real studios. The main **exhibition gallery** is on the school's Navarro campus, which opened in 1998 and stands opposite San Antonio's central public library. It hosts temporary exhibitions by local, regional and national artists.

A short walk away, the historic campus is at the former all-girls Ursuline Academy and Convent opened by French nuns in 1851, San Antonio's first all-girls school. A good place to start off is the **visitor center museum** (❧ 10am-5pm Mon-Sat, 11am-4pm Sun). Exhibits cover the history of the beautiful national historic landmark, and also its woman-centric history, in some depth. Doors opening onto the main cloister lead toward the convent's former chapel, now an events space, inside of which hangs a wall-size tapestry. Both upstairs and on the ground level are several more working art studios. The **sales gallery shop** (❧ 10am-3pm Mon-Fri) exhibits and sells works by the school's artists and visiting artists as well. It's downstairs near the rustic Copper Kitchen restaurant.

You'll probably feel like the heel you are if you don't make a donation to this wonderful place, whose admission is otherwise free. At the beginning of Fiesta

San Antonio each year, the school's Ursuline campus hosts a family-friendly arts fair.

BUCKHORN SALOON & MUSEUM

This odd **museum** (Map pp126-7; ☎ 210-247-4000; www.buckhornmuseum.com; 318 E Houston St; adult/child 3-11 $10/8; ⚘ 10am-5pm, extended hrs in summer) is one of the best kitsch values around. The Buckhorn got its kick-start as a rustic saloon back in 1881, when the owner promised patrons a free beer or whiskey shot for every pair of deer antlers they brought. Halls of mounted stuffed animals from around the world are now the epitome of the collection, and one features such oddities as a two-headed cow and an eight-legged lamb.

But another reason to come is for the cheezoid Americana – there are maps of Texas made from rattlesnake rattles and a jaw-dropping collection of Lone Star Beer paraphernalia (such as a guitar made from pull-tabs). The pièce de résistance is the wax museum, which was clearly assembled by buying wax figures from other wax museums and merrily changing the costumes. In one diorama, Teddy Roosevelt consults with what's gotta be Alan Ladd, and in another, it's Tom Selleck as Magnum PI as General Robert E Lee. Another figure has been recast as the famous writer O Henry, who used to imbibe here during his San Antonio years.

Even if you don't have the willpower for visiting the museum, at least get a taste of the place by having a drink in its saloon. A taxidermist's nirvana, this place contains more stuffed animals than you'll ever want to see again in your entire life. The Buckhorn's adjacent curio shop sells bucketloads of Texas stuff, including silver belt buckles, cowboy hats and odder items that must be seen to be believed. It's a wonderland for kids.

LA VILLITA

La Villita, 'the little village,' was a settlement of Coahuiltecan Indians first, then Spanish colonists second. General Martín Perfecto de Cós surrendered to Texas revolutionaries in the **Cós House** at the northeast corner of King Phillip V Walk and Villita St. Later in the 19th century, European immigrants

founded the village itself, which developed alongside what became downtown San Antonio, and is now the Riverwalk's southern end.

The village went into decline around the beginning of the 20th century. After a few decades it was overhauled by the city, giving birth to **La Villita** (Map pp126-7; ☎ 210-207-8610; lavillita.com; 418 Villita St; admission free; ⚘ most shops 10am-6pm Tue-Sun), a heavily touristed and touristy collection of arts-and-crafts shops. It's basically a legitimate national historic landmark district charmingly restored as a tourist trap. That said, it's fun – certainly no more kitschy than other places of the same ilk – and the architecture and grounds make it a lovely place to walk through.

Just off King Philip V Walk in the center of the complex, the San Antonio Conservation Society sponsors exhibits on the history of the area, with interesting textured displays about the sundry building methods and materials used during centuries past. You'll find these exhibits next to the post office above the Bolivar Cafe. Closer to Alamo St, La Villita's **Little Church** opens for services at 11am on Sunday and noon Thursday. Performances are held throughout the year at the Arneson River Theater, situated where King Philip Walk drops down onto the Riverwalk.

SPANISH GOVERNOR'S PALACE

Built in the mid-18th century, the **Spanish Governor's Palace** (Map pp126-7; ☎ 210-224-0601; 105 Plaza de Armas; adult/child 7-13 $1.50/75¢; ⚘ 9am-5pm daily, from 10am Sun), west of city hall, was originally the quarters for the *presidio capitan* of the area's Spanish colonial troops. In 1722 it became the seat of Texas' colonial government – it was from bureaucrats in this palace that Moses Austin sought permission to import American settlers to the area. After Texan independence, the house was used in a variety of ways (including as a saloon), but it was bought and refurbished by the city in 1928. Today, it's a museum filled with period furniture that provides a charming foreground against the backdrop of the palace's adobe walls, brick ovens and fireplaces. Out back is a cobblestone patio and a fountain set among gardens. A self-guided tour pamphlet is available upon entry.

SAN FERNANDO CATHEDRAL

The nation's oldest surviving chapel, the **San Fernando Cathedral** (Map pp126-7; ☎ 210-227-1297; donations welcome; 115 Main Plaza) was established in 1731 by settlers from the Canary Islands. Today it's the parish church of the Archbishop of San Antonio. The original dome collapsed in 1872, and the center of the replacement dome is considered the geographical center of the city. During the Battle of the Alamo, Santa Anna used the church as an observation post, and the battle kicked off when a 'no quarter' flag was raised from the tower. Remains (including charred bones and fragments of uniforms) uncovered in 1936, wildly purported to be those of Davy Crockett, William Travis and James Bowie, are now kept in a marble casket at the rear of the church. The church also features impressive stained-glass windows and a pipe organ dating to 1884.

James Bowie was, in fact, married here. Modern-day wedding parties streaming through the cathedral doors may prevent all but the most persistent visitor from getting inside to take a peek. Your best bet may be to attend mass. Bilingual services in English and Spanish are held at 5:30pm on Saturday and 5pm Sunday. On Sunday there's also a televised Spanish-language mass at 8am, a 10am service in Latin, English and Spanish, a Spanish-only service at noon and one in English at 2pm.

HEMISFAIR PARK

Site of the 1968 World's Fair, HemisFair Park is south of downtown and has provided it with one of its landmark structures, the 750ft **Tower of the Americas** (Map pp126-7; ☎ 210-207-8615; adult/senior/child 4-11 $3/2/1; ☺ 9am-10pm daily, till 11pm Fri-Sat), which is taller than Seattle's Space Needle. At 579ft, the tower's observation deck offers views of the city far and wide. If heights aren't making you queasy yet, there's always the revolving Tower Restaurant (reservations strongly advised) and the High in the Sky lounge.

The 15-acre park fell on bad times in the 1950s and was quite a scoundrel magnet until a renovation that was completed in 1990. Today, it's home to fountains, playgrounds, a number of wonderful Victorian homes and the **Instituto de Mexico** (Mexican Cultural Institute; map pp126-7; ☎ 210-227-0123; admission free; ☺ 10am-5pm Tue-Fri, noon-5pm Sat), the cultural wing of the Mexican consulate. It offers concerts, art exhibits, food fairs, dance performances and other cultural events. Also visit its nearby **Casa Mexicana Gallery** (☎ 210-227-0123; admission free; ☺ 9:30am-5pm Mon-Fri), which has excellent art exhibitions. Spanish-language instruction at all levels is offered throughout the year at the campus here for the **Universidad Nacional Autonoma de México** (☎ 210-222-8626; 600 HemisFair Plaza).

INSTITUTE OF TEXAN CULTURES

Originally slated for a six-month run during HemisFair, the **institute** (Map pp126-7; ☎ 210-458-2330; www.texancultures.utsa.edu/public; 801 S Bowie St; adult/senior/child 3-12 $5/3/2; ☺ 9am-5pm Tue-Sun) is now a permanent museum and the state of Texas' official center for

---

FREE FOR ALL

Some of the best things in San Antonio don't cost a penny (or even a peso), including:

- Ambling inside the **Alamo** and along the **Mission Trail**
- Live jazz on the **Riverwalk**
- Exhibitions at the **McNay Art Museum**, the **Instituto de Mexico**, **ArtPace**, the **San Antonio Art League Museum** and, on Tuesday after 3pm, **SAMA**
- Amateur hour and 'After Midnight Madness' shows at the **Rivercenter Comedy Club**
- Gallery-hopping at the **Southwest School of Art & Craft**, **La Villita** and the **Blue Star Arts Complex**
- Strolling the **Japanese Tea Gardens**
- Peeking inside **Sunset Station**, **San Fernando Cathedral**, the **Guenther House** and historic **Fort Sam Houston**
- Experiencing **Fiesta San Antonio** or any of the city's other colorful celebrations

the interpretation of its history. Run by the University of Texas at San Antonio, the somewhat outdated displays explore the diverse backgrounds of the settlers of Texas. The main exhibit, spread out over an enormous single-floor space, has sections devoted to over two dozen ethnic and national groups of settlers in Texas, including Anglo-Americans, Mexicans, Germans, European Jews, Irish and African Americans, among others. The Native American and Tejano sections are the most interesting.

There's a puppet theater where interpretive shows are held daily, a real chuck wagon, displays on fibers and fabrics and a working post office. Near the front entrance don't miss the displays of footwear donated by famous Texans, everything from a pair of vanity cowboy boots once worn by Dubya to the sparkly high heels of novelist Sandra Cisneros. The Back 40 Area, behind the main exhibition, has reconstructed living-history buildings such as a fort, schoolhouse, log cabin and a windmill. Except during the Texas Folklife Festival, parking is validated free for two hours at the lot beside the museum.

ARTPACE

This unique contemporary arts **gallery** (Map pp126-7; ☎ 210-212-4900; www.artpace.org; 445 N Main Ave; admission free; ☒ noon-5pm Wed-Sun, till 8pm Thu) hosts temporary exhibitions by its outstanding artists-in-residence, who are selected from a pool drawn from across Texas, the USA and abroad. Inside a 1920s automobile showroom, the renovated gallery space is inspiring and the works are often experimental. ArtPace also schedules special community events, including lectures, films, artist conversations and more.

SUNSET STATION

Just north of the Alamodome, **Sunset Station** (Map pp126-7; ☎ 210-222-9481; www.sunset -station.com; 1174 E Commerce St) is worth a look. Originally the Southern Pacific Railroad Depot and the city's Amtrak station (which moved next door), and a stop along the Sunset Limited line between San Francisco and New Orleans, the station has been fully restored to its old glory, complete with stained-glass windows and a colorful, bold interior. Don't overlook

the vintage 1916 steam engine either. The station is open to visitors during the day, but is usually hired out in the evening, for concerts, private parties or whoever can afford it. The attached entertainment complex can be a good place for a night out.

NAVARRO STATE HISTORIC SITE

José Antonio Navarro (1795–1871), who served in the Mexican government and later as a state legislator, was a lawyer and rancher who became one of two native Texans to sign the Texas Declaration of Independence. The wealthy Tejano built a large residence and office in downtown San Antonio, which is now open to the public as a **state historical park** (Map pp126-7; ☎ 210-226-4801; 228 S Laredo St; adult/child 6-12 $2/1; ☒ 10am-4pm Wed-Sun). Not far from Market Square, the 1-acre park consists of three separate adobe, caliche block and limestone buildings that were his home, office and kitchen. Call ahead for guided tours and demonstrations of equipment and household gadgets.

O HENRY HOUSE MUSEUM

A block away from the Navarro State Historic Site, this humble 19th-century adobe **home** (Map pp126-7; no ☎ ; cnr Laredo & Houston Sts; admission free; ☒ open daily, hrs vary) has been moved here from its original location in Southtown. The street corner has an interesting interpretive sign about the historic site, but can also be a magnet for some pretty unsavory types. The O Henry Museum in Austin is more interesting anyway.

King William District & Southtown

South of downtown on the banks of the San Antonio River, the charming King William District (once nicknamed 'Sauer Kraut Bend') was built by wealthy German settlers at the end of the 19th century. The architecture here is mostly Victorian, though there are fine examples of Italianate, colonial-revival, beaux-arts, and even art-moderne styles. Most of the district's houses have been renovated and are privately owned or run as B&Bs. It's a very pleasant area for a stroll. Stop by the **San Antonio Conservation Society** (Map p134; ☎ 210-224-6163; 107 King William St) for self-guided walking tour brochures.

SAN ANTONIO

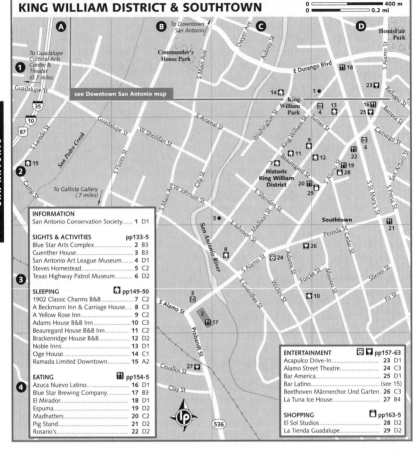

KING WILLIAM DISTRICT & SOUTHTOWN

0 ————— 400 m
0 ————— 0.2 mi

INFORMATION
San Antonio Conservation Society...... 1 D1

SIGHTS & ACTIVITIES   pp133-5
Blue Star Arts Complex.................... 2 B3
Guenther House................................ 3 B3
San Antonio Art League Museum....... 4 D1
Steves Homestead............................ 5 C2
Texas Highway Patrol Museum.......... 6 D2

SLEEPING   pp149-50
1902 Classic Charms B&B................. 7 C2
A Beckmann Inn & Carriage House.... 8 C3
A Yellow Rose Inn............................ 9 C2
Adams House B&B Inn.....................10 C3
Beauregard House B&B Inn..............11 C2
Brackenridge House B&B..................12 D2
Noble Inns......................................13 D1
Oge House.......................................14 C1
Ramada Limited Downtown.............15 A2

EATING   pp154-5
Azuca Nuevo Latino.........................16 D1
Blue Star Brewing Company.............17 B3
El Mirador.......................................18 D1
Espuma..19 D2
Madhatters......................................20 C2
Pig Stand...21 D2
Rosario's..22 D2

ENTERTAINMENT   pp157-63
Acapulco Drive-In............................23 D1
Alamo Street Theatre......................24 C3
Bar America......................................25 D1
Bar Latino..................................... (see 15)
Beethoven Männerchor Und Garten. 26 C3
La Tuna Ice House............................27 B4

SHOPPING   pp163-5
El Sol Studios..................................28 D2
La Tienda Guadalupe.......................29 D2

see Downtown San Antonio map

Generally speaking, South Alamo St divides the King William District lying to the west and Southtown, a vibrant arts district, to the east. Many art galleries schedule their exhibition openings, and art studios open their doors to the public, on the first Friday of each month. These **'First Friday'** events also feature live entertainment, longer shopping hours and a lot of pedestrian traffic on the streets of Southtown. Visit www.southtown.net for more information.

VIA's Blue Line streetcars stop nearby all of the following sights, including the storefront **Texas Highway Patrol Museum** (Map p134; ☎ 210-231-6030, 800-795-8472; 812 S Alamo St; admission $2; ☼ 10am-4pm Tue-Sun), a

small memorial hall with a few simple educational displays.

BLUE STAR ARTS COMPLEX

At the south end of the district, this enormous **complex** (Map p134; www.bluestarcomplex.com; 1400-1414 S Alamo St; admission free; ☎ complex open daily, gallery hrs vary) is a working arts center, featuring several galleries and more than 30 art studios. It's more commercially minded than the smaller Southwest School of Art & Craft, but also more multicultural. It's still very much the real McCoy, with regular gallery openings and art shows. Within the sprawling complex you'll find the **Joan Grona Gallery** (☎ 210-225-6334; 112 Blue Star; ☼ 11am-5pm Wed-Sat, noon-5pm Sun) for innovative contemporary art; the **San Angel Folk Art** (☎ 210-226-6688; ☾ noon-5pm daily) shop; and the main **Blue Star Art Space** (☎ 210-227-6960; 116 Blue Star; ☾ noon-6pm Wed-Sun), which is a series of contemporary art studios. Blue Star Brewing Company and the Jump-Start Theater are also part of the complex.

GUENTHER HOUSE
German immigrant Carl Hilmar Guenther founded the Pioneer Flour Mill in Fredericksburg in 1851, moving it to San Antonio in 1859 and building his family house right next to the river. The house has been restored to a small-scale **museum** (Map p134; ☎ 210-227-1061; www.guentherhouse.com; 205 E Guenther St; admission free; ☾ 8am-4pm Mon-Sat, 8am-3pm Sun). Although the period furnishing and historical displays aren't much of an attraction, the café is a pleasant place for lunch and the river mill gift shop has a few unusual souvenirs for sale, such as custom stoneware and gourmet baking goods. Look for the 'Pioneer Flour Mills' sign directly opposite the Blue Star Arts Complex on S Alamo St.

SAN ANTONIO ART LEAGUE MUSEUM
This tiny **museum** (Map p134; ☎ 210-223-1140; www.saalm.org; 130 King William St; admission free; ☾ 10am-2pm Tue-Sat) houses art from regional 20th-century American artists. In the 1920s, the San Antonio Art League was famous for annual exhibitions of paintings of Texas wildflowers. The museum's early patron was Marion McNay, who also founded the excellent McNay Art Museum. Here, the permanent collections include textiles, paintings, sculpture, furniture and photography. If you're in the neighborhood, it's worth a short visit, especially since you'll likely have the place all to yourself.

STEVES HOMESTEAD
Volunteer docents from the San Antonio Conservation Society run guided tours through this Italianate villa and French Second Empire-style **home** (Map p134; ☎ 210-225-5924; 509 King William St; adult/child under 12 $5/free; ☾ 10am-4:15pm daily, last tour at 3:30pm) dating from 1876. Built for Edward Steves, a wealthy lumber merchant, this stately house has been restored to demonstrate the life of the affluent at the end of the 19th century.

Incidentally, San Antonio's first indoor swimming pool is on the property.

Brackenridge Park & Around
A couple of miles north of downtown, Brackenridge Park has been for over a century now a favorite San Antonian getaway spot, lovers' lane and gentle amusement park, with offerings including boat rentals, playgrounds, rides and gardens. Its main attraction – other than a serene green setting – is that it's the headspring for the San Antonio River. Many of the park's sights are designed for children, but may be equally interesting for adults, such as the impressive **Witte Museum** (p142).

SAN ANTONIO MUSEUM OF ART
Housed in the original 1880s Lone Star Brewery, which is a piece of artwork itself, the **San Antonio Museum of Art** (SAMA; map pp136-7; ☎ 210-978-8100; www.sa-museum.org; 200 W Jones Ave; bus Nos 8, 9 or 14; adult/senior/student/child 4-11 $6/5/4/1.75; ☾ 10am-5pm Tue-Sat, till 8pm Tue & Thu, noon-6pm Sun) is off Broadway just north of downtown. It houses an impressive trove of Spanish colonial, Mexican, pre-Columbian, folk, modern and contemporary works from Latin America.

On the ground floor is Egyptian art (boggle at the *Seated Statue of a God*), serving trays and ancient glassworks, as well as a fine series of Greco-Roman sculpture. After the brand-new Asian wing opens in fall 2004, expect to see Chinese porcelain from the Ming and Qing dynasties, including bowls, vases, urns and tomb figures of horses and warriors. SAMA's Asian collection also has Thai pottery, Vietnamese dishes, Korean bronze works, Japanese folding screens and more. In addition to the permanent collections and touring exhibitions (which are charged separately), SAMA hosts regular poetry readings, films, classes, lectures and other events; on Tuesday from 3pm to 9pm the museum is free. There's a gift shop, museum café and free parking across the street.

SAN ANTONIO BOTANICAL GARDENS
This expertly tended, 33-acre **garden complex** (SABA; map pp136-7; ☎ 210-207-3250; www.sabot.org; 555 Funston Place; bus Nos 9 or 14; adult/senior/child 3-13 $4/2/1; ☾ 9am-5pm), northeast of downtown,

SAN ANTONIO

BRACKENRIDGE PARK & AROUND

A   **B**   **C**   **D**

INFORMATION
Broadway News.................................. **1** D5
Cheever Books.................................. **2** E3
E-Z Wash Laundry **3** D4
Half Price Books, Records,
    Magazines............................... (see 26)
Kinko's.. **4** F2
The Twig Bookshop; The Red Balloon.. **5** F1

SIGHTS & ACTIVITIES   pp135-7
Japanese Tea Gardens...................... **6** D3
Kiddie Park...................................... **7** E4
San Antonio Botanical Gardens
    (SABA).. **8** F3
San Antonio Museum of Art (SAMA).. **9** C6
Texas Pioneer & Ranger Museum..... **10** E3
Witte Museum................................ **11** E3

SLEEPING   pp150-1
Bullis House.................................... **12** F5
HI San Antonio International
    Hostel....................................... (see 12)
Rodeway Inn Downtown.................. **13** B6
Terrell Castle.................................. **14** E5
The Inn at Craig Place..................... **15** B4
Villager Lodge Downtown............... **16** C5

EATING   pp155-6
Bill Miller BBQ................................ **17** F2
Candlelight Coffee House................. **18** C4
Earl Abel's...................................... **19** D5
Josephine Street............................. **20** D5
Koi Kawa.. **21** E2
La Madeleine French Bakery & Cafe.. **22** F1
Liberty Bar..................................... **23** D5

Olmos Pharmacy.............................. **24** B2
Pig Stand....................................... **25** D6
WD Deli.. **26** E3
Willard's Jamaican Jerk
    Bar-B-Que................................... **27** C4

ENTERTAINMENT   pp157-63
Banana's Billiards............................ **28** A4
Carmen's de la Calle Café............... (see 27)
Electric Company............................ **29** A5
Heat... **30** B5

Josephine Theatre........................... **31** C5
Laurie Auditorium........................... **32** C2
Pegasus... **33** B5
Salute.. **34** C4
Sam's Burger Joint.......................... **35** D5
San Pedro Playhouse....................... **36** A4
Silver Dollar Saloon........................ (see 33)
Sin 13.. **37** B5
The Annex...................................... **38** B6
The Saint.. **39** B5
White Rabbit................................... **40** C5

Melrose Dr

Annie Ave   44
Holland Ave   24
Hilderbrand Ave
Lullwood Ave
Rosewood Ave
Hollywood Ave
Schreiner Place   Oakmont Ct

Bushnell Ave
Laurel Heights Place
Kings Hwy

Shook Ave
Joy Dr
Thelma Dr
Devine Rd
Mt Erin Pass

32
San Antonio Zoo
6
N St Mary's St

Trinity University

McAllister Freeway

Pastores St
Alvin St
Mulberry Ave

Mulberry Ave
Huisache Ave

Magnolia Ave
Mistletoe Ave
Woodlawn Ave   28
Craig Place   15
Russell Place
French St

Howard St
N Main Ave
Breeden Ave
N Flores St

Magnolia Ave
Mistletoe Ave   18
Woodlawn Ave   27
Craig Place
Russell Place   34
French St
Rose Place

Kings Ct
N St Mary's St
Valdez St
Terry Ct

Magnolia Ave
Magnolia Dr
Lindell Place
Woodlawn Ave
Armour Ave
Craig St

Brackenridge Municipal Golf Course

Ashby Place
Courtland Place   42
Dewey Place
Locust St
Myrtle St   46
W Park Ave

36
37   40
31
Ashby Place
Josephine St
Grayson St
Locust St
Myrtle St
Schiller St
E Park Ave

McAllister Freeway

23   20
35
16
Newell St

Avenue B
Avenue A
IS 35
SPUR 368
281
Broadway
N Alamo St
Austin St

San Pedro Park
San Pedro Ave
Maverick St

W Evergreen St   30
39
W Laurel St   33
29   Crockett Park
W Cypress St
W Poplar St

Howard St
Ogden St
N Main Ave
43
McCullough Ave

Erie Ave
Alleta Ave
E Euclid Ave

E Elmira St
Pan Am Expressway

10
87
Marshall St
38   13

W Euclid Ave
W Elmira St
N Frio St
N Flores St
San Pedro Ave
Jackson St
Lewis St

Lexington Ave
McCullough Ave
E Quincy St
E Camden St
Madison Square Park

W Jones Ave   9
9th St
10th St
12th St
Maverick Park

37
281
Austin St

see Downtown San Antonio map

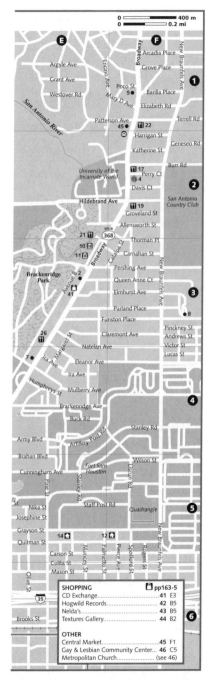

showcases native Texas flora. There's also a fragrance garden and a wonderful conservatory, with a bit of everything from equatorial rainforest to alpine flowers to a tropical lagoon. The strolling garden was designed and created by a 26th-generation gardener and one of Japan's living national treasures from the island of Kyūshū, specifically the city of Kumamoto, which is also home to one of Japan's most revered traditional gardens, Suizenji-kōen. A few of that famous garden's elements appear here at SABA. Call or go online for a calendar of special events, anything from concerts under the stars to bonsai workshops to summer classes for children.

JAPANESE TEA GARDENS

At Brackenridge Park's northwestern end, an eyesore of a quarry has been transformed into a Japanese-style strolling **garden** (Map pp136-7; 3800 N St Mary's St; bus No 8; admission free; ☽ 8am-dusk), with stone bridges, floral displays and a 60ft waterfall. Popular with families and senior citizens, it's a pretty spot near the San Antonio Zoo. But it's not worth a special trip, especially if you've already seen the San Antonio Botanical Gardens. The curious sign over the front entrance still says 'Chinese Tea Gardens,' lingering evidence of America's backlash against all things Japanese during WWII. ('Freedom Fries,' anyone?)

TEXAS PIONEER & RANGER MUSEUM

Next door to the Witte Museum in Brackenridge Park, the dusty place officially known as the **Texas Pioneer, Trail Driver and Texas Rangers Museum** (Map pp136-7; ☎ 210-822-9011; 3805 Broadway; bus Nos 9 or 14; adult/senior/child 6-12 $4/1.50/1; ☽ 10am-5pm May-Aug, 11am-4pm Sept-Apr) is exactly what it sounds like. Housed in a rather impressive WPA building (1936) specifically designed for it, the museum is not a must-see attraction. However, staff and volunteers (some former rangers themselves) are interesting guides, and the barbed wire displays are also a hoot. Look for an annual Western art show during February.

Greater San Antonio

San Antonio's major theme parks, including SeaWorld and Six Flags Fiesta Texas, are described in 'San Antonio for Children,' p141. With all the firepower in the area, the city is teeming with military museums. But note that access to the bases is restricted, and for all, you'll need to get visitor's passes (obtainable only through certain gates, and even then subject to change), so bring photo ID. Sometimes the bases may be closed entirely except to military personnel and their dependents, so always call ahead.

MCNAY ART MUSEUM

This museum, housed within the **McNay Art Institute** (Map pp122-3; ☎ 210-824-5368; www.mcnayart.org; 6000 N New Braunfels Ave; bus No 14; admission free; ☽ 10am-5pm Tue-Sat, grounds 7am-6pm daily), north of Brackenridge Park, is in a spectacular Spanish colonial revival–style mansion that was the private residence of Marion Koogler McNay. It's worth venturing outside of downtown San Antonio just to visit this place.

Upon her death in 1950, McNay left her impressive collection of European and American modern art to the city. It has been supplemented since by other Texas family collectors. Now the collection is among the best in the Southwest, with works by van Gogh, Chagall, Cézanne, Hopper, Pissarro, O'Keeffe and Dalí. Unusual works from the Tobin Collection of Theatre Arts include over 10,000 design pieces for operas and ballets. Smaller exhibitions, including rotating shows, the galleries of medieval and Renaissance art and diverting documentaries of Koogler's life, are located upstairs. In the courtyard, colorful tiles tell the story of Don Quixote.

Downstairs, the **research library** (☽ 10am-4:45pm Tue-Fri) is also open to the public. Admission and parking for both the library and the museum are free.

FORT SAM HOUSTON

Fifth US Army headquarters and home of Brooke Army Medical Center, **Fort Sam Houston** (Map pp122-3; ☎ public affairs 210-221-1151), just northeast of downtown, is a working collection of historic buildings with designated museums that are open to the public. Incidentally, the first military aircraft took flight at Fort Sam Houston in 1910.

The **Quadrangle** (Map pp136-7; ☎ 210-221-1232; cnr E Grayson St & Liscum Rd, west of New Braunfels Ave; admission free; ☽ usually 8am-6pm Mon-Fri, noon-6pm

Sat-Sun) was built in 1876. The base briefly held prisoner Apache chief Geronimo. Today, the Quadrangle is open as a museum of the history of the fort, and it leads through to sort of a petting zoo – deer have been kept here for more than 100 years, and rabbits, ducks and chickens abound. The hours can change depending on the army's schedule.

The **US Army Medical Department Museum** (AMEDD; map pp122-3; ☎ 210-221-6358, 210-221-6277; 2310 Stanley St; admission free; ☽ 10am-4pm Tue-Sun), in the northeast section of the fort's grounds, has a display of army medical gear from the US and several other countries, including Germany, the former Soviet Union, Vietnam and China, and a cool collection of restored ambulances, helicopters and a hospital rail car. But what makes the AMEDD museum really worth the trip is the collection of Civil War surgical gear, notably the disturbing saws and portable amputation kits.

The public entrance to Fort Sam Houston is a short drive northeast of downtown. By car, take I-35 north (exit at Wilson Rd or Stanley Rd), then head west to the fort's security checkpoint, where all visitors must stop to obtain a free day pass.

US AIR FORCE HISTORY & TRADITIONS MUSEUM

This fascinating **museum** (Map pp122-3; ☎ 210-671-3055; 2051 George Ave, base entrance off SW Military Drive; admission free; ☽ call for hrs) at Lackland Air Force Base, 13 miles southwest of downtown off US 90, has vintage historical aircraft on display. It's a must for flight buffs. At press time it was closed to the general public, but call ahead to check if it's since been reopened to visitors.

HANGAR 9

Getting a bit more esoteric is Hangar 9 – the Edward H White II Museum at **Brooks Air Force Base** (Map pp122-3; ☎ museum 210-536-2203; 8008 Inner Circle Rd; admission free; ☽ museum 7am-2pm Mon-Fri). Located 8 miles southeast of downtown, the museum is inside the oldest wooden aircraft hangar in the air force, and it's named after a San Antonio native who perished in the Apollo I capsule fire after becoming the first American astronaut to walk in space. Displays concern early manned flight and the evolution of aerospace medicine. Another exhibit is dedicated to flight nurses. A rare JN-4D 'Jenny' biplane inside the hangar is one of only a dozen left in the world.

TEXAS TRANSPORTATION MUSEUM
This modest volunteer-run **museum** (TTM; map pp122-3; ☎ 210-490-3554; www.txtransportation museum. org; 11731 Wetmore Rd, off Wurzbach Pkwy; adult/child $5/3; ☺ 9am-4pm Thu, Sat & Sun) boasts full-size, miniature and indoor scale model railroads. Train rides are included with the price of admission, and there are special holiday events for kids. By car from downtown, take I-35 north to exit 167, turn left onto Starlight Terrace (which turns into Thousand Oaks Dr). Merge left onto Wurzbach Pkwy for about 3 miles; exit onto Wetmore Rd, then turn left (south) again. The entrance is down on the right. Call ahead to check opening hours before making the trip.

ACTIVITIES
Apart from **Brackenridge Park** (p135) and the **Mission Trail** (p128), San Antonio is short on places to enjoy the great outdoors. You've usually got to head into the Hill Country or drive north on I-35 to the aquatic wonderlands of New Braunfels, Gruene and San Marcos, where you can go swimming and tubing to your heart's content on local rivers and at amusement parks. Golfers are in luck, however.

Golf Courses
San Antonio is a favorite golfing vacation destination, thanks to the region's mild year-round climate. Rates vary from $35 for toting your own bag around a public course to over $150 to play a round at a private resort.

Municipal golf courses include the following:

Brackenridge Park (Map pp136-7; ☎ 210-226-5612; 2315 Ave B) The original site of the PGA winter tour and inducted into the Texas Golf Hall of Fame, this 18-hole championship golf course dates from 1916.
Olmos Basin (Map pp122-3; ☎ 210-826-4041; 7022 N McCullough Ave) North of Brackenridge Park, this challenging 18-hole, 6890-yard course is the site of amateur tournaments.
Cedar Creek (☎ 210-695-5050; 8250 Vista Colina) A hilly 18-hole, 7150-yard course in a suburban subdivision, with an on-site driving range.

Willow Springs (Map pp122-3; ☎ 210-226-6721; E Houston St, at SBC Parkway) Also a venue for the Texas Open golf tournament, this championship 18-hole, 7100-yard course is near the Coliseum.

Nationally renowned public golf courses include the following:

The Quarry (Map pp122-3; ☎ 210-824-4500, 800-347-7759; 444 E Basse Rd) Designed by Keith Foster, this 18-hole, 5600-yard urban course winds through grasslands and a century-old old quarry pit.
Canyon Springs Golf Club (☎ 210-497-1770, 888-800-1511; 2440 Canyon Golf Rd) Out where the Hill Country begins, Canyon Springs has twice been rated one of the USA's best public golf courses.
Westin La Cantera (☎ 210-558-4653, 800-446-5387; 16401 La Cantera Pkwy) A stop on the PGA tour, this premier golf resort boasts two championship courses, with one designed by Arnold Palmer.

Hiking & Cycling
Your best options are the 12-mile paved recreational path along the **Mission Trail** (p128) or a visit to **Brackenridge Park** (p135). Otherwise try the following places, which are both far from downtown.

MCALLISTER PARK
For a taste of the Hill Country without venturing outside the city limits, head to this 850-acre **suburban park** (☎ 210-207-3000; 13102 Jones Maltsberger Rd; admission free; ☺ dawn-dusk). The park, which is about 12 miles northeast of downtown (just north of the airport), is covered in woods, and during the summer months, it's home to some shorebirds. It has about 7 miles of trails for walking and cycling; one of the trails is also wheelchair-accessible. By car from downtown, take US 281 north to the Nakoma Rd exit, turn right and continue to Jones Maltsberger Rd. Turn left and drive for another 1½ miles; the park entrance is on the right.

FRIEDRICH WILDERNESS PARK
Close to Six Flags Fiesta Texas, this 230-acre 'wilderness' park (☎ 210-698-1057; 21480 Milsa, north of Loop 1604; admission free; ☺ 8am-5pm, till 8pm Apr-Sep) has 5½ miles of walking trails that are especially worth a detour when wildflowers are blooming in spring. The park is also a nesting ground for two endangered species of birds, the golden-cheeked warbler and

the black-capped vireo. It's about a half-hour's drive from downtown; take I-10 north to exit 554 (Camp Bullis Rd), turn left to pass under the interstate, then right onto the access road. After about a mile, take another left onto Oak Dr, then turn right at the T-intersection onto Milsa; the park entrance is on the left.

DOWNTOWN SAN ANTONIO WALKING TOUR

This 2¾-mile walking tour starts at the Alamo, meanders along the southern part of the **Riverwalk** and ends up by the Southwest School of Art & Craft at the northern edge of downtown; it doesn't cover the historic King William District.

Starting outside the **Alamo (1)** in Alamo Plaza, opposite the downtown visitors center, stroll down to Crockett St, turning east. Pass the historic **Menger Hotel (2)** and the equally venerable **Crockett Hotel (3)**. Walk south, then east around the Rivercenter Mall and detour into **St Joseph's Church (4)**, dating from the 1850s; self-guided booklets are available at the door.

After exiting the church, turn around and go west to Alamo St. Head south past the ugly duckling **Hilton Palacio del Rio (5)** hotel until you reach La Villita, a tourist-thronged art studio collection. Turn right onto Paseo de la Villita and amble past the **Little Church (6)** and historic **Cós House (7)**. Continue to the intersection of Villita and Navarro Sts. Immediately ahead on the left is the **Mexican Consulate (8)**, a building with the still stolid appearance it was given in its former life as one of the USA's Federal Reserve banks. A block farther on is one of the lynchpins of SA's skyline, the soaring and octagonal art deco **Tower Life Building (9)**. Some say the tower's gargoyles were designed to protect the building, which was erected in the aftermath of the stock market crash of 1929.

Heading north on St Mary's St, walk up a block and you will come to Paseo del Rio, more commonly referred to as **Riverwalk**. Walk down the little staircase and wind along the south bank of the San Antonio River. If you're hungry, snack at **Wild About Harry's (10)**, then keep going past

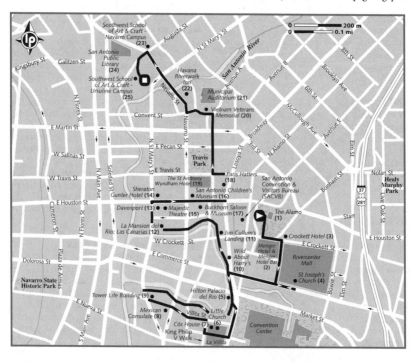

Jim Cullum's Landing (11), a landmark jazz club on the river. Finally, at the end of a string of luxury hotels, the 19th-century **La Mansion del Rio (12)** is favored by celebrity guests. Its Las Canarias restaurant is an tempting stop for breakfast or lunch.

At N St Mary's St, ascend the staircase to street level and walk north past the **Davenport (13)** cocktail lounge to Houston St. Standing on the opposite corner is the **Sheraton Gunter Hotel (14)**, another grand downtown hostelry. Promenade east on Houston St by the splendid 1920s **Majestic Theatre (15)**, a beautifully renovated Spanish revival theater that's currently home to the San Antonio Symphony. On the next block is the **San Antonio Children's Museum (16)**. Also be sure to take a peek inside the **Buckhorn Saloon & Museum (17)**, which has an attached curio shop.

Turn left onto Losoya St for window shopping at **Paris Hatters (18)**, then cut west over to the **St Anthony Wyndham Hotel (19)**. Breeze north past Travis Park, and up by the **Vietnam Veterans Memorial (20)** is the neoclassical **Municipal Auditorium (21)**. Walk west to Navarro St, then head north past the gorgeous **Havana Riverwalk Inn (22)** up to Augusta St. Ahead on your right are the exhibition galleries of the Navarro campus of the **Southwest School of Art & Craft (23)**; off to the left is **SA's central public library (24)**, a massive building of cubes and spheres painted in what everyone in town now refers to as 'enchilada red.'

For now, turn left onto Augusta St. . Finally, amble a half block beside the old convent stone walls, then turn left into the driveway of the charming **Ursuline campus (25)** of the Southwest School of Art & Craft. Here you'll find a small visitors museum, art galleries and the Copper Kitchen, an excellent place for lunch.

SAN ANTONIO FOR CHILDREN

San Antonio is a very popular family destination, thanks to its theme parks and mild year-round climate. Day trips worth taking include those out to **New Braunfels** and **San Marcos**. Inside the city limits, the Riverwalk and Brackenridge Park are the centers for family-oriented fun. For more on outdoor activities, see p139. See individual reviews of hotels and restaurants for some great family options.

See p192 for general practical advice on traveling with kids.

Downtown

Throughout the year, SA's **central public library** (p123) runs special programs for children. Another popular open-house event at the **Southwest School of Art & Craft** (p130) is **Saturday Morning Discovery**, a free program from September to May, designed for kids between the ages of five and 16. Programs last for a month of Saturdays and include workshops in batik, drawing, painting, ceramics, silk-screening and other art techniques. Reservations are required (☎ 210-224-1848 ext 321). If you live in the area or will be around for a few weeks, check it out.

SAN ANTONIO CHILDREN'S MUSEUM

Set in a former dime store, the **San Antonio Children's Museum** (Map pp126-7; ☎ 210-212-4453; www.sakids.org; 305 E Houston St; admission $6, child under 2 free; ☪ 9am-5pm Mon-Fri, 9am-6pm Sat, noon-4pm Sun in summer, shorter hrs in winter) is one of the state's best kids' museums. It has two floors of exhibits, including the Good Cents Bank, where kids open an account and can use an ATM; the Kidz Cafe, where they can explore the inner working of a diner; a compost room, where about a billion worms are helping to make our world a better place; and a hard-hat area, where kids can try out a front-end loader. Community volunteers and local businesses come in for special events, such as when PBS films its hands-on kids science show *Zoom Zone* twice a week. Check the website or call for a schedule of workshops and events. Parking is validated for one hour at the MidCity parking garage, at the corner of Navarro and College Sts.

MAGIK CHILDREN'S THEATRE

Not far from the Riverwalk, this merry theater troupe (Map pp126-7; ☎ 210-227-2751; www.magiktheatre.org; 420 S Alamo St; adult/child/infant $8/6/2; ☪ box office 9am-5pm Mon-Fri, 10am-5pm Sat) stages adaptations of favorite children's books, hilarious original musicals and modern retellings of Texas legends and classic fairy tales, like the witty (and bilingual!) *La Cinderella*. The theater's regular season lasts from September to May, and includes a contemporary play series for adults, too.

Brackenridge Park

In the center of the park near the zoo, there's a **miniature railroad**, an old-fashioned **carousel** and a **skyride** (3910 N St Mary's St; ☎ 210-734-5401; each ride adult/child 3-11 $2.25/1.75; ✆ 9:30am-5pm, extended hrs in summer), a Swiss-made cable car that grants so-so views of the city.

WITTE MUSEUM

Pronounced 'witty,' this top-notch **museum** (Map pp136-7; ☎ 210-357-1900; www.wittemuseum .org; 3801 Broadway; bus Nos 9 or 14; adult/senior/child 4-11 $6/5/4; ✆ 10am-5pm Mon-Sat, till 9pm Tue, noon-5pm Sun, extended hrs in summer), north of downtown along the east edge of Brackenridge Park, is a great place to spend the day with kids; the Science Treehouse, a high-tech activity center in back of the museum building, is a marvelous diversion. Kids begin downstairs with lots of cool physical-property displays designed to tire out the little darlings before they even get to the more cerebral displays upstairs, which include music makers, a video-light microscope and an Internet room. Outside the treehouse, a deck overlooks the San Antonio River; there's a real treehouse as well. Inside the main museum are excellent permanent exhibits on Texas natural history and the indigenous peoples of the Lower Pecos region, including a replica of their cave dwellings. Downstairs is Texas Wild, which covers the flora and fauna of all Texas ecological regions. Especially noteworthy are special temporary exhibitions on the history, culture and peoples of the River City, aimed at both adults and children. On Tuesday from 3pm to 9pm, the museum is free.

SAN ANTONIO ZOO

Established in 1914, the **San Antonio Zoological Gardens & Aquarium** (Map pp136-7; ☎ 210-734-7183; www.sazoo-aq.org; 3903 N St Mary's St; bus No 8; adult/senior & child 3-11 $8/6; ✆ 9am-6pm, till 5pm Labor Day–Memorial Day) is famous for its animal breeding conservation programs, which have given it one of the largest endangered-animal collections in the country. But parts of the zoo still need renovation and expansion, so don't be surprised to find some of the exhibitions looking cramped. There are more than 3500 animals here, representing some 750 species. Things to see include enormous free-flight tropical aviaries and a petting zoo and playground. A recent addition is the Conservation Research Center, which has a number of endangered species on show, including the wonderfully creepy Goliath bird-eating spider.

KIDDIE PARK

This 1920s-vintage kiddie **amusement park** (Map pp136-7; ☎ 210-824-4351; 3015 Broadway; bus Nos 9 or 14; single-ride tickets from 35¢, unlimited day pass from $6; ✆ 10am-dusk daily, from 11am Sun) has a wonderful old carousel, a tiny roller coaster, a Ferris wheel, skee-ball alleys and more. It's a slice of carnival atmosphere year-round. Bargain discount days are on Wednesday.

Greater San Antonio

SEAWORLD

One in a chain of parks owned by brewery giant Anheuser-Busch, perhaps to redeem itself to the world for bringing it Budweiser beer, **SeaWorld Adventure Park** (☎ 210-523-3611, 800-700-7786; www.seaworld.com, 10500 SeaWorld Dr; bus No 64; adult/child 3-9 $40/30; ✆ 10am-6pm Mar-Nov, later in high season) claims to be the world's largest marine-life park, and it gives aid to real scientific research and conservation efforts and contributes to education (see www.seaworld.org) throughout the country. It's also got a whopping couple of rides – such as the 'Steel Eel' hypercoaster and the 'Great White,' an inverted 'heels-over-head' roller coaster – and marine-life displays that'll have the kids in awe; if you're in the mood for a theme park, it's your best bet in the area. Pay an extra $10 for a behind-the-scenes tour and you'll get to touch a shark.

Peak summer season can be unbelievably crowded, but it's also the best time for free events like evening fireworks and concerts by country music stars. SeaWorld is a half-hour's drive west of downtown, just off Hwy 151 between Loop 410 and Loop 1604. By car, take I-37 south to US 90 west, and take that to exit 153 for TX 151 west. After about 5½ miles, turn left at Westover Hills Blvd, which takes you right to the front entrance. Parking is $7.

SIX FLAGS FIESTA TEXAS

Besides SeaWorld, the city's other major **theme park** (☎ 210-697-5000, 800-473-4378; www .sixflags.com; 17000 IH-10 W, exit 555; bus No 94; adult/ senior/child under 48in tall $37/25/23; ✆ 10am-6pm

Mar-Oct, later in high season) has great roller coasters, swimming pools, water rides and kiddie rides. The setting – against a limestone quarry that looks similar to the Arizona desert – is dramatic, and there's plenty of music and shows. It's broken into several sections, and there is some semblance of a theme celebrating the diversity of Texas and the Southwest – with Batman and Bugs Bunny thrown in, that is. The park is owned by Time Warner Inc, owner of rights to a gazillion licensed comic book and cartoon characters, so you may well see a guy dressed as the Green Lantern in a Hispanic village–themed area.

Six Flags Fiesta Texas, north of the intersection of I-10 and Loop 1604, is about a 20-minute drive northwest of downtown. From downtown, take I-10 westbound (heading north) to the La Cantera-Fiesta Texas exit and follow the signs. Parking is $7.

SPLASHTOWN
Offering Texas' biggest wave pool, a seven-story aquatic bobsled run, and inner-tubing in total darkness, this **water amusement park** (Map pp122-3; ☎ 210-227-1400; www.splashtownsa .com; 3600 N IH-35; bus No 21; adult/child under 48in tall $22/17, all $14 after 5pm; ☜ 11am-8pm daily Jun–mid-Aug, Sat-Sun only mid-Apr–May & mid-Aug–mid-Sep) certainly has its thrills, as well as gentler floating rides and a special 'Kids Kove' for preschoolers. Call to confirm exact hours.

STEVEN STOLI BACKYARD THEATRE
Especially for kids, this **outdoor theater** (☎ 210-408-0116; www.stolientertainment.com; 11838 Wurzbach Rd, east of I-10 exit 562; adult/child $5.25/4.75; ☜ showtimes usually 10am Wed, Thu & Sat) puts on musical shows year-round, mainly fairy tales and holiday extravaganzas for younger children. It's about a 20-minute drive northwest of downtown.

TOURS
There are several good options for tours of the city.

Yanaguana Cruise (Map pp126-7; ☎ 210-244-5700, 800-417-4139; www.sarivercruise.com; adult/child under 6 $6/1.25; ☜ tours 10am-8pm) offers 40-minute narrated tours along the Riverwalk in kitschy boats. Tickets are just $3 on Tuesday and Wednesday mornings, and if you're with a group, the boats make a nice charter option ($90 for the first hour before 5:30pm

and $45 for each additional 30 minutes). Almost every restaurant along Riverwalk will book you onto the boats for dinner – it's romantic and fun, but the food's no better on the water than on land.

The downtown visitors center (p124) sells tickets for many of the following tours, and has more information about other possibilities.

Lone Star Trolley Tours (☎ 210-226-1706, 800-472-9546; 217 Alamo Plaza; adult/child 2-12 $9.50/4; ☜ tours 10am-4:45pm) runs hop-on/hop-off streetcar tours through downtown San Antonio. Trolleys run along the one-hour route every 45 minutes. Boarding is at Ripley's Believe It or Not!, where you can also buy tickets.

The Texas Trolley Hop (☎ 210-225-8587; adult/child $10/5) offers one-hour, hop-on/hop-off trolley tours of either the downtown area or attractions lying just north of the center. You can buy combination tickets (adult/child $17/9) for both tours.

San Antonio City Tours (☎ 210-228-9776; www.sanantoniocitytours.com) runs one-hour narrated trolley tours and 3½-hour walking and bus tours of the city ($28). Also offered is an all-day tour including admission to the IMAX cinema and a riverboat cruise for $45. It runs Hill Country Magic tours ($45) as well, which last eight hours and visit Hill Country areas, such as Fredericksburg and the LBJ Ranch.

Coach USA (☎ 210-226-1706, 800-472-9456; www.coach usa.com) also runs bus tours ranging from simple city orientation trips to more elaborate full-day programs, including half-day tours of the Alamo and Mission Trail ($22), full-day trips out to the Hill Country ($38) and shopping excursions to San Marcos' factory outlet malls or Nuevo Laredo, Mexico.

Alamo City Paranormal Club (☎ 210-227-3286; adult/child 7-17 $10/5) runs ghost-hunting tours on many evenings (call to see if one is scheduled). The one-hour tours usually leave from the defender's monument in front of the Alamo and visit what are purported to be downtown San Antonio's most haunted addresses.

FESTIVALS & EVENTS
San Antonio is a city with a full calendar of festivals and events; visitors are bound to run into at least one. For a complete list, check with the downtown visitors center (p124). Advance tickets for many of the

SAN ANTONIO

biggest events are sold through **Ticketmaster** (☎ 210-224-9600; www.ticketmaster.com).

JANUARY
San Antonio Mud Festival (mid-Jan) This 'dirty' celebration fetes the draining of the San Antonio River with an arts-and-crafts fair, live music and the annual crowning of the Mud King and Queen at the Kangaroo Court on the Riverwalk.

FEBRUARY
San Antonio Stock Show & Rodeo (☎ 210-225-5851; www.sarodeo.com; 3201 E Houston St; adult/senior/child $5/3/2; mid-Feb) Two weeks' worth of buckin' broncos and other Western hoopla comes to the SBC Center (Map pp122-3); Texan rock, country and Latin music stars also perform on rodeo days.
Mardi Gras (☎ 210-227-4262; thesanantonioriverwalk.com; date varies) On the weekend before Ash Wednesday, the riverfront fills up with decorated barges and all manner of local musicians playing everything from adagio to zydeco, including all the Texan twang most folks can take.

MARCH
St Patrick's Day (Mar 17) On the weekend closest to the 17th, the city dyes the river green and celebrates the feat by tossing back downright Irish quantities of beer. Many festivities are at downtown's La Villita and the Arneson River Theater.

APRIL
Fiesta San Antonio (mid-Apr) The city's biggest bash of the year, and definitely worth planning any trip around. See the special feature on p129 for full details.
Tejano Music Festival (☎ 210-222-8862; tickets 800-500-8470; www.tejanomusicawards.com; early Apr)

A star-studded showcase of Tejano singers and bands kicks off at Sunset Station with a free extravaganza of dance and live music, then heads to the Alamodome for the Tejano Music Awards ceremonies.

MAY
Cinco de Mayo (May 5) In celebration of Mexico's defeat of French troops at the 1862 Battle of Puebla, there's food, music and dances taking place around the city, especially at Market Square.
Tejano Conjunto Festival (☎ 210-271-3151, www.guadalupeculturalarts.org; mid-May) Feast on five days of the world's best *conjunto* musicianship to progressive Tejano sounds, along with plenty of Tex-Mex cooking and dancing.
Return of the Chile Queens (☎ 210-207-8600; date varies) Banned by public health officials in the 1930s, the Chile Queens once set out their dishes of *chile con carne* and other delights in the downtown plaza. Now you'll find a new generation cooking up traditional fiery concoctions, all while being serenaded at Market Square.
Fiesta Noche del Rio (late May through early Sep) All summer long, the Fiesta Noche del Rio brings Latin music to the Arneson River Theater (p131) in a series of concerts and dance performances.

JUNE
Texas Folklife Festival (mid-Jun) A multicultural celebration with food, storytellers, artisans, dancers and live music held over four days at the Institute of Texan Cultures.
Juneteenth (Jun 19) Commemorating the date when the news of the Emancipation Proclamation freeing slaves finally reached Texas, the city comes alive with African American cultural festivities and a multimedia Freedom Fair.

DETOUR: LULING
Luling trumpets that it's the 'crossroads to everywhere.' But pretty much the only reason to stop here these days as you whiz through on the way to Shiner (p160) is to see the famous annual **Luling Watermelon Thump** (covered in *People* magazine and the *New York Times*), a fruit-growing contest, complete with a crowned queen, that takes place the last full weekend of June (visit www.watermelonthump.com for exact dates). Incidentally, Luling is also the two-time holder of the world watermelon seed-spitting championship as documented in the *Guinness Book of World Records*.

Luling was founded as the western end of the Sunset branch of the Southern Pacific Railroad in 1874, and in 1922 oil was discovered beneath it. The downtown **Central Texas Oil Patch Museum** (421 E Davis St; admission by donation; 9am-noon & 1-3pm Mon-Fri, noon-3pm Sat) is dedicated to Luling's history and heritage. In the same building, the Luling **Chamber of Commerce** (☎ 830-875-3214; www.lulingcc.org) has more information on the area, including its antiques shops.

Luling is on US 183 where it meets Hwys 80 and 90, just north of I-10; it's about an hour's drive from San Antonio or Austin. Greyhound buses bound for Luling depart from San Antonio ($11, 1¼ hours, three per day) and Austin ($15, 45 minutes, once daily).

JULY

Contemporary Art Month (☎ 210-222-2787; www.sanantonio.gov/art/website; Jul) With over 400 exhibitors at several dozen venues around town, this series of gallery events, talks and festivities is the USA's only month-long contemporary arts fair. For information and schedules, contact the city's Office of Cultural Affairs .

Fourth of July (Jul 4) Expect concerts, fireworks and plenty of partying throughout the city for the nation's Day of Independence.

Annual Conjunto Shootout (mid-Jul) Dueling *conjunto* groups face off in traditional *mano a mano* style on stages at Market Square.

SEPTEMBER

Fotoseptiembre USA (www.safotofestival.com; Sep 1-30) Held at the same time as the one in Mexico City, this international photography festival takes place at various venues around town. It's sponsored by SAFOTO, which curates online photography exhibitions throughout the year.

Mexican Independence Day (Sep 16) Held on the weekend closest to the 16th, the Diez Y Sies festival is celebrated with food, music and theater all across the city, including at Market Square.

Jazz 'SAlive (☎ 210-212-8423; www.sanantoniopark sfoundation.org; admission free; mid-Sep) A top-tier jazz festival in downtown's Travis Park and other venues, with past performances by Branford Marsalis and Sergio Mendes Brasil 2003.

OCTOBER

New World & Wine Festival (☎ 210-930-3232; www. newworldwinefood.org; mid-Oct) Celebrity chefs, wine and food from all around the Americas, with workshops and events at top restaurants around the city.

International Accordion Festival (☎ 210-222-2787; www.sanantonio.gov/art/website; mid-Oct) A two-day outdoor marathon featuring dancing and accordion music of all styles, from cumbia to conjunto and zydeco to klezmer. The city's Office of Cultural Affairs has details.

NOVEMBER

El Día de los Muertos (Nov 2) Altars, religious services, processions and cultural activities celebrate the Day of the Dead, especially along the old Spanish colonial Mission Trail and at many museums.

DECEMBER

Feast of the Virgen de Guadalupe (Dec 12) This is a festive, Mexican traditional gathering.

Las Luminarias & Las Posadas (mid-Dec) Following up the feast of the Virgen de Guadalupe on the two weekends preceding Christmas, the San Antonio Conservation Society (p133) stages candlelit nativity pageant processions and bilingual caroling along the riverbanks.

Alamo Bowl (☎ 210-226-2695; www.alamobowl.com; late Dec) A college football championship of Big 10 vs Big 12 conference teams draws up to 65,000 spectators to the Alamodome.

New Year's Eve (Dec 31) Family-friendly celebrations with fireworks and live music on South Alamo St, near HemisFair Park and La Villita.

SLEEPING

San Antonio has loads of places to stay that become booked solid, and much more expensive, during major NCAA

GAY & LESBIAN SAN ANTONIO

Despite its conservative outlook (at least compared with Austin), the River City is one of the most tolerant places in Texas for gay, lesbian, bisexual and transgendered travelers. Although this ain't San Francisco or NYC, there's definitely a vibrant community here. One of the best times to visit is during Fiesta San Antonio (p129). June's Pridefest SA is another big event. For more on the gay and lesbian entertainment scene, see p160.

The **Gay & Lesbian Community Center of San Antonio** (GLCCSA; ☎ 210-223-6106, 866-452-2724; www.glccsa.org; 611 E Myrtle St) publishes a newsletter, *OutWrite SA*, and has social events a few times weekly. GLCCSA also runs the San Antonio Gay and Lesbian Chamber of Commerce, which provides lists of gay-owned and gay-friendly bars, clubs, businesses and other services. **Beauregard House B&B Inn** (p149), **A Beckman Inn & Carriage House** (p149) and **Oge House** (p149), all in the historic King William District, are especially welcoming to same-sex couples. Women should try the lesbian-owned **Painted Lady Inn** (p147).

Out in San Antonio (www.outinsanantonio.com) is an online source of news, events calendars, advice columns, chat rooms and more. **Texas Triangle** (www.txtriangle.com), a free statewide monthly publication, is available at gay bars, restaurants and queer-friendly businesses around town. For more general information on traveling in Texas, see p194.

games, city festivals and large conventions. Most motels and hotels raise their rates substantially during summer, too. Even though the city has plenty of hotels, really cheap places downtown are few and far between and aren't particularly attractive options. The downtown area does have a good selection of reasonably priced motels, and there is a multitude of choices out by the airport and along the interstates. Many are new or have been remodeled, and lots have perks like morning coffee, continental breakfast, newspapers and shuttle services. So it's worth considering spending a few extra dollars for a place that is comfortable, clean and accommodating.

Motels and hotels are the best bet when staying in San Antonio, and there are a fair number of good deals to be had right downtown. On the city's outskirts, motels charge from $35 to $65 per night; downtown places run higher. Check with the visitors center to see if there are coupons – many times you can get a discounted motel or hotel price just by asking. The city's mid-range options are essentially better-end motels and lower-end hotels; these types of places may offer special deals on their own websites, or through www.orbitz.com and other online travel discounters. Many luxury hotels inhabit venerable downtown buildings, and are often priced from just $100 a night – less than standard chain hotels found on the Riverwalk itself. San Antonio also has its fair share of B&Bs, and generally speaking they are good value, ensconced in fine old homes in the more historic areas of the city, especially the King William District.

Downtown
BUDGET
Red Roof Inn San Antonio Downtown (Map pp126-7; ☎ 210-229-9973, 800-733-7663; www.redroof.com; 1011 E Houston St; s & d winter/summer from $45/75; P ☎) Within walking distance of the Riverwalk, motel rooms are totally spotless and standard rooms are huge. There's an outdoor pool and one small pet allowed per room. Kids under 18 stay free.

Downtowner Motel (Map pp126-7; ☎ 210-227-6233; 100 Starr St; s & d from $50; P) This motel is owned and managed by the Days Inn across

the street. It's often a better deal, with clean rooms at reasonable prices.

Most cheap hotels are located disconcertingly near pawn shops, in marginal parts of downtown and not worth the money. The following two will do if you're desperate; they are not great but both are cheap and run by friendly (if sometimes suspicious) management.

Traveler's Hotel (Map pp126-7; ☎ 210-226-4381; 220 N Broadway; s from $25) The shootout scene between Steve McQueen and the bad guys in *The Getaway* could easily have been filmed here. It's very handy to downtown, and the rooms are cleanish (cheaper rooms share a bath).

Alpha Hotel (Map pp126-7; ☎ 210-223-7644; 315 N Main Ave; s/d from $30/35) At first it looks like a dive, with ratty hallways festooned with armchairs, but the owners are friendly. Rooms are clean and comfortable, if very worn. Those with private bath cost slightly more.

MID-RANGE
Most chain motels provide free parking for guests.

La Quinta Inn Market Square (Map pp126-7; ☎ 210-271-0001, 800-531-5900; www.laquinta.com; 900 Dolorosa St; s/d from $80/90; P ☎) Even closer to Market Square, La Quinta is just as nice as the Fairfield Inn. The complimentary continental breakfast includes coffee, pastries, yogurt, milk, juices and fresh fruit. Kids stay free; small pets are allowed.

Fairfield Inn Market Square (Map pp126-7; ☎ 210-299-1000, 800-228-2800; www.mariott.com/fairfieldinn; 620 S Santa Rosa St; s/d from $90/100; P ☎) This Marriott-run motel is a decent choice away from the hustle and bustle of the exact center but within walking distance of all you need. There's an indoor heated swimming pool, exercise room and complimentary continental breakfast.

Hampton Inn Riverwalk (Map pp126-7; ☎ 210-225-8500, 800-445-8667; www.hamptoninn.com; 414 Bowie St; s/d from $70/80; P ☎) This upmarket motel is another good downtown option for families. It has an outdoor pool, and complimentary breakfast is included.

Days Inn Alamo/Riverwalk (Map pp126-7; ☎ 210-227-6233, 800-329-7466; www.daysinn.com; 902 E Houston St; s & d winter/summer from $60/80; P) This chain motel, which has clean, cheerful rooms and an outdoor pool, includes a continental breakfast in the rates.

TOP END
With only slightly higher rates, these B&Bs have loads more character than better-end motels. Most are found south of downtown near the San Antonio River, with many more nearby in the King William Historic District.

Riverwalk Inn (Map pp126-7; ☎ 210-212-8300, 800-254-4440; www.riverwalkinn.com; 329 Old Guilbeau St; d from $150; P) In a quiet spot overlooking the river, this welcoming B&B has a distinctly rustic feel. It was constructed from 19th-century cottonwood log cabins hauled over from Tennessee, and it now houses nearly a dozen antique-filled rooms. All rooms have phones, cable TV and a private bath with stone floors and a walk-in shower. Most rooms also have fireplaces. The continental breakfast buffet is not skimpy, and there are homemade desserts in the evening. On weekends, there's a two-day minimum stay. Ask about off-season discounts.

Inn on the River (Map pp126-7; ☎ 210-225-6333, 800-730-0019; www.innonriver.com; 129 Woodward Pl; s, d & tr from $100; P) Presided over by a venerable pecan tree, this B&B is in a beautiful, peaceful setting by the river. Each cheery room has its own private bath, with the more expensive digs equipped with a Jacuzzi, private porch or balcony. Children are welcome in the cottage, and the owner is a licensed pilot who runs hot-air balloon tours. Off-street parking is free.

Arbor House Suites B&B (Map pp126-7; ☎ 210-472-2005, 888-272-6700; www.arborhouse.com; 109 Arcienega St; ste $110-195; P) This place seems to have the best of both worlds: it has much of the character of a B&B and the amenities of a hotel. It's a charming, small outfit run by a very friendly owner who happens to be a Son of the Republic of Texas, which means he can trace his direct lineage back to the Alamo. In a peaceful residential area

between the Riverwalk and Southtown, there are a few buildings, each with three or so suites.

Painted Lady Inn (Map pp126-7; ☎ 210-220-1092; www.thepaintedladyinn.com; 620 Broadway; d & ste $110-230; P) This romantic 1920s Southern colonial-style guesthouse is on a deserted stretch of Broadway, but it's worth the trip. A woman-owned property, it caters predominantly to same-sex couples, with tasteful antique furnishings and luxury boutique hotel–type amenities. Its upstairs balcony and rooftop hot tub look onto Broadway and right out over the madness of Fiesta San Antonio. All accommodations have a refrigerator, microwave, TV/VCR and CD player; some suites have fireplaces, kitchenettes or whirlpool tubs. Guest parking is free, and the streetcar stops just two blocks away.

Riverwalk Vista (Map pp126-7; ☎ 210-223-3200, 866-898-4782; 262 Losoya St; www.riverwalkvista.com; d from $150, ste from $180; 🖳) This bed-and-breakfast boutique hotel occupies the top floors of a downtown Victorian-era building overlooking the Riverwalk. The interior spaces have a timeless feel, yet boast leather chairs, panoramic windows, feather blankets on the beds, flat-screen TVs with DVD players and high-speed Internet access in every room. There's a small business center and guests enjoy access to a fitness studio in Travis Park. Rates include continental breakfast only. You need to call for the address.

As befits a major city, San Antonio has no shortage of luxury hotels, most of which have business and fitness centers for guests. Valet parking costs about $15 per day, and self-parking only slightly less.

Havana Riverwalk Inn (Map pp126-7; ☎ 210-222-2008, 800-224-2008; www.havanariverwalkinn.com; 1015 Navarro St; d $140-195, ste $250-600; 🖳) Even

---

AUTHOR'S CHOICE

Hotel Valencia (Map pp126-7; ☎ 210-227-9700, 866-842-0100; www.hotelvalencia.com; 150 Houston St; s & d from $100; 🖳) Easily a steal at twice the price, San Antonio's hippest luxury digs are astonishing, starting with the stone waterfall with delightful feng shui by the main entrance and the ultra-sleek minimalist lobby. The fully-equipped yet elegant rooms have Californian bath products, high-speed Internet access and more amenities. Spa and executive services, a fitness center, kids club activities and multilingual staff are all fabulous, but it's curbside Wi-Fi express check-in and **Citrus** (p154), the hotel's creative restaurant, that really put this place over the top. Check the website for romantic B&B and Majestic Theatre package deals.

if you're not staying under its roof, be sure to have a look inside the Havana. It's a completely renovated hotel in a national historic landmark building. It aims to evoke 1920s San Antonio, and the rooms are stocked with colonial-style furnishings from India and furniture from French hotels and bistros. Ask for a room with a river view. **Club Cohiba** (p159) is a big draw if you enjoy a good cigar and a dry martini.

The Fairmount Wyndham Hotel (Map pp126-7; ☎ 210-224-8800, 800-996-3426; www.wyndham.com; 401 S Alamo St; s/d from $115/125; 🖳) Things are highly exclusive in the three dozen rooms and suites at this Victorian-era hotel opposite HemisFair Park, and service is wonderful. The hotel also makes it into the Guinness Book of Records for being the largest hotel in the world to be physically moved from one location to another. Boutique rooms have classy turn-of-the-century touches like canopy beds and verandas, as well as modern amenities. There's a great bar and restaurant downstairs, **Polo's**.

La Mansion del Rio (Map pp126-7; ☎ 210-518-1000, 800-292-7300; www.lamansion.com; 112 College St; d from $140; 🖳 🖴) This is another fabulous downtown property, born out of 19th-century religious school buildings in the Spanish-Mexican hacienda style. It's on a quiet stretch of the Riverwalk, and its discreet oasis attracts stars and other notables. Enjoy in-room spa services, swim in the outdoor heated pool or unwind at the hotel's exceptional restaurant, **Las Canarias** (p152). Small pets are allowed.

Menger Hotel (Map pp126-7; ☎ 210-223-4361, 800-345-9285; www.historicmenger.com; 204 Alamo Plaza; s & d from $110; 🖳 🖴) The Menger has an ideal location in the shadow of the Alamo. Service is appropriately hushed, and the place is quite aware of its historical importance (the hotel was built in 1859) while managing not to be snooty. Mae West and Babe Ruth are just a few of the famous folks who've stayed here; at the end of the 19th century, Teddy Roosevelt liked to hang out in the bar. Rates are a lot less than they could be, and there's a large outdoor pool and gym. Ask for a room with a view.

Sheraton Gunter Hotel (Map pp126-7; ☎ 210-227-3241, 888-999-2089; www.gunterhotel.com; 205 E Houston St; s/d from $90/140; 🖴) This is another fine old dame with plenty of luxury added by the

Sheraton outfit. The boutique hotel rooms are appropriately plush, and there's a fitness center, whirlpool and outdoor heated pool. Although parts of downtown can be seedy, this corner is anchored by the Majestic Theatre, with a few trendy restaurants and bars nearby on Houston St. Don't miss the hotel's revered bakery and café, either.

The St Anthony Wyndham Hotel (Map pp126-7; ☎ 210-227-4392, 800-996-3426; www.wyndham.com; 300 E Travis St; s/d from $90/100; 🖳 🖴) Tucked discreetly between Jefferson and Navarro Sts, this place has that understated elegant look. It's a historic hotel built in 1909 and swallows up nearly a full city block. Inside, the atmosphere is intimate, and common areas are furnished with French Empire antiques. Rooms have botanical bath products and high-speed Internet access (including Wi-Fi in the common areas and meeting rooms). There's a health club, heated outdoor pool and whirlpool, and a business center. The hotel fronts Travis Park.

Emily Morgan Hotel (Map pp126-7; ☎ 210-225-5100, 800-824-6674; www.emilymorganhotel.com; 705 E Houston St; d from $140; 🖳 🖴) Right behind the Alamo, this historic hotel dating from 1926 alleges to have been the first skyscraper (at 13 stories) west of the Mississippi River. Rooms are clean, large and enjoy all the luxury amenities, from Tazo teas and Aveda bath products to high-speed Internet access. There's a lap pool, Jacuzzi and fitness center, a library with business services and a remarkable restaurant, **Oro** (p154), on the classy premises.

Crockett Hotel (Map pp126-7; ☎ 210-225-6500, 800-292-1050; www.crocketthotel.com; 320 Bonham St; d from $120; 🖴) Sitting almost atop the Alamo, the historic Crockett Hotel dates from 1909 and has been fully renovated with an eye toward historic conservation. Rooms are basic, but Southwest artwork adorns the walls, and there's an outdoor pool, Jacuzzi and rooftop sundeck. It's managed by the Holiday Inn motel next door.

Marriott Rivercenter (Map pp126-7; ☎ 210-223-1000, 800-228-9290; www.marriott.com; 101 Bowie St; d from $140; 🖳 🖴) Looking like an architect's rendering, this fantastically huge (1000-room) superhotel is adjacent to the convention center and the Rivercenter Mall. It's a small city of its own, with shops, restaurants, bars and cafés, and a Hertz car rental outlet. There's an indoor/outdoor pool, sauna and health club. Rooms have high-speed Internet access.

Marriott Riverwalk (Map pp126-7; ☎ 210-224-4555, 800-228-9290; www.marriott.com; 711 E Riverwalk; d from $160; ☐ ☎) Directly opposite the Marriott Rivercenter, this fine older option has a more conventional hotel size, and some room balconies directly overlook the Riverwalk. Guests have access to all facilities at the Marriott Rivercenter.

Also recommended are:

Adam's Mark San Antonio Riverwalk (Map pp126-7; ☎ 210-354-2800, 800-444-2326; www.adamsmark.com; 111 E Pecan St; d from $125; ☐ ☎)
Hawthorn Inn & Suites (Map pp126-7; ☎ 210-527-1900, 800-527-1133; www.hawthorn-riverwalk.com; 830 N St Mary's St; ste from $95; ☐)
Holiday Inn San Antonio Downtown (Map pp126-7; ☎ 210-224-2500, 800-445-8475; www.holiday-inn.com; 217 N St Mary's St; d from $120; ☐ ☎)
Hilton Homewood Suites (Map pp126-7; ☎ 210-222-1515, 800-225-5466; www.homewood-suites.com; 432 W Market St; ste from $130; ☐ ☎)
Plaza San Antonio (Map pp126-7; ☎ 210-229-1000, 800-727-3239; www.mariott.com; 555 S Alamo St; d from $150; ☐ ☎)
Watermark Hotel & Spa (Map pp126-7; ☎ 866-605-1212; www.watermarkhotel.com; 212 W Crockett St; ☐ ☎) Due to open winter 2003.

King William District & Southtown
The historic King William District, within walking distance of downtown and the Riverwalk, is bursting with B&Bs. Many are historic San Antonio landmarks, even national trust properties. On-street parking is usually freely available in the nearby residential streets; VIA streetcars run frequently from stops along S Alamo St directly into downtown.

BUDGET
Ramada Limited Downtown (Map p134; ☎ 210-229-1133, 800-272-6232; 1122 S Laredo St; s/d from $40/45; ☐ ☎) Just south of downtown, the Ramada has clean and comfortable rooms. There's free parking and an outdoor pool.

MID-RANGE
Adams House Bed & Breakfast Inn (Map p134; ☎ 210-224-4791, 800-666-4810; www.adams-house.com; 231 Adams Street; s/d from $50/85, ste from $130; ☐) This modest turn-of-the-century property was built by two immigrant woodworkers, and

the craftsmanship is apparent in the details. All rooms have private bath, TV and phone, as well as fresh flowers, chocolates, soft drinks and juices. Some have a two-person Jacuzzi tub. The owners also provide free unlimited streetcar rides and give AAA and AARP discounts. A two-night minimum stay is required on weekends.

1902 Classic Charms Bed & Breakfast (Map p134; ☎ 210-271-7171, 800-209-7171; www.1902classiccharms .com; 302 King William St; d $90-145; ☐) A turn-of-the-century Queen Anne home, this quiet B&B serves a generous hot breakfast, including a hearty main dish, breads and fresh fruit. Many of the rooms have large windows and octagon ceilings; all have private bath. Helen's Room is decorated in rich shades of burgundy with an antique brass bed and a parlor stove.

TOP END
Oge House (Map p134; ☎ 210-223-2353, 800-242-2770; www.ogeinn.com; 209 Washington St; d $110-225; ☐) Offering the most impressive lodgings in the King William District, this 19th-century mansion sits quietly beside the river. Oak and pecan trees shade the beautifully landscaped grounds. Each of the ten guestrooms and suites has a small refrigerator, telephone, TV and private bath.

Beauregard House B&B Inn (Map p134; ☎ 210-222-1198, 888-667-0555; www.beauregardhouse.com; 215 Beauregard St; d $115-140; ☐ ☐) At this Victorian home, the movie-worthy accommodations reflect an exquisite taste in fabrics and antiques. The Whitman and Faulkner rooms have access to a computer for business travelers, while the Hemingway Suite has Egyptian carpets, original paintings and a king-size bed. Each has a phone, cable TV and private bath.

Noble Inns (Map p134; ☎ 210-225-4045, 800-221-4045; www.nobleinns.com; 107 Madison St; d $120-225, ste $175-250; ☐ ☎) Noble Inns runs two separate properties, the Jackson House and the Aaron Pancoast Carriage House suites, but all with little luxuries like Godiva chocolates beside your pillow at night. Guests in the main house enjoy a full breakfast, afternoon refreshments and evening sherry. Airport pick-ups in a vintage Rolls Royce can be arranged.

A Beckmann Inn & Carriage House (Map p134; ☎ 210-229-1449, 800-945-1449; www.beckmanninn.com; 222 E Guenther St; d $110-150; ☐) Mixing

SAN ANTONIO

Victorian-era architecture and Southern-style elegance, this B&B is graced with flower boxes, gardens and wraparound porches. Floral-inspired rooms have ceiling fans, air-conditioning, TVs, phones and private bath. A daily-changing gourmet breakfast served in the formal dining room includes dessert.

Brackenridge House Bed & Breakfast (Map p134; ☎ 210-271-3442, 800-221-1412; www.brackenridgehouse .com; 230 Madison St; d $90-200, ste $100-300; (P)) This hospitable and elegant B&B lets you indulge in sherry and chocolate anytime you like. Rooms have private baths with clawfoot tubs, phones, cable TV, mini-fridge and microwaves. The detached carriage house has two bedrooms, a full kitchen and a screened-in porch for lazing.

A Yellow Rose Inn (Map p134; ☎ 210-229-9903, 800-950-9903; www.ayellowrose.com; 229 Madison St; d from $130; (P)) True to its name, this butter-scotch-colored house is a bloomin' beauty. Spacious rooms are tastefully furnished, with well-thought-out amenities like fresh flowers, snacks, sodas and juice. All have TVs, and some have VCRs. Choose either an in-room breakfast basket or a full hot breakfast delivered to your door.

Brackenridge Park & Around

Not many travelers stay this far north of downtown, but its peaceful atmosphere and proximity to quiet attractions make it a reasonable alternative for those with their own transport.

BUDGET

HI San Antonio International Hostel (Map pp136-7; 210-223-9426, fax 210-299-1479; hisananton@aol.com; 621 Pierce St; dm $20, s/d with shared bath from $41/46; (Ⓨ) office 8am-10pm) Situated next to a large colonial ranch-style historic house with a swimming pool and day-only common area, this basic hostel offers a kitchen and Internet access, but no laundry facilities. The hostel is 2 miles north of downtown. From downtown, take bus No 9 or 14 heading north and let the driver know you're heading for the hostel. From the Amtrak station, take bus No 516 along Hackberry St to Grayson St.

Villager Lodge Downtown (Map pp136-7; ☎ 210-222-9463, 800-328-7829; www.villager.com; 1126 E Elmira St; bus No 8 from downtown; s/d from $35/45, weekly $150-275; (P)(Ⓡ)) This rapidly aging motel

turns into party central during Fiesta week, when it becomes what seems to be the world headquarters for drag queens. The property has seen better days, and most of the clientele are here for the long haul. Management donates rooms to HIV-positive people waiting for housing or treatment elsewhere.

Rodeway Inn Downtown (Map pp136-7; ☎ 210-223-2951, 877-424-6423; www.rodewayinn.com; 900 N Main Ave; s/d from $55/60; (P)(Ⓡ)) A good option nearer downtown, this Rodeway has a coin laundry, free parking and an outdoor pool. Continental breakfast is complimentary. There's also a café on site. Kids stay free.

MID-RANGE

Bonner Garden (www.bonnergarden.com; 45 E Agarita Ave; s/d from $70/80, ste $115-125; (P)(💻)(Ⓡ)) This lovely Italianate villa dates from 1910 and was built for artist Mary Bonner. Original works by Texas artists hang on the walls, and there's a fireplace with antique tiles. The detached studio suite, which has white-washed stone walls and saltillo tile floors, is a steal, while the upstairs Garden Suite has views, European tapestries and high-speed Internet access.

Bullis House (Map pp136-7; ☎ 210-223-9426, 877-477-4100; www.bullishouseinn.com; 621 Pierce St; s & d $55-90; (P)(Ⓡ)) This national historic trust property is under the same hos-pitable management as the youth hostel. Take your continental breakfast on the outdoor veranda, then splash in the private swimming pool. Some rooms have fireplaces and French doors, but all share a hall telephone and bathrooms.

TOP END

Terrell Castle (Map pp136-7; ☎ 210-271-9145, 800-481-9732; www.terrellcastle.net; 950 E Grayson St; d $105-120, ste $140; (P)) Built at the end of the 19th century by a lawyer and former US ambassador to Belgium, this 'castle' was constructed for Edwin Terrell's bridge. It's a magnificent Victorian-era construction, though by no means excessively imposing. The rooms have an elegant European flavor, and cost far less than similar lodgings closer to downtown. There's a two-night minimum stay on most weekends.

The Inn at Craig Place (Map pp136-7; ☎ 210-736-1017, 877-427-2447; www.craigplace.com; 117 W Craig Pl; d $115-200; (P)) A quiet getaway in the historic

Monte Vista neighborhood, this national trust property is popular for weddings and honeymoons. Each of the romantic rooms has its own breakfast table, bath and telephone. Fresh-baked cookies and chocolates appear in the evening, plus there's a three-course hot breakfast every morning. Peruse the library or simply relax in the antique-furnished parlor.

Greater San Antonio
BUDGET
Many of the city's chain motels are found near the airport off Loop 410 and also by the SeaWorld and Six Flags Fiesta Texas theme parks.

Motel 6 (Map pp122-3; ☎ 210-533-6667, 888-897-0202; www.motel6.com; 748 Hot Wells Blvd, off I-37 & US 281; s/d from $45/50; P ⚲) The reliable, if ultra-basic, Motel 6 has numerous locations around San Antonio, including a couple of extended-stay Studio 6 options. Kids always stay free; small pets are welcome.

Super 8 Motel SeaWorld (☎ 210-678-0888; 2211 SW Loop 410; s/d winter from $45/55, summer from $70/80; P ⚲) This Super 8 motel is slightly flashier than the norm, with an outdoor pool.

Super 8 Motel Six Flags Fiesta Texas (☎ 210-696-6916; 5319 Casa Bella, at I-10; s/d from winter $40/50, summer from $50/60; P ⚲) As you might have guessed, this Super 8 is handy to Six Flags. Ask about weekly rates in the off-season.

The greater San Antonio area is also home to a surprising number of campgrounds.

Dixie Campground (Map pp122-3; ☎ 210-337-6501, 800-759-5267; 1011 Gembler Rd; bus No 24; tent sites with electricity $20, RV sites with full hookups $25, cabins $30; P ⚲) Dixie is northeast of downtown San Antonio near the SBC Center. It's about as flashy as your typical KOA and slightly cheaper, too. By car, take I-35 north and exit at SBC Parkway, turn south and then left (east) onto Gembler Rd and follow the signs for the KOA, which you'll reach before Dixie Campground.

San Antonio KOA Kampground (Map pp122-3; ☎ 210-224-9296, 800-562-7783; 602 Gembler Rd; bus No 24; tent sites $24, RV sites $28-50, kabins for 2/4 people $36/51; P ⚲) The cheery-as-usual KOA campground has a few creekside sites, an outdoor swimming pool and bicycle rentals.

Traveler's World (Map pp122-3; ☎ 210-532-8310, 800-755-8310; www.travelersworldrv.com; 2617 Roosevelt Dr; bus No 42; RV sites daily/weekly $28.50/155; P) Traveler's World is the closest to downtown, only 5 miles southeast of the Alamo and convenient to the Mission Trail. Tenters can be accommodated. There are some trees for shade, hot showers and organized activities during winter.

Greentree Village RV Park (☎ 210-655-3331; www.greentreevillage.com; 12015 O'Connor Rd; RV sites daily/weekly $27/155; P ⚲) This peaceful RV Park is about 13 miles northeast of the city. It has a swimming pool and an exercise room. From downtown, take I-35 north to exit 169, then head west for about a half mile; the campground is on the left.

Admiralty RV Resort (☎ 210-647-7878, 800-999-7872; www.admiraltyrv.com; 1485 N Ellison Dr; RV sites daily/weekly $32/192; P ⚲) This top-notch RV park with a junior Olympic-size swimming pool is convenient to SeaWorld, which runs a free shuttle service to the campground during summer. By car, take US 90 west to TX 151, then keep heading west to Military Dr. Turn left and drive for half a mile, then turn right at the Diamond Shamrock gas station onto Ellison Dr; the campground is on the left.

MID-RANGE & TOP END
Ramada Inn Six Flags (☎ 210-558-9070; www.ramada.com; 9447 I-10 W; s/d from $55/65; P ⚲) Close to Six Flags and a reasonable distance from downtown, this Ramada Inn has an outdoor pool.

Also recommended are:

Radisson Hill Country Resort (☎ 210-509-9800, 800-333-3333; www.radisson.com/sanantoniotx_resort; 9800 Westover Hills Blvd; d from $140; P ⌨ ⚲)
The Westin La Cantera Resort (☎ 210-558-6500, 888-625-5144; www.westinlacantera.com; 16641 La Cantera Parkway; d from $200; P ⌨ ⚲)

EATING
The Riverwalk alone has more restaurants than you'll ever need in a visit to the city, but if you only frequent these establishments, you'll be letting your taste buds down. Many top-notch eateries are found outside the downtown area, and there is an excellent selection to be had. Naturally some of the best cooking is Tex-Mex and Mexican-style. Both the *San Antonio Current* and the *San Antonio Express-News'* 'Weekender' section regularly list their top pick of restaurants and are worth checking out.

Riverwalk

Generally speaking, you go to Riverwalk for the atmosphere, not the food. All of the restaurants along the walk set up tables outside most of the year, and the view is truly lovely. The vast majority of the food has a Mexican or at least Tex-Mex theme, and all establishments serve large, multicolored and frozen cocktails. Our advice is to stick to those and appetizers, practicing the Tourist Trap Theory of Perpetual Motion – one drink and maybe a little something to nibble per stop.

BUDGET & MID-RANGE

Wild About Harry's (Map pp126-7; ☎ 210-299-1099; 245 Losoya St; $3-7; ☼ 7am-4pm) This carnival-colored café serves frozen custard sundaes, malts and shakes, as well as gourmet hot dogs – including New York–style dogs with sauerkraut and veggie soy franks. Or stop by just to jumpstart the morning with New Orleans–style beignets and café au lait.

County Line Smokehouse (Map pp126-7; ☎ 210-229-1941; 111 W Crockett St; BBQ from $5, platters $10-20; ☼ 11am-11pm) Right next to the Hard Rock Cafe, this Texas cowboy–style chain has pretty good barbecued ribs and brisket and a hugely tumultuous (and on weekends, meat-market) ambience. The

mixed barbecue platter comes with hearty beef ribs, brisket and sausage.

Casa Rio (Map pp126-7; ☎ 210-225-6718; 430 E Commerce St; mains $5-10; ☼ 11am-11pm) One of SA's oldest Mexican restaurants, it's unmistakable for its colorful array of umbrellas. Although it may look like a Hollywood movie set, the Spanish hacienda here dates back to the colonial period of Texas history. It has some nice touches, like cedar doors and a fireplace.

When it's unbearably hot and humid, cool off at **Justin's Ice Cream Company** (Map pp126-7; ☎ 210-222-1457; 510 Riverwalk; ☼ noon-11pm), where you can enjoy a dish of pink grapefruit gelato at a table overlooking the river.

TOP END

There's no end of very expensive places to dine on the Riverwalk, but few are recommendable. Many of the following happy exceptions have entrances both on the Riverwalk and above at street level. Reservations are essential; long lines of people waiting on the riverbanks for a table are a common sight every weekend.

Las Canarias (Map pp126-7; ☎ 210-225-2581, 800-292-7300; 112 College St; breakfast & lunch $6-15, dinner mains $25-30; ☼ 6:30am-10:30pm, Sun brunch 10:30am-

---

EATIN' ON THE CHAIN GANG

All the major national fast-food chains are well represented in San Antonio, but forget them all and head to the following local chains instead.

Pig Stand (Map pp136-7; ☎ 210-222-2794; 1508 Broadway; meals $4-10; ☼ 24hrs) How can you not at least look inside a place called 'Pig Stand'? Part of the chain that invented the drive-in restaurant in 1921, Pig Stand has a few locations in town. The signature pig sandwich consists of barbecued pork and relish on a bun. This location, which holds drive-in classic car shows on Friday nights, looks like it hasn't changed much since the '50s. All serve breakfast around the clock, including breakfast tacos, huge three-egg omelets and totally awesome cinnamon rolls. There's another branch in **Southtown** (Map p134; ☎ 210-225-1321; 801 S Presa St; ☼ 24hrs).

Bill Miller BBQ (Map pp126-7; ☎ 210-212-4343; 501 N St Mary's St; fried chicken from $3, BBQ plates $4.50-6.50; ☼ 7am-4pm Mon-Fri) Every year, this chain sells more than 4lb of beef brisket for every man, woman and child in San Antonio. The sauced BBQ sandwiches are beyond succulent, and for only $5 you can get one with a large iced tea, a side of potato salad and a slice of meringue pie. Bill Miller's has several outlets in SA, including the one listed here, which is opposite the Greyhound bus station – a good thing while you're waiting.

Bob's Smokehouse (Map pp122-3; ☎ 210-333-9611; 3306 Roland Ave; BBQ plates $5.50-8; ☼ 11am-7:30pm Mon-Thu, 11am-8:30pm Fri-Sat) One of the best places in town for barbecue is Bob's. The issue is: 'Better for Texas than the Alamodome!' The decor is a little off-putting – just cheap tables and chairs – but you don't come here to admire the surroundings, only what's on your plate. You'll find another branch north of **Loop 410** (Map pp122-3; ☎ 210-344-8401; 5145 Fredericksburg Rd).

2pm) In the historic **La Mansion del Rio** hotel (p148) overlooking a beautiful section of the Riverwalk, this three-tiered restaurant rates at the top of anyone's list. Adventures in regional cuisine here might include deviled Texas blue crab cakes or yellowfin tuna ceviche. Las Canarias also does a fine breakfast and Sunday champagne brunch. The name refers to the Canary Islanders who settled in Texas during the 18th century.

Biga on the Banks (Map pp126-7; ☎ 210-225-0722; 203 S St Mary's St; mains $18-35; ☽ jazz brunch 11am-2:30pm Sun, dinner 5:30-10pm daily, till 11pm Fri-Sat) This is one of the most justifiably praised restaurants in town, run by Bruce Auden, who is also the chef. The menu is a wonderful mix of European, Tex-Mex, American and Asian influences that probably don't cost as much as they should (certainly not what they could). It's stylish, yet welcoming, and the wine list is impressive.

Zuni Grill (Map pp126-7; ☎ 210-227-0864; 223 Losoya St; lunch $7-11, dinner mains $10-25; ☽ 7:30am-11pm) The Southwest-style food at this modern bistro is served with fresh locally grown vegetables, a real bonus in Texas. The artwork and outlook are both contemporary. Breakfast is as indulgent as you dare to order it, perhaps with cinnamon buttermilk pancakes. Be sure to try one of Zuni's cactus pear margaritas with dinner.

Boudro's (Map pp126-7; ☎ 210-224-8484; 421 E Commerce St; lunch $7-12.50, dinner mains $15-33; ☽ 11am-11pm daily, till midnight Fri-Sat) This brightly colored restaurant is hugely popular even with locals. Fresh guacamole is made right at your table. The upscale Tex-Mex menu reveals some gourmet surprises, such as black bean soup made with sherry and white cheddar, lobster tail fajitas drizzled with pineapple pico de gallo and wines from Texas and California.

Downtown
Away from the Riverwalk, the restaurants may not be as scenic, but neither are they generally overpriced.

BUDGET & MID-RANGE
Twin Sisters Bakery & Café (Map pp126-7; ☎ 210-354-1559; 124 Broadway; meals $4-10; ☽ 8am-5pm Mon-Fri) The downtown storefront branch of this café is a wholesome, if efficient, spot for breakfast or lunch; see p156 for a full review. There's also a branch of **Bill Miller BBQ** (p152) near the bus station.

Copper Kitchen (Map pp126-7; ☎ 210-224-0123; 300 Augusta St; sandwiches & specials $4-7.50; ☽ 11:30am-2pm Mon-Fri) This quiet, rustic-looking café on the historic Ursuline Campus of the Southwest School of Art & Craft does great home-style soups, salads and sandwiches, and has daily lunch specials. Gallery art by the school's students make the dining space even more cozy.

Pecan St Deli (Map pp126-7; ☎ 210-227-3226; 152 E Pecan St; sandwiches $4-6; ☽ 10am-2:30pm Mon-Fri) Close to the Greyhound bus station, looking as though it belongs in the heart of New York City, this bustling little deli is popular with downtown workers. Even though 'haste' seems to be the deli's motto at lunchtime, sandwiches are still made to order right in front of you.

Schilo's Delicatessen (Map pp126-7; ☎ 210-223-6692; 424 E Commerce St; meals $3-6; ☽ 7am-8:30pm Mon-Sat) This is the real thing – an eatery that's been operating for 80 years. Some of the furniture looks like it's never been replaced. It's one of the few truly great options near the Riverwalk that has kept its traditional atmosphere, right down to the excellent selection of German beer and the 'almost over the hill' waitresses. Specialties include wonderful split-pea soup, fresh pumpernickel bread and homemade root beer. There's live Alpine folk music after 5pm on Friday and Saturday nights.

Market Square (p163) has lots of kiosks selling Mexican snacks and food, and if you think music's good for the digestion, you're in luck: mariachi bands and Mexican guitar players constantly make the rounds. Especially look for them at **Mi Tierra Cafe & Bakery** (Map pp126-7; ☎ 210-225-1262; 218 Produce Row; meals $7-12; ☽ 24hrs), which serves $6 lunch specials from 11am until 3pm on weekdays. Parking is validated for the first 90 minutes for restaurant patrons at the small lot off Dolorosa St.

TOP END
Reservations are strongly advised for the following places.

Little Rhein Steak House (Map pp126-7; ☎ 210-225-2111; 231 S Alamo St; mains $18-35; ☽ 5-11pm) Right downtown and almost on Riverwalk, this steak house is filled with pieces of history – note the brass light fixtures from a federal courthouse in Chicago – and also has a lovely outdoor sitting area. For a carnage fest of flesh, you could do a lot worse – it serves solidly dependable steaks, lamb and pork.

Fig Tree (Map pp126-7; ☎ 210-224-1976; 515 Villita St; mains $18-35; ♥ 6-10pm) Inside what was once the last of La Villita's private dwellings, Little Rhein's sister restaurant serves a hearty Eurasian grill menu. Offered are Kobe beef carpaccio, pan-seared ahi tuna and lemon-pudding cake with fresh pomegranate.

Oro (Map pp126-7; ☎ 210-225-5100; 705 E Houston St; breakfast & lunch $5-13, dinner mains $18-35; ♥ 6: 30am-2pm Sun-Fri & 6-11pm Tue-Sat) With a name meaning 'gold' in both Spanish and Italian, this gorgeous restaurant at the **Emily Morgan Hotel** (p148) beckons with seasonal, creative Mediterranean cuisine and an equally fine wine list. The chef hails from one of Santa Fe's finest hotels, so high expectations are in order. Breakfast is especially grand, with Creole eggs benedict, lemon-blueberry French toast with mint maple syrup, and more.

Citrus (Map pp126-7; ☎ 210-227-9700; 150 E Houston St; lunch $8-12, dinner mains $23-31; ♥ 6:30am-10pm)

GOOD MORNING, RIVER CITY

Among your best bets for breakfast are these:

On the Riverwalk
- Wild About Harry's (p152)
- Zuni Grill (p153)
- Las Canarias (p152)

Around Downtown
- Twin Sisters Bakery & Café (p153)
- Schilo's Delicatessen (p153)
- Oro (p154)

King William District & Southtown
- Madhatters (p154)
- Guenther House (p154)

Brackenridge Park
- La Madeleine Bakery & Cafe (p155)
- Earl Abel's (p155)

Elevated inside the chic **Hotel Valencia** (p147), this New American dining space is certainly a sleek destination, with food that hints of Spain and Asia. The hotel's Vbar lounge also overlooks the San Antonio River.

Le Rêve (Map pp126-7; ☎ 210-212-2221; 152 E Pecan St; chef's tasting menu per person $85-95, with wine pairing $105-135; ♥ 5:30-11pm Tues-Sat) Chef Andrew Weissman has made this intimate, very modern French restaurant into a top-notch dining destination, despite its location in an unlikely corner of downtown. The menu changes seasonally, with French delicacies like foie gras and also hints of Asia. Make reservations as far in advance as possible. Jackets are required for men.

King William District & Southtown
Southtown is the place for authentic Mexican and Latin fusion cuisine. The adjacent King William District has a handful of pretty places for a light lunch.

BUDGET
Espuma (Map p134; ☎ 210-226-1912; 928 S Alamo St; soups, salads & sandwiches $4-6.50; ♥ 7am-10pm Mon-Thu, 7am-midnight Fri, 8am-midnight Sat, 8am-2pm Sun) An artistic haven serving rich coffee, Espuma has fresh edibles for lunch, including vegetable wraps, salads and gourmet deli sandwiches. The café also has live music on weekends and a notice board for community events.

Madhatters (Map p134; ☎ 210-212-4832; 320 Beauregard St; bakery $1-5, meals $5-8; ♥ 9am-9pm Mon-Fri, 9am-7pm Sat, 9am-6pm Sun) With over 70 types of tea on hand, this little bakery and café is the perfect stop for an afternoon snack. During the week, club sandwiches, spinach salads and sirloin burgers are served; there's French toast, eggs benedict with chipotle hollandaise and mimosas for weekend brunch.

Guenther House (Map p134; ☎ 210-227-1061; 205 E Guenther St; breakfast $3.50-6.50, lunch $6-8; ♥ 7am-3pm) The Guenther's lovely indoor/outdoor garden café does dependable Southern and Tex-Mex specialties for breakfast and lunch. A favorite is the champagne chicken enchiladas with tossed salad. Breakfast is served all afternoon.

MID-RANGE & TOP END
Blue Star Brewing Company (Map p134; ☎ 210-212-5506; 1414 S Alamo St; burgers, pizza & pasta $4-10,

grilled mains $10-20; 11am-midnight Mon-Sat, till 2am Sat) Inside the Blue Star Arts Complex, this relaxed brewpub (p160) and restaurant serves reliably good food. Dinner has more substantial offerings than lunch, with rib-eye steaks, roast lamb and pecan-encrusted pork tenderloin.

Rosario's (Map p134; ☎ 210-223-1806; 910 S Alamo St; lunch $6, mains $8-12; 11am-3pm Mon, 11am-10pm Tue-Sat, till 11pm Sat) This colorful and lively restaurant has huge windows that allow in loads of sunlight. All the typical Mexican dishes are available, along with a few extras, and although the food is nothing special, it's a great place for dancing to live salsa bands (p157).

El Mirador (Map p134; ☎ 210-225-9444; 722 S St Mary's St; lunch $6-13, dinner mains $8-15; 6:30am-9pm Tue-Sat, till 10pm Fri-Sat, 9am-2pm Sun) Ask many San Antonians to name one Mexican place that's reliable for excellent food, and invariably they will mention El Mirador. Absolutely everything on the menu is exquisitely done. One of the biggest drawcards is Sopa Azteca Saturday, when it serves up portions of justifiably famous shredded chicken soup with cheese, tortilla strips and avocado. People line up out the door for it.

Azuca Nuevo Latino (Map p134; ☎ 210-225-5550; 713 S Alamo St; mains $10-18; 11am-9:30pm Mon-Sat, till 10:30pm Fri-Sat) A new hot spot in Southtown, this sleek restaurant and bar has a daring Latin American menu, with sizzling shrimp diablo and chicken azteca, as well as a great selection of tapas.

Brackenridge Park & Around

These neighborhoods are havens for some of the best-value eateries in the city, and most are worth a trip from downtown.

BUDGET

WD Deli (Map pp136-7; ☎ 210-828-2322; 3123 Broadway; lunch $5-7; 10:30am-3pm Mon-Fri, 11am-3pm Sat) This gourmet deli's staff gets top marks for not cracking under the pressure of the daily lunchtime crush. Folks are always lined up waiting for hot deli sandwiches, cool salads and fresh-baked cookies. You can get a boxed lunch to picnic in Brackenridge Park nearby.

Earl Abel's (Map pp136-7; ☎ 210-822-3358; 4200 Broadway; meals from $6; 6:30am-1am) This classic diner has been around for years, and the decor shows it; don't miss the very

cool art deco neon outside. The waitresses are genuinely friendly, the food is great (real home-style cooking) and locals just keep coming back for more. A sign above the bar reads, 'It was a brave man who ate the first oyster.'

Willard's Jamaican Jerk Bar-B-Que (Map pp136-7; ☎ 210-736-5375; 726 E Mistletoe Ave; meals $7-10; call for hours) It's often a one-man magic show at this tiny smokehouse, just off the N St Mary's St strip. Follow your nose inside for some of the most memorable jerk chicken you'll ever have, not to mention a friendly chat with the owner while you wait (it's always worth it).

Candlelight Coffee House (Map pp136-7; ☎ 210-738-0999; 3011 N St Mary's St; meals $5-10; 4pm-midnight Tue-Sun, till 1am Fri-Sat) Possessing quite a fabulous vibe, this is really more of an upscale bar and restaurant serving light meals, cocktails and more. You can eat at wrought-iron tables on the back patio, or at the bar stools in front.

Near Brackenridge Park, the **Olmos Pharmacy** (Map pp136-7; ☎ 210-822-3361; 3902 McCullough Ave; $2-5; 7am-6pm Mon-Sat, from 10am Sun) is a 1930s drugstore with a beloved grill counter. **La Madeleine French Bakery & Cafe** (Map pp136-7; ☎ 210-829-7291; 4820 Broadway; $2-6; 6:30am-10pm daily, till 11pm Fri-Sat) is a soothing spot for breakfast.

MID-RANGE & TOP END

On weekends, swing by **Carmen's de la Calle Café** (p158).

Koi Kawa (Map pp136-7; ☎ 210-805-8111; 4051 Broadway; meals $7-13; 11:30am-9:30pm daily, till 10pm Fri-Sat) The two Koi Kawa locations reflect the two faces of Japan; the **Alamo Quarry Market** branch (p165) represents modern-day Japan (steel-and-glass interior design, and a sushi-delivering conveyor belt), while the Brackenridge Park restaurant reflects traditional Japan: lots of natural wood and a riverside setting. Both branches serve decent sushi.

Josephine Street (Map pp136-7; ☎ 210-224-6169; 400 E Josephine St; mains $8-15; 11am-10pm Mon-Sat, till 11pm Fri-Sat) Always a tremendous bang for the buck, this creaky old Victorian house offers exactly what the signs in the window say – 'Steaks' and 'Whiskey.' It serves up an incredible 12oz blackened sirloin steak, or steak and grilled shrimp for the same reasonable price.

Liberty Bar (Map pp136-7; ☎ 210-227-1187; 328 E Josephine St; sandwiches & salads $6-10, mains $6-20; ⏰ 11:30am-10:30pm daily, till midnight Fri-Sat) Liberty Bar's walls are so delightfully crooked it seems as if the place is sliding downhill, and the floor is so uneven it's like being at sea. Yet it's worth trying anything on the creative American menu, which includes several vegetarian options. If you can't make up your mind, let the knowledgeable servers decide for you.

Greater San Antonio

These restaurants may seem out of the way, but many of them are convenient to outlying accommodations and attractions. Others are destinations in and of themselves.

BUDGET

Olmos Coffeehouse (Map pp122-3; ☎ 210-829-4546; 518 Austin Hwy; $2-6; ⏰ 7am-8pm Mon-Wed, 7am-10pm Thu, 7am-11pm Fri, 8am-11pm Sat, 10am-6pm Sun) Come here for rich espresso, a yummy selection of homebaked goods, simple lunches and eclectic gifts. It's not far from the McNay Art Museum, but is nicely tucked away from the well-beaten tourist paths.

Casbeers (Map pp122-3; ☎ 210-732-3511; 1719 Blanco Rd; enchiladas $3-6, grilled mains $4-12; ⏰ 11am-11pm Tue-Thu, 11am-midnight Fri, 5pm-1am Sat) This social club doesn't look like much from the outside (or the inside for that matter), but people have been coming to this spot northeast of downtown for the past 65 years to enjoy the famous truck-stop enchiladas. Not only are they soft, tender, and covered in a rich sauce, they're also cheap. This is also a good spot for live music, including the once-a-month Sunday gospel brunch.

Señor Burrito Grill (Map pp122-3; ☎ 210-736-6522; 504 W Hildebrand Ave; burritoes $4-6; ⏰ 11am-5pm Mon-Sat) It's the only place in south-central Texas for a gigantic West Coast–style burrito with all the healthy fixins. The owner provides a bewildering variety of tortilla wraps, homemade salsas, rice and beans to choose from. The Hildebrand Ave antiques stores are nearby.

DeWese's Tip Top Cafe (Map pp122-3; ☎ 210-732-0191; 2814 Fredericksburg Rd; meals $5-8; ⏰ 11am-8pm Tue-Thu, 11am-9pm Fri-Sat, 11am-7pm Sun) Some of the best chicken-fried steak and onion rings in the known universe are at this diner, which has been around since 1938. There's more – the freshly baked rolls are

heavenly, and pies (chocolate or banana meringue, chocolate, apple, coconut or egg custard) are good enough to fight over. It's all made here from scratch. The decor and the cooking haven't changed much at all, and customers almost always come back.

Twin Sisters Bakery & Café (Map pp122-3; ☎ 210-822-0761; 6322 N New Braunfels Ave; meals $5-8; ⏰ 7am-9pm Mon-Fri, 7am-3pm Sat, 9am-2pm Sun) Near the McNay Art Museum, this laidback café is a great spot for breakfast, when you'll find a hearty selection of American and Mexican food. Vegetarians are well catered to, and the vegetable sauté is an excellent choice. Listen for live music on select Friday nights.

For Mexican-style frozen fruit treats, visit **La Palatera** (Map pp122-3; 4426 Blanco Rd).

MID-RANGE

Some of the best ethnic and comfort food in San Antonio is found off Loop 410.

Thai Taste (Map pp122-3; ☎ 210-520-6800; 5520 Evers Rd; dishes $6-12, lunch special under $5; ⏰ 11am-2:50pm & 5-9:45pm Mon-Sat) Located in a row of nondescript shops in northwest San Antonio, this local fave has an enormous menu of Thai dishes. The food is expertly cooked, and despite a serious lack of ambience, it's no wonder the place can be packed at lunchtime.

410 Diner (Map pp122-3; ☎ 210-822-6246; 8315 Broadway; meals $7-11; ⏰ 11am-10pm) Don't be misled by the name, as it's certainly no greasy spoon. The 410's amazing kitchen puts forth exceptional comfort fare, for example blackened snapper, zucchini casserole and chicken Caesar salads. Service can be inattentive, but the food is so satisfying you'll hardly notice.

Saffron (Map pp122-3; ☎ 210-930-8463; 6450 N New Braunfels Ave; lunch $8-14, dinner tapas $6-15; ⏰ lunch 11am-2:30pm Mon-Sat, dinner 5-10pm daily, till 11pm Fri-Sat) In the Sunset Ridge shopping center, this rosy-hued Spanish restaurant often has flamenco guitarists to serenade diners in the evenings, when escargot, barbecued quail and Galician scallops all appear on the menu.

Acadiana Café (Map pp122-3; ☎ 210-674-0019; 1289 SW Loop 410; meals $6-15; ⏰ 11am-10pm daily, till 11pm Fri-Sat) On the way out of town to SeaWorld, this great family-friendly restaurant has a Cajun kitchen that turns out hush puppies, corn bread, fried catfish, seafood gumbo and other delightful Louisiana specialties.

El 7 Mares (Map pp122-3; ☎ 210-436-6056; 3831 W Commerce St; meals $8-20; 🕑 10am-10pm daily, till midnight Fri-Sat) Although it's a fair drive west of downtown, by all accounts this is the place for Mexican seafood. A family-owned restaurant, 'The Seven Seas' cheerfully serves up shrimp enchiladas, fish tacos, sparkling ceviche and more.

See p155 for a review of **Koi Kawa** (Map pp136-7; ☎ 210-930-6042; Alamo Quarry Market, 255 E Basse Rd; meals $7-13; 🕑 Tue-Sun).

TOP END

Barn Door (Map pp122-3; 210-824-0116, 8400 N New Braunfels; mains $10-30; 🕑 lunch 11am-2pm Mon-Fri, dinner 5-10pm Mon-Sat, till 10:30pm Fri-Sat) North of downtown, this popular local steak house is a cavernous barn of a place with good service, steaks, homebaked pies and appetizers. It's kid-friendly, too, and packed with fascinating old-timey antiques.

Silo Elevated Cuisine (Map pp122-3; ☎ 210-824-8686; 1133 Austin Hwy, at Exeter Rd; lunch $8-15, dinner mains $18-35; 🕑 lunch 11:30-2:30pm Mon-Fri & Sun, dinner 5:30-9:30pm daily, till 10:30pm Fri-Sat) Housed inside what once was a gourmet produce market, this eclectic restaurant preserves a seasonally fresh menu. Expect creative New American ideas like blue crab spring rolls, garlic-roasted mashed potatoes or pork tenderloin with cherry sauce over sweet corn risotto. The chefs' new experimental dishes appear on the prix fixe dinner menu, offered from 5:30pm until 6:45pm nightly. Silo's bar hosts tango and jazz nights, too.

Grey Moss Inn (☎ 210-695-8301; 19010 Scenic Loop Rd, 3mi east of Hwy 16; mains $20-45; 🕑 5-10pm) A short drive into the Hill Country lying northwest of the city is this romantic country inn, dating from the 1920s. The recipes adhere lovingly to tradition and feature seafood, roasted meats basted in a secret 'witches brew' and chocolate pecan pie. Children are welcome. It's also near the John T Floore Country Store (p158).

ENTERTAINMENT

Although the live-music scene isn't as jumping as in Austin, there's still plenty of entertainment in San Antonio. Check the *San Antonio Current* or Jim Beal's 'Night Lights' column in the 'Weekender' section of the *San Antonio Express-News*

for upcoming concerts. Both publications also have comprehensive listings of art exhibitions and openings, touring shows, theater, classical music and cinema.

Most bars stay open until 2am daily (unless otherwise noted), while a few clubs stay hoppin' until 4am. Club schedules vary (as do club cover charges, which vary from $3 for local bands to $25 or more for big-name acts). Tickets for major sports and performing arts events can be purchased through **Ticketmaster** (☎ 210-224-9600; www .ticketmaster.com), which has over a dozen city-wide ticket outlets.

Live Music

North of downtown along N St Mary's St, **the Strip** was once a very vibrant music and bar scene at the center of the university student's universe. Though not what it was, it's still a good place to start your search for live local shows (and the occasional international act) in San Antonio. There are also a few places by the Riverwalk and on the city's outskirts.

DOWNTOWN & SOUTHTOWN

Jim Cullum's Landing (Map pp126-7; ☎ 210-325-2495; www.landing.com; riverwalk level, Hyatt Regency Hotel, 123 Losoya St) Jazz at the Landing is a San Antonio tradition. The seven-piece Jim Cullum Jazz Band plays at 8pm Monday to Saturday, and local jazz group Small World plays on Sunday night. Live jazz duos play, weather-permitting, starting at noon on the outside riverside patio. NPR's syndicated show *Riverwalk, Live from the Landing* broadcasts live on Saturday nights, when advance reservations are required.

Sunset Station (Map pp126-7; ☎ 210-222-9481; www.sunset-station.com; 1174 E Commerce St; 🕑 box office 10am-6pm Mon-Fri, 5-11pm on show days) The renovated South Pacific Railroad Depot is now home to this complex, which houses a number of restaurants, clubs and music venues under one roof. Regular outdoor concerts for touring international bands are held here, under the shadow of the Alamodome. For information on future gigs, check out the website, call or go in person to the box office inside the Sunset Saloon.

Rosario's (Map p134; ☎ 210-223-1806; 910 S Alamo St) This restaurant (p155) has live music Friday and Saturday night. On Friday you'll find the small dance floor packed with salsa, cumbia and merengue dancers, and Saturday it's all about jazz. There's no cover charge, and the bar stays open until 1:30am.

There's regularly scheduled live rock and blues at a few downtown chain venues, including the group at 111 W Crockett St on the south bank of Riverwalk: the **Hard Rock Cafe** (Map pp126-7; ☎ 210-224-7625), **Fat Tuesday's** (Map pp126-7; ☎ 210-212-7886) and the piano bar **Howl at the Moon** (Map pp126-7; ☎ 210-212-4695).

Plus, strolling mariachi players frequent the restaurants in Market Square both day and night, and there's also live jazz at Swig Martini Bar (p159).

BRACKENRIDGE PARK & AROUND

The following venues are all on or near the Strip.

White Rabbit (Map pp136-7; ☎ 210-737-2221; www.sawhiterabbit.com; 2410 N St Mary's St) This is one of the best places for indie, metal and punk sounds, with two stages, slates of several bands per night and often no cover. These days, it has diversified into a college bar scene on Thursday nights. Acoustic acts take over Tuesday nights.

Sam's Burger Joint (Map pp136-7; ☎ 210-223-2830; www.samsburgerjoint.com; 330 E Grayson St) Its neon sign visible from the highway overhead, Sam's hosts plenty of rockabilly, ska and punk bands all week long. It's also SA's main venue for open-mic poetry slams, often held Tuesday nights.

Carmen's de la Calle Café (Map pp136-7; ☎ 210-737-8272; 720 E Mistletoe Ave; ☽ 6pm-midnight Thu-Sat) This garden venue located just off the Strip offers live jazz and paella Thursday night and live flamenco with a tapas menu on Friday. All shows start at 8:30pm.

Saluté (Map pp136-7; ☎ 210-732-5307; 2801 N St Mary's St) This tiny place looks like a dive at first, especially with its siren-red neon sign. Inside there's great live music of all stripes, from funk to soul to Latin jazz to blues-rock and beyond.

Sin 13 (Map pp136-7; ☎ 210-313-5789; 1902 McCullough Ave) Though the look runs more to goth than punk, the club manages to book a full lineup of local indie bands on select weeknights. Weekends, it's a dance club (p160).

GREATER SAN ANTONIO

Don't imagine that staying outside of central SA will deprive you of great live music.

Casbeers (Map pp122-3; ☎ 210-732-3511; www.casbeers.com; 1719 Blanco Rd) Tuesday through Saturday, you'll find live local acoustic, folk, rock, or blues gigs here, and beer for only $2. There's usually a small cover charge, except on Tuesday and Wednesday nights. Proceeds from the once-a-month Sunday gospel brunch ($10) support a neighborhood food bank.

Martini's (Map pp122-3; ☎ 210-344-4747; 8507 McCullough Ave) For a taste of Las Vegas in the heart of San Antonio, head to what can only be described as a kitsch lounge bar. Wayne, the owner/singer/guitarist/trumpeter/saxophonist, fronts a three-piece band. He can impersonate anyone by request, from Neil Diamond to Willie Nelson, to perfection. Wayne and his cohorts don't come on stage until 9:30pm, but get there at least half an hour before that if you want to secure a seat. The only problem with Martini's is finding it. It's located in a strip mall next to the Avon shop, and the only indication of the bar's existence is a small brass plaque reading 'Martini's' screwed to the wall next to the entrance.

Re-Bar (Map pp122-3; ☎ 210-320-4091; 8134 Broadway) Just off of Loop 410 next to Beto's Empanadas grill, this stylish lounge is not only a place to meet and mingle, but it also books live local bands a few nights a week. Sit on the open-air patio, if you can.

Rox Club (Map pp122-3; ☎ 210-545-0229; www.skytravel.org; 502 Embassy Oaks, cnr Embassy Row) Owned by the same folks as Austin's Red Eyed Fly, this place has a more suburban vibe (maybe it's the strip mall locale), but the lineup includes great live local music and DJs. There's often no cover during the week; on weekends, admission charges may skyrocket to $20 for big-name bands.

John T Floore Country Store (☎ 210-695-8827; www.liveatfloores.com; 14464 Old Bandera Rd, Helotes; ☽ live music usually Thu-Sun) Northwest of town, this dance hall has been around for years, and rivals **Gruene Hall** (p168) for authenticity. The hall hosts plenty of country-and-western concerts; Willie Nelson, Bob Wills, Patsy Cline and Elvis have all done shows here. Sunday is family night, with free admission and dancing after 6pm.

There are lots of places to hear Tejano bands and *conjunto* music, but which place is hottest tends to shift; check the Spanish-language newspapers for listings. **Hacienda Salas Party House** (Map pp122-3; ☎ 210-923-1879; 3127 Mission Rd), north of the San José mission, and **Lerma's Night Club** (Map pp122-3; ☎ 210-732-0477; 1602 N Zarzamora St) are long-running local venues.

Bars & Pubs

It often seems that San Antonio's watering holes are all crowded as close to the Riverwalk as possible. But there are also a few convivial spots scattered elsewhere around downtown and the Southtown arts district.

DOWNTOWN & THE RIVERWALK

The Esquire (Map pp126-7; ☎ 210-222-2521; 155 E Commerce St) This classic pressed-tin ceiling dive is a San Antonio favorite, with what's billed as the longest wooden bar in Texas. It's the real McCoy but a little rough, with a Tejano and college-student crowd all taking advantage of really cheap tequila shots and beer. There's waiter service in the booths – if he gets around to it. Women may want to avoid this place.

Club Cohiba (Map pp126-7; ☎ 210-222-2008; 1015 Navarro St) At the other end of the scale from Esquire is this fantastic little bar behind the **Havana Riverwalk Inn** (p147). Come here to sink into deep couches or just prop yourself up at the bar and enjoy a cigar in the decadent surroundings, reminiscent of the 1920s. During summer you can sip margaritas overlooking a peaceful, less-touristed section of the Riverwalk.

Mark's on the Riverwalk (Map pp126-7; ☎ 210-222-2444; 245 E Commerce St, ste 200; ☺ 5pm-2am Tue-Sat) Like a modern gentleman's club, Mark's on the Riverwalk has sophisticated

---

GOLD STAR HOTEL BARS

Menger Hotel Bar is a great rainy-day bar – dark, woody, serious but laidback. It's modeled on the British House of Lords and was a hangout of Teddy Roosevelt back in his Rough Rider days.

Polo's at the Fairmount is a cigar-friendly restaurant and bar downstairs at the Fairmount Wyndham Hotel (p148), and it is a classy place to have a martini or a good whiskey, with live piano music and attentive service.

---

appeal. Well-heeled patrons of both sexes recline by marble-top bars. Libations, not drinks, are served. Indulge with a little jazz on Thursday evenings. There's also an impressive list of wines by the glass and a humidor.

Zinc (Map pp126-7; ☎ 210-224-2900; 207 N Presa St) Head to Zinc's for an atmosphere that's nicely chilled-out, helped along by a good range of music and an array of wines, champagnes and ports that are simply stunning. There's also a nice garden bar and an extensive selection of cigars.

Davenport (Map pp126-7; ☎ 210-354-1200; 200 E Houston St) Handy to the Majestic Theatre, this Houston-owned outpost is a hip cocktail lounge worth stopping for, especially before hitting the Riverwalk nearby. Its stemware, mod-looking furniture and backlit bar are to die for. There's also a fireplace and over 50 different martinis.

Swig Martini Bar (Map pp126-7; ☎ 210-476-0005; 111 W Crockett St, entrance off N Presa St) Right on the Riverwalk, this 1940s-style establishment has a constant tinkling piano. There's live jazz after 8pm Monday to Thursday, and from 9pm on Friday and Saturday nights. The bar's Red Slipper is a potent mix of tequila and Cointreau in a Cabernet Sauvignon–lined glass.

Mad Dog's (Map pp126-7; ☎ 210-222-0220; 123 Losoya St) Authenticity is not in high demand along the Riverwalk, but this Britishy pub (named for the bar started by two Scots over in Hong Kong) has ales on tap, billiards, pool tables and darts. Occasionally there's live entertainment, too.

For a bird's-eye perspective, visit the revolving **High in the Sky Lounge** (☺ till 11pm Sun-Thu, till midnight Fri-Sat) at the **Tower of the Americas** (p132).

SOUTHTOWN

A Latin-flavored scene that's refreshingly unpretentious is what you'll find in this neighborhood, near all of the King William District's B&Bs.

La Tuna Ice House (Map p134; ☎ 210-224-8862; 100 Probandt St) When the sun starts to set over Southtown, scoot down by the railroad tracks to this back-to-basics watering hole for a few cold beers and nostalgic school-size snacks. Locals, even families, crowd around outdoor tables until well after dark, especially on weekends when there's live music.

SAN ANTONIO

Blue Star Brewing Company (Map p134; ☎ 210-212-5506; 1414 S Alamo St) At the back of the Blue Star Arts Complex, this brewpub and restaurant (p154) has been open for almost a decade. The beers are eminently respectable (only $1 per 4oz sample) and the vibe casual enough to linger all night long.

Bar America (Map p134; ☎ 210-223-7462; 723 S Alamo St; ⊙ closed Mon) Owned by the same family since the 1940s, this old-school dive bar has cheap beer (in fact, that's all they've got), a jukebox and a pool table. It's a few doors down from the lively Bar Latino in Azuca Nuevo Latino.

Other spots for a beer around Southtown include the outdoor **Acapulco Drive-In** (Map p134; ☎ 210-224-2452; 609 S Alamo St) and German-style **Beethoven Männerchor Und Garten** (Map p134; ☎ 210-222-1521; 422 Pereida St; ⊙ hrs vary), which hosts a summer beer garden and Oktoberfest entertainment.

Dance Clubs

San Antonio doesn't have a great clubbing scene, but it does have a few spots to get down. Check in the local papers about schedules and drop-in classes for tango, salsa, folk and country two-step dancing.

Bonham Exchange (Map pp126-7; ☎ 210-271-3811; www.bonhamexchange.net; 411 Bonham St; cover varies, free before 10pm some nights; ⊙ usually Wed-Sun) Right behind the Alamo, this club has a mixed, predominantly gay crowd that likes to gyrate to house, R&B and Latin beats. It's inside a 19th-century Victorian mansion with five bars, three huge dance floors and laser and light shows – definitely a scene. Check the website for special events.

Sin 13 (Map pp136-7; ☎ 210-313-5789; 1902 McCullough Ave; cover under $5, free before 10pm Fri or 11pm Sat; ⊙ till 3am Fri-Sat) Goth and industrial music is not dead. No, really, we swear. On Friday and Saturday nights, this midtown club spins '80s and '90s retro from New Wave to synth-punk and electro grooves. Drinks are unbelievably cheap.

Far West Rodeo (Map pp122-3; ☎ 210-646-9378; www.cowboysdancehall.com; 3030 NE Loop 410, east of I-35; cover from $5, concert tickets $8-20; ⊙ usually 7pm-2am Thu, 8pm-2am Fri, 8pm-3am Sat) With an amusing Old West facade, this giant country-and-western dance hall hosts performances by big-name artists like Dwight Yoakam and Cory Morrow. Ladies usually get in free every Thursday and on weekends for $1 before 10pm. If no concert is scheduled, swing by for a free dance lesson at 7pm on Thursday.

Jewels (Map pp122-3; ☎ 210-691-3000; 5500 Babcock Rd, cnr Eckhert Rd; cover varies; ⊙ call for schedule) In a strip mall far, far away from the Riverwalk, this retro-style cocktail lounge bops with live jazz, soul and R&B bands several nights a week. It's north of Loop 410.

Most mainstream dance clubs lie along the city's outskirts, including DJ-driven **Club Antro** (Map pp122-3; ☎ 210-949-5131; 7959 Fredericksburg Rd; ⊙ usually Thu-Sat), north of Loop 410, and **Joe's Volcano** (Map pp122-3; ☎ 210-680-7225; 6844 Ingram Rd, off Loop 410; ⊙ usually Thu-Sun), near Ingram Park Mall.

Gay & Lesbian Venues

Apart from **Bonham Exchange**, the River City's gay scene is concentrated along Main and San Pedro Aves, just north of downtown. Venues change, but the strips remain the

---

DETOUR: SHINER

The highlight of any trip to Shiner, the self-proclaimed 'cleanest little city in Texas,' is a tour of the **Spoetzl Brewery** (☎ 512-594-3383; www.shiner.com; 603 E Brewery St; tours free; ⊙ tours usually 11am & 1:30pm Mon-Fri) where America's best-selling bock beer, Shiner Bock, is produced. Czech and German settlers who began making beer under brewmaster Kosmos Spoetzl (pronounced shpet-zul) founded the brewery more than 90 years ago. Today the brewery still produces several types using the same methods, including bock, blonde, honey wheat, summer stock and winter ale. You can sample the beers for free after the tour in the little bar. Shiner's 'Bocktoberfest,' featuring rock and country music concerts, is held in mid-October; admission is $30 to $35 per adult (children under 12 free).

By car from San Antonio, take I-10 past Luling to US 95 and go south right to the very doors of Spoetzl Brewery. From Austin, take US 183 south through Luling to Gonzales, then turn east (left) and follow US 90A, which brings you right into the center of town; cross the railroad tracks and make a left turn on US 95 to reach the brewery.

same. Visit www.outinsanantonio.com or www.txtriangle.com for the latest listings.

The Hideout (Map pp122-3; ☎ 210-828-4222; Yard Shopping Center, 5307 McCullough Ave; no cover) If you're looking for a neighborhood bar that welcomes everybody with open arms, look no farther. Later in the week, the Hideout also boasts **The Den**, a quieter jazz and video lounge, and **Club Lava** for high-energy dancing; both open only after 9pm.

The Saint (Map pp136-7; ☎ 210-227-2468; 1430 N Main Ave; no cover before 11pm; ☺ 9pm-2am) This glittery (some say it's semi-trashy) show bar is an after-hours player on the scene. Nightly drag performances (some of the best in Texas, if not the country) start at 11:30pm sharp.

Electric Company (Map pp136-7; ☎ 210-212-6635; 820 San Pedro Ave; ☺ 9pm-3:30am Wed-Sun) This lesbian-owned bar and dance club attracts both genders and all ages. Even a few straight folks get caught up here in the house, hip-hop and R&B mix. This dance floor grooves into the wee hours.

The Annex (Map pp136-7; ☎ 210-223-6957; 330 San Pedro Ave; www.theannex-satx.com) SA's best-known Levis-and-leather bar has a small outdoor patio, cheap drinks and weekly steak nights.

Pegasus (Map pp136-7; ☎ 210-299-4222; 1402 N Main Ave) is a laidback bar with pool tables and darts, just a few doors down from both the Saint and the two-steppin' **Silver Dollar Saloon** (Map pp136-7; ☎ 210-227-2623; 1418 N Main St). Or you could always boogie over with the beautiful boys at **Heat** (Map pp136-7; ☎ 210-227-2600; 1500 N Main Ave).

Comedy

There are also comedy performances from visiting headliners at venues such as the downtown **Majestic Theatre** (p162) and Trinity University's **Laurie Auditorium** (p162); check the *Current* or the *Express-News'* 'Weekender' section for more information.

Rivercenter Comedy Club (Map pp126-7; ☎ 210-229-1420; www.hotcomedy.com/rivercenter.htm; 3rd level, Rivercenter Mall, 849 E Commerce St; tickets $9-12; ☺ showtimes 8:30pm Sun-Thu, 8:30pm & 10:45pm Fri-Sat) This club has nightly comedy featuring major headliners and up-and-coming local comedians. Saturday from 5:30pm until 7:30pm are the local amateur hours, when there's no cover charge. There's also a free adults-only 'After Midnight Madness' show

on Saturday night. Three-hour parking is validated free at the Rivercenter Mall garage.

Cinema

Check the *Current* or the *Express-News'* 'Weekender' section for cinemas and showtimes.

San Antonio IMAX Alamo Theatre (Map pp126-7; ☎ 210-247-4629, 800-354-4629; www.imax-sa.com; Rivercenter Mall, 849 E Commerce St; adult/senior & youth 12-17/child 3-11 $9/8/5.50) Films shown here include the 45-minute award-winning film *Alamo: The Price of Freedom*, about guess what. If you've never seen a film on a six-story-high screen in six-track surround sound, this theater plays several movies in the IMAX format – it's worth the admission price just for the experience.

The Texas Adventure (Map pp126-7; ☎ 210-227-8224; www.texas-adventure.com; 307 Alamo Plaza; adult/child 3-11 $9/5.50; ☺ 8:30am-8pm, call for showtimes) Opposite the Alamo, this multimedia special-effects show based on the Texas War for Independence focuses on the Battle of the Alamo. The show is pretty amazing and an exciting (if overly dramatic) depiction of the battle.

Santikos Mission 4 Outdoor Theater (Map pp122-3; ☎ 210-532-3259; 3100 Roosevelt Ave; adult/child $5/3) Dating from the 1940s, this old-fashioned drive-in cinema close to the Mission Trail shows mainstream first-run Hollywood flicks. It's a perfect excursion on those long, hot Texas summer evenings.

Although it mostly shows blockbusters, **AMC Huebner Oaks** (Map pp122-3; ☎ 210-558-9988;

FILM FIESTAS

In February **Cinefestival** is a pivotal event that brings together Texan, Mexican, Chicano and Latino filmmakers at the **Guadalupe Cultural Arts Center** (☎ 210-271-3151; www.guadalupeculturalarts.org; 1301 Guadalupe St). June's experimental **San Antonio Underground Film Festival** (☎ 210-977-9004; www.safilm.com) is all about video, whether that means documentary, animated or narrative. The organizers' do-it-yourself punk attitude can be summed up as 'This ain't no Cannes. This ain't no Sundance.' Grand prizes include a low-rider bicycle and a miniature accordion.

11075 IH-10 W, at Huebner Rd) and **Regal Fiesta 16** (☎ 210-333-3456; 12631 Vance Jackson Rd, off De Zavala Rd east of I-10) also screen a few arthouse films. During the summer at AMC Huebner Oaks cinema, **Texas Public Radio** (TPR; ☎ 210-614-8977; www.tpr.org; tickets $12) hosts a 'Cinema Tuesday' classic film series.

There are plenty more googolplex cinemas in San Antonio, including the convenient **AMC Rivercenter 9** (Map pp126-7; ☎ 210-558-9988; Rivercenter Mall, 849 E Commerce St) and the **Regal Alamo Quarry 14** (Map pp122-3; ☎ 210-333-3456; Alamo Quarry Market, 255 E Basse Rd), with stadium seating.

Bowling & Billiards

Hermann Sons Bowling Alley (Map pp126-7; ☎ 210-226-5432; 525 S St Mary's St; game $1.75, shoe rental 75¢; ☉ usually 5-11pm Tues & Fri) This vintage 1940s bowling alley on the south side of downtown is unbelievably hip without even trying to be. Automatic scoring machines? Who needs 'em. Best of all, it's usually not crowded.

Banana's Billiards (Map pp136-7; ☎ 210-226-2627; 2003 San Pedro Ave; ☉ noon-2am daily) At this neighborhood hall not too far of a drive from Brackenridge Park, ladies always play free. Otherwise, plug quarters into the tables before cueing up at this haunt opened by legendary Alejandro 'Banana' Rodriguez back in the '70s.

Spectator Sports

Paid for by what could be called a local sports-team extortion tax, the **Alamodome** (Map pp126-7; ☎ 210-207-3663, 800-884-3663; 100 Montana St; ☉ box office 10am-5pm Mon-Fri), just east of I-37, near the southeast corner of HemisFair Park, is an extraordinary 65,000-seat stadium that is home to the city's NBA basketball team. One of the most flexible stadiums in the world, the seating system can be configured to hold as many as 77,200 people and is the largest of its kind. The building's dome roof stands, at its highest point, at about 170ft, and the Sony JumboTron monitor – which hypnotizes spectators with ads during breaks in the action – weighs in at an amazing 30 tons. The annual **Alamo Bowl** college football championship game is held here. Finding a parking lot close to the Alamodome is the only problem you'll have attending a game; there's only limited public parking provided on the grounds.

The big news in town is the **San Antonio Spurs** (☎ 210-225-8326; www.nba.com/spurs; tickets from $10), currently one of the top NBA teams in the country. No matter how the team performs during the October-to-April season, San Antonians are simply psychotic in their support of the men's professional basketball team. Games held at the **SBC Center** (Map pp122-3; cnr Houston St & SBC Center Pkwy, off I-35 exit 159B/160; bus No 24) are exciting, action-packed spectacles.

Winners of the Texas League championships in 2003, the **San Antonio Missions** (☎ 210-675-7275; www.samissions.com; Nelson W Wolff Municipal Stadium, 5757 US 90 W; tickets $4-8; regular season Apr-Aug) play minor league baseball at Wolff Stadium, a short drive west of downtown. There's horse racing at **Retama Park** (☎ 210-651-7000; 1 Retama Pkwy, off I-35 exit 174A; www.retamapark.com; admission $1.50-3.50, parking on race days $2), a gracious place with mission-style architecture in northeast San Antonio, north of Loop 1604. Thoroughbred races are held several days per week, year-round.

Performing Arts

San Antonio's most historic downtown venue for the performing arts is the **Majestic Theatre** (Map pp126-7; ☎ 210-226-3333; www.themajestic.com; 226 E Houston St; ☉ 10am-5pm Mon-Fri, 10am-3pm Sat), which hosts a variety of musical concerts, Broadway plays and other events year-round. In La Villita (p131), the **Arneson River Theater** (Map p131) is an outdoor venue for anything from Latin dance to plays to festival processions. Trinity University's **Laurie Auditorium** (Map pp136-7; ☎ 210-999-8117; 715 Stadium Dr) also hosts a few musical concerts and dance and theatre performances year-round. May is the month to celebrate dance in San Antonio, with recitals by local troupes, national touring companies and new choreographers' works at both indoor and outdoor venues around the city; contact **San Antonio Dance Umbrella** (SADU; ☎ 210-212-7775; www.sadu.org) for details.

THEATER

Visit www.satheatre.com for information on the venues below, as well as other theatres and dramatic companies performing year-round.

San Pedro Playhouse (Map pp136-7; ☎ 210-733-7258; 800 E Ashby Pl, at San Pedro Ave) This beautiful Greek revival-style mansion in San Pedro Park is the performance venue for the nonprofit San Antonio Little Theatre (SALT), which stages several shows a year, usually classics. It's also home to the SALT Cellar Theater, a 60-seat venue that holds scaled-down and experimental works.

Alamo Street Theatre (Map p134; ☎ 210-271-7791; www.alamostreetrestaurantandtheatre.com; 1150 S Alamo St; performances with dinner $25-28, without dinner $7-15) In a restored former church, the Alamo Street Theatre has two playhouses. Popular revivals and murder mysteries appear on the dinner theater stage. Other performances are mainly modern classics. Occasionally, there are special children's shows.

Guadalupe Theatre (☎ 210-271-3151; www.guadalupeculturalarts.org; 1301 Guadalupe St, cnr Brazos St) You never know what to expect at this community arts center, whether it's a poetry reading, dance recital, contemporary drama or ballet folklorico performance, but it's always worth the trip.

Other places to catch performances, from musicals to dramas to children's plays, include downtown's **Majestic Theatre** (p162), the adult drama series at **Magik Children's Theatre** (p141), the Blue Star Arts Complex's innovative **Jump-Start Performance Co** (Map p134; ☎ 210-227-5867; www.jump-start.org; 108 Blue Star, off S Alamo St) and the nonprofit **Josephine Theatre** (Map pp136-7; ☎ 210-734-4646; 339 W Josephine St) in an old movie house near Brackenridge Park.

CLASSICAL MUSIC
The Majestic Theatre and Laurie Auditorium are the main performance venues for both local and touring orchestras and chamber groups.

San Antonio Symphony (☎ 210-554-1010; www.sasymphony.org; box office: 2nd floor, Majestic Tower, 222 E Houston St; tickets from $16) The symphony performs a wide range of classical concerts, operas and ballets at the spectacular Majestic Theatre. Tickets (which range in price wildly) can be bought from the symphony's box office or from Ticketmaster outlets.

Alamo City Men's Chorale (☎ 210-495-7464; www.acmc-texas.org) This is a community group of about 40 gay singers who perform a large

repertoire of classics, pops, spirituals and new works, sometimes alongside the San Antonio Symphony but more often on its own at various venues.

SHOPPING
Don't overlook San Antonio's museum gift shops, especially SAMA and the McNay Art Museum, which can be exceptional. Popular attractions like the Alamo, Buckhorn Saloon and Guenther House also make for unique souvenir shopping. If you're just desperate because you forgot to get gifts until the last minute, Texas-made goods are sold at stores in both terminals of San Antonio's airport.

Markets, Art & Crafts
Before Christmas you'll find more than a few of SA's special holiday markets, for example Mexican-style **Bazar Sabado** at SAMA, **Hecho a Mano** (literally, 'made by hand') at the Guadalupe Cultural Arts Center and **Kristkindlmarkt** at the Beethoven Männerchor Und Garten

Market Square (Map pp126-7; ☎ 210-207-8600; 514 W Commerce St; ☉ 10am-6pm, until 8pm in summer) A short ride from the Riverwalk, 'El Mercado' is a re-creation of a Mexican marketplace. As far as tourist traps go, you

PAPA JIM'S BOTANICA

If you have never visited a botanica before, be sure to make a special trip out to **Papa Jim's** (Map pp122-3; ☎ 210-922-6665; www.stjudesbotanica.com; 5630 S Flores St; bus No 44; ☉ 9:30am-6:30pm Mon-Sat, 10:30am-5pm Sun) in the southern part of the city. It's basically a religious and Santeria superstore (mixed with a bit of voodoo), selling items to rid you of the problem of your choice: Get-Rich candles; Do-As-I-Say floor wash; Jinx Removal air-freshener; Run-Devil-Run and Get-out-of-Jail oil; and Stop-Gossip soap, all for a few dollars a piece. The store also has books, herbal teas, incense, good-luck charms and other items related to Santeria, a synthesis of Catholicism and the Nigerian Yoruba folk beliefs of slaves brought to the Caribbean. Papa Jim's motto is 'Whatever Works,' and obviously it works for some: the botanica has been around since 1980.

SAN ANTONIO

could do worse, with about 100 merchants selling blankets, handbags, rugs, craftwork, clothing and reasonable Mexican food. Prices will seem decent if you've haven't been south of the border.

La Tienda Guadalupe (Map p134; ☎ 210-226-5873; 1001 S Alamo St; ☽ noon-6pm Mon-Tue & Thu-Sun, closed on rainy days) One of the most authentic Mexican folk arts shops in the city, La Tienda imports goods from across Central America, too. Although prices may be higher here than at Market Square, you'll be glad you spent the extra few coins.

El Sol Studios (Map p134; ☎ 210-226-9700; 1036 S Alamo St; h10am-5pm Tue-Sun) In a quaint house tucked behind Espuma coffeehouse (p154), this is another of Southtown's laudable Mexican folkcraft shops. The artist-owner sells Día de los Muertos figurines, unique silver and beaded jewelry, hand-printed cards and more.

Guadalupe Cultural Arts Center (☎ 210-271-3151; www.guadalupeculturalarts.org; 1301 Guadalupe St, cnr Brazos St ; ☽ 9am-5pm Mon-Fri) Folk art, jewelry, books for kids and adults, Latin music, original posters and prints all are on display here at this nonprofit store. Proceeds support the arts center's programs, and all the work is high-quality; it's worth the trip.

Gallista Gallery (☎ 210-212-8606; 1913 S Flores St; ☽ hrs vary) A diverse art gallery attached to a coffeehouse, Gallista is run by a convivial Chicano watercolorist, Joe Lopez, who makes exhibition space available to young and emerging visual artists from the neighborhood and around south-central Texas. It's a welcoming space.

Many of the art galleries around town are excellent for buying crafts by contemporary Texas and Mexican artists. Seek out the **Southwest School of Art & Craft's** sales gallery shop (p130), touristy **La Villita** (p131) and workshops inside the **Blue Star Arts Complex** (p134).

Clothing

For spectacular bargains, head to the **factory outlets** in New Braunfels and San Marcos.

FASHION & VINTAGE

Although the River City isn't as red-hot for tracking down new designers and vintage finds as Austin is, there are a few places worth a detour.

Adelante Boutique (Map pp122-3; ☎ 210-826-6770; Sunset Ridge shopping center, 6414 N New Braunfels Ave; ☽ 10am-5:30pm Mon-Sat) Like a romantic breath of fresh air, this shop has mix-and-match pieces in vibrant prints and fabrics you won't find anywhere else, along with designer jewelry imports. Sale items are downright beautiful, too.

Textures Gallery (Map p136-7; ☎ 210-822-9727; 4026 McCullough Ave; ☽ 10am-5:30pm Tue-Fri, 10am-4pm Sat) At this Olmos Park co-op shop, run by women artists, you'll find unconventional 'artwear' made with fabrics that just beg to be touched, as well as jewelry, home decor and other odds and ends.

Nelda's (Map p136-7; ☎ 210-271-7111; 1621 N Main Ave; ☽ 11am-6pm Tue-Sat) The queen of vintage shopping in the River City, Nelda's offers hand-picked clothes, hats and shoes (along with fabulous jewelry and accessories) that span the decades from the swinging '40s to the flared '70s.

WESTERN WEAR

If you're not headed for the Hill Country, buy here.

Paris Hatters (Map pp126-7; ☎ 210-223-3453; 119 Broadway; ☽ call for hrs) A humble downtown storefront, Paris Hatters has been around a long, long time. It's one of the best places in the state to get a Stetson (or any other brand of cowboy hat).

Little's (Map pp122-3; ☎ 210-923-2221; www.davelittleboots.com; 110 Division Ave; ☽ call for hrs) This high-quality bootmaker's shop established in 1915 now caters to country music stars, actors and locals alike. Get your custom pair with a belt to match made from calf, crocodile, 'gator, lizard, eel, ostrich or even kangaroo skin. Allow a few months for delivery.

Lucchese (Map pp122-3; ☎ 210-828-9419, 800-548-9755; Alamo Quarry Market, 255 E Basse Rd; ☽ 10am-7pm Mon-Fri, 10am-6pm Sat, noon-5pm Sun) This 19th-century boot company is one of the top sellers of upscale Western gear in town. It's a must for those on a serious quest to get rigged out cowboy-style. Handmade cowboy boots are shaped specially for your feet. They have ready-made items, jewelry and accessories, too.

Affordably priced Western-wear chains around town include **Sheplers** (Map pp122-3; ☎ 210-681-8230; 6201 NW Loop 410), next to Ingram Park Mall, and **Cavender's Boot City**

(Map pp122-3; ; ☎ 210-520-2668; 5075 NW Loop 410; ☯ 9am-9pm Mon-Sat, noon-6pm Sun).

Antiques

West of San Pedro Ave on the 500 and 600 blocks of **Hildebrand Avenue** you'll find specialty antiques shops ranging from mid-century modern to rustic Texan-ware.

Echoes of the Past (Map pp126-7; ☎ 210-225-3714; 517 E Houston St; ☯ 10am-5:30pm Mon-Sat) This antiques shop is just a short stroll from the Alamo. Apart from Alamo Records in the basement, there's all manner of collectibles for sale, from kids' toys to old Texas license plates and some vintage Lone Star Beer paraphernalia.

Center for Antiques (Map pp122-3; ☎ 210-804-6317; 8505 Broadway, north of Loop 410; ☯ 10am-5:30pm Mon-Fri, 10am-6pm Sat, noon-5pm Sun) At the Airport Convention Center, this mini-mall of individual antiques vendors has the city's widest selection of treasures, such as Wurlitzer jukeboxes, snooker tables, amber hatpins and Marvin the Martian Pez dispensers.

Music

Alamo Records (Map pp126-7; ☎ 210-225-3714; 517 E Houston St; ☯ 10am-5:30pm Mon-Sat) Alamo Records, in the basement of the great antiques store Echoes of the Past, is *the* place to look for that long-lost Bucks Fizz album on vinyl. The selection is enormous, covering every type of music imaginable.

CD Exchange (Map pp136-7; ☎ 210-828-5525; 3703 Broadway; ☯ 10am-9pm Mon-Sat, noon-7pm Sun) This reliable chain music store has lots of cheap second-hand CDs, DVDs and videotapes in all genres. DJs occasionally spin at in-store shows. Call for other locations around San Antonio; this one is nearby Brackenridge Park.

Hogwild Records (Map pp136-7; ☎ 210-733-5354; 1824 N Main Ave; ☯ 10am-9pm Mon-Sat, noon-8pm Sun) With an expert selection of vinyl, Hogwild also vends tapes and CDs. If you're after alt-country, punk 'zines or rare drum 'n bass records, this independent music store is the place. Just look for the front door, plastered with band flyers and deep layers of stickers.

Other favorites for vinyl are **The Record Collector** at the Center for Antiques, with rare vinyl jazz, blues and other genres, and **Spider Records** (Map pp122-3; ☎ 210-736-1697; 502

Fredericksburg Rd; ☯ hrs vary), another local vinyl shop with an indie-punk attitude.

Malls

The malls below all keep the same hours: from 10am to 9pm Monday to Saturday, and noon to 6pm Sunday.

Rivercenter Mall (Map pp126-7; ☎ 210-225-0000; 849 E Commerce St) It's the most accessible mega-mall in town, and its setting on the Riverwalk isn't bad at all. Because of the cinemas, IMAX theater, comedy club, restaurants and dozens of shops, you'll probably end up here at some point in your stay.

Alamo Quarry Market (Map pp122-3; ☎ 210-225-1000; 255 E Basse Rd; bus No 505) Making fine use of an old 19th-century cement plant is this outdoor mall, which has plenty of top-brand stores, a multiplex cinema and restaurants. A few Austin-based chains here include Whole Foods Market for groceries, Amy's Ice Creams and the outdoors outfitter Whole Earth Provision Co.

Other malls around the city include **Ingram Park Mall** (Map pp122-3; ☎ 210-684-9570; 6301 NW Loop 410 at Ingram Rd), **North Star Mall** (Map pp122-3; ☎ 210-340-6627; 7400 San Pedro Ave at Loop 410) and **Crossroads of San Antonio** (Map pp122-3; ☎ 210-735-9137; 4522 Fredericksburg Rd at Loop 410).

GETTING THERE & AWAY

See the Transport chapter for toll-free contact numbers, websites, car rental and other regional transportation information.

Air

San Antonio International Airport (SAT; ☎ 210-207-3411; www.ci.sat.tx.us/aviation; 9800 Airport Blvd) is about 9 miles north of downtown, just north of the intersection of Loop 410 and US 281. It's served by taxis, public transportation and shuttles.

The airport offers frequent flights to destinations in Texas and the rest of the USA via the following airlines: American, America West, Delta, Midwest Express, Northwest-KLM, Southwest and United-Lufthansa. AeroLitoral runs flights between San Antonio and Monterrey, with connecting flights throughout Mexico. There is also direct or connecting air service to Mexico with Continental, Mexicana, American and America West airlines.

Bus

Greyhound (☎ 210-270-5824) and **Kerrville Bus Co** (☎ 210-226-7371, 800-256-2757) share a **terminal** (Map pp126-7; 500 N St Mary's St) right downtown.

Bus services from San Antonio, and the highest standard published fares for same-day tickets, include the following:

to/from	frequency (per day)	duration	one way/ round-trip
Austin	14	1½ to 2 hrs	$14/22
Dallas	14	5 to 7½ hrs	$34/59
El Paso	3	10½ hrs	$84/126
Houston	13	3¼ to 6¼ hrs	$22/39
Kerrville	4	1 to 1¼ hrs	$17/28
Laredo	17	2½ to 6¼ hrs	$17/31
Lubbock	3	8¾ to 10 hrs	$76/130
Waco	5-8	3½ to 5¼ hrs	$27/39

Car & Motorcycle

San Antonio radiates from the convergence of I-35, I-10 and I-37. For the Texas Hill Country, you can take I-10 north to many of the larger towns, or US 281, which is the northbound continuation of I-37. All of the major rental car agencies have outlets at San Antonio International Airport, and some have outlets downtown as well.

Train

Squeezed between Sunset Station and the Alamodome, the **Amtrak station** (Map pp126-7; ☎ 210-223-3226; 350 Hoefgen St) is served by *Sunset Limited* and *Texas Eagle* trains. It's a fully staffed Amtrak station, with an enclosed waiting area and free short-term parking. VIA streetcars (50¢) on the yellow line connect Sunset Station with the downtown Riverwalk, where you can transfer to other streetcar and bus lines.

GETTING AROUND
To/From the Airport

VIA bus No 2 runs at least hourly between the airport and downtown from around 6am (8am on weekends) until 9:30pm. The regular service costs 80¢, the express service $1.60; the journey takes between 45 minutes and an hour. Slower bus No 550 (clockwise) and 551 (counter-clockwise) circumnavigate the city on Loop 410, taking three hours and stopping at the airport on the way.

Major downtown hotels have free airport courtesy shuttles; be sure to ask. A taxi ride from the airport to downtown costs between $15 and $20 for up to four people.

All of the major rental car agencies have outlets at San Antonio International Airport.

Boat

Operated by **Yanaguana Cruise** (☎ 210-244-5700, 800-417-4139; www.sarivercruise.com), the River Shuttle (aka 'Rio Trans') operates between 10am and 9pm daily, stopping every 20 minutes or so at several points along the Riverwalk. Fares are steep: $3.50 per one-way ticket, or $10 for an all-day pass. A better value are their regular riverboat tours or dinner cruises (see p143). Cash is not accepted on board the boats; buy tickets and passes from various hotels or restaurants along the Riverwalk.

Car & Motorcycle

There are plenty of public parking lots downtown, including by most of the major hotels. The lots generally cost $3 per hour, $5 to $8 for 24 hours (go figure). Otherwise you can park for free in the residential streets of the King William District and Southtown, then walk or ride VIA's blue line streetcars (see below) north into downtown.

Public Transport

San Antonio's public transport network, **VIA Metropolitan Transit** (☎ 210-362-2020; www.viainfo.net), operates more than 100 regular bus routes, plus four streetcar routes. VIA passes, bus schedules and streetcar route maps are available at VIA's downtown **information center** (Map pp 126-7; ☎ same phone; 260 E Houston St; ☾ 7am-6pm Mon-Fri, 9am-2pm Sat) and the San Antonio CVB's downtown visitors center (p124), opposite the Alamo.

Local VIA bus fares are 80¢ (15¢ for a transfer), and exact change is required. VIA express buses, which use interstate highways and include buses to theme parks, cost $1.60. VIA streetcars cost 50¢ per ride. Discount fares are available for children, seniors and the mobility impaired. Otherwise, a $2 Day Tripper Pass allows unlimited rides on all VIA buses and streetcars for one day. VIA's monthly pass, which is just $20 (or $10 for the streetcars only), is a real bargain if you plan to use public transit regularly.

Note that the streetcars look more like trolleys, since there is no overhead cable. The streetcar routes are occasionally served by buses, too, although the fare remains the same in that case. VIA streetcars run to and from the Alamo, Market Square, HemisFair Park, the Alamodome, Sunset Station, Southtown and the King William Historic District. There are stops throughout downtown and at several hotels. The main transfer station for all streetcar lines is near the Rivercenter Mall.

Most streetcar routes operate every 10 minutes from 9am until 7:30pm daily; there are extended hours for some lines, especially on weekdays. VIA bus schedules vary, but the last buses leave downtown between 10:30pm and 11:30pm, depending on the route. Night buses may only cover part of the daytime route, so call to check.

Bicycle

Getting around by bicycle isn't very feasible in San Antonio. Downtown streets are too congested for cycling, and the spread-out nature of the city makes it even more difficult to travel. That said, biking around Brackenridge Park and the Mission Trail are two attractive options.

To rent bicycles, contact the following:

Abel's Bicycle Repair & Rental (☎ 210-533-9927) Rents bikes for $21.50 a day, and will deliver bikes free of charge to the downtown area.
Bike City (Map pp122-3; ☎ 210-308-0812; West Ave Center, 3122 West Ave, at Basse Rd)
Britton's Bicycle Shop (☎ 210-656-1655; 4230 Thousand Oaks, cnr Uhr Lane, off I-35 exit 167)

Taxi

Taxi stands are found at major downtown hotels, the Greyhound and Amtrak stations and the airport. Otherwise you'll probably need to telephone for one. Taxi rates are $1.60 at flag-fall ($2.60 between 9pm and 5am), then $1.50 for each additional mile. Bigger companies include **Yellow Checker Cab** (☎ 210-222-2222) and **San Antonio Taxis** (☎ 210-444-2222, 877-731-7111). For six-passenger vans and ADA-accessible vehicles, contact **All Taxi Dispatch Service** (☎ 210-444-1111).

AROUND SAN ANTONIO

The area directly north of San Antonio is known primarily as a haven for shoppers who stream by the hundreds of thousands into the factory outlet malls in the cities of San Marcos and New Braunfels, off I-35. It's definitely something every bargain shopper should put on his or her itinerary. But these towns are also great destinations for outdoor recreation on local rivers, perfect for families or anyone else who needs to cool off on a hot summer's day!

NEW BRAUNFELS

The richly historic town of New Braunfels (named for its Prussian founder, Prince Carl of Solms Braunfels) was the first German settlement in Texas. Today residents from Austin and San Antonio flock to New Braunfels in the summer for its main attraction: the easy-flowing icy waters of the Guadalupe and Comal Rivers. For a more controlled – but just as exhilarating – experience, there are two excellent water parks.

Visit the Greater New Braunfels **Chamber of Commerce** (☎ 830-625-2385, 800-572-2626; 390 S Seguin Ave; 🕑 8am-5pm Mon-Fri) or the highway **visitors center** (☎ 830-625-7973; off I-35 exit 190A; 🕑 9am-5pm) to pick up maps, historic downtown walking tour brochures and loads of more information on local attractions. The town's annual sausage festival, **Wurstfest**, is held on November 1 and 2.

Sights & Activities

The watery fun starts at Bavarian-themed **The Schlitterbahn** (☎ 830-625-2351; 305 W Austin; all-day pass adult/child $26.50/22; 🕑 10am-6pm or later daily May-Sep, weekends only early May), Texas' largest water park featuring about 30 different slides and water pools all using water from the Comal River. It's one of the best places to be with kids on a hot day.

Landa Park (☎ 830-608-2160, golf course 830-608-2174; Garden St & Union Ave; admission free, train ride $2, pool entry $4, picnic table fee $5; 🕑 6am-midnight) has an 18-hole golf course, a miniature railroad, shady picnic facilities and an Olympic-size swimming pool. In Price Solms Park, **The Chute** (☎ 830-608-2165; entry $5, tube rental $5, weekend parking $5; 🕑 10am-7pm Sat-Sun May-Aug) lets you fly down rapids in the Comal River.

For a day of doing nothing but chilling in the Guadalupe River, you don't have to go far in New Braunfels. For the most part, the river is calm with a few good rapids to make things exciting – it's something the whole family can enjoy.

Dozens of tubing outfitters rent rafts, kayaks, canoes and tubes and arrange shuttles to pick up and drop off floaters. Most offer tubes with built-in bottoms, so you won't scrape your backside on the bottom of the rocky river (and it gets rockier the longer the region goes without rain – which can be for months during the summer – so check current water levels at the visitors centers). Don't forget to bring sunscreen, a hat and drinking water and also be sure to wear some kind of water-soakable shoes or sandals.

The following rental agencies also provide shuttle services:

The Rockin' 'R' River Rides (☎ 830-629-9999, 800-553-5628; Gruene Rd, a mile off Hwy 46; tubes $14-16)
Gruene River Company (☎ 830-625-2800, 888-705-2800; 1404 Gruene Rd; tubes $12-14)
Janie's Riverbank Outfitters (☎ 830-625-4928; 6000 River Rd; tubes $12-14)

Sleeping & Eating
For an extensive list of wonderful B&Bs around town, contact the **Bed & Breakfast & Getaways Reservation Service** (☎ 830-625-8194, 800-239-8282; 295 E San Antonio St; ☯ 9am-9pm).

With a convenient downtown location, the popular **Prince Solms' Inn** (☎ 830-625-9169, 800-625-9169; 295 E San Antonio St, d $125-175; **P**) is one of the oldest still-operating inns in Texas. Its flowery Victorian and rustic Western-themed rooms offer authentic furnishings (some also have bunk beds, a great option for families). The romantic cabin out back has a full kitchen. Wines and desserts are specialties of the house at the classy, attached **Piano Bar**.

For Czech kolaches and German strudels, try **Naegelin's Bakery** (☎ 830-625-5722; 129 S Seguin Ave; ☯ 6:30am-5:30pm Mon-Sat), one of the oldest continuously operating bakeries in Texas (it opened in 1868). Hearty American breakfasts and German-style lunches are served at popular **Krauses Cafe** (☎ 830-625-7581; 148 South Castell Ave; mains $6-9; ☯ 6:30am-8:30pm Mon-Fri, 7am-9pm Sat, 7:30am-4pm Sun), which also sells burgers and Texas

barbecue. **Huisache Grille** (☎ 830-620-9001; 303 W San Antonio St; mains $7-17; ☯ 11am-11pm), just across the railroad tracks from the plaza, serves up imaginative Southwestern cuisine, like 'Pork Chop Lollipop' in a rum-butter pecan sauce. For an eclectic upscale atmosphere and some serious steaks, try **Myrons Steakhouse** (☎ 830-624-1024; 136 N Castell St; mains $20-35; ☯ 4-10pm Mon-Sat, till 11pm Fri-Sat), located inside an old movie theater.

Shopping
Good deals can be had at the **New Braunfels Factory Stores** (☎ 830-620-6806; off I-35 exit 189; ☯ 9am-8pm Mon-Sat, noon-6pm Sun), one of the area's many factory outlet malls.

GRUENE
The charming and historic town of Gruene (pronounced 'green') is just 4 miles northeast of New Braunfels, and in many ways, it's a much nicer place to stay. It's close to all of the Guadalupe River tubing outfitters (p168) and loaded with antique and crafts shops besides. **Old Gruene Market Day** is held the third weekend of the month from February through November.

The town is best known for Texas' oldest dance hall, **Gruene Hall** (☎ 830-606-1281; 1281 Gruene Rd; cover $8-12, advance show tickets $22-25; ☯ 11am-9pm Mon-Wed, 11am-midnight Thu-Fri, 10am-10pm Sat, 10am-9pm Sun). There's no air-conditioning, but it's got cold beer and great bands. It seems that anyone who's anyone has played here, from Jerry Lee Lewis to Willie Nelson. On Friday and Saturday night it's always packed with San Antonio partygoers.

Gruene's **Museum of Art & Music** (☎ 830-625-5636; 1259 Gruene Rd; adult/student $3/2; ☯ 10am-6pm Mon & Wed, 10am-9pm Thu-Sat, noon-6pm Sun) is an in-depth look at the Lone Star State's folkcraft and contemporary arts.

Sleeping & Eating
For a rural escape from the big city, **Gruene Mansion** (☎ 830-629-2641; 1275 Gruene Rd; d $120-220; **P**) is a pretty Victorian house with double-decker wraparound porches; rooms are clean and each comes with its own balcony overlooking the oak-lined grounds. Inside a converted grain silo, **The Silo Inn B&B** (☎ 830-643-1791; www.siloinn.com; 1609 Waterway; d from $120; **P**) is a unique choice: it's a split-level vacation rental loaded with antiques, two queen-size beds (one's up in the loft) and

a kitchenette. Rock on the front porch and watch the windmill go 'round, or sink into the whirlpool bath – ah, heaven.

Chicken-fried steak and other Texas savories can be found behind Gruene Hall at the **Gristmill River Restaurant & Bar** (☎ 830-625-0684; 1287 Gruene Rd; mains $8-15; 🕙 11am-10pm daily, till 11pm Fri-Sat), which is picturesquely sited inside the brick remnants of an 80-year-old cotton gin. On the Guadalupe River next to all of the tubing action, the **Guadalupe Smoked Meat Company** (☎ 830-629-6121; 1299 Gruene Rd; mains $4-8; 🕙 11am-10pm) is a more laidback spot, with a fine selection of Texas barbecue, salads and lemonade. There's also a pretty patio on which to drink margaritas after a day spent floating down the river.

SAN MARCOS

While practically every one of the tens of thousands who come through here daily are heading to the factory outlet malls (maybe the best around), San Marcos also is home to Wonder World, Texas' most visited cave, and natural attractions around Southwest Texas State University, including tubing on the San Marcos River

The **San Marcos Convention & Visitors Bureau** (☎ 512-393-5930, 888-200-5620; www.sanmarcostexas.com; 617 N IH-35 exit 204B/205; 🕙 9am-5pm Mon-Sat, 10am-4pm Sun) has maps, brochures and information on trolley tours of the town's historic districts. Since San Marcos is so close to San Antonio, visitors rarely need to avail themselves of any overnight accommodations.

Sights & Activities

Owned by Southwest Texas State University, the enjoyable **Aquarena Center** (☎ 512-245-7570, 800-999-9767; www.continuing-ed.swt.edu/aquarena; 921 Aquarena Springs Dr, west of I-35 exit 206; admission free, boat tours adult/senior/child 4-14 $6/5/4; 🕙 9:30am-6pm) is home to family-oriented exhibitions on ecology, history and archaeology and includes the ruins of a Spanish mission founded here on the Feast of San Marcos. This educational center also offers hour-long glass-bottom boat tours of the lake formed by the town's namesake springs, which gush forth 1½ million gallons of artesian water every day.

Just south of the Aquarena Center, the **Lions Club** (☎ 512-396-5466; City Park, next to the Texas National Guard Armory; single/double tubes without bottoms $6/12, with bottoms $8/14) rents tubes to tackle the usually docile stretch of the San Marcos River from 10am to 7pm daily between Memorial Day and Labor Day, as well as on weekends in May and September. The last tube is rented at 5:30pm and the last shuttle pickup from Rio Vista Dam is at 6:45pm sharp.

A mini-theme park has been built around the USA's largest earthquake-created cave, **Wonder World** (☎ 512-392-3760; www.wonderworldpark.com; Wonder World Dr, off I-35 exit 202; combination tickets adult/senior/child 4-11 $16/13/12; 🕙 8am-8pm daily Jun-Aug, 9am-5pm Mon-Fri & 9am-6pm Sat-Sun Sep-May), which is the most-visited cave in Texas. Take a one-hour tour through the Balcones Fault Line Cave, where you can look at the Edwards Aquifer up close; tours begin every 15 to 30 minutes year-round. Outside, in the 110ft Tejas Observation Tower, you can make out the faultline itself. Other attractions include a petting park filled with Texas animals, a train ride around the park and the quaint 'Anti-Gravity House,' a holdover from family vacations of yesteryear. There's a picnic area on the grounds.

Adults may want to detour onto the university campus to visit the excellent free exhibitions at the **Witliff Gallery of Southwestern & Mexican Photography** and the **Southwestern Writers Collection**, both found on the 7th floor of the Alkek Library. Hours vary, so call ahead (☎ 512-245-2313). Take Aquarena Springs Dr about three-quarters of a mile west of the Aquarena Center, then turn right onto University Dr and take another right less than a half mile later onto Guadalupe St. Follow the signs to the LBJ Student Center parking garage ($2/hour). The library is a short walk downhill from the student center.

SHOPPING

There are more than 100 name-brand factory outlet stores at **Prime Outlets** (☎ 512-396-2200, 800-628-9465; off I-35 exit 200; 🕙 10am-9pm Mon-Sat, 11am-6pm Sun), an enormous shopping complex. Located off the same interstate exit, equally big **Tanger Outlets** (☎ 512-396-7446, 800-408-8424; 4015 S IH-35; 🕙 9am-9pm Mon-Sat, 11am-7pm Sun) has similar offerings. Outlet shops at both malls offer at least a 30% discount on regular retail prices, and sometimes as much as 75% off brands. Stores include Calvin Klein, Tommy Hilfiger and Levi's, to name just a few.

Hill Country

Driving through the natural beauty of the Texas Hill Country can be like visiting Provence in the south of France (never mind the longhorns and the cowboy hats). You'll find peaceful, picturesque towns and superb restaurants, art galleries, vineyards and even an olive press tucked into the gently rolling limestone hills. In fact, about the only thing missing are the truffles, though you can be sure some enterprising Texan is figuring out how to grow those, too. It's no wonder so many folks from Austin and San Antonio drop out and head for the hills, since the area is as far from the big cities as you can get in under two hours.

Sitting in the center of the state, the Hill Country is formed by the Balcones Escarpment and the limestone ledges and hills of the Edwards Plateau. Giant oak trees, cool lakes, spring-fed creeks and easy flowing rivers round out the geography. It's because of this natural beauty that the area was settled by freethinking Europeans, mostly German doctors, artists, carpenters and dreamers over 150 years ago. Today there's still a large population of their descendants in the Hill Country, especially in and around the town of Fredericksburg, a touristy destination that has embraced its heritage with 'vilkomen' arms (and cash registers). Yet the true character of the Hill Country is most evident on its winding back roads, which go between the big towns ('big' here is a relative term; the biggest towns, Kerrville and Fredericksburg, are both pretty small). There you'll find the Hill Country's beautiful parks, rivers and dude ranches, along with locals' generous, friendly smiles.

HILL COUNTRY

HIGHLIGHTS

- **Cowboy Arts** Kerrville's National Center for American Western Art (p181)
- **Dining** A taste of Bavaria in Fredericksburg (p175)
- **Wining** Sipping Chenin Blanc in the Texas wine country (p173)
- **Kickin' Back** Country music under the oak trees of Luckenbach (p179)
- **Antiques** Comfort, a 19th-century German settlement (p180)
- **Honky Tonk** Drinkin' beer, dancin' and dude ranches in Bandera (p185)

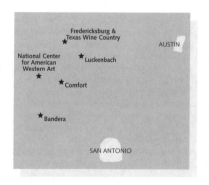

| ■ TELEPHONE CODE: 03 | ■ POPULATION: 4.7 MILLION | ■ AREA: 227,420 SQ KM |

INFORMATION

You can spend an entire vacation in the Hill Country and not see it all. One of the best times to visit is December, when the regional **Christmas Lighting Tour** (☎ 830-997-8515) goes around the whole place stringing up lights and making everything look romantic. Visit www.hill-country-visitor.com for information on special events, accommodations, outdoor recreation and other Hill Country destinations.

ORIENTATION

The Hill Country makes up most of the area between Austin and San Antonio. It extends west all the way to US 83, while I-35 runs north-south along its easternmost edge. Ask 10 people the boundaries of the Hill Country and you'll get 11 different answers, but for travelers this is close enough. The capitals of activity are Fredericksburg and Kerrville. Most people make their base in one of those towns. Nearer San Antonio, San Marcos, New Braunfels and Gruene are often considered part of the Hill Country as well.

JOHNSON CITY

☎ 830 population 1300

Long before Lyndon Baines Johnson made it to the White House, the Johnson family had made a name for itself in the Texas Hill Country as ranchers, farmers and businessmen. In fact, it was LBJ's second cousin, James Polk Johnson, who lopped off 320 acres of the family's land on the Pedernales River so Johnson City could get its start in 1879. The town is named for him. Still, Johnson City is better known for the former US president, who grew up here and spent so much time here during his administration that the ranch became known as the 'Texas White House.'

The working **LBJ Ranch** and **Johnson's boyhood home** are now open as state and national historical sites (☎ 830-868-7128; admission free; ✆ 9am-4:30pm). There are two distinct sites – the boyhood home and settlement in Johnson City and the ranch area (now LBJ State Historic Park), about 14 miles west of town on US 290. Ninety-minute **bus tours** of the ranch ($3; ✆ 10am-4pm) start from the state park visitors center.

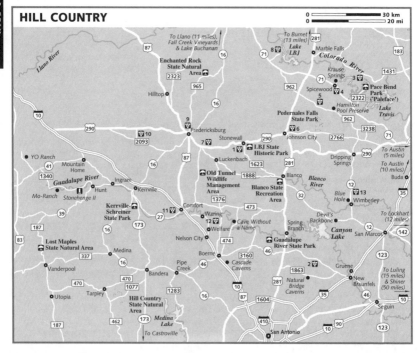

If you're looking for beautiful scenery, excellent swimming holes, mountain biking and hiking trails, head 9 miles east of town to **Pedernales Falls State Park** (☎ 830-868-7304; 2585 Park Road 6026, off FM 2766; day-use adult/senior $4/2, campsites $8-18). This 5000-acre park's

---

HILL COUNTRY WINERIES

When most people think of Texas, they think of cactus, Cadillacs and cowboys...not grapes. But the fact is, grapes – the kind that eventually get crushed, fermented and bottled – are the reason Texas is gaining notice for its wine. The Lone Star State has become the fifth-largest wine-producing state in the country (behind California, Washington, New York and Oregon). The Hill Country, with its robust Provence-like limestone and hot South African–style climate, has become the most productive wine-making region in the state. These rolling hills are home to more than a dozen wineries scattered throughout the region.

Most wineries are open daily for tastings and tours. Many also host special events, such as grape stompings and annual wine and food feasts. Local visitor bureaus stock the handy *Texas Hill Country Wine Trail* leaflet, which details the wineries and schedules of wine trail weekends (or visit www.texaswinetrail.com).

The largest concentration of Hill Country vineyards is around Fredericksburg. **Becker Vineyards (1)** (☎ 830-644-2681; www.beckervineyards.com; Jenscheke Lane; ☽ 10am-5pm Mon-Thu, 10am-6pm Fri-Sat, noon-5pm Sun) is one of the state's most decorated wine producers. Located 10 miles east of Fredericksburg, just off US 290, the vineyard has 36 acres of vines and allegedly Texas' largest underground wine cellar. Its tasting room is housed in a beautiful old stone barn. Becker Vineyards also has the advantage of lovely B&B accommodations. For $125 you get a bottle of wine, continental breakfast and a fully renovated log cabin dating from the 1890s all to yourself. Call ☎ 830-997-5612 for reservations.

Another well-known vineyard is **Fall Creek Vineyards** (☎ 915-379-5361; www.fcv.com; 1820 CR 222; ☽ 11am-4pm Mon-Fri, noon-5pm Sat, noon-4pm Sun), located just over 2 miles north of the town post office in Tow, close to Llano and perched beautifully on the shores of Lake Buchanan. Now in its 28th year, Fall Creek churns out several different French- and German-style varietals, including a popular Chenin Blanc and a tasty Riesling. The winery offers a colorful, modern tasting room as well.

A smaller vineyard with wines that have begun to turn heads is unique **Dry Comal Creek (2)** (☎ 830-885-4121; www.drycomalcreek.com; 1741 Herbelin Rd, off Hwy 46; ☽ noon-5pm Wed-Sun), located about 7 miles west of New Braunfels. Proprietor Franklin Hauser gives his own tours around the tiny winery, which is constructed of stone and cedar trees.

No matter where you find yourself swirling, sniffing and sipping a Texas-made wine, you're in for a palate-pleasing surprise. Other wineries you'll encounter on the Texas Wine Trail include these:

Flat Creek Estate (3) (☎ 512-267-6310; www.flat creekestate.com; off Singleton Bend Rd, 3mi south of RM 1431, Marble Falls; ☽ noon-5pm Tue- Sun, from 10am Sat)

Spicewood Vineyards (4)(☎ 830-693-5328; www.spicewoodvineyards.com; 1419 Burnet CR 409, Spicewood; ☽ noon-5pm Wed-Sun, from 10am Sat)

McReynolds Winery (5) (☎ 830-825-3544; www .mcreynoldswines.com; 706 CR 304, Cypress Mill; ☽ usually noon-5pm Sat-Sun)

Texas Hills Vineyard (6) (☎ 830-868-2321; www.texashillsvineyard.com; RR 2766, 1mi east of Johnson City; ☽ 10am-5pm daily, from noon Sun)

Grape Creek Vineyard (7) (☎ 830-644-2710; www.grapecreek.com; on US 290, 4mi west of Stonewall; ☽ 10am-5pm daily, from noon Sun)

Lost Creek Vineyard (8) (☎ 325-388-3753; on Hwy 2233, 1mi off Hwy 71; ☽ 10am-5pm daily, from noon Sun)

Fredericksburg Winery (9) (☎ 830-990-8747, www .fbgwinery.com; 247 W Main St, Fredericksburg; ☽ 10am-6pm Mon-Thu, 10am-8pm Fri-Sat, noon-6pm Sun)

Chisholm Trail Winery (10) (☎ 830-990-2675; www.chisholmtrailwinery.com; 2367 Usener Rd, off US 290, Fredericksburg; ☽ noon-6pm Thu-Mon)

Comfort Cellars Winery (11) (☎ 830-995-3274; 723 Front Street, Comfort; ☽ noon-6pm daily) See also p180.

Sister Creek Vineyards (12) (☎ 830-324-6704; www .sistercreekvineyards.com; on FM 1376, 12mi north of Boerne in Sisterdale; ☽ noon-5pm daily, from 11am Fri-Sat)

Driftwood Vineyards (13) (☎ 512-858-4508; www.driftwoodvineyards.com; RR 12, 6mi south of US 290; ☽ 11am-6pm Fri-Sat, 12:30-6pm Sun)

camping is some of the best in the Hill Country. Primitive sites accessible only by foot are beautifully situated next to the river. Campsites with water and electricity are also available. Call ahead to reserve either.

There aren't many hotels or motels in town, although a few B&Bs do a solid business. One spot worth checking out is **A Room With a View B&B** (☎ 830-868-7668, 888-588-8439; www.hillcountryaroomwithaview.com; on RR 3232 east of town, 2mi east of Pedernales Falls; d $80-90; P). It's far off the beaten path, with a charming Hill Country atmosphere, two comfy rooms and yes, great views.

The best dining in Johnson City – and what could become some of the best in the

Hill Country – can be found at the perfectly rustic **Silver K Cafe** (☎ 830-868-2911; Main St; mains $10-22; ☺ lunch 11am-2pm daily, dinner 5-9pm Fri-Sat). In the Old Lumber Yard, the Silver K serves up imaginative Texas-style home cookin' with a Mediterranean flair, along with 'Texas wines, Texas beers, and Texas music.'

For beer, pool and live acoustic tunes, the **Friendly Bar** (☎ 830-868-2347; 106 N Nugent St, off US 290) is a Johnson City original that's been serving thirsty patrons since 1916.

Getting There & Away

By car, it's almost a 50-mile drive along US 290 between Austin and Johnson City. Getting to Johnson City by bus from Austin

FREDERICKSBURG

0 — 500 m
0 — 0.3 mi

INFORMATION
Broadway National Bank....................1 B3
Fredericksburg Convention & Visitors
  Bureau..2 C3
Pioneer Public Library.......................3 B3
The Main Bookshop...........................4 C3

SIGHTS & ACTIVITIES pp175-6
Fredericksburg Winery......................5 B3
Gillespie County Historical Pioneer
  Museum..6 B3
Hill Country Bike Shop......................7 D4
National Museum of the Pacific War...8 C3
Vereinskirche......................................9 B3

SLEEPING p177
B&B of Fredericksburg......................10 A2
Bed & Brew...11 C3
Deluxe Inn Budget Host Hotel.........12 D4
Dietzel Motel......................................13 A2
Gästehaus Schmidt............................14 B3
Hill Country Lodging & Reservation
  Service...15 B3
Main Street B&B.................................16 B3
Sunday House Inn & Suites...............17 C4

EATING pp177-8
Altdorf Restaurant & Biergarten........18 B3
Centre Fredericksburg Brewing
  Company..(see 11)
Dietz Bakery..19 C3
Friedhelm's Bavarian Inn & Bar.........20 A2
Navajo Grill...21 C3
Old German Bakery............................22 B3
Rather Sweet Bakery & Cafe.............23 C3
Silver Creek Restaurant.....................24 C3

ENTERTAINMENT p178
Dog Trot..25 C3
Lincoln Street Wine Bar.....................26 C3

SHOPPING p178
Fredericksburg Herb Farm.................27 A3
Texas Wine Cellars.............................28 C3
The Peach Basket...............................29 B2

is a troublesome prospect. Greyhound has two buses departing daily at 4:15am and 12:15pm for Lampasas, where you transfer to Century Texas Bus Lines, which takes you the rest of the way. It takes four hours total and costs $51 roundtrip. From San Antonio, Kerrville Bus Co sends out several buses per day; the trip takes 1½ hours each way and costs $21 roundtrip.

FREDERICKSBURG

☎ 830 population 8900

Smack dab in the middle of the Hill Country, the 19th-century German settlement of Fredericksburg is what smaller Hill Country towns with struggling economies like to call 'a destination.' Fredericksburg has gourmet restaurants, homemade beer, vintage Victorian architecture, quaint B&Bs and plenty of colonial German history. The problem – as it is for any town that's put all of its economic eggs into the tourism basket – is that sometimes it takes on the cheap air of a souvenir shop at Disney World.

Nonetheless, the town boasts some of the best dining and architecture in the Hill Country, as well as the stellar Museum of the Pacific War, a homage to local hero Admiral Chester W Nimitz who was commander of the US Pacific naval forces during WWII. Plus, Fredericksburg is a great base for checking out the surrounding peach orchards, vineyards and natural getaways, such as Enchanted Rock and Johnson City.

History

In 1846 Fredericksburg was established by 120 determined and thrifty German doctors, teachers, craftsmen and artists, all led by Baron Ottfried Hans von Meusebach, who quickly dropped his title and changed his name to John O Meusebach to blend in better. Named for Prince Frederick of Prussia, the town was part of a string of German outposts set up near New Braunfels, about 90 miles to the south. After a bad first year, the German settlers quickly turned their patch of Texas wilderness into a regional trade center and way station for travelers heading west. In 1847 Meusebach signed a treaty with the Comanches that was never broken despite years of bloodshed and false promises elsewhere in the state. Today German is still spoken among some of Fredericksburg's old-timers.

Orientation

The intersection of Adams St and Main St is the center of town. Most of the action on Main St happens between Washington and Adams St (the latter divides Fredericksburg addresses into east and west). The town's grid is actually oriented about 45 degrees off true compass bearings, but locals say anything northeast of Main St is north, southwest of it is south. Most shops and restaurants are on (or a block off) Main St, starting near the prow-like facade of the former Nimitz Hotel (now the Museum of the Pacific War) and continuing to Friedhelms Bavarian Inn, where US 290 and US 87 split.

Information

Fredericksburg Convention & Visitors Bureau (CVB; ☎ 830-997-6523, 888-997-3600; www.fredericksburg-texas.com; 302 E Austin St; 8:30am-5pm Mon-Fri, 9am-noon & 1-5pm Sat, noon-4pm Sun) has a friendly (if overworked) staff and a new building a block off Main St, behind the Museum of the Pacific War.

The **Main Bookshop** (☎ 830-997-2375; 143 E Main St; 9:30am-5:30pm Mon-Fri, 9am-6pm Sat, 10am-5pm Sun) has a decent collection of Texana titles and some travel books. There is no currency exchange in Fredericksburg, but there's a 24-hour ATM at **Broadway National Bank** (204 W Main St, cnr Crockett St). Internet access is free at the **Pioneer Public Library** (☎ 830-997-6513; 115 W Main St; 9am-6pm Mon-Thu, till 7pm Wed, 9am-2pm Fri-Sat). The **Hill Country Memorial Hospital** (☎ 830-997-4353; 1020 S Adams St) has 24-hour emergency services.

Sights

NATIONAL MUSEUM OF THE PACIFIC WAR

This state-run **museum complex** (☎ 830-997-4379; www.nimitz-museum.org; 340 E Main St; adult/senior & child 6-17 $5/3; 10am-5pm) consists of three galleries: the Admiral Nimitz Museum, the George Bush Gallery of the Pacific War and the Pacific Combat Zone.

Inside the former Nimitz Hotel, the **Admiral Nimitz Museum** has details of the city's history and the life and times of its favorite son, WWII fleet admiral Chester Nimitz. His family ran the hotel, and the list of luminaries who stayed there is interesting reading. There are extensive exhibits on the war in the Pacific, including a large Pearl Harbor display, war photos and, best of all, the recording of Franklin D Roosevelt's famous 'day that will live in infamy' radio address. The serene Japanese Peace Garden at the back was a gift from the Japanese government.

Next door, the **George Bush Gallery of the Pacific War** explains America's involvement in the war by telling stories about people, battles and campaigns. Highlights include a Japanese mini-sub captured at Pearl Harbor and dioramas of Guadalcanal. Next to the gallery is the **Plaza of the Presidents**, a monument to the US leaders.

Last but not least, the price of admission includes a guided tour of the **Pacific Combat Zone**, a 3 acre site that's been transformed into a South Pacific battle zone, complete with amphibious assault vehicles, a PT-309 boat, a field hospital and an airplane hangar housing a TBM Avenger.

VEREINSKIRCHE
The city's **Vereinskirche** (Society Church; Marktplatz, off W Main St; admission $1; ☉ 10am-4pm Mon-Sat, 1-4pm Sun) was the original town church, meeting hall and school. Rebuilt in 1935–36, the compound now houses a small collection of archival photos and dusty historical artifacts gathered by the Gillespie County Historical Society.

PIONEER MUSEUM
The **Gillespie County Historical Pioneer Museum** (☎ 830-997-2835; www.pioneermuseum.com; 309 W Main St; combined admission with Vereinskirche $4; ☉ 10am-5pm Mon-Sat, 1-5pm Sun) centers on the well-preserved Kammlah family house and store, with furnished rooms and a wine cellar dating from 1849. There are several other houses and a blacksmith shop on-site.

FORT MARTIN SCOTT
This pre-Civil War **fort** (☎ 830-997-9895; 1606 E Main St; admission free; ☉ 10am-5pm Tue-Sun) was one of the US Army's first frontier outposts in Texas. Only one original building remains – the stockade, of course – but others have been recreated for a fine glimpse into frontier life in the 1850s.

Activities
Mid-May through June is peach-pickin' season around town, when almost every restaurant in town sells desserts that are just, well, peachy. **Hallford Orchards** (☎ 830-997-3064; ☉ 8am-2pm Tue-Sun May-Sep), 1 mile east of downtown on Hwy 1631, offers pick-your-own peaches, along with cut flowers and fresh herbs. **The Peach Basket** (☎ 830-997-4533; 334 W Main St) sells fresh peaches and jams.

For bat viewing between May and October, head 12 miles south of town to the site of the old Fredericksburg & Northern Railroad tunnel, now designated the **Old Tunnel Wildlife Management Area** (☎ 830-238-4487; Old San Antonio Rd; upper/lower deck viewing area free/$5; ☉ daily). Three million Mexican free-tailed bats call this state-run facility home. It's best to visit during August around dusk, when the air hums with bats leaving the abandoned tunnel to feast on Hill Country insects.

Tours
Despite having more than its share of tacky tourist shops, Fredericksburg's historic district has retained the look (if not the feel) of 125 years ago. Beautiful limestone-clad buildings with gingerbread-style storefronts, hand-hewn ceiling joists and longleaf pine floors line Main St from end to end. A free self-guided walking tour map of the district is available at the visitors center. The **Fredericksburg Carriage Co** (☎ 830-868-4144; $45) conducts one-hour horse-drawn buggy tours through the historic district. Ninety-minute guided walking tours are available through **K&K Historic Tours** (☎ 830-456-8344; $10), but call ahead for availability.

Festivals and Events
Hardly a weekend goes by in Fredericksburg where there isn't some kind of festival or event, but the premiere one is the state's largest **Oktoberfest** (☎ 830-997-4810; www.oktoberfestinfbg.com; day-pass $6, 2-/3-day pass $10/15), which lasts for three days around the first weekend in October and features endless kegs of German beer, oom-pah-pah bands, schnitzels and other revelry. Toward the end of the month, the festivities continue with the **Fredericksburg Food and Wine Fest** (☎ 830-997-8515; www.fbgfoodandwinefest.com; admission $20), which is a tamer version of Oktoberfest. In nearby Stonewall, the **Peach JAMboree & Rodeo** (☎ 830-644-2735; admission $7-12) takes place in mid-June, at the height of peach season.

Sleeping

Chain motels abound in Fredericksburg, and there are some interesting locally owned spots along US 290 to the east and west of the city. Rates for these are about $10 higher on the weekends. Many people, however, stay in one of the scores of B&Bs or guesthouses, which offer everything from 19th-century limestone cottages to basic beds above a brewery; doubles average $80 to $140 per night. During special events, prices skyrocket, and it's essential to book ahead, even for camping. For more B&Bs, use one of the city's reliable and efficient reservation services:

Bed & Breakfast of Fredericksburg (☎ 830-997-4712; bandbfbg@ctesc.net; 240 W Main St)

Gästehaus Schmidt (☎ 830-997-5612; gasthaus@ktc .com; 231 W Main St)

Hill Country Lodging & Reservation Service (☎ 830-990-8455, 800-745-3591; jimclark@fbg.net; 215 W Main St)

Main St Bed & Breakfast (☎ 830-997-0153, 888-559-8555; mainstbb@ktc.com; 337 E Main St)

BUDGET

Deluxe Inn Budget Host Hotel (☎ 830-997-3344; 901 E Main St; s $35-60, d $45-75; P) This downtown spot and its across-the-street extension, the Miller Inn, have both been in Fredericksburg for decades and offer friendly service and clean rooms at a good value. Soak your weary feet in the hot tub.

Dietzel Motel (☎ 830-997-3330; junction US 290 & Hwy 87; s $45-75, d $55-75; P) This good budget option is located at the west end of town away from the hustle and bustle. Rates are higher during special events, lower in winter; all in all, it's a good deal.

Lady Bird Johnson Municipal Park (☎ 830-997-4202; 432 Lady Bird Drive; camp/RV sites $8/18) This pretty country park sits 3 miles south of town on the Pedernales River. There are plenty of RV hookups but no tent sites per se, just a big field behind the park's headquarters.

KOA Fredericksburg (☎ 830-997-4796, 800-562-0796; cnr US 290 & FM 1376; camp/RV sites $19/25, kamping kabins $40; P ⊠) Located 6 miles east of town, this nicely shaded campground has lots of amenities, including electrical hookups, hot showers, a pool and a laundromat.

Not far from the Dietzel, both the **Frontier Inn and RV Park** (☎ 830-997-4389; 1704 US 290 W; s/d $45/55; P) and **The Country Inn** (☎ 830-997-2185; 1644 US 290 West; s/d Fri-Sat $60/75, Sun-Thu $42/48; P ⊠) are good choices. Each has small yet clean rooms and the management may be willing to cut you a deal on slow weekends.

MID-RANGE & TOP END

Sunday House Inn & Suites (☎ 830-997-4484, 800-274-3762; www.sundayhouseinnandsuites.com; 501 E Main St; d $75-125; P ⊠) Helpful staff, good-size rooms and being within easy strolling distance of the restaurants all make the Sunday House a popular choice.

Bed & Brew (☎ 830-997-1646; www.yourbrewery .com/bed.htm; 245 E Main St; d $90; P) The Fredericksburg Brewing Company owns 12 rooms scattered around Main St, each with its own private bath and queen-size bed. The accommodations are for adults only – no kids, no pets, no smoking, no phones – and instead of breakfast you get a free sample of each beer from the brewery every day. What a trade-off! Check-in is at the brewery.

Settlers Crossing Bed & Breakfast (☎ 830-997-2722, 800-874-1020; www.settlerscrossing.com; FR 1376, off US 290 E; d $135-195; P) This 35-acre estate stands out from the rest of the crowd for its collection of period antiques, elegant *fachwerk* farmhouses and 19th-century log cabins (some of them moved here from as far away as Pennsylvania). Families are welcome, but guests need their own transport since the guesthouse is located 5 miles outside town, close to Luckenbach.

Eating

Dietz Bakery (☎ 830-997-3250; 218 E Main St; ☒ Tue-Sat) This third-generation family bakery makes some of the best pastries this side of Bavaria. Donuts and danishes cost just 50¢, and fresh oven-baked breads and baguettes are $2 or less each. Be sure to get here before noon, because they always sell out.

Old German Bakery (☎ 830-997-9084; 225 W Main St; mains $7-9; ☒ 7am-3pm Thu-Mon) This is also pleasantly authentic, with good soups, lots of schnitzel and plenty of pastries.

Rather Sweet Bakery & Cafe (☎ 830-990-0498; 249 E Main St; $2-8) This bright, cheery bakery is a welcome addition. Tucked behind the old Henke Meat Market (now a gift shop), there's outdoor seating and a fine selection of pastries. At lunch, you'll find fresh soups, salads and sandwiches.

HILL COUNTRY

Fredericksburg Brewing Company (☎ 830-997-1646; www.yourbrewery.com; 245 E Main St; mains $5-20; ☺ 11:30am-9pm Mon-Thurs, till 10pm Fri-Sat, till 7pm Sun) The town's brewpub is a fun place, serving good ol' American and German American food, such as meat loaf, a sausage sampler with German potato salad and even wild game plates. Enjoy beers made right on the premises while sitting in the enclosed beer garden.

Ken Hall and Company Texas Barbecue (☎ 210-997-2353; 1679 S Hwy 87; mains $5-10; ☺ closed Mon) The Fredericksburg culinary scene wouldn't be complete without some Texas barbecue, and this spot run by a former professional football player won't disappoint. Savor the fall-off-the-bone pork ribs.

Silver Creek Restaurant (☎ 830-990-4949; 310 E Main St; mains $6-10; ☺ 4-9pm Mon, Wed & Thu, 11:30am-2:30pm & 5-10pm Fri-Sun) Silver Creek's big draw is its beer gardens – one out front for watching the world go by, and one out back to escape the crowds. There's occasionally live music on the weekends.

Altdorf Restaurant & Biergarten (☎ 830-997-7865; 301 W Main St; mains $10-13; ☺ closed Tue) This is the biggest German place in town, with lots of big mugs of beer, oom-pah-pah bands and typical Bavarian specialties.

Friedhelm's Bavarian Inn & Bar (☎ 830-997-6300; 905 W Main St; mains $10-15; ☺ closed Mon) This architectural behemoth at the west end of town features hearty German fare and waitresses wearing traditional *trachten*, complete with bodices, aprons and *unterhosen*.

AUTHOR'S CHOICE

The best dining experience in town is actually *out* of town at the **Hill Top Café** (☎ 830-997-8922; 10661 US 87; mains $12-25; ☺ 11am-2pm & 5-9pm Wed-Sun), about 10 miles north of Fredericksburg. Inside a renovated 1950s gas station, this cozy roadhouse serves up an imaginative mix of spicy Cajun seafood, fresh Greek salads and good ol' chicken-fried steaks. On weekends there's live blues from the owner, Johnny Nicholas, a former member of the West Coast swing band Asleep at the Wheel. Trust us, this is the Texas Hill Country at its best. Reservations are recommended.

Navajo Grill (☎ 830-990-1169; 209 E Main St; mains $16-25; ☺ lunch 11am-2pm, dinner 5:30-9pm Mon-Thurs, till 10pm Fri-Sat, till 8pm Sun) For something more upmarket, head straight for the Navajo Grill, which boasts a lovely patio, creative Southwestern cuisine and a list of about 40 different wines to choose from.

Entertainment

There's no shortage of beer along Main St, including the homemade kind at Fredericksburg Brewing Company, and at the slick-looking **Dog Trot** (☎ 830-990-9900; 329 E Main St). For a change of pace, head to **Lincoln Street Wine Bar** (☺ 830-997-8463; 111 S Lincoln St), where staff sommeliers will guide you through the over 200 different wines on the premises while you snack on imported olives, cheeses and breads or perhaps enjoy a cigar in one of the overstuffed leather armchairs.

There is live music (generally oom-pah-pah) at several spots in town on weekends, including the Fredericksburg Brewing Company and the Altdorf Restaurant.

Shopping

Antiques are a big thing in Fredericksburg, and it sometimes seems as though every other store is selling something old and dilapidated. The tourist bureau stocks the handy *Fredericksburg Antique Directory* leaflet, which will help you find that rare gem in town.

Texas Wine Cellars (☎ 830-997-0123; 217A E Main St; ☺ 10:30am-5:30pm Mon-Fri, 10:30am-6:30pm Sat, noon-5:30pm Sun) sells an unrivaled selection at its Fredericksburg storefront, and tastings are always free. Out back they've got beers from around the world (however, don't expect free tastings of these).

For cooking herbs, aromatherapy goods, gardening books, or a jar of rosemary-infused honey worth sending home to mom, visit **Fredericksburg Herb Farm** (☎ 830-997-8615; 402 Whitney St off S Milam St; ☺ 9:30am-5:30pm Mon-Thu, 9:30am-9pm Fri-Sat, noon-4pm Sun). While you're there, stroll through the herb gardens, have a glass of wine under the live oaks or get a full-body massage ($35-60).

Getting There & Around

Heading west from Austin, US 290 becomes Fredericksburg's Main St. Highway 16, which runs between Fredericksburg and

Kerrville, is S Adams St in town. From Austin, **Greyhound** (see p201) will get you to San Antonio, where you'll transfer to a **Kerrville Bus Co** (☎ 210-227-5669) bus bound for Fredericksburg (three daily). The one-way trip costs $20 from San Antonio or $32 from Austin (3½–5 hours). In town buses leave and depart from the Fredericksburg **bus station** (☎ 830-997-2249; 758 S Washington St). You can rent bicycles at **Hill Country Bike Shop** (☎ 830-990-2609; 702 E Main St) for $25 per day. For longer excursions, **87 Auto Rental** (☎ 830-990-0562; 729 S Washington St) rents cars for $30 a day.

ENCHANTED ROCK STATE NATURAL AREA

South of Llano, this popular **park** (☎ 915-247-3903, camping reservations 512-389-8900; 16710 RR 965; $5, primitive/standard campsites $8/10; ⏰ 8am-10pm) is about 18 miles north of Fredericksburg off RR 965. The round dome-like mound of Enchanted Rock rises out of the surrounding cedar and oak trees for a memorable sight. The rock is actually the second-largest granite batholith in the USA. The part that you can see (most of the rock formation is underground) is 425ft high and covers 640 acres. It makes for great hiking and rock climbing, and there's camping as well.

The park can be very crowded, especially during weekends, spring break and holidays. Staff may close the park when it reaches maximum occupancy (and they won't say how many people that is), and then you'll only be able to enter if you already have a reservation, so call ahead.

The exposed granite of Enchanted Rock dates from the Proterozoic era. Tonkawa Indians, hearing crackling and snapping noises from the rock at night, believed that ghost fires were burning. Park staff say that as the granite cools at night, it crackles. There are 7 miles of hiking trails, including the easy 4-mile loop that wraps around the granite and the 0.6-mile Summit Trail, which gains 425ft in elevation on its way to the top of the rock. Rock climbers head for the 1000ft Enchanted Rock Fissure, one of the world's largest granite caves; a list of climbing routes is available at the ranger office.

The park has open oak woodlands, mesquite grasslands and floodplains, and there are rock and fox squirrels, rabbits, white-tailed deer, armadillos and turkeys as well. The park issues permits for walk-in tent camping (no vehicles or RVs are allowed), and reservations are required.

LUCKENBACH
☎ 830 population 3

In 1977, Waylon Jennings and Willie Nelson told the world that in 'Luckenbach, Texas, ain't nobody feeling no pain.' This tiny Hill Country community has been a pilgrimage zone for zealous country-music fans ever since. Luckenbach has a couple of old buildings worth poking around, but the real attraction is all about kicking back and relaxing. Time is best spent sipping your Shiner Bock under a shady tree listening to

HILL COUNTRY

THE STORY BEHIND THE SONG

A famous saying in Luckenbach goes something like this: 'We have discovered that, on the globe, Luckenbach is at the center of the world.' And while today's casual visitor may question that logic over a cold beer and a lazy afternoon, not so in 1977, when the town was at the center of the world – or at least the country music world – as Waylon Jennings' and Willie Nelson's hit song 'Luckenbach, Texas (Back to the Basics of Love)' stayed at number one on the country music charts for nearly the entire summer.

What's odd about one of the most catchy country tunes ever recorded is that it was written by Bobby Emmons and Chips Moman, two Nashville producers who'd never been to Luckenbach. Even Jennings couldn't say he'd actually set foot in any one of the three buildings in town until the first and only time he made the trip in 1997, 20 years after the song's original release. Still 'Luckenbach, Texas' was and remains a well-loved tribute to the Hill Country hamlet, partly because Nelson is a Texas fixture and has held his famous 4th of July Picnic here off and on for years. Also, since Jennings' death in 2002, Luckenbach has thrown an annual mid-July tribute party to the musician, giving the town's regulars (and its three permanent residents) one more reason to call Luckenbach the center of the world.

local guys and gals strum guitars and sing country-and-western classics.

The only way to get here is to drive. From Fredericksburg, take US 290 east then take FM 1376 south for about 3 miles. From San Antonio, take I-10 north to FM 1376 and follow it north for about 25 miles.

Sights & Activities

Luckenbach basically consists of its 120-year-old **general store** (☎ 830-997-3224, 888-311-8990; ☼ 10am-9pm Mon-Sat, noon-9pm Sun), which also serves as the local post office, dance hall, saloon and community center. Its walls are decorated with the hand-scrawled howdies of pilgrims and devotees, its floor with six generations of scuff marks. The **dance hall** periodically hosts weekend musical performances by both amateur crooners and some of country music's finest, but about the only times you can count on a crowd are during the Labor Day and 4th of July weekend concerts. In mid-July the town pays tribute to the late Waylon Jennings with music, drinking and not a few Harley Davidsons. The annual **Cowboy Christmas Ball**, held on December 26 in the dance hall, is a cowboy-style Christkindlmarkt (Christmas Market) with carols by the fire, mulled wine and dancing; admission costs $5 to $10.

COMFORT

☎ 830 population 1477

Another 19th-century German settlement tucked into the hills, Comfort is perhaps the most idyllic of the Hill Country bunch, with pristine rough-hewn limestone homes – many of which were built in the 1880s and '90s by architect Alfred Giles, of San Antonio fame – as well as traditional *fachwerk* (or half-timber construction), plus a beautifully restored business district that looks as if it were lifted straight off a Victorian postcard. In fact, most of the buildings in downtown Comfort are on the National Register of Historic Places. Shopping for antiques is the number-one activity, but you'll also find a few good restaurants, a winery, some rich history and, as the town's name suggests, an easy way of life.

Comfort was founded in 1854 by a group of politically active and freethinking German families from nearby Sisterdale. This new group was so opposed to any type

of local government or organized religion that a church wasn't built in Comfort until 40 years after the original settlement. The settlers were also staunchly antislavery and pro-Union during the Civil War. The 1866 **Treue der Union Monument** (True to the Union), a shrine to the town's young men who were killed by Confederate soldiers in the battle of the Nueces in 1862, is on High St between 3rd and 4th Sts. The bones of the dead are interred beneath the monument.

About halfway between Kerrville and Boerne, Comfort is on TX 27, just 2 miles west of I-10.

Sleeping & Eating

Comfort Common B&B (☎ 830-995-3030; www.comfortcommon.com; 717 High St; d $80, cabins & cottages $110-175; P) This B&B also moonlights as an antique store (but then again, what doesn't in Comfort?). With two rooms in the historic 1880s Ingenhuett-Faust Hotel and three nearby cabins, this is a friendly place to put up your feet.

Meyer Bed & Breakfast (☎ 830-995-2304; www.meyerbedandbreakfast.com; 845 High St; d $80-110; P ☼) At the other end of High St, right on the beautiful shores of Cypress Creek, this collection of cabins and duplexes, some old and some new, includes a former stage coach stop built in 1857. Decor in the newer rooms won't be winning interior design awards anytime soon, but they're relaxing nonetheless.

For a fresh lunch (and Friday night steak dinners), check out **Mimi's Cafe** (☎ 830-995-3470; 814 High St; mains $5-8; ☼ lunch 11am-2pm Tue-Fri & 11am-3pm Sat, dinner 6-8:30pm Fri). Another popular spot for soups, salads and sandwiches is **Arlene's Country Cafe** (☎ 830-995-3330; 426 7th St; mains $4-8; ☼ 11am-3pm Thu-Sun), in an immaculate Victorian house owned by a former food columnist for the *San Antonio Express-News*. Head to local favorite **Los Jarritos** (☎ 830-995-4112; 1005 Hwy 87 S; mains $4-7; ☼ 7am-8:30pm Mon-Sat), next door to the Texaco station, for a dang good Mexican dinner. The place may look a bit divey, but the green-chile chicken enchiladas and homemade corn tortillas will melt in your mouth.

Comfort also boasts its own winery. **Comfort Cellars Winery** (☎ 830-995-3274; 723 Front Street; ☼ 11am-6pm daily, from noon Sun) offers free tastings inside a turn-of-the-20th-century building on the town's main road.

Shopping

Take your pick of antique stores in Comfort, which sell everything from weathered old Mexican doors to beautifully restored collectibles.

Ingenhuett Store (☎ 830-995-2149; 834 High St; ☺ 8am-5:30 Mon-Fri, 8am-4:30pm Sat) Don't miss this general store for groceries, outdoor gear, local maps, hardware and some living history. Ingenhuett has been owned and operated by the same family since it opened in 1867. Gregory Krauter, the great-great grandson of the original owner, now runs the place and has a firm handle on the comings and goings of Comfort over the past 135 years or so. According to Krauter, Pancho Villa once watered his horses at the store's well.

KERRVILLE

☎ 830 population 21,700

Friendly Kerrville's not the most jumping of towns – except during its annual springtime folk festival – but it's a great Hill Country base that offers easy access to kayaking, canoeing and swimming on the Guadalupe River. It's also home to one of the world's best museums of cowboy life.

Orientation & Information

Just south of I-10, Hwy 16 (Sidney Baker St) bisects Hwy 27 (aka Junction Hwy) before continuing south and crossing the Guadalupe River. Five blocks east of Sidney Baker St, Kerrvile's Main St becomes Junction Hwy. Almost any place downtown is within a five-block walk of the intersection of Sidney Baker and Main Sts.

Kerrville has got its tourist infrastructure down pat. Its excellent **visitors center** (☎ 830-792-3535, 800-221-7958; www.ktc.net/kerrcvb; 2108 Sidney Baker St; ☺ 8:30am-5pm Mon-Fri, 9am-3pm Sat, 10am-3pm Sun) has everything you'll need to get out and about in the Hill Country, including heaps of brochures and coupon books for accommodations.

Wolfmueller's Books, Records & Antiques (☎ 830-257-7323; 703 Water St; ☺ 9am-5pm Mon-Sat) has an eclectic collection of old books and records; **Hastings Books, Music & Video** (☎ 830-896-8233; 501 Main St; ☺ 9am-11pm) has all the newest stuff. The **Butt-Holdsworth Memorial Library** (☎ 830-257-8422; 505 Water St; ☺ 10am-6pm Mon-Sat, till 8pm Tue, Wed & Thu, 1-5pm Sun) provides free Internet access. You can

change money at **Bank of America** (☎ 830-896-3111; 741 Water St; ☺ 9am-4pm Mon-Thu, 9am-5pm Fri), which has an ATM. **Sid Peterson Hospital** (☎ 830-896-4200; 710 Water St) is central and has 24-hour emergency services.

Sights

In town, the former residence of Charles Schreiner (see YO Ranch, p184) has been restored and opened as the **Hill Country Museum** (☎ 830-896-8633; 622 Earl Garrett St; adult/child 6-12 $5/2; ☺ 10am-4:30pm Mon-Sat), which features period costumes and furniture. The historical museum is at least as interesting for its architecture as the exhibits, which can be ho-hum. In Kerrville's old post office, the **Kerr Arts & Cultural Center** (☎ 830-895-2911; www.kacckerrville.com; 228 Earl Gattett St; admission free; ☺ 10am-4pm Tue-Sat, 1-4pm Sun) exhibits works by many local artists. There are permanent art gallery displays, and the center holds workshops, classes and lectures throughout the year.

NATIONAL CENTER FOR AMERICAN WESTERN ART

This **museum** (☎ 830-896-2553; www.caamuseum.com; 1550 Bandera Hwy; adult/senior/child $5/3.50/1; ☺ 9am-5pm Mon-Sat, 1-5pm Sun) is a nonprofit showcase for cowboy art. In 1965 in Sedona, Arizona, a group of folks who worked the range by day and were illustrators of (among other things) Western novels by night joined to form the Cowboy Artists of America (CAA). Although the museum's association with the CAA has formally ended, the collections retain their focus on Western Americana. The quality and detail of the work – paintings and bronze sculptures mostly – is astounding; all depict scenes of cowboy life, the Western landscape or vignettes of Native American life. The scenes themselves are moving and detailed, and the museum has permanent displays of two artists' studios, the equipment of cowboy life (where kids can climb on saddles, feel a lasso and play with spurs) and a research library available to anyone interested in learning more about the frontier. The staff is very knowledgeable about both the art and cowboys in general. The building itself is fabulous, with handmade mesquite parquet and unique bóveda (vaulted) domes overhead. From downtown Kerrville, take Hwy 16 south to

Hwy 173 (Bandera Hwy) and turn left; the museum is a half mile ahead on the right. There's no public transport.

Activities

Near the river at the south end of downtown, the **Riverside Nature Center** (☎ 830-257-4837; 150 Francisco Lemos St; admission free; ☼ dawn-dusk) has walking trails, a wildflower meadow and Guadalupe River access. Take a refreshing swim in the river at **Louise Hays City Park** (Thompson Dr, west of Sidney Baker St S; admission free; ☼ 7:30am-11pm) or **Guadalupe Street City Park** (1001 Junction Hwy; ☼ 7:30am-11pm), behind the Inn of the Hills Resort. **Kerrville Kayak & Canoe Rentals** (☎ 830-459-2122, 800-256-5873; 130 W Main St) rents watercraft by the half day or full day (rates $20 to $30); you can pick up the vessels or have them delivered right to your B&B. There's also a riverside stand located behind Chili's Grill & Bar (1185 Junction Hwy) that rents paddleboats, kayaks and canoes by the hour ($8 to $12).

Three miles southeast of town, **Kerrville-Schreiner State Park** (☎ 830-257-5392, camping reservations 512-389-8900; 2385 TX 173, off Hwy 16; day-use per person $3; ☼ 8am-5pm) is a beautiful place for cycling, hiking, canoeing, tubing and camping. The park's concession stand rents inner tubes ($4/day) and four-person canoes (from $7/hour) for lazy floats along the Guadalupe River. Every year on the Thursday before Easter, the Hill Country Bicycle Tour starts here. See p183 for bicycle rentals. From town, head south on Hwy 16, then turn left on Hwy 173 (Bandera Hwy) and go past the National Center for Western American Art; the park entrance is down on the right.

Festivals & Events

An 18-day musical extravaganza, the **Kerrville Folk Festival** (☎ 830-257-3600; tickets 800-435-8429; www.kerrville-music.com) is held at Quiet Valley Ranch, 9 miles south of town on Hwy 16. Beginning the Thursday before Memorial Day, there's music by national touring acts and local musicians, great food and lots of fun. One-day tickets cost $12 to $22 in advance, slightly more at the gate; advance-purchase multiday festival tickets start at $50. Camping at Quiet Valley during the festival is free if you have tickets for three or more consecutive days; otherwise, it's $5 per person and $15 per vehicle.

Held over Labor Day weekend, September's **Kerrville Wine and Music Festival** is a four-day mini-version of the folk festival. The **Hill Country Bike Tour** and Kerrville's **Chili Cook-Off** (☎ 210-656-3759) take place around Easter weekend, and they're both huge events. Weekend rodeos are held at various venues throughout the summer.

Sleeping

If you're planning on heading to Kerrville during any of the festivals, book months in advance.

BUDGET

There are plenty of motels along Sidney Baker St.

Flagstaff Inn Motel (☎ 830-792-4449, 888-896-0379; 906 Junction Hwy; s/d Sun-Thu $35/40, Fri-Sat $50/55; ᴘ) A great choice for the price range, the rooms here are standard but clean and situated around a quiet grassy courtyard.

Budget Inn Motel (☎ 830-896-8200, 800-219-8158; 1804 Sidney Baker St; s/d $40/50; ᴘ) This place has clean, simple rooms, some with microwaves and refrigerators. Breakfast is included in the rates.

There's also tent and RV camping within easy reach of town.

Kerrville-Schreiner State Park (day-use per person $3, camp/RV sites $10/15, screened shelters $16) This is a beautiful park. Well-tended campsites come with running water as well as full RV hookups; the primitive shelters sleep up to eight people and from December through February, the seventh night is free. There's also a cabin (see below).

MID-RANGE & TOP END

Best Western Sunday House Inn (☎ 830-896-1313, 800-677-9477; www.bestwestern.com; 2124 Sidney Baker St; d $65-80; ᴘ ☎) This is a standard option, where breakfast is included in the rates (except on Monday, when the restaurant is closed).

Kerrville-Schreiner State Park (six-person cabin $75; ᴘ) The staff-built cabin at this state park (see above) is a spotless place in the middle of the wilderness. It has a full kitchen, satellite TV/VCR and your own campfire and barbecue pit – what a deal! Reserve early.

Inn of the Hills Resort (☎ 830-895-5000, 800-292-5690; www.innofthehills.com; 1001 Junction Hwy; d winter $60-90, summer $90-140; ᴘ ☎) This inn is one of the better ones in town, with an Olympic-size pool, sauna, river access and tons of amenities. Everything's spacious and clean.

YO Ranch Resort (☎ 830-257-4440, 877-967-3767; www.yoresort.com; 2033 Sidney Baker St; s & d $100-120, 1-/2-bedroom ste $170/260; **P** **≋**) Affiliated with the YO dude ranch (p184), this is the biggest place in town. It has tennis, basketball and volleyball courts, a walking track and a kids' playground. Even if you're not staying, swing by to check out the lobby; branding-iron chandeliers hang over a grand room packed with cowboy paraphernalia and mounted stuffed animals, including giraffes and a huge grizzly bear.

Eating

Taco To Go (☎ 830-896-8226; 428 Sidney Baker St; meals $5-7; 🕒 6am-9pm daily, from 7am Sun) Right downtown, this doesn't look like much, but it has terrific breakfast tacos.

Hill Country Cafe (☎ 830-257-6665; 806 Main St; $2-8; 🕒 6am-2pm Mon-Fri, 6-11am Sat) This tiny diner near the historic district serves up good old-fashioned omelets, as well as breakfast tacos and turkey sandwiches.

Big Mamou Cajun Corner (☎ 830-895-7867; 1028 Water St; mains $5-9; 🕒 lunch 6am-2pm, dinner 6-9pm Mon-Sat, till 11pm Fri-Sat) The chef cooks up real-deal Cajun dishes at this converted old gas station.

Jefferson Street Cafe (☎ 830-257-2929; 1001 Jefferson St; mains $7-17; 🕒 lunch 11am-2pm Mon-Fri, dinner 5-9pm Mon-Sat) East of downtown, this home-cookin' café is located in a beautifully renovated two-story Victorian house. The chicken-fried steaks are awesome.

The Lakehouse (☎ 830-895-3188; 1655 Junction Hwy; mains $6-12; 🕒 11am-8:30pm daily, till 9pm Fri-Sat) For a friendly, family atmosphere with great lake views, come to this place for the chicken-fried steak, fried catfish and other country cooking.

Franciscos (☎ 830-257-2995; 201 Earl Garret St; lunch $4-8, dinner mains $10-23; 🕒 lunch 11am-3pm Mon-Sat, dinner 5:30-9pm Thu-Sat) This colorful, bright and airy bistro and sidewalk café is housed in an old limestone building in the historic district. It serves Tex-Mex fare for lunch and dinner.

Annemarie's Alpine Lodge Restaurant (1001 Junction Hwy; buffet $8-13; 🕒 6am-10pm) At the Inn of the Hills Resort (p182) restaurant, it's all-you-can-eat all the time, including

a pretty good Sunday brunch. Inside, you'll also find the **Alpine Pub**, a fine place to grab a pint or cut a rug on the weekly cowboy music night.

La Fours (☎ 830-896-1449; 1129 Junction Hwy; mains $9-15; 🕒 11am-2pm & 4-9pm Tue-Sat) This stucco-walled local spot is known for its excellent fried shrimp and Cajun-influenced fare like frogs legs and spicy jalapeño hush puppies.

Cowboy Steakhouse (☎ 830-896-5688; 416 Main St; mains $12-25; 🕒 5-10pm) For no-frills buffalo steaks, lobster and Texas quail, head on over to this meat-lover's paradise. Locals name it as the best steak house in town.

Patrick's Lodge (☎ 830-895-4111; 2190 Junction Hwy; mains $12-19; 🕒 lunch 11am-2pm Tue-Fri, dinner 5-9pm Mon-Sat) If you're looking for escargot or filet mignon *au poivre*, look no further than Patrick's, where white tablecloths and good wine make for a decidedly French setting (never mind the chicken-fried steak on the menu).

Getting There & Around

By car from Austin, take US 290 west to Fredericksburg, then turn south onto Hwy 16, which meets Kerrville south of I-10. From San Antonio, take I-10 north to Hwy 16, then head south. **Kerrville Bus Co** (☎ 830-257-7454; 701 Sidney Baker St) sends out one morning bus daily to Austin ($29, 3¼-5 hours) and five or six buses every day to San Antonio ($17, 1¼ hours). In town **Bicycle Works** (☎ 830-896-6864; 1412 Broadway; half-/full-day rental $15/25) rents cycles.

INGRAM

☎ 830 population 1615

Everything in this pokey ol' town can be readily explained by the **West Kerr County Chamber of Commerce** (☎ 830-367-4322; www.wkcc.com; 113 Hwy 27 E, just west of town; 🕒 10am-3pm Mon-Fri). There are a few **craft shops** along the Old Ingram Loop, an area worth visiting just to grab a frosty Schlitz beer at the delightfully dilapidated **Miss Kitty's Social Club** (☎ 830-367-5783; 208 Old Ingram Loop). There's free **swimming** at the nice little park at the Ingram Dam, a couple of miles west of downtown Ingram.

A theater and fine-arts complex, the **Hill Country Arts Foundation** (☎ 830-367-5122; www.hcaf.com; 507 W Hwy 39, near Hwy 27; 🕒 10am-4pm Mon-Sat, 1-4pm Sun) is the main reason people come to Ingram, and it's packed in summer. The Point Theatre, a riverside outdoor complex, and the indoor pavilion are both respected community-theater stages (Tommy Tune himself worked here before hitting the big time on Broadway), where classics and musicals are performed in summer. Its 1700-sq-ft exhibition space is host to three national art shows annually; the smaller Duncan-McAshan Gallery holds about 10 exhibitions per year. The foundation also runs children's classes and, in summer, classes in sculpture, photography and other crafts taught by professionals in the field. The complex is 2 miles west of downtown.

The **Lazy Hills Guest Ranch** is a friendly place with a magnificent spread about 10 miles west of Kerrville. You can ride horses (Western only) on dozens of trails or go whole hog and stay overnight for the full-blown dude ranch experience. One-hour guided trail rides cost $15; children must be at least six years old to ride.

Ingram is about 5 miles west of Kerrville on Hwy 27, which cuts north just to the west of the center of town. Hwy 39 continues west toward Hunt.

Sleeping & Eating

The **Hunter House Motor Inn** (☎ 830-367-2377, 800-655-2377; 310 Hwy 39; d from $45) has nice, clean rooms, which are more expensive in summer. The hotel also has the **River Road Cafe** (☎ 830-367-3383; mains $4-9; ⏰ 7am-2pm Tue-Sun).

After a long day of sightseeing, you can relax at **Lazy Hills Guest Ranch** (☎ 830-367-5600, 800-880-0632; www.lazyhills.com; Henderson Branch Rd; per day adult/youth/child $120/55/40, weekly $770-1190; P ⏰). Rates include cabin accommodations with three meals, plus all the tennis, fishing and horseshoes you can squeeze into three days and nights (which is the minimum stay). Weekly rates include six horseback rides per person. Special winter rates for B&B-only accommodations are lower. A 10 ☎ gratuity is added to every bill. The ranch is located about 2 miles northwest of town, off Hwy 27.

STONEHENGE II

Stonehenge II is a 60%-scale model of the ancient megalithic structure near Salisbury, England, and it's definitely worth driving

a couple of miles north of the hamlet of Hunt to see it. Two locals built the thing (out of concrete) and threw in some Easter Island statues for good measure. Now it's open to the public – for free. Watch out for fire ants if you lie down in the grass. The reason for the construction of this replica is as enigmatic as the construction of the original, but they moved London Bridge to Arizona, so why not Stonehenge in Texas? From Hunt, which is 6 miles west of Ingram on Hwy 39, turn north on FM 1340 for 2 miles; the monument is on the left.

MO-RANCH

Ten miles west of Stonehenge II, this 475-acre ranch and Christian **retreat** (☎ 830-238-4455, 800-460-4401; www.moranch.com; FM 1340; day-use $8, horseback rides $15-25, campsites $25, cabins $50, d $75-85) is well equipped for outdoor activities and fellowship. A day pass to the ranch includes use of the hiking trails and access to the Guadalupe River swimming area and canoes. There's horseback riding at the North Fork Riding Stables offered several times daily. Accommodations range from campsites to basic eight-person cabins to hotel rooms. You can purchase meals at the ranch's dining hall for under $10.

YO RANCH

The famous **YO Ranch** (☎ 830-640-3222, 800-967-2624; www.yoranch.com; accommodations adult/child 4-12 $75/40, Fri-Sat $95/50), founded by Texas Ranger captain Charles Armand Schreiner in 1880, is a 40,000-acre cattle ranch. It's also home to imported exotic animals, including zebra, giraffe, oryx and eland. The ranch is open to the public for horseback riding ($25 to $30 per hour) and overnight stays. On a more controversial note, the ranch is also open for hunting year-round of all animals – both imported and domestic – that shed their antlers annually. According to the staff, the people who come to hunt do so mainly in November and December, and hunting areas don't overlap with areas used for other ranch activities. Rates for the ranch's rustic cabins include all meals and beverages (yes, even the alcoholic variety). There's an Old Western bar here, too, and a wonderful fireplace in the lodge.

To get there from Kerrville, follow Hwy 27. Bear right in Ingram, staying on Hwy 27 for about 15 miles until you hit the town of

Mountain Home. Take Hwy 41 west toward Rocksprings for another 20 miles or so, and the entrance to the YO Ranch will appear on the right. Turn onto the ranch road and follow it to the padlocked gate, where you phone the main office for the combination. From there it's 7 miles to the chuck wagon.

BANDERA

☎ **830 population 1296**

Bandera has the look and feel of an old Western movie set, and that's just the effect the locals want – they claim the town as the cowboy capital of Texas. There are certainly lots of dude ranches around, and you can come here to get outfitted for a day of kayaking or tubing down the Medina River.

But perhaps one of the best reasons to come to Bandera is to drink beer and dance in one of the many hole-in-the-wall cowboy bars and honky-tonks. You'll find friendly locals, good live music and rich atmosphere. Nearby, the **Hill Country State Natural Area** is a very pleasant diversion.

Orientation & Information

Main St is roughly north-south through the center of town. At the south edge of downtown, Cypress St heads east-west, continuing as Hwy 16 at the east end of town.

For more information and friendly advice, drop by the **Bandera Convention and Visitors Bureau** (CVB; ☎ 830-796-3045, 800-364-3833; 1206 Hackberry St; ☿ 9am-5pm Mon-Fri, 9am-2pm Sat). For an excellent collection of Texana and contemporary fiction, visit the mother-daughter run **Backroads Books** (☎ 830-796-7748; 1107 Cedar St; ☿ 10am-6pm Mon-Fri, 10am-5pm Sat, noon-4pm Sun).

Sights & Activities

The visitors center stocks a handy historical walking tour brochure covering many of the old buildings scattered around town, including the St Stanislaus Catholic Church and adjacent Convent Cemetery and the First Bandera Jail. The **Frontier Times Museum** (☎ 830-796-3864; 510 13th St; adult/child 4-16 $3/1; ☿ 10am-4:30pm Mon-Sat, 1-4:30pm Sun) displays guns, branding irons and cowboy gear, and there are various temporary exhibitions.

Local rodeos are held during summer twice weekly at **Mansfield Park** (contact the CVB for information), on Hwy 16 toward

Medina, and **Twin Elm Guest Ranch** (☎ 830-796-3628; www.twinelmranch.com; on Hwy 470), which lets the bulls loose on Saturday at 8pm.

A mile north of downtown on the west side of Hwy 16, the **Medina River Company** (☎ 830-796-3553) rents tubes for $5 per day, plus $2 for shuttle service. Sit-on-top single/double kayaks rent for $25/35 per day, plus $10 for the shuttle service. The shuttle drives you to Medina, then you tube or kayak back to Bandera on the river – it's usually pretty tame, but when it runs, it runs fast; count on six hours to kayak the 18 miles between Medina and the Bandera landing. The **Bandera Beach Club** (☎ 830-796-7555; 703 Main St, cnr Cottonwood St) rents tubes for the same price.

The CVB knows nearly a dozen places in and around town were you can go **horseback riding**. There are also more than a dozen dude ranches in the area, all with hundreds of acres, enormous ranch houses, resort features and heaps of riding opportunities. Most of them also offer horseback riding to nonguests, usually for around $20 per hour, $80 for a half-day ride with lunch or $180 for overnight rides with meals.

The CVB can makes reservations at all of the following:

Dixie Dude Ranch (☎ 830-796-4481, 800-375-9255; www.dixieduderanch.com; FM 1077, 8mi west of Bandera)
Yellow Rose Ranch (☎ 210-698-2001; www.yellow roseranch.com; in Tarpley, 22mi northwest of Bandera)
Silver Spur (☎ 830-796-3037; www.silverspur-ranch .com; RR 1077, near Hill Country State Natural Area)
Running-R Ranch (☎ 830-796-3984; www.rrranch.com; 9059 Bandera Creek Rd)
LH7 Ranch and Resort (☎ 830-796-4314; off FM 3240, 3½ mi northwest of Bandera; cabins $65)

Sleeping & Eating

Overnight stays at the dude ranches all cost about the same; plan on spending about $100 per person per night (usually there's a two-night minimum stay). Ask if rates include meals or horseback riding, too.

Mansion in Bandera (☎ 830-460-7134; www .mansioninbandera.com; 1005 Hackberry St; d Sun-Thu $60-125, Fri-Sat $75-155; Ⓟ) This lovely limestone-clad home has several rooms, romantic porches and a great hammock out back for sunny days. A full breakfast is included in the price, and there's prix fixe fine dining on Friday and Saturday nights (by reservation only), when $40 gets you a five-course meal including wine.

At the south end of town, the friendly, family-run **River Front Motel** (☎ 830-460-3690, 800-870-5671; 1004 Maple St; s/d Sun-Thu $55/60, Fri-Sat $74/79; **P**) offers 11 cabins on the river, each with a fridge, coffeemaker and cable TV. It's your best bet for the money. Another good choice is the **River Oak Inn** (☎ 830-796-7751; 1105 Hwy 16; d $50-110; **P**), where all of the clean rooms have a fridge and microwave.

For breakfast, head to **Fool Moon Cafe** (☎ 830-460-8434; 204 Main St; mains $6; ☽ closed Mon), an inviting place that's more like New England than Texas, with real cappuccino and huge Sunday breakfasts. Across the street from the 11th St Cowboy Bar is the tiny but tasty **Boudreaux's Cajun Kitchen** (☎ 830-796-8887; 306 11th St; mains $4-7; ☽ 11am-9pm daily, till 3am Fri-Sat) serving up spicy crawfish etoufée, gumbo and shrimp po' boys.

Billy Gene's Restaurant (☎ 830-460-3200; behind the River Oak Inn; mains $5-12; ☽ 7am-9pm daily, till 10pm Fri-Sat) is a particularly friendly place that serves steaks and home cooking in a seating area overlooking the river. Protein cravings can be further satiated at the **Meat Works** (☎ 830-460-4608; 706 Main St; mains $5-8; ☽ 11am-7pm Tue-Sat), which serves up barbecued brisket, ribs and turkey, or at **Busbee's BBQ & Catering** (☎ 830-796-3153; 319 Main St; mains $4-8; ☽ 10:30am-8pm), where you can get smoked meat by the pound, plate meals and decent burgers.

OST (☎ 830-796-3836; 305 Main St; mains $6-14; ☽ 6am-10pm daily, from 7am Sun) – the name stands for Old Spanish Trail – does hearty chuck-wagon-style breakfasts, along with Tex-Mex and the ubiquitous chicken-fried steaks at dinner. There's an entire wall devoted to the likeness of John Wayne.

Entertainment
If it's honky-tonkin' and beer drinkin' you're looking for, you've come to the right place. **Arkey Blue's Silver Dollar Bar** (☎ 830-796-8826; 308 Main St) is a dance hall where you can cotton-eyed-Joe with the best of them. Look for Hank Williams Sr's carved signature in one of the wooden tables. **Cabaret** (☎ 830-796-8166; 801 Main St) is another rootin' tootin' dance hall that's bigger than Arkey's and has been around since 1936. Bandera resident Robert Earl Keen and Austin yodeler Don Walser have been known to play its stage.

Right next door to the Cabaret, **Bandera Forge** (☎ 830-796-7184; 807 Main St) is a working iron forge that has live music and $2 beers. The not-to-be-missed **11th St Cowboy Bar** (☎ 830-796-4849; 301 N 11th St), just north of Cypress St, is a tiny hole in the wall with a fun crowd and, if you're lucky, guitar playing.

Getting There & Away
From Kerrville, the most direct route is Hwy 173 (Bandera Hwy). The more pleasant and scenic way – through hill and dale and past Medina – is to take Hwy 16 south.

HILL COUNTRY STATE NATURAL AREA
About 10½ miles southwest of Bandera (State Rd 1077 runs into the main entrance), this **park** (☎ 830-796-4413; per car $3, primitive campsites $10-12) is a protected wilderness area lined with 35 miles of trails open for hiking, bicycling and horseback riding. Park maps can be obtained at the CVB office in Bandera. Bury human waste in cat holes and pack out anything you've brought in – this is the most litter-free park in Texas. The park has no services (not even water), so you'll have to bring everything you'll need. For guided **horseback rides**, contact the Silver Spur or Running-R Ranch in Kerrville.

BRIGHTER DAYS HORSE REFUGE
The little town of Pipe Creek, about 10 miles southeast of Bandera, is home to **Brighter Days Horse Refuge** (☎ 830-510-6607; Hwy 46; all donations appreciated; ☽ 10am-3pm Tue, Thu & Sat), a nonprofit center that nurses abused and injured horses back to health. It's home to more than 50 horses and ponies. Bring along a bag of carrots or apples, which is the suggested price of admission. The entrance is on Hwy 46, less than 2 miles south of its intersection with Hwy 16.

BOERNE
☎ 830 population 6178
Twenty-three miles east of Bandera on Hwy 46 is the bustling little center of Boerne (rhymes with 'journey'), settled by German immigrants in 1849. The town clings strongly to its German roots – Main St is signposted Hauptstrasse and events like the Oktoberfest Konzert and Weihnachts (Christmas) Fest are held each year – but it's less overrun with tourists

than Fredericksburg. It's a pleasant place to spend a few hours, and the **Greater Boerne Chamber of Commerce** (☎ 830-249-8000, 888-842-8080; www.boerne.org; 126 Rosewood Ave; ☻ 9am-5pm Mon-Fri, 9am-noon Sat) has brochures covering historical markers around town. The stretch of Main St from Main Plaza to Cibolo Creek seems to be exclusively devoted to **antiques stores**; most stock a handy leaflet that will help you navigate around the plethora of shops.

East of Main St, the **Cibolo Nature Center** (☎ 830-249-4616; City Park Rd, off Hwy 46; admission free; ☻ 8am-dusk) is a small park with rewarding nature trails that wind through native Texan woods, marshland and along Cibolo Creek. Call the park visitors center to ask about a series of live music concerts and events held here during summer.

Natural attractions outside town include popular **Cascade Caverns** (☎ 830-755-8080; 226 Cascade Caverns Rd, off I-10 exit 543; adult/child 3-11$12/8; ☻ 9am-4pm Sat-Sun Sep-Feb, later in summer), about 3 miles south of Boerne. The caverns include a 140ft-deep cave that features giant stalagmites and stalactites and a 100ft waterfall. The only way to see the cae is by taking a 45-minute tour, which departs every 30 minutes. Also nearby is the **Cave Without a Name** (☎ 830-537-4212; 325 Kreutzberg Rd; adult/child $11/6; ☻ 10am-5pm winter, 9am-6pm summer), another living cave with a small stream running through it; from Boerne, take Hwy 474 for 6 miles to Kreutzberg Rd, then it's another 5 miles to the cave.

Sleeping & Eating

Ye Kendall Inn (☎ 830-249-2138; www.yekendall inn.com; 128 W Blanco St; d $100-200, cabins $140-170; **P**) This national landmark hotel is the nicest place to stay in Boerne. The creekside main house is made of hand-cut limestone and features a two-story, 200ft-long front porch; the building dates to 1859 and has 14 rooms. There are also three cabins and a small church, all of which date from the 1800s and were relocated to the property from various places around the state (the stunning Enchanted Cabin was built near Enchanted Rock). Prices at the inn include a three-course gourmet breakfast from the attached **Limestone Grille** (mains $13-25; ☻ breakfast, lunch & dinner daily), an upscale spot serving good food in a somewhat stuffy atmosphere.

For a fresh, delicious breakfast buffet, don't look any further than **Bear Moon Bakery & Cafe** (☎ 830-816-2327; 401 S Main St; mains $3-7, buffet $8; ☻ 8am-3pm Tue-Sun, breakfast till 10:30am Tue-Fri & noon Sat-Sun). On weekends, be sure to arrive early – it's always packed. There are plenty of home-baked goodies to tempt you as well, along with fresh soups, salads and sandwiches for lunch. Another prime choice for early morning coffee and tea is **The Daily Grind** (☎ 830-249-4677; 143 S Main St), a cute little spot right on the main strip.

For a tasty mix of Mexican and German fare and homemade beers in an eclectic atmosphere, head to **The Dodging Duck Brewery** (☎ 830-248-3825; 402 River Rd; mains $7-13; ☻ 11am-9pm Tue-Sun, till 11pm Fri-Sat). A good choice for families is **Hungry Horse Restaurant** (☎ 830-816-8989; 109 S Saunders St; ☻ 11am-9pm), behind the courthouse. If your sweet tooth has you on the prowl for pies, cookies or a dang good apple turnover, check out **The Boerne Apple Co** (☎ 830-249-4706; Old Towne Shopping Center, 233 S Main St; ☻ 10am-4pm Wed-Sat).

WARING-WELFARE ROAD

Just up the road from Boerne on I-10 is the tiny town of Nelson City, which is notable mainly as the starting point for a drive along the Waring-Welfare Rd (SR 1621), a lazy country lane that dips and meanders past some beautiful scenery and a few hidden Hill Country escapes.

Nelson City is really just a smattering of buildings off I-10 at the Waring-Welfare Rd exit. One of these is **Nelson City Dance Hall** (☎ 830-537-3835; 825 Waring-Welfare Rd, ½mi off I-10 exit 533; ☻ 5-11pm Wed-Thu, 4pm-2am Fri-Sat, 2-10pm Sun), a family-friendly honky-tonk where you can show off your new cowboy boots and do a little two-steppin'. On the weekends, live bands play everything from country and bluegrass to zydeco and Tejano.

Drive north on SR 1621 for about 3 miles to the town Welfare, named for the German word *wohlfarht,* which roughly means 'pleasant trip.' About 10 people call Welfare home, including Gaby McCormick and David Lawhorn, the chef-owners of the **Welfare Cafe** (☎ 830-537-3700; 223 Waring-Welfare Rd; mains $10-22; ☻ brunch 11am-3pm Sat-Sun, dinner 5-9pm Wed-Sun, till 10pm Sat), a gourmet restaurant housed inside a 1920s general store and post office. American-style seafood as well as German schnitzel are on the eclectic menu; dinner reservations are recommended. The Welfare also offers a superb selection of beer and wine, as well as live music in a beautiful outdoor beer garden on Thursday and Sunday evenings.

About 7 miles north of Welfare, the **Waring General Store** (☎ 210-434-2331, 800-749-2332; Waring-Welfare Rd) is a worn, wooden and cozy retreat selling Bowie knives and beer. There's live music under a giant old oak tree on the first Saturday of each month. Wednesday between 6pm and 9pm is steak night: for $15 you get a 10oz rib-eye (or two chicken breasts), spinach and chicken quesadillas, gorditas, a baked potato, salad, desert, iced tea and live music. If you're looking for the spirit of the Hill Country, it doesn't get much more spirited than this.

NATURAL BRIDGE CAVERNS
About halfway between San Antonio and New Braunfels, this **national landmark cave** (☎ 210-651-6101; Hwy 3009, west of I-35 exit 175; adult/senior/child 4-12 $14/13/8.50; ☺ 9am-4pm, till 7pm Jun-Aug) is one of the state's largest underground formations. Its name comes from the 60ft natural limestone bridge that spans the entrance, but inside (where it's always 70°F) are simply phenomenal formations, including the Watchtower, a 50ft pedestal that looks like a crystallized flower. You can only see the caverns as part of a guided tour; they leave every half hour. Attached is the Natural Caverns Wildlife Park, a small zoo with rare animals.

GUADALUPE RIVER STATE PARK
Thirty miles north of San Antonio, this exceptionally beautiful **state park** (☎ 830-438-2656; 3350 Park Rd 31; Spring Branch; adult/child under 12 $4/free, camp/RV sites $12/15; ☺ dawn-dusk) straddles a 9-mile stretch of the sparklingly clear, bald-cypress-tree-lined Guadalupe River, and it's great for canoeing and tubing. There are also 3 miles of hiking trails through the park's almost 2000 acres. Two-hour guided tours of the geology, flora and fauna of the nearby Honey Creek State Natural Area are included in the price of admission. The tours leave at 9am on Saturday morning from the Guadalupe ranger station. There are picnic areas along the river. By car from San Antonio, take US 281 north to Hwy 46, and turn west (left) for 8 miles to

Park Rd 31. From Austin take I-35 south to New Braunfels, then go west on Hwy 46 for 30 miles to Park Rd 31.

WIMBERLEY
☎ 512 population 2100
Pretty Wimberley is an artist and artisan's retreat on the serene Cypress Creek that has as much in common with Tuscany as it does with Texas. Here you can visit a glassblowing studio, taste olive oil in one of the state's only commercial olive orchards, eat expertly baked homemade pies or simply kick back at one of the many B&Bs along the creek.

On the first Saturday of each month from April to December, local art galleries, shops and craftspeople set up booths for **Wimberley Market Days**, a bustling collection of live music, food and over 400 vendors at Lion's Field on RR 2325. For more information on market days and other happenings around town, contact the **Wimberley Convention & Visitors Bureau** (CVB; ☎ 512-847-2201; www.visitwimberley.com; 14001 RR 12, near Brookshires grocery store; ☺ 9am-4pm Mon-Sat, noon-4pm Sun).

If you're wondering why none of the grocery stores in town sell beer, it's because the village of Wimberley is 'dry,' a peculiar Prohibition-era holdover that occasionally still lingers in this part of the country. Local restaurants get around the law by charging patrons an annual 'membership fee,' which usually costs $1.

Sights & Activities
An unusual sight in Wimberley (and the rest of Texas, for that matter) is the only producing olive orchard in the Hill Country, found at **Bella Vista Ranch** (☎ 512-847-6514; 3101 Mt Sharp Rd, off CR 182; ☺ 10am-4pm Mon-Sat). There's a gift shop with free tastings as well as tours of the orchard and the olive press, one of only two in Texas. The town's Italian influence continues at **Wimberley Glass Works** (☎ 512-847-9348, 800-6686; RR 12; ☺ 10am-5pm), about 1 mile south of Wimberley. This working studio offers free glassblowing exhibitions and an art gallery.

For excellent scenic views of the surrounding limestone hills near Wimberley, take a drive on FM 32, otherwise known as the **Devil's Backbone**. From Wimberley, head south on RR 12 to FM 32, then turn right

---

DETOUR: LOST MAPLES STATE NATURAL AREA

The foliage spectacle in October and November at **Lost Maples State Natural Area** (☎ 830-966-3413, reservations 512-389-8900; on RR 187, 5mi north of Vanderpool; day-use $2-5, primitive camping $8, tent sites $15) is as colorful as any you'd see in New England. In autumn, big-tooth maple trees turn shocking golds, reds, yellows and oranges. In the summertime there's good swimming in the Sabinal River. At any time of the year, campers will find back-country primitive areas where they can pitch a tent as well as more convenient sites supplied with water, electricity and nearby showers. Hiking trails will take visitors into rugged limestone canyons and prairie-like grasslands populated by bobcat, javelina and gray fox. Bird-watching is another popular attraction at Lost Maples due to the green kingfisher who takes up residence in the park year-round.

---

toward Fischer and Canyon Lake. The road gets steeper, then winds out onto a craggy ridge – the 'backbone' – with a 360-degree vista. About the only establishment on this stretch of road, **Devil's Backbone Tavern** (☎ 830-964-2544; 4041 FM 32), a perfectly tattered and dusty beer joint with a country music jukebox, has live acoustic music on Wednesday and Friday.

The famous **Blue Hole** (☎ 512-847-9127; off CR 173; $1; ☺ 9am-8pm) is one of the Hill Country's best swimming holes. It's a privately owned spot in the calm, shady and crystal-clear waters of Cypress Creek. To get here from Wimberley, head down Hwy 12 south of the square, turn left on County Rd 173, and then after another half mile, turn onto the access road between a church and a cemetery.

Sleeping & Eating

There are dozens of B&Bs and cottages in Wimberley; call the CVB or visit its website for more information. Close to the action and just a quarter mile east of the square, the **Wimberley Inn Motel** (☎ 512-847-3750; www.wimberleyinn.com; on RR 3237; d $60-150; P) offers large, no-frills rooms at a fair price. Two miles south of town, **Blair House** (☎ 512-847-1111, 877-549-5450; www.blairhouseinn.com; 100 Spoke Hill Rd; d $125-230, cabins $275; P) is a quiet, lovely B&B with eight rooms and two cabins. On Saturday nights, its fine-dining restaurant offers a perfectly presented Mediterranean-influenced meal with five courses and wine for $55 per person (reservations strongly advised).

For great Tex-Mex and an outdoor patio try **Christos Comidas Mexicanas** (☎ 512-847-8111; 1 River Rd; mains $6-10; ☺ 11am-9pm Tue-Sun), located

behind the Ozona Bank. Gourmet deli-style sandwiches and pizzas, including a good vegetarian selection, are served at **Idle Wild** (☎ 512-847-0430; Poco Rio shopping center, 1539 RR 12; mains $4-10; ☺ 11am-8pm Tue-Sat). Barbecue fans shouldn't miss out on family-run **Miss Mae's Bar-B-Q** (☎ 512-847-9808; 419 FM 2325; mains $3-10; ☺ 10:30am-7pm Mon-Sat) west of town.

You haven't eaten until you've wrapped your mouth around a pie from the **Wimberley Pie Company** (☎ 512-847-9462; 13619 RR12; ☺ 9:30am-5:30pm Tue-Fri, 10am-5pm Sat, noon-4pm Sun), a small but popular bakery that supplies many of the area's restaurants (and a few in Austin) with every kind of pie and cheesecake you can imagine, and then some. It's south of the square.

Shopping

Art galleries, antique shops and craft stores surround **Wimberley Square**, located where Ranch Rd 12 crosses Cypress Creek and bends into an 'S.' The best browsing is 1½ miles north of the square on Ranch Rd 12 at **Poco Rio** (15406 RR 12), a shopping center with boutique clothing stores, artists' galleries, eateries, a health spa for acupuncture and massage and an 18-hole putt-putt golf course, all set among lush gardens and tree-shaded pathways.

Getting There & Away

There is no public transportation to Wimberley. To make the 1½-hour drive from Austin, take US 290 west to Dripping Springs, then turn left onto Ranch Rd 12. From San Antonio, take I-35 north to San Marcos, where you can pick up Ranch Rd 12 headed west and then north into town.

HILL COUNTRY

Directory

ACCOMMODATIONS

Motel and hotel prices vary tremendously from urban to rural areas and from season to season. Prices considered expensive in the Hill Country could be mid-range rates in Austin and budget options in San Antonio, and a motel charging $55 for a double during peak periods may drop its rates to $30 in the off-season and then raise them to $75 for a special event. B&B rates vary less dramatically, although they're typically higher on weekends and holidays. Prices in this book can only be an approximate guideline at best. Also, be prepared to add room tax of about 15% to all rates quoted here. Online discounters such as www.orbitz.com can save you quite a bit of money off chain motel and hotel rates, even at the very last minute.

Festivals and conventions can fill up accommodations quickly and prices soar, so call ahead to find out what will be going on during your visit. Reservations are always a good idea during Texas' busy periods (most of March, May through August and the Christmas-New Year's holidays), and they are essential during special events. Better motels and all hotels will take reservations

days or months ahead of time. Most chains have toll-free reservations numbers, but it sometimes pays to call the motel or hotel direct to learn of any manager's specials. Be sure to let the hotel know if you plan a late arrival – many motels will give your room away if you haven't arrived or called by 6pm, unless you've guaranteed it on a credit card. Cancellation policies vary, so ask to avoid being charged a penalty fee later.

As a rule of thumb, the price ranges for our accommodations listings are as follows: budget is less than $50 or $60 per night, mid-range starts under $100 and top end starts over $100.

B&Bs

European visitors should be aware that North American B&Bs are rarely the casual, inexpensive sort of accommodations found on the continent or in Britain. While they are usually family-run, many B&Bs require

---

PRACTICALITIES

Electricity Voltage is 110V 60Hz and the plugs have two (flat) or three (two flat, one round) pins. Most European appliances designed to work on 220V 50Hz won't work.

Media Easily one of the best regional-interest magazines in the US, *Texas Monthly* (www.texasmonthly.com) has strong reporting and excellent photography. Molly Ivins writes for the *Texas Observer* (www.texasobserver.org), a left-wing rag of news, politics, culture and the arts.

Photography Remember that film is susceptible to heat, so protect your film by keeping it cool and processing it as soon as possible. New US airport security x-ray machines will damage unprocessed film, whether exposed or not.

Video North American videotape uses the NTSC system, which is incompatible with the PAL or SECAM formats.

Weights & Measurements The USA ignores the metric system. Temperatures are degrees Fahrenheit, not Celsius. Distances are measured in inches (in), feet (ft), yards (yd) and miles (mi). Dry weights are ounces (oz) and pounds (lb). Gasoline is dispensed by the US gallon, which is about 20% less than the imperial gallon.

advance reservations, though some will be happy to oblige the occasional drop-in (call first). Most B&Bs prohibit smoking. Nearly all have hot breakfasts included in their rates, but light continental breakfasts are not unheard of. The cheapest establishments, with rooms starting at $50, may have clean but unexciting rooms with shared bath. More expensive places have rooms with private baths, perhaps in historical buildings, quaint country cabins or luxurious urban townhouses. Most of these B&Bs charge $70 to $125 per double, but some rates go from $150 on up. The best are distinguished by a friendly attention to detail by hosts who can provide you with local sightseeing information and added amenities, such as Internet access, VCRs and if you're lucky, a swimming pool.

Camping

Private and public campgrounds and RV parks charge $10 to $20 per night, or even less for primitive tent camping. Sites arc often on a 'first-come, first-served' basis, so plan on an early arrival, preferably during the week, as sites fill up fast on Friday and weekends. More popular campgrounds may accept or require reservations, in which case you'll need a major credit card. Smaller campgrounds usually only accept cash as payment upon entry. Primitive walk-in sites are exclusively for tents and require campers to pack out all trash; some don't have any drinking water. Developed camping areas usually have toilets, drinking water, fire pits (or charcoal grills) and picnic benches. Some have electricity, showers and full RV hookups. Most private campgrounds are designed with RVs in mind; tenters can camp, but fees are several dollars higher than at public campgrounds. In addition, state and city taxes apply. Facilities may include hot showers, coin laundry, Internet access and a swimming pool. **Kampgrounds of America** (KOA; ☎ 406-248-7444; www.koakampgrounds.com) is a national network of private campgrounds that, although expensive, are among the most reliable for service and amenities.

Extended-Stay Accommodation

The past few years have seen an explosion of all-suites hotels and extended-stay motels, most with rooms from $50 to $100 a night. Rates drop as much as 50% if you book for a week or more. These are especially popular with business travelers, but they can be excellent for families or couples traveling together, too. Any property billed as a suite has, at minimum, a kitchenette (at least a mini-refrigerator and microwave) and a bit more space than the typical motel room. The better ones are like apartments, with full kitchens and separate sleeping and living quarters with sliding doors for privacy.

Hotels

Texas has a variety of excellent historic hotels. Most have been completely updated with modern plumbing and amenities, but they still have plenty of quirks and charm. Rates may start at just $100 per night, even for the big-city classics.

The USA also has many hotel chains, where the level of quality and style tends to be standard. Chains in the $85-and-up category include Radisson, Doubletree, Clarion and Hilton. Many are full-service hotels with room service, fitness facilities and other niceties.

Other hotels are part of top-tier chains (like the Four Seasons, Omni and Wyndham brands), which can easily run $200 or more a night during the week; rates often fall dramatically on weekends. These luxury hotels have bellhops and a concierge, restaurants and bars, exercise rooms, business centers, room service and more.

Prices advertised by hotels are called 'rack rates' and are not written in stone. If you simply ask about specials and discounts, you can often save quite a bit of money. Booking through a travel agent or via the Internet can also mean big savings.

Hostels

The US hostel network is less widespread than in the rest of the world, and the Texas hostel network is smaller than that of most states. **Hostelling International-American Youth Hostels** (HI-AYH; www.hiayh.org) has facilities in Austin and San Antonio; you can make reservations online. Dormitory beds cost less than $20 a night; private rooms, when available, cost at least $35 for one or two people. You can purchase membership on the spot when checking in to a hostel, although it's advisable to purchase it

DIRECTORY

before you leave home. Most hostels allow nonmembers to stay but charge them a few dollars more. Dormitories are segregated by sex. Kitchen and laundry privileges are usually available. There are information boards, TV rooms and lounge areas. Alcohol and smoking may be banned.

Motels

Motels with $30 rooms are found mostly in small towns along major highways and near the airports and outlying interstate loops in Austin and San Antonio. Rooms are usually small, and although a minimal level of cleanliness is maintained, expect scuffed walls, atrocious decor, old furniture and strange noises from your shower. Even these rooms normally have a private bathroom, air-conditioning and a TV. The cheapest budget places may not accept reservations, but at least phone from the road to see what's available.

All of the national chain motels accept reservations by phone or over the Internet. Chains like Red Roof Inn, Travelodge and Econo Lodge are typically just a few dollars more than your basic Motel 6, which costs from around $35 per night. At the slightly more expensive Super 8 Motels and Days Inns, expect firmer beds and free continental breakfast. Stepping up, chains in the $55-to-$85 range have more spacious rooms, indoor swimming pools and other niceties; La Quinta is a major player in this category, as are Ramada Inn, Marriott-owned Fairfield Inn and for some properties, Holiday Inn.

Ranches

Dude ranches and guest ranches welcome visitors as paying guests. All offer horseback riding; some are working cattle ranches where you may also learn how to rope and herd cattle. Many are pretty rustic, though others are quite upscale. For a few Hill Country possibilities, check around Bandera.

University Accommodation

A handful of independent student cooperatives near Austin's **University of Texas** campus open their doors to hostellers on a space-available basis. Most accommodations are in private en-suite dorm rooms that sleep one or two people. Perks usually include a shared kitchen, living area and Internet access. Rooms are commonly available during summer vacation, but harder to get during the school year.

BUSINESS HOURS

Most businesses are open 9am to 5pm weekdays. Retail shop hours are usually 10am to 6pm Monday to Saturday, noon to 5pm on Sunday. Shopping malls may stay open later, particularly on Thursday. Most restaurants are open for lunch between 11am and 2pm and for dinner from 5pm daily, but if they take a day off, it's Monday. They are characteristically open until at least 9pm, later on Friday and Saturday nights. A few specialize in breakfast or serve weekend brunch. Bars usually open in the late afternoon around 4pm or 5pm, but some unlock their doors before noon. Live music clubs open in the early evening around 6pm or 7pm, but rarely get busy before 9pm. Bars serve liquor until 2am; a few dance clubs stay open until 4am. In the big cities it's usually not a problem finding 24-hour supermarkets, pharmacies, convenience stores or gas stations. Tourist attractions often keep longer hours during summer, but some also close in the winter.

CHILDREN

Texas is very child-friendly – Texans love li'l cowpokes, and kids will usually get fussed over aplenty. There are several theme parks in the region, including **SeaWorld** (p142) and **Six Flags Fiesta Texas** (p142). Both Austin and San Antonio have museums, parks, playgrounds, zoos and other attractions specifically aimed at the younger set. Still, try to take the kids away from the urban areas and into the Hill Country, where you'll see the Texas of your imagination: wide-open spaces, working cowboys, cool geology and unusual animals.

Lonely Planet's *Travel with Children* has more information on what to do when on the road with little ones. To help you plan your family's south-central Texas vacation, we've suggested a special Tailored Trip ('Just Kiddin' Around,' p14), and you can turn to the sections 'Austin for Children' (p76) and 'San Antonio for Children' (p141) in the destination chapters.

In this book we list as often as possible attractions that kids might like as well as the discounted prices for children. There's rarely an extra charge for kids staying with their parents at motels and hotels. Ask hotel staff or the concierge about licensed babysitting services. Public restrooms often have diaper-changing tables, usually on the women's side, but it's rare to see women breast feeding in public. Rental car companies will rent car seats, which are legally required for young children, for about $5 per day or $25 per week. AAA members may be entitled to reimbursement for car seat rentals.

CLIMATE CHARTS

Texas leads the nation in tornadoes, with an average of almost 130 per year. Generally speaking, south-central Texas enjoys a mild subtropical climate year-round, with average temperatures of 50°F (10°C) in January and 85°F (30°C) in July. But weather varies throughout the region; evenings in the Hill Country are often cool enough for a jacket or even a coat in winter. Areas of San Antonio are among the most humid in the state, with effective summer daytime temperatures rising over 100°F (38°C), with Austin only marginally less heat-stricken. See also 'When to Go,' p9.

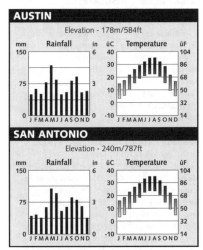

DISABLED TRAVELERS

Public buildings (including hotels, restaurants, theaters and museums) are required by the Americans with Disabilities Act (ADA) to be wheelchair accessible and have available restroom facilities. Public transportation services (buses, trains and taxis) must be made accessible to all, including those in wheelchairs. Texas has gone a long way toward ensuring accessibility at kid-friendly attractions. Telephone companies are required to provide relay operators for the hearing impaired. Many banks now provide ATM instructions in Braille, and you will find audible crossing signals as well as dropped curbs at busier roadway intersections. Guide dogs may legally be brought into restaurants, hotels and other businesses.

Larger private and chain hotels have suites for disabled guests. Most local buses are wheelchair-accessible, and some bus companies offer paratransit services in addition to regular service for those with disabilities. Many car rental agencies offer hand-controlled vehicles or vans with wheelchair lifts at no extra charge, but only with advance reservations. Disabled parking at blue-colored curbs and specially-designated spots in public lots is by permit only. All major airlines, Greyhound buses and Amtrak trains allow service animals to accompany passengers and frequently sell two-for-one packages when seriously disabled passengers require attendants. Airlines will also provide assistance for connecting, boarding and deplaning the flight – ask for assistance when making your reservation (note: airlines must accept wheelchairs as checked baggage and have an onboard chair available, though advance notice may be required).

A good website listing resources for the disabled is www.access-able.com, or try the following useful organizations:

Mobility International USA (MIUSA; ☎ 541-343-1284, fax 541-343-6812; www.miusa.org; PO Box 10767, Eugene, OR 97440) Advises disabled travelers on mobility issues. Offers a limited free information and referral service.
Society for Accessible Travel & Hospitality (SATH; ☎ 212-447-7284, fax 212-725-8253; www.sath.org; 347 Fifth Ave, ste 610, New York, NY 10016) Publishes *Open World*, a magazine for disabled travelers. Has information sheets on a wide range of destinations around the world, or they can research your specific requirements for a fee.

DISCOUNT CARDS
Student & Youth Cards

An ISIC or official school or university ID card entitles students to discounts on

(Continued on page 196

INTERNATIONAL VISITORS

ENTERING THE COUNTRY

To enter the USA, you must have a nonrefundable, roundtrip ticket, except when entering overland from Canada or Mexico (in which case sufficient funds for the duration of your stay must be shown).

Thanks to heightened security measures, travelers can expect long waits at immigration and security checkpoints. The Department of Homeland Security is phasing in the US-VISIT program, which will track every single one of the 35 million visitors who come to the USA every year. Visitors may be photographed and fingerprinted, and in the future, may be subject to iris scanning and facial recognition technology. The program should be fully implemented by 2005; check www.dhs.gov for current procedures and requirements.

No matter what your visa says, US immigration officers have an absolute authority to refuse or impose conditions on admission. Public health, customs and agricultural inspections may be carried out separately or together with immigration clearance.

No immunizations are required to enter the USA, but you should have adequate health insurance before setting out.

Passports

Your passport must be valid for at least 6 months after your intended stay in the USA. Technically Canadians don't need a passport, but official proof of citizenship with photo ID is necessary.

Visas

The USA is in the middle of overhauling its entry requirements as it establishes new national security guidelines post-9/11. It is imperative that travelers double- and triple-check current regulations before coming to the USA, as changes will continue for several years. There is a new website with comprehensive visa information: www.unitedstatesvisas.gov.

Under the Visa Waiver Program, citizens of certain countries may enter the USA without a US visa for stays of up to 90 days. Currently, 27 countries are in the program, including most EU countries, Australia and New Zealand. For other eligible countries in this program, check with the Bureau of Citizenship and Immigration Services (www.immigration.gov). All other travelers, for example, South African nationals, will need a visitor's visa. These can be obtained at most US consulates or embassies overseas; it is usually best to obtain a visa from an office in your home country.

International Drivers License

With few exceptions, you can legally drive in the USA as long as you have a valid driver's license issued by your home country. If your home country license is not in English, you may be required to show an international driving permit.

CUSTOMS

Amounts in excess of $10,000 in cash, traveler's checks, money orders and other cash equivalents must be declared. Each visitor can import 1L of liquor, 200 cigarettes and 100 cigars (provided they are not Cuban), but you must be at least 21 years old to possess the former and 18 years old for the latter.

EMBASSIES & CONSULATES

USA Embassies & Consulates

US Embassies and Consulates overseas can be found on the government's website (usembassy.state.gov), including:

Australia (☎ 02-6214-5600) Moonah Place, Yarralumla, ACT 2600
Canada (☎ 613-238-5335) 490 Sussex Dr, Ottawa, ON K1N 1G8
France (☎ 01-43-12-22-22) 2 avenue Gabriel, 75008 Paris
Germany (☎ 030-8305-0) Neustädtische Kirchstrasse 4-5, 10117 Berlin
Ireland (☎ 1-668-8777) 42 Elgin Rd, Dublin 4
Mexico (☎ 01-55-5080-2000) Paseo de la Reforma 305, Col. Cuauhtémoc, 06500 Mexico, DF
Netherlands (☎ 70-310-9209) Lange Voorhout 102, 2514 EJ, The Hague
New Zealand (☎ 4-462-2000) 29 Fitzherbert Terrace, Thorndon, Wellington
UK (☎ 20-7499-9000) 24 Grosvenor Square, London W1A 1AE

Embassies & Consulates in Texas

Most foreign diplomatic representation in Texas is found in Dallas or Houston, except for two Mexican consulates in **Austin** (☎ 512-478-

2866 200 E 6th St, ste 200, Austin, TX 78701) and **San Antonio** (☎ 210-227-9145) 127 Navarro St, San Antonio, TX 78205

MONEY

Currency
The US dollar ($) is divided into 100 cents (¢). Gas stations, convenience stores and fast-food eateries may not accept bills over $20.

ATMs
Almost all ATMs accept cards from the Cirrus, Visa, Star and Global Access networks. They are found everywhere, especially at banks and convenience stores. Most ATMs charge a service fee of $1.50 or so per transaction for foreign bank cards, but exchange rates usually beat traveler's checks.

Traveler's Checks
American Express, VISA and Thomas Cook traveler's checks are widely known issuers. Restaurants, hotels and most shops readily accept US-dollar traveler's checks, same as cash, but small businesses, markets and fast-food chains may refuse them.

Changing Money
Banks offer better rates than most bureaux de change. Always ask about commissions and any other surcharges when exchanging money. Most banks are typically open 10am to 5pm Monday to Thursday, until 6pm Friday, and sometimes Saturday morning.

Taxes
A state sales tax of 6.25% is charged in addition to city and county taxes.

POST
The **United States Postal Service** (USPS; ☎ 800-275-8777; www.usps.gov) is reliable and inexpensive. Call the toll-free number for the nearest branch, including those that accept post restante. Most post offices have after-hours stamp vending machines. You can also buy stamps from hotel concierges, convenience stores and supermarkets.

At press time, 1st-class mail within the US is 37¢ for letters up to 1oz (23¢ each additional ounce) and 23¢ for postcards. International airmail rates are 80¢ for a 1oz letter and 70¢ for a postcard, 20¢ less respectively to either Canada or Mexico. Aerograms cost 70¢.

TELEPHONE

Dialing Codes
Always dial '1' before toll-free (800, 888, etc) and domestic long-distance numbers. If you dial the code when you shouldn't or don't dial the code when you should, a recording from the phone company will set you straight. International rates apply for calls to Canada, even though the dialing code (+1) is the same as for US long-distance calls. Dial ☎ 011 followed by the country code for all other overseas direct-dial calls.

Phones
Public **pay phones** are either coin- or card-operated; some also accept credit cards. Local calls usually cost 25¢ minimum and increase with the distance and length of call. Pay phones in airports and better hotels have data ports for laptop Internet connections.

Private prepaid **phonecards** are available at newsstands, convenience stores, supermarkets and pharmacies. Cards sold by major telecommunication companies like AT&T may actually offer better deals than upstart companies, whose cards have catchy names.

The USA uses a variety of **mobile phone** systems, 99% of which are incompatible with the GSM 900/1800 standard used throughout Europe, Asia and Africa. Check with your cellular service provider before departure about using your phone in Texas. Sometimes calls are routed internationally, while US travelers should beware of roaming surcharges (either way, it can become very expensive for a 'local' call).

TIME
Central Standard Time (CST) is six hours behind GMT. During Daylight Saving Time (from first Sunday in April to last Saturday in October), the clock moves ahead one hour.

At noon in Texas it's:
10am in Los Angeles
noon in Mexico City
1pm in New York
6pm in London
7pm in Paris
4am (the next day) in Sydney
6am (the next day) in Auckland

(Continued from page 193)
museum admission, theater tickets and
other attractions.

Senior Cards
People over the age of 65 (sometimes
even 50) typically qualify for the same
discounts as students, and then some. Be
sure to inquire about such rates at hotels,
museums and restaurants. Any photo ID is
usually sufficient proof of age. The **American
Association of Retired Persons** (AARP; ☎ 800-424-
3410; www.aarp.org; 601 E St NW, Washington, DC 20049;
one-year membership $12.50) is an advocacy group
for US residents 50 years and older and is a
good resource for travel bargains. Citizens
of other countries can also join.

AAA Membership Cards
For its members, the **American Automobile
Association** (AAA; ☎ 800-765-0766; www.aaa-texas.com)
provides great travel information, distributes
free road maps and driving guides, and sells
American Express traveler's checks without
commission. The AAA membership card
will often get you discounts on motel and
hotel accommodations, car rental and
admission charges. AAA also provides
emergency roadside service to members
in the event of an accident, breakdown or
locking your keys in the car. Service is free
within a given radius of the nearest service
center, and service providers will tow your
car to a mechanic if they can't fix it. The
nationwide toll-free roadside assistance
number is ☎ 800-222-4357. The AAA has
reciprocal agreements with other motoring
associations; members of some foreign auto
clubs are entitled to AAA services, so bring
your membership card and/or a letter of
introduction from home.

FESTIVALS & EVENTS
See p79 for festivals in Austin and p143
for festivals in San Antonio. Elsewhere
throughout this guidebook you'll find full
reviews of special regional and local events,
including in the Hill Country. For our Top
10 festivals, see p11.

FOOD
For Texas' regional cuisine, consult the
Food & Drink chapter (p45). In this book
our restaurant reviews are usually sorted by
geographical area, then arranged by price.

'Budget' diners, cafés and coffee shops
generally cost around $5 for a meal, or up
to $10 including taxes and a tip. 'Mid-range'
restaurants charge $8 to $15 just for the main
dish (often called an entrée). At 'Top End'
dining establishments, expect to pay from
$45 per person for an appetizer, a main
course, drinks and dessert, all inclusive.

GAY & LESBIAN TRAVELERS
The larger cities in Texas have gay, lesbian,
bisexual and transgender community centers (or at least a gay chamber of commerce)
that offer tips on everything from gay-owned
businesses to medical care to information
on bars, clubs and accommodations. As
you travel into the boondocks, it is often
much harder to be open. In some rural
areas, public displays of affection may land
you in serious trouble. That said, Austin
and San Antonio are known to be much
more tolerant than the Texas norm, and
both cities have pride festivals and well-
established gay communities. The **Lesbian/
Gay Rights Lobby of Texas** (LGRL; ☎ 512-474-5475;
lgrl.sitestreet.com) has excellent online coverage
of news and politics.

For travel advice and information while in
San Antonio, see p145. In the Capitol City,
check in with the **Austin Gay & Lesbian Chamber
of Commerce** (☎ 512-474-4422; www.aglcc.org),
which can guide you to queer-friendly
businesses, organizations and events. Statewide publications, such as *This Week in
Texas* (www.thisweekintexas.com) and the *Texas
Triangle* (www.txtriangle.com), have guides to
the bar and club scene, as well as special
events calendars, directories of gay-friendly
businesses, personal ads and news. The
Gay & Lesbian Yellow Pages (www.glyp.com)
publishes separate phone directories to
Austin and San Antonio; browse them
online or pick up a copy at local businesses.

The following national resources may
also prove useful:

Gay and Lesbian National Hotline (☎ 888-843-
4564; www.glnh.org; ✆ 4pm-midnight Mon-Fri,
noon-5pm Sat) Referrals to local doctors, attorneys and
other professionals.
National Gay and Lesbian Task Force (☎ 202-393-
5177; www.ngltf.org; 1325 Massachusetts Ave NW, ste
600, Washington, DC 20005) A civil rights and political
advocacy group for GLBT issues. Great national news
coverage is found on its website.

Lambda Legal (☎ 214-219-8585; www.lambdalegal .org; 3500 Oak Lawn Ave, ste 500, Dallas, TX 75219) Dedicated to achieving recognition of full civil rights for GLBT people and those living with HIV or AIDS.

HOLIDAYS

National public holidays are celebrated throughout the USA. Banks, schools and government offices (including post offices) are closed on major holidays, when public transit, museums and other services opt for a Sunday schedule. Private businesses and restaurants may also close on the 4th of July, Thanksgiving, Christmas and New Year's Day. Many public holidays are observed on the following Monday.

Public Holidays

Jan 1st	New Year's Day
3rd Mon in Jan	Martin Luther King Jr Day
3rd Mon in Feb	President's Day
Mar 2nd	Texas Independence Day
Mar/Apr	Easter Sunday
last Mon in May	Memorial Day
July 4th	Independence Day
1st Mon in Sept	Labor Day
2nd Mon in Oct	Columbus Day
Nov 11th	Veterans Day
4th Thur in Nov	Thanksgiving
Dec 25th	Christmas Day

INSURANCE

Taking out a travel insurance policy to cover theft, lost tickets and medical problems is a good idea, especially in the USA, where some privately run hospitals will refuse care without evidence of insurance. (Public hospitals must treat everyone, though standards are lower and, except in the most serious of cases, waits can last for hours.) There are lots of different insurance policies, and your travel agent will have recommendations, but always check the fine print. International policies handled by STA Travel and other student-travel organizations are usually a good value. For more advice on health insurance, see p203, and for important information regarding auto insurance, see p202.

INTERNET ACCESS

Major Internet service providers (ISPs) such as **Earthlink** (☎ 800-327-8454; www.earthlink.net), **AOL** (☎ 800-827-6364; www.aol.com) and **CompuServe** (☎ 800-848-8990; www.compuserve.com) each have dozens of dial-up numbers across Texas. Most motel and hotel rooms have phones equipped with data ports, and some offer high-speed Internet access. Deluxe hotels often have fully-equipped business centers with computers, photocopiers, fax and Internet services. Copy centers, such as **Kinko's** (☎ 800-254-6567 for nationwide locations), offer Internet access from 20¢ per minute. A few coffee shops may also offer Internet access, either via pay kiosks or free Wi-Fi for laptop users. Logging on at public libraries is usually free. For local advice, check out 'Internet Access' in Austin and San Antonio.

LEGAL MATTERS

Speed limits in smaller towns are strictly enforced, and rural Texans don't usually hurry, so you should get used to driving a bit slower than usual. Watch for school zones, which can have strictly enforced speed limits as low as 15mph during school hours. Speeding tickets are expensive, and could easily land you a fine of more than $100. Littering is illegal, too. For information about Texas' concealed handguns law, see p25.

You could incur stiff fines, jail time and penalties if caught driving under the influence (DUI) of alcohol or any illegal substance (eg, marijuana). Statewide, the blood-alcohol limit over which you are considered legally drunk is .08%, which is reached after just two beers. If you're younger than 21 years old, it is illegal to drive after you have consumed *any* alcohol – zero tolerance. During festive holidays and special events, roadblocks are sometimes set up to catch and deter drunk drivers. If you are stopped by the police for any reason, bear in mind that there is no system of paying fines on the spot. For traffic offenses, the police officer will explain your options to you. Attempting to pay the fine to the officer is frowned upon at best and may compound your troubles by resulting in a charge of bribery.

There is no legal reason to speak to a police officer if you don't wish, but never walk away from an officer until given permission. If you are arrested for any offense, the law says you are innocent until proven guilty. All persons who are arrested

DIRECTORY

are legally allowed to make one telephone call. You're also given, as viewers of any cop show can tell you, the right to remain silent and to refuse to answer questions and the right to representation by an attorney, which will be appointed to you free if you request it from the office of the public defender. If you don't have a lawyer or family member to help you, call your embassy; the police will give you the number upon request.

MAPS

Texas-based **Mapsco** (☎ 866-277-7264; www.mapsco .com) publishes a huge array of detailed maps and atlases of major Texas cities. Their stores around Texas also sell the entire catalog of USGS topographical maps for Texas and surrounding states. Order online or visit Mapsco retail stores in Austin (☎ 512-302-9036, 888-674-6277; 6406 N IH-35; ✆ 9am-6pm Mon-Fri, 10am-4pm Sat), near Highland Mall; or in San Antonio (☎ 210-829-7629, 800-798-2112; 610 W Sunset Rd; ✆ 9am-6pm Mon-Fri, 10am-4pm Sat), west of US 281.

The **Texas Department of Transportation** (☎ 800-452-9292, 512-832-7000 in Austin, 210-615-1110 in San Antonio) produces the helpful *Texas Official Travel Map*, available free at many visitors centers and tourist offices, including the Austin CVC. The American Automobile Association offers good driving maps. Other city and regional map products are available in bookstores, pharmacies and gas stations.

SOLO TRAVELERS

Travel, including solo travel, is generally safe and easy. In general, women need to exercise more vigilance in large cities than in rural areas. Women traveling by themselves may raise a few eyebrows, especially in rural areas, and some men interpret a woman drinking alone in a bar as a bid for male company, whether intended it that way or not. Everyone should avoid hiking, cycling long distances or camping alone, especially

in unfamiliar places. For more safety advice, see p61 in Austin and p124 in San Antonio.

TOURIST INFORMATION

Larger cities and towns have tourist information centers run by local convention and visitors bureaus (CVBs). They're good sources of information, offering details on attractions and events and sometimes providing free trip-planner kits, reservation services for hotels and B&Bs, and tickets for tours, transport and other activities. In smaller towns, local chambers of commerce often perform the same functions.

State tourist offices give out free maps and vacation planners. The free *Texas State Travel Guide* is a glossy magazine-style guidebook that lists information offices and major sights and attractions for almost every city and town in the state. It's available at all **Texas Travel Information Centers** (☎ 800-452-9292; www.traveltex.com); in Austin.

WOMEN

Let's face it, Texas is part of the South, and women can expect to be called 'honey' and 'sweetheart' a lot. Some women might find this offensive, but many opt to accept it graciously. More traditional Southern gentlemen will hold open doors, doff hats and call you 'ma'am' quite a lot. The upside of this overly solicitous attitude is that women who find themselves in genuine trouble can just ask the nearest bystander for assistance, and help is usually forthcoming. Cities and larger towns have rape crisis centers and women's shelters that provide help and support; they are listed in the telephone directory, or if not, the police should be able to refer you to them. Note that you need not report a rape to the police to receive treatment at a rape crisis center.

Useful nationwide organizations with affiliates in Texas include:

Planned Parenthood (☎ 210-736-2244; www.ppsctx .org, www.plannedparenthood.org; 104 Babcock Rd, off Fredericksburg Rd, San Antonio, TX 78201) Referrals to clinics throughout the region and free advice on medical issues.
National Organization for Women (NOW; ☎ 202-628-8669; www.now.org; 733 15th Street NW, 2nd Floor, Washington, DC 20005) A good resource for all kinds of information. Ask about state and local chapters.

HOW OLD IS OLD ENOUGH IN TEXAS?	
Driving a car	16
Voting in an election	18
Age of consent for heterosexual sex	17
Drinking alcoholic beverages	21

Transport

CONTENTS

WARNING

The information in this chapter is particularly vulnerable to change – prices, routes and schedules change, special deals come and go, and rules and visa requirements are amended. Check directly with the airline or travel agency to make sure you understand how a fare (or a ticket you may buy) works. Get opinions, quotes and advice from as many airlines and travel agencies as possible before you part with your hard-earned cash. The details given in this chapter should be regarded as pointers: they are not a substitute for careful, up-to-date research.

GETTING THERE & AWAY

Texas is big, but it's not hard to reach, even from abroad. You can get to and from other larger cities in the USA by Greyhound bus, but flying is by far your best option if time is short. Don't assume that it will cost an arm and a leg, either. With Southwest's special fares, flying sometimes beats the bus for cost. There's also limited train service.

AIR

US domestic airfares vary tremendously depending on the season you travel, the day of the week you fly, the length of your stay and the flexibility the ticket allows for flight changes and refunds. Still, nothing determines fares more than demand, and when things are slow, airlines lower their fares to fill empty seats. There's a lot of competition,

and at any given time any one of the airlines could have the cheapest fare.

From Abroad

The main international gateways to Texas are, from Europe, Dallas/Fort Worth International Airport (DFW), and, from Latin America and some Pacific points, Houston's George Bush Intercontinental Airport (IAH). Houston and Dallas are the major hubs as well for US domestic carriers, though some also have direct flights into Austin-Bergstrom International Airport and San Antonio International Airport. San Antonio's airport also offers some flights to Mexico.

From Within the USA

Most larger domestic airlines have connecting services through either Dallas or Houston; you can fly within the state on these flights as well, but the price will probably be higher than with a regional carrier.

See the individual chapters for small carriers that serve various destinations in Texas, but over the past several years the best deals have come consistently from Southwest, which serves Amarillo, Austin, Corpus Christi, Dallas (Love Field), El Paso, Harlingen–Rio Grande Valley, Houston, Lubbock and Midland-Odessa, and offers a host of special fares, including frequent $35 one-way fares between Texas destinations. Southwest also offers Internet special fares from its website (www.iflyswa.com).

For other special Internet-only airfares, try www.orbitz.com and other online travel discounters. Websites like www.travelzoo.com and www.smarterliving.com do not sell air tickets themselves, but can link you to a wealth of Internet-based flight deals.

Airports & Airlines

The following airports are in or around south-central Texas:

Austin-Bergstrom International Airport (AUS; ☎ 512-530-2242; www.ci.austin.tx.us/austinairport)
Dallas/Fort Worth International Airport (DFW; ☎ 972-574-8888; www.dfwairport.com)
Dallas Love Field (DAL; ☎ 214-670-6073; www.dallas-lovefield.com)

Houston's George Bush Intercontinental Airport
(IAH; ☎ 281-443-4551; www.houstonairportsystem.org)
Houston's William P Hobby Airport (HOU; ☎ 713-641-7770; www.houstonairportsystem.org)
San Antonio International Airport (SAT; ☎ 210-207-3411; www.ci.sat.tx.us/aviation)

Seveal major airlines fly in and out of south-central Texas:

AeroLitoral (☎ 800-237-6639; www.aerolitoral.com)
Aeromar (☎ 877-237-6627; www.aeromarairlines.com)
American Airlines (AA; ☎ 800-433-7300; www.aa.com)
America West (AWA; ☎ 800-235-9292; www.americawest.com)
Continental (☎ 800-523-3273; www.continental.com)
Delta (☎ 800-221-1212; www.delta.com)
Mexicana (☎ 800-531-7921; www.mexicana.com)
Midwest Express (☎ 800-452-2022; www.midwest express.com)
Northwest Airlines-KLM (NWA; ☎ 800-225-2525; www.nwa.com)
Southwest (SWA; ☎ 800-435-9792; www.iflyswa.com)
United Airlines-Lufthansa (UAL; ☎ 800-864-8331; www.ual.com)

LAND
Bus
Greyhound (☎ 800-229-9424; www.greyhound.com), the only nationwide bus company, has reduced local services considerably but still runs cross-country. It has extensive fixed routes and its own terminal in major cities, albeit often in undesirable parts of town. Buses are generally comfortable, the company has an exceptional safety record and buses usually run on time. Still, schedules are often inconvenient, fares are relatively high and bargain airfares can undercut buses on long-distance routes; in some cases, for shorter routes, it can be cheaper to rent a car than to ride the bus.

Long-distance bus trips are often available at rock-bottom prices by purchasing or reserving tickets at least a week in advance. Keep in mind travel times can vary dramatically depending on the time of day and the route you take.

Car
Interstate 35 runs south from the Dallas–Fort Worth metro area past Austin, San Antonio and eventually Laredo, where you can cross into Mexico. Customs officials along the entry points between the US and Mexico can be strict and often wary of anyone who doesn't look straitlaced. The transcontinental interstate for the southern USA is I-10, and it runs from Florida to California, passing through much of Texas, including San Antonio. Interstate 37 runs between San Antonio and Corpus Christi on the Gulf of Mexico. Drivers of cars and motorcycles will need to carry the vehicle's registration papers, proof of liability insurance and a driver's license. For road rules and information about renting a car, see p201.

Train
Amtrak (☎ 800-872-7245; www.amtrak.com) provides cross-country passenger service, stopping in both Austin and San Antonio. Train travel is fairly comfortable, even in its reclining coach seats (though if you can spring for a sleeper, they're worth it). Trains have lounge and dining cars, and there's usually plenty of entertainment. Amtrak attracts a higher class of clientele than most Greyhound bus routes. The frequent service delays are the only real downside to US train travel.

Schedules usually vary from the published timetables the farther you are from your starting point. Amtrak services through Texas are the *Sunset Limited*, which runs between Florida and Los Angeles, and the *Texas Eagle*, which runs between Texas and Chicago. Fares for train travel vary greatly, depending on different promotional fares and destinations. Reservations (the sooner made, the better the fare) can be held under your surname only; tickets can be purchased by credit card over the phone, via the website, from a travel agent or at an Amtrak depot. Most small train stations don't sell tickets, and trains may stop there only if you have bought a ticket in advance.

GETTING AROUND

The easiest way is to get around south-central Texas is to rent a car, but you can also get to some destinations by bus. If you're just visiting Austin or San Antonio for a few days, you can get around easily enough on public transport. For a real taste of Texas' Hill Country, you'll need your own vehicle. The good news is that renting a car for a day or two often costs less than two long-distance bus tickets.

BUS

Greyhound (☎ 800-229-9424; www.greyhound.com) is the main line for the region, with terminals in Austin and San Antonio. In many small towns, Greyhound no longer maintains terminals, but merely stops at a given location. Boarding passengers usually pay the driver with exact change. Elsewhere local bus companies often pick up the slack, like the **Kerrville Bus Co** (☎ 800-256-2757, or reserve through Greyhound), which runs buses in the Texas Hill Country. Although the buses will eventually get you where you are going, the frequency of service (except between a few major destinations) is not very good and schedules are often inconvenient. Reservations are advisable during peak periods and on less-traveled routes.

CAR & MOTORCYCLE

By far the most convenient and popular way to get around Texas is by car. Motorcycles are also very popular, and with the exception of rainy days, conditions are perfect: good, flat roads and generally warm weather. Texans are rather unsafe drivers, and you'll have to get used to being the smallest thing on the road – give way to vehicles larger than you, which is most of them. Speed limits in smaller towns are strictly enforced, and rural Texans don't usually hurry, so you should get used to driving a bit slower than usual.

Rental

All major car rental companies in the USA have offices throughout Texas. Typically a small car costs at minimum $25 per day and $130 a week. On top of that there will be a 10% state rental tax, plus a heap of local taxes, and additional daily fees for each insurance option you take.

Rates go up and down like the stock market, and it's always worth phoning around to see what's available. Generally speaking, the best deals come on weekly or weekend rental periods. Reserving ahead of time usually ensures the best rates – and reserving ahead can even mean calling from the pay phone in the rental office to the company's toll-free reservation line before

you approach the counter. Sometimes the head office can get you a better price than the branch office, so always call ahead, or check the website for Internet-only offers.

Most car-rental companies include unlimited mileage at no extra cost – be sure to check this point, because you can rack up hundreds of miles even just in the city, and at 25¢ per mile, this could lead to an unhappy surprise when you get the bill. If you plan to drop off the car at a different location than the one where you originally rented it, check and make certain that there won't be any penalty.

National car rental agencies with locations in Austin and San Antonio include:

Advantage	(☎ 800-777-5500; www.arac.com)
Alamo	(☎ 800-462-5266; www.alamo.com)
Avis	(☎ 800-230-4898; www.avis.com)
Budget	(☎ 800-527-0700; www.budget.com)
Dollar	(☎ 800-800-4000; www.dollar.com)
Enterprise	(☎ 800-736-8222; www.enterprise.com)
Hertz	(☎ 800-654-3131; www.hertz.com)
National	(☎ 800-227-7368; www.nationalcar.com)
Thrifty	(☎ 800- 847-4389; www.thrifty.com)

Age & Credit Requirements

Most operators require that you be at least 25 years old and have a major credit card in your own name. Some will rent to younger drivers (minimum age 21), but you must pay outrageous surcharges. Renting without a credit card – if you can even accomplish it – will require a large cash deposit, and you'll have to

---

DRIVERS BEWARE

Uninsured drivers are a widespread epidemic in Texas. Your chances of being hit by someone here who doesn't carry liability insurance, even though it is legally required for all drivers, is higher than in any other state in the USA. By some estimates, at least one out of every five drivers in Texas is uninsured. Be sure your own insurance policy covers damages and medical injuries caused by uninsured motorists, and also that the deductible isn't unreasonably high. A thousand dollars can be a lot of money to pay out for a fender-bender that wasn't your fault in the first place.

work things out well in advance with the company. The minimum age for renting motorcycles is usually 21 years old; you'll need to show a valid motorcycle license. The minimum age for renting a scooter or moped (scooters are OK at highway speeds, while mopeds are only for around town) is 16.

Insurance

Note that in Texas, liability insurance is not included in rental costs. Some credit cards offer a Loss/Damage Waiver (LDW; sometimes also called CDW, or Collision/Damage Waiver), which means that you won't have to pay if you or someone else damages the car itself. Liability insurance means that you won't have to pay if you hit someone and he or she sues you. If you own a car and have insurance at home, your liability insurance may extend to coverage of rental cars, but be *absolutely* certain before driving on the roads in the litigious USA. Also, if you opt out of the LDW, be certain that your credit card really will cover you for it. If it doesn't, make sure you buy liability coverage when you rent, which costs from $10 to $25 a day in addition to the cost of the car, but may be worth it.

Road Rules

The minimum age for driving a car in Texas is 16. Speed limits are posted *and* enforced. Speed limits are 70mph daytime, 65mph nighttime on interstates and freeways unless otherwise posted. (In urban areas, the speed limit often dips to 55mph.) Speed limits in cities and towns can vary from 25mph to 45mph. Watch for school zones, which can have strictly enforced speed limits as low as 15mph during school hours.

Driving while intoxicated (DWI) is legally defined as having a blood alcohol level of greater than 0.08%. Texas requires the use of seat belts for drivers and front-seat passengers. Children under age four, or under 36 inches tall, must be secured in a federally approved child safety seat; kids between four and 17 must wear regular safety belts.

Texas also requires those riding motorcycles to wear helmets. Exceptions are only granted for those who are at least 21 years old and have applied for a state helmet exemption sticker.

LOCAL TRANSPORT
Bicycle

Cycling is a feasible way of getting around only in the central parts of Austin and San Antonio. Spare parts are widely available and repair shops are found only in the cities, so it's important to be able to do basic mechanical work, like fixing a flat, yourself. Enthusiasts could plan a tour of the Hill Country by bicycle, where pleasantly hilly conditions and less traffic make cycling more enjoyable.

There are more bicycle rental shops in Austin than San Antonio. If you're cycling around for more than a few days, it pays to bring your bike with you from home. Be aware that some airlines will welcome bicycles, while others will treat them as an undesirable nuisance and do everything possible to discourage them. Greyhound buses will accept bicycles as checked baggage for a $15 to $25 free; bicycle boxes can be purchased for $10. Amtrak usually accepts bicycles as part of regularly checked baggage, although a carrying case is required and a nominal fee may be charged on smaller trains.

Bus

Local bus service is available only in Austin and San Antonio. Pay as you board; exact change is usually required, though some buses accept $1 bills. Operating hours differ from city to city and route to route, but buses generally run from about 6am to 10pm, with shorter hours on weekends.

Taxi

Taxis can be hailed down only at airports, major hotels and busy downtown areas. Otherwise, you'll usually need to telephone ahead for one.

TRAIN

It's possible to take Amtrak's *Texas Eagle* between San Antonio and Austin for slightly less than the bus. But it takes twice as long (three hours, if you're lucky) and schedules in the reverse direction (Austin to San Antonio) may be inconvenient.

Health by David Goldberg MD

CONTENTS

BEFORE YOU GO

INSURANCE

The United States offers possibly the finest health care in the world. The problem is that, unless you have good insurance, it can be prohibitively expensive. If you're coming from abroad, you're advised to buy supplemental travel health insurance if your regular policy doesn't cover you for overseas trips. (Check the Subway section of the Lonely Planet website at www.lonelyplanet.com/subwwway for more information.) If you are covered, find out in advance if your insurance plan will make payments directly to providers or reimburse you later.

Domestic travelers who have insurance coverage should check with their insurance company for affiliated hospitals and doctors. US citizens who don't have regular health coverage can purchase domestic travel insurance, but be aware that most plans only cover emergencies.

Bring any medications you may need in their original containers, clearly labeled. A signed, dated letter from your physician describing all medical conditions and medications, including generic names, is also a good idea.

ONLINE RESOURCES

There is a wealth of travel health advice on the Internet. The World Health Organization publishes a superb book, called *International Travel and Health*, which is revised annually and is available online at no cost at www.who.int/ith. Another website of general interest is MD Travel Health at www.mdtravelhealth.com, which provides complete travel health recommendations, updated daily, also at no cost.

It's usually a good idea to consult your government's travel health website before departure, if one is available:

United States www.cdc.gov/travel
Canada www.hc-sc.gc.ca/pphb-dgspsp/tmp-pmv/pub_e.html
United Kingdom www.doh.gov.uk/traveladvice/index.htm
Australia www.dfat.gov.au/travel

IN TEXAS

AVAILABILITY & COST OF HEALTH CARE

In general, if you have a medical emergency, the best bet is to find the nearest hospital and go to its emergency room. If the problem isn't urgent, you can call a nearby hospital and ask for a referral to a local physician, which is usually cheaper than a trip to the emergency room. You should avoid standalone, for-profit urgent care centers, which tend to perform large numbers of expensive tests, even for minor illnesses.

Pharmacies are abundantly supplied, but international travelers may find that some medications that are available over-the-counter at home require a prescription in the United States, and as always, if you don't have insurance to cover the cost of prescriptions, they can be shockingly expensive.

INFECTIOUS DISEASES

In addition to more common ailments, there are several infectious diseases that are unknown or uncommon outside North America. Most are acquired by mosquito or tick bites.

West Nile Virus

This virus was unknown in the United States until a few years ago, but has now been reported in almost all 50 states. The virus is transmitted by Culex mosquitoes, which are active in late summer and early fall and generally bite after dusk. Most infections are mild or asymptomatic, but the virus may infect the central nervous system, leading to fever, headache, confusion, lethargy, coma, and sometimes death. There is no treatment for West Nile virus. For the latest update on the areas affected by West Nile, go the US Geological Survey website at http://westnilemaps.usgs.gov/.

Lyme Disease
The disease has been reported from many states, but most documented cases occur in the northeastern part of the country, especially New York, New Jersey, Connecticut and Massachusetts. A smaller number of cases occur in the northern Midwest and in the northern Pacific coastal regions, including northern California. Lyme disease is transmitted by deer ticks, which are only 1mm to 2mm long. Most cases occur in the late spring and summer. The CDC has an informative, if slightly scary, web page on Lyme Disease: www.cdc.gov/ncidod/dvbid/lyme.

The first symptom is usually an expanding red rash that is often pale in the center, known as a bull's-eye rash. However, in many cases, no rash is observed. Flu-like symptoms are common, including fever, headache, joint pains, body aches and malaise. When the infection is treated promptly with an appropriate antibiotic, usually doxycycline or amoxicillin, the cure rate is high. Luckily, since the tick must be attached for 36 hours or more to transmit Lyme disease, most cases can be prevented by performing a thorough tick check after you've been outdoors, as described in 'Tick Bites,' later.

Rabies
Rabies is a viral infection of the brain and spinal cord that is almost always fatal. The rabies virus is carried in the saliva of infected animals and is typically transmitted through an animal bite, though contamination of any break in the skin with infected saliva may result in rabies. In the US, most cases of human rabies are related to exposure to bats. Rabies may also be contracted from raccoons, skunks, foxes and unvaccinated cats and dogs.

If there is any possibility, however small, that you have been exposed to rabies, you should seek preventative treatment, which consists of rabies immune globulin and rabies vaccine and is quite safe. In particular, any contact with a bat should be discussed with health authorities, because bats have small teeth and may not leave obvious bite marks. If you wake up to find a bat in your room, or discover a bat in a room with small children, rabies prophylaxis may be necessary.

Giardiasis
This parasitic infection of the small intestine occurs throughout North America and the world. Symptoms may include nausea, bloating, cramps and diarrhea, and may last for weeks. To protect yourself from Giardia, you should avoid drinking directly from lakes, ponds, streams and rivers, which may be contaminated by animal or human feces. The infection can also be transmitted from person to person if proper hand washing is not performed. Giardiasis is easily diagnosed by a stool test and readily treated with antibiotics.

HIV/AIDS
As with most parts of the world, HIV infection occurs throughout the US. You should never assume, on the basis of someone's background or appearance, that they're free of this or any other sexually transmitted disease. Be sure to use a condom for all sexual encounters.

ENVIRONMENTAL HAZARDS
Insect Bites & Stings
Commonsense approaches to these concerns are the most effective: wear boots when hiking to protect from snakes, wear long sleeves and pants to protect from ticks and mosquitoes. If you're bitten, don't overreact. Stay calm and follow the recommended treatment.

Heat Exhaustion
Dehydration or salt deficiency can cause heat exhaustion. Take time to acclimatize to high temperatures and make sure that you drink enough liquids. Salt deficiency is characterized by fatigue, headaches, giddiness and muscle cramps; salt tablets are overkill; just adding extra salt to your

food is probably sufficient. Vomiting or diarrhea can deplete your liquid and salt levels. Always carry – and use – a water bottle.

Heatstroke

Long, continuous periods of exposure to high temperatures can leave you vulnerable to this serious, sometimes fatal, condition that occurs when the body's heat-regulating mechanism breaks down and body temperature rises to dangerous levels. Avoid excessive alcohol intake or strenuous activity when you first arrive in a hot climate. Symptoms include feeling unwell, lack of perspiration and a high body temperature of 102°F to 106°F (39°C to 41°C). Where sweating has ceased, the skin becomes flushed and red. Severe, throbbing headaches and lack of coordination will also occur, and the sufferer may be confused or aggressive. Hospitalization is essential for extreme cases, but meanwhile get out of the sun, remove clothing, cover with a wet sheet or towel and fan continually.

Mosquito Bites

When traveling in areas where West Nile or other mosquito-borne illnesses have been reported, keep yourself covered (wear long sleeves, long pants, hats, and shoes rather than sandals) and apply a good insect repellent, preferably one containing DEET, to exposed skin and clothing. In general, adults and children over 12 should use preparations containing 25% to 35% DEET. Children ages two to 12 should use preparations containing no more than 10% DEET, applied sparingly. Neurologic toxicity has been reported from DEET, especially in children, but appears to be extremely uncommon and generally related to overuse. DEET-containing compounds should not be used on children under age two.

Insect repellents containing certain botanical products, including oil of eucalyptus and soybean oil, are effective but last only 1½ to 2 hours. Products based on citronella are not effective. Visit the Center for Disease Control's (CDC's) web site (www.cdc.gov/ncidod/dvbid/westnile/prevention_info.htm) for information.

Tick Bites

Ticks are parasitic arachnids that may be present in brush, forest and grasslands, where hikers often get them on their legs or in their boots. Adult ticks suck blood from hosts by burrowing into the skin and can carry infections such as Lyme disease.

Always check your body for ticks after walking through high grass or thickly forested area. If ticks are found unattached, they can simply be brushed off. If a tick is attached, press down around the tick's head with tweezers, grab the head and gently pull upwards – do not twist it. (If no tweezers are available, use your fingers, but protect them from contamination with a piece of tissue or paper.) Do not rub oil, alcohol or petroleum jelly on it. If you get sick in the next couple of weeks, consult a doctor.

Animal Bites

Do not attempt to pet, handle, or feed any animal, with the exception of domestic animals known to be free of any infectious disease. Most animal injuries are directly related to a person's attempt to touch or feed the animal.

Any bite or scratch by a mammal, including bats, should be promptly and thoroughly cleansed with large amounts of soap and water, followed by application of an antiseptic such as iodine or alcohol. The local health authorities should be contacted immediately for possible post-exposure rabies treatment. It may also be advisable to start an antibiotic.

Snake Bites

There are several varieties of venomous snakes in the USA, but unlike those in other countries, they do not cause instantaneous death, and antivenins are available. First aid is to place a light constricting bandage over the bite, keep the wounded part below the level of the heart and move it as little as possible. Stay calm and get to a medical facility as soon as possible. Bring the dead snake for identification if you can, but don't risk being bitten again. Do not use the mythic 'cut an X and suck out the venom' trick; this causes more damage to snakebite victims than the bites themselves.

HEALTH

Behind the Scenes

THE LONELY PLANET STORY

The story begins with a classic travel adventure: Tony and Maureen Wheeler's 1972 journey across Europe and Asia to Australia. There was no useful information about the overland trail then, so Tony and Maureen published the first Lonely Planet guidebook to meet a growing need.

From a kitchen table, Lonely Planet has grown to become the largest independent travel publisher in the world, with offices in Melbourne (Australia), Oakland (USA), London (UK) and Paris (France).

Today Lonely Planet guidebooks cover the globe. There is an ever-growing list of books and information in a variety of media. Some things haven't changed. The main aim is still to make it possible for adventurous travelers to get out there – to explore and better understand the world.

At Lonely Planet we believe travelers can make a positive contribution to the countries they visit – if they respect their host communities and spend their money wisely. Since 1986 a percentage of the income from each book has been donated to aid projects and human rights campaigns, and, more recently, to wildlife conservation.

THIS BOOK

This is the first edition of *Austin, San Antonio & the Hill Country*. It was researched and written by Sara Benson. Sam Martin wrote the Music chapter and the Health chapter was written by David Goldberg MD.

THANKS from The Author

SARA 'SAM' BENSON Many thanks to Kathleen Munnelly, Jay Cooke and Jeff Campbell for their many ideas and helpful suggestions during the course of this project. Mariah Bear started things rolling back in Oakland. In San Antonio the good samaritans at Fiesta Shave Ice on Babcock Rd helped me out in the aftermath of a car accident. Likewise I'm grateful for the warm-hearted welcome of Sam Martin and Denise Prince-Martin, who were always generous with help, advice and tea in Austin. Without the brilliant editing skills of Josh Lucas, this book would never have been finished – thank you.

CREDITS

This book was commissioned and developed in the US office by Kathleen Munnelly with the help of Jay Cooke and Wendy Taylor. Series Publishing Manager Susan Rimerman oversaw the redevelopment of the regional guides series and Regional Publishing Manager Maria Donohoe steered the development of this title. The guide was edited by Jeff Campbell and proofed by Valerie Sinzdak and Alex Hershey. Cartographers Bart Wright and Kat Smith drew the maps. Candice Jacobus designed the color pages and oversaw layout by Andreas Schueller and Shelley Firth. Pepi Bluck designed the cover. Ken DellaPenta compiled the index. Darren Burne and David Burnett helped with coding.

SEND US YOUR FEEDBACK

We love to hear from travelers – your comments keep us on our toes and help make our books better. Our well-traveled team reads every word on what you loved or loathed about this book. Although we cannot reply individually to postal submissions, we always guarantee that your feedback goes straight to the appropriate authors, in time for the next edition. Each person who sends us information is thanked in the next edition – and the most useful submissions are rewarded with a free book.

To send us your updates – and find out about LP events, newsletters and travel news – visit our award-winning website: www.lonelyplanet.com.

Note: we may edit, reproduce and incorporate your comments in Lonely Planet products such as guidebooks, websites and digital products, so let us know if you don't want your comments reproduced or your name acknowledged. For a copy of our privacy policy, email privacy@lonelyplanet.com.au.

Index